PRAISE FOR *VALUE STRUGGLES*

With deep empirical insight and theoretical rigor, *Value Struggles* reveals how wine value chains expose the power asymmetries of contemporary capitalism. This book is a powerful examination of the moral and economic tensions at the heart of global capitalism. A must-read for anyone interested in inequality, sustainability, and the politics of taste.

> Filippo Barbera, Professor of Economic Sociology, School of Cultures, Politics and Society University of Torino and Fellow, Collegio Carlo Alberto

This fascinating book examines wine from a holistic perspective. It combines analysis of the commercial dynamics of wine global value chains (focusing on South Africa and Italy) and the art of wine making. It investigates power imbalances across a range of stakeholders and explores how value struggles are shaped by place, nature and people. *Value Struggles* highlights class, race and gender – so often neglected or ignored in the literature – as central dimensions in how contradictory pressures and embedded inequalities play out across fragmented wine value chains. A highly recommended and insightful read.

> Stephanie Barrientos, Emeritus Professor, Global Development Institute, University of Manchester

If you're interested in the global economy of wine – how it is produced by people and nature, how value is unevenly captured among firms, how valuations of 'fine wines' are constructed, and the conflicts over each of these – then *Value Struggles* is for you. Stefano Ponte brings together years of careful research in Italy and South Africa to trace relations of race, class and gender in the reproduction of enduring inequalities in and through wine value chains, ultimately providing novel insights into how we think about capitalism.

> Liam Campling, Professor of International Business and Development, School of Business and Management Queen Mary University of London

Value Struggles is a brilliant account of the ways in which tensions over the valorization of places, nature, and people intersect with power in the wine industry. Illustrated with examples from South Africa and Italy, Stefano Ponte's careful research uncovers the myriad ways in which capitalism's contradictions are reflected in a glass of wine.

> Jennifer Clapp, University Professor & Canada Research Chair, School of Environment, Resources and Sustainability University of Waterloo

Stefano Ponte takes us on a captivating journey through the wine industries of Italy and South Africa. His spirited analysis reveals strikingly original insights into the environmental and social consequences of producing wine. Along the way, he deepens our understanding of how power struggles to produce, capture, and allocate value within modern capitalism impact people and the planet. This book is a *tour de force*.

> Peter Dauvergne, Professor of International Relations,
> Department of Political Science University of British Columbia

In a world of climate change, inequality and economic uncertainty, rethinking capitalism has never been more urgent. Understanding global value chains – and unpacking the power dynamics and value struggles in and around them – is key to assess the potential and myths of sustainable development. Drawing on rich cases from Italy and South Africa, Stefano Ponte guides us through the fascinating world of wine with a critical eye, unveiling how value is created, appropriated and redistributed across different 'worlds of valuation.' *Value Struggles* is essential reading for scholars in political economy, economic geography and international business – and a treat for wine lovers!

> Valentina De Marchi, Associate Professor,
> Department of Society, Politics and Sustainability, ESADE, Ramon Llull University

Value Struggles is a masterful and lucid exploration of the complexities of a paradoxical commodity. Stefano Ponte has distilled twenty years of fine-grained empirical research into an account of struggles around the creation, appropriation, and distribution of value in the production, retail and consumption of wine in two very different sites of global capitalism. His analysis bridges the global North and the global South in a coherent framework that links traditional value chain analysis with a nuanced account of the constitutive role played by the normative work of social value creation. A full bodied and nuanced analysis!

> Andries du Toit, Professor, School of Government,
> University of the Western Cape

Industries are microcosms of global capitalism. In this ingeniously designed and highly readable book, Stefano Ponte uses his detailed field research on the wine industry in South African and Italy to offer intriguing insights into how power dynamics and value struggles jointly shape human-scale winners and losers in contemporary capitalism. Highly recommended for general readers and experts alike.

> Gary Gereffi, Professor Emeritus of Sociology, Duke University

In *Value Struggles*, Stefano Ponte wrests value from the sidelines, situating it in its rightful place at the center of global value chain analysis. His conceptually expansive and empirically rich narration of value struggles over places, natures and people's lived experiences in the heterogenous world of wine leads directly to a pressing modern question: what do we value most? *Value Struggles* is a must-read for anyone seeking to understand and/or resist contemporary capitalism and the forms of power therein.

> Elizabeth Havice, Bowman and Gordan Gray Distinguished Professor, Department of Geography and Environment, University of North Carolina at Chapel Hill

Exploring the contradictions and crises endemic to capitalism through wine, *Value Struggles* expertly shows how the bitter taste of exploitation – of labour and nature – tarnishes this increasingly global and powerful industry. Empirically rich and theoretically sophisticated, like a vintage wine, this book comes highly recommended and will suit a number of palates.

> Peter Newell, Professor of International Relations, School of Global Studies University of Sussex

In this book Stefano Ponte not only makes another major contribution to knowledge about the economics and politics of Global Value Chains. He does so by theorizing the 'value struggles' which structure both in an original and convincing way. Using robust and creative first-hand data, his analysis clearly demonstrates that the world is deeply structured by values and, moreover, can only be changed by tackling them head on.

> Andy Smith, Directeur de recherche, Centre Emile Durkheim, Sciences Po Bordeaux

Stefano Ponte succeeds in the *tour de force* of making an elusive and almost ineffable question, the value of wine, the luminous revealer of contemporary capitalism. A lesson in state-of-the-art political economy, *Value Struggles* is informed by extensive field research. It opens up critical understandings of the exploitation of nature and people (by class, race and gender), and unpacks the complex relationship between humanity and its spatial anchoring. *A grand cru*.

> Laurent Thévenot, Directeur d'études honoraire, School for Advanced Studies in the Social Sciences (EHESS), Paris

Value Struggles is a fascinating and accessible read for scholars, practitioners and wine enthusiasts alike. It presents an impressively detailed contribution on how we understand value, and how our construction of what is valuable is created and sustained – a sobering reality check about the power dynamics, values and falsehoods that belie the glam in value chains like that for wine. *Value Struggles* compels us to (re)think how value and values interact to (re)produce stark inequities.

> Thando Vilakazi, Associate Professor, School of Economics, University of Johannesburg

This outstanding monograph offers a well-developed conceptual tool to decipher capitalism's many contradictions and exploitative tendencies. With three decades of proper wine experience, Stefano Ponte takes us through the intricate contours of wine growing, marketing, and consumption across places, environments, and people. After reading this incredible book, your wine will never taste the same – much better and more reflexive of his 'worlds of valuation'!

Henry Yeung, Choh-Ming Li Professor of Geography and Resource Management, The Chinese University of Hong Kong, China

VALUE STRUGGLES

VALUE STRUGGLES

Looking at Capitalism through the Wine Glass

Stefano Ponte

BLOOMSBURY ACADEMIC
LONDON • NEW YORK • OXFORD • NEW DELHI • SYDNEY

BLOOMSBURY ACADEMIC
Bloomsbury Publishing Plc
50 Bedford Square, London, WC1B 3DP, UK
1359 Broadway, 12th Floor, New York, NY 10018, USA
29 Earlsfort Terrace, Dublin 2, Ireland

BLOOMSBURY, BLOOMSBURY ACADEMIC and the Diana logo are trademarks of
Bloomsbury Publishing Plc

First published in Great Britain 2025

Copyright © Stefano Ponte, 2025

Stefano Ponte has asserted his right under the Copyright, Designs and Patents
Act, 1988, to be identified as Author of this work.

Cover design and illustration by Grace Ridge

This work is published open access subject to a Creative Commons Attribution-NonCommercial-NoDerivatives 4.0 International licence (CC BY-NC-ND 4.0, https://creativecommons.org/licenses/by-nc-nd/4.0/). You may re-use, distribute, and reproduce this work in any medium for non-commercial purposes, provided you give attribution to the copyright holder and the publisher and provide a link to the Creative Commons licence.

Bloomsbury Publishing Plc does not have any control over, or responsibility for, any third-party websites referred to or in this book. All internet addresses given in this book were correct at the time of going to press. The author and publisher regret any inconvenience caused if addresses have changed or sites have ceased to exist, but can accept no responsibility for any such changes.

A catalogue record for this book is available from the British Library.

A catalog record for this book is available from the Library of Congress

ISBN:	HB:	978-1-3503-7863-6
	PB:	978-1-3503-7862-9
	ePDF:	978-1-3503-7865-0
	eBook:	978-1-3503-7864-3

Typeset by RefineCatch Limited, Bungay, Suffolk
Printed and bound in Great Britain

To find out more about our authors and books visit www.bloomsbury.com
and sign up for our newsletters.

To Lisa, for opening the door to wine for me ... and much else

CONTENTS

List of Tables	xv
List of Figures	xvi
List of Images	xvii
List of Acronyms	xviii
Preface	xix

Part I
VALUE(S) AND VALUATION

Chapter 1
INTRODUCTION 3
  1.1 The allure of Bacchus: Why wine to understand contemporary capitalism? 3
  1.2 'Value chains' and 'chains of values' 5
  1.3 Empirical cases and sources of data 8
  1.4 How to read through the book 10

Chapter 2
VALUE CHAINS AND CHAINS OF VALUES 13
  2.1 Introduction 13
  2.2 Governance and power in value chains 14
  2.3 On value in value chains 19
      Value as price 19
      Value as rent 20
      Value as surplus labour time 22
      Value struggles 23
  2.4 The sociology of value and valuation 25
  2.5 Worlds of valuation: An analytical framework 28

Chapter 3
THE GLOBAL, SOUTH AFRICAN AND ITALIAN VALUE CHAINS FOR WINE 33
  3.1 Introduction 33
  3.2 The global value chain for wine 35
      Key trends in production and exports 35
      Value chain configurations 39
      Wine regulation and reform in the EU 42
  3.3 South African wine 46

	Brief history and recent trends	46
	Value chain characteristics	48
	Production and exports	50
	Profitability	55
	Regulation	57
	The Wine of Origin scheme	58
	The 'Porto Agreement'	59
	Wine tourism	60
3.4	Italian wine	61
	Brief history and recent trends	61
	Regulation	65
	Wine tourism	66
	Prosecco and Valpolicella: A brief introduction	66
3.5	What's next	69

Part II
THREE SITES OF VALUE STRUGGLE

Chapter 4
PLACE 73

4.1	Introduction	73
4.2	'Placeless wines'	74
4.3	Tasting place in wine: Tradition and authenticity	77
	Terroir	77
	Geographical indications and appellations	78
	The (re)invention of Prosecco	81
	Geographical indications in South Africa	84
	Immutable tradition or flexible bricolage?	85
	Is Amarone della Valpolicella 'traditional'?	88
4.4	Heritage	91
	UNESCO recognition of 'The Prosecco Hills of Conegliano and Valdobbiadene'	92
	Amarone and the 'famiglie storiche'	95
	Heritage vineyards in South Africa	96
4.5	Place and 'fine wines'	99
	Distinction vis a vis the 'democratization of taste'	99
	The market for fine wines	100
	Conspicuous production	101
4.6	Tasting wine in place: Wine tourism	103
4.7	Worlds of valuation and value struggles related to place	107
	Placeless wines	107
	Place wines	108
	Fine wines	110
	Wine tourism	112
4.8	Conclusion	112

Chapter 5
NATURE — 115
- 5.1 Introduction — 115
- 5.2 Regulation and governance of environmental sustainability — 117
  - Driving change: Alcohol monopolies, finance and wine experts — 118
  - Broad sustainability certifications and initiatives in South Africa and Italy — 121
  - Towards a global wine sustainability certification? — 123
- 5.3 Ecology, biodiversity conservation and beauty — 124
  - Organic wine — 124
  - Biodynamic wines and regenerative viticulture — 128
  - Biodiversity conservation and beauty — 132
  - Environmental value struggles in Prosecco and Valpolicella — 138
- 5.4 'Natural' wines — 142
- 5.5 Wine and climate change — 144
  - The Confronting Climate Change programme in South Africa — 145
  - New packaging forms and the weight of bottles — 146
  - Technology and innovation — 147
- 5.6 The limited valorization of sustainability at wine trade fairs — 151
- 5.7 Worlds of valuation and value struggles related to nature — 155
  - Regulation and governance — 158
  - Ecology, biodiversity conservation and beauty — 159
  - Natural wine — 159
  - Climate change — 160
- 5.8 Conclusion — 161

Chapter 6
PEOPLE (CLASS, RACE AND GENDER) — 163
- 6.1 Introduction — 163
- 6.2 Racialized and gendered labour exploitation in wine — 164
  - Labour relations in South Africa and Italy — 164
  - Certification systems on social and labour conditions — 168
    - Fairtrade wine — 168
    - The Wine and Agricultural Ethical Trading Association (WIETA) — 172
    - Equalitas — 173
- 6.3 Ownership and control: 'Black Economic Empowerment' in South Africa — 175
  - Brief history and current status — 176
  - Land ownership initiatives — 178
  - Brand ownership and business support initiatives — 179
- 6.4 Worlds of valuation and value struggles related to people (class, race and gender) — 182
- 6.5 Conclusion — 183

Chapter 7
LOOKING AT CAPITALISM THROUGH THE WINE GLASS　　　　　187
  7.1 Introduction　　　　　187
  7.2 Value struggles, constitutive power and inequality in wine　　　　　188
      Place　　　　　188
      Nature　　　　　191
      People (class, race and gender)　　　　　193
      Worlds of valuation and inequality　　　　　194
  7.3 Learning from wine to understand contemporary capitalism　　　　　196

Appendix Tables　　　　　203
Notes　　　　　207
References　　　　　221
Index　　　　　241

TABLES

1	Key features of different worlds of valuation.	31
2	World top ten wine-producing countries by volume (2014–2023).	36
3	World top ten wine-exporting countries by value (2014–2023).	37
4	World top ten wine-consuming countries by volume (2014–2023).	38
5	Number of players at each node of the value chain for South African wine.	49
6	Packaged and bulk South African wine exports by volume (2005, 2021).	53
7	Italian wine production (2009–2023).	62
8	Wine production in Italy: the Veneto region and by province in Veneto (2014–2023).	64
9	Top 10 Italian winemaking firms (2021–2022).	65
10	Worlds of valuation and value struggles in wine (place).	109
11	Main environmental demands by international retailers on wine suppliers.	119
12	Worlds of valuation and value struggles in wine (nature).	156
13	Worlds of valuation and value struggles in wine (people).	184
14	Worlds of valuation and value struggles in wine.	189

FIGURES

1	Example of a value chain for wine (Italy).	41
2	South African wine production by volume (2005–2022).	50
3	South African wine production of red and white wines by volume (2005–2022).	51
4	Domestic and export sales of South African wine (2005–2022).	51
5	South African wine exports by value (2001–2022).	52
6	Top 25 export destinations for South African wine by volume (May 2023–April 2024).	52
7	South African wine exports by destination, by value (2001–2023).	53
8	Wine grape farming profitability in South Africa (2013–2022).	55
9	Continued profitability decline at farm level, South Africa (2012–2022).	56
10	Vinpro cost breakdown of a bottle of wine, South Africa (2021).	57
11	Total area under vineyard cultivation for wine grapes in Italy (2006–2023).	63
12	Italian wine production by type of denomination (2006–2023).	63
13	Italian wine exports by value (2010–2023).	64

IMAGES

1	Bacchus (*c.* 1596), oil painting by Michelangelo Merisi da Caravaggio.	4
2	Winegrowing areas of South Africa.	58
3	Map of the Prosecco area of production, Italy.	67
4	Map of the Valpolicella areas of production, Italy.	68
5	Modern wine amphoras.	86
6	Map of the UNESCO site 'Prosecco Hills of Conegliano and Valdobbiadene', Italy.	93
7	Typical vineyard landscape in Valdobbiadene, Italy.	94
8	A Certified Heritage Vineyard (bushvine), South Africa.	98
9	Tasting room with winemaking facility in the background, South Africa.	104
10	Depiction of 'heroic viticulture', Italy.	107
11	Pergola veronese semplice (left) and Guyot (right) vineyard training systems, Italy.	131
12	'Clean' vineyards (left) and more biodiverse vineyards (right), South Africa.	136
13	Main design of the Veneto pavilion at Vinitaly 2024.	152
14	The 'organic world' space at ProWein.	153
15	South Africa's collective designs at ProWein.	155

ACRONYMS

AOC	Appellation d'Origine Contrôlée
BEE	Black Economic Empowerment
BiB	Bag-in-Box
CAP	EU Common Agricultural Policy
CBAM	Carbon Border Adjustment Measures
CC	Conservation Champion
CCC	Confronting Climate Change
CFK	Cape Floral Kingdom
DOC	Denominazione d'Origine Controllata
DOCG	Denominazione d'Origine Controllata e Garantita
EU	European Union
FederDoc	Confederazione Consorzi Volontari Tutela Denominazioni Vini Italiani
FIVS	International Federation of Wines and Spirits
IGT	Indicazione Geografica Tipica
INAO	Institut National des Appellations d'Origine
IPW	Integrated Production of Wine
KWV	Ko-öperatieve Wijnbouwers Vereniging van Zuid-Afrika
NFI	Net Farm Income
OIV	International Organisation of Vine and Wine
PDO	Protected Designation of Origin
PGI	Protected Geographical Indication
RRR	Reduce, Retrench, Respect
SADC	Southern African Development Community
SAWB	South African Wine and Brandy Company
SAWIS	South African Wine Industry Information System
SAWIT	South African Wine Industry Trust
SQNPI	Sistema Qualità Nazionale Produzione Integrata
SWR	Sustainable Wine Roundtable
TDCA	Trade, Development and Cooperation Agreement
TRIPS	WTO Agreement on Trade-Related Aspects of Intellectual Property Rights
TUV	Testo Unico Vino
UNESCO	United Nations Educational, Scientific and Cultural Organization
VDT	Vino da Tavola
WBA	World Biodiversity Association
WIETA	Wine and Agricultural Ethical Trading Association
WO	Wine of Origin
WOSA	Wines of South Africa
WWF	World Wildlife Fund
ZAR	South African Rand

PREFACE

When I was nine years old, during one of the regular visits to my extended family's farmhouse in northeast Italy, my maternal grandfather took me aside. He whispered that it was time for me to 'become a man'. What he meant was that I was allowed to taste a sip of red wine diluted with water. My *nonno* had been a farmer and a mason – a tall, silent and imposing figure. One could not say no to him very easily. Plus, we visited the extended family only three times a year from the city where we lived, a three-hour train ride away. It would have been impolite to decline. So, I pulled myself together and tasted it. It was horrible. I thought that I had avoided making a bad face, but nonetheless, he understood that I did not like what 'men' drink. My *nonno* did not try to make me taste wine ever again. And I decided at nine that wine was not something I had to subject myself to.

My father never offered me wine. I suspect that because my mother did not drink alcohol, he was afraid of being reprimanded by her. Her own mother also claimed to abstain, but several times, I found her surreptitiously dipping cookies in Marsala – I guess it does not count as 'drinking'. One of my childhood chores was fetching wine from a cramped space under the communal stairs in our 1950s-built apartment house. I had to wiggle through a tiny door and transfer wine from the jug to the 2-litre bottle for daily use. To do so, I had to suck air from a plastic tube so the wine would flow from the jug into the bottle. Needless to say, sometimes I was too slow to let it go and happened to get some liquid in my mouth. We also kept vinegar in a separate jug, but to tell you the truth, I could not taste much of a difference between the two – the olive oil though was delicious. This was wine my father bought directly from a farmer friend in Valpolicella. He told me this wine was much better than the one my *nonno* kept. Because my father was an agronomist, I thought he knew better. I was disappointed. That did it for me and wine for quite a long time. Teenagers in the urban working-class area where I grew up drank beer, so did I. Wine was for 'old people'.

Fast forward to my mid-twenties. A string of luck, hard-headedness and a scholarship had brought me to study for a Master's in the social sciences at the University of Chicago. I was interested in agricultural policy and rural livelihoods in East Africa and won a fellowship to study Kiswahili at Michigan State University for the summer. We were all graduate students but formed a tight-knit group and lived the lifestyle of undergrads in a dorm. I got invited with a small group to have drinks in Lisa's room – apparently, she had bought 'really good wine' and even had proper wine glasses. I thought, 'here we go again'. The wine (a Cabernet Sauvignon from California, if I remember correctly), came in a nice, heavy bottle not from a non-descript glass container. I liked Lisa and wanted to impress her. I tried the wine and . . . was amazed at how much I liked it. An American teaching an Italian how to drink wine – the world felt upside down.

A decade passed and in 2005 Lisa and I (and our three children) were living in Cape Town, South Africa for a year. We were spending our maternity and paternity leave for our newborn together (thanks to the Danish welfare state) before going back to work on our separate research projects in South Africa – hers on the politics of access to anti-retrovirals for HIV/AIDS; mine on the political economy of quality in . . . wine. By then I was drinking wine, but I needed to learn a lot more before doing interviews in the farms and cellars around Stellenbosch. So, I enrolled at the Cape Wine Academy and went through six months of intensive courses on viticulture, winemaking, wine markets and, most importantly, tasting. By the end of our stay, I was fully immersed in the world of wine. At the same time, I became deeply aware of what lurked behind the fancy cellars and neatly tended vineyards – appalling labour conditions and an industry that was (and, to some extent, still is) mainly in the hands of white South Africans. My parents came to visit us in South Africa and I had the chance to talk about wine and to go on tasting tours with my father. He was learning from me. I was pleased. It was just in time, before we discovered his terminal illness.

In early 2020, Covid-19 was upending our lives, but fortunately, we had not yet caught it in our family. Whenever possible during the following eighteen months, we spent our time holed up in our own holiday home on the hills not far from Valpolicella. While teaching online, I was working on a new research project on power and inequality in global value chains, including case studies on wine in South Africa and Chile. In South Africa, when allowed to travel, I was doing research on wine with a group of wonderful colleagues at the University of Johannesburg (Reena das Nair and Shingie Chisoro), while Juliane Lang (the PhD fellow in the project) was working in Chile. But since I was often in Italy, why not learn more about the wine made where I come from? As a visiting scholar at the University of Padova, I did some fieldwork together with Valentina de Marchi, Marco Bettiol and Eleonora di Maria. We became fellow travellers in the world of wine. I also hopped on the Vespa and interviewed grape farmers and winemakers closer to my home – and discovered that Valpolicella wine was not what it used to be, or at least not what my father used to drink. My son Zeno, by then in his late teens, had become interested in wine too. He interned in the wine sector in South Africa and in Italy and has acquired far more sophistication than I had at his age.

This book is in a way the story of a thirty-year personal journey that began when I drank that glass of Cabernet Sauvignon in Lisa's dorm room. It is an ode to wine as a convivial product but also a critical reflection on the exploitation and inequalities that also make up the political economy of wine. In order to sift through the massive amount of fieldwork material, trade journals and academic literature that I had amassed in the past two decades, I needed to put aside everything else and focus on writing. Winning the Carlsberg Foundation Monograph Fellowship made it possible to take a sabbatical year to do just that. Among my friends and colleagues, the joke goes that Stefano wrote a book on wine . . . with beer money!

I wrote this book in the form of a monograph, but this does not mean that it was a lone effort. In addition to my closest and wonderful collaborators already mentioned (Reena das Nair, Shingie Chisoro and Juliane Lang), I would like to thank Filippo Barbera, David Monciardini and Andy Smith for reading early full drafts of the manuscript and providing incisive and constructive feedback – along with two anonymous reviewers. Heated conversations and conviviality with other friends and colleagues at the University of Johannesburg (especially Pamela Mondliwa, Simon Roberts and Thando Vilakazi) allowed me to hone my argument and avoid some pitfalls. Gianluca Perillo offered invaluable research assistance. My commissioning editor, Nick Wolterman, and production manager, Nadine Staes-Polet, at Bloomsbury Academic provided unwavering support and encouragement. The Department of Cultures, Politics and Society at the University of Torino (arguably the Italian capital of good taste in food and wine) hosted me as a visiting scholar in 2023/24 during the writing of the book. Colleagues and support staff at the Department of Management, Society and Communication, Copenhagen Business School kindly covered my teaching and administration duties in my absence. Most of all, I am thankful to the around 250 people who patiently lent their time in interviews, plus all those with whom I had informal chats at various wine trade fairs.

Thanks also to all those from whom I received useful feedback at a number of conferences and invited seminars between late 2021 and late 2024: the 2021 and 2023 International Studies Association (ISA) annual conferences; three annual conferences of the Society for the Advancement of Socio-Economics (2021, 2022 and 2024); the international symposium 'Structural transformation and inclusive industrial development', Centre for Competition, Regulation and Economic Development (CCRED), University of Johannesburg; a seminar hosted by the Institute for Poverty, Land and Agrarian Studies, University of the Western Cape; the international workshop 'Environmental and social upgrading in Global Value Chains: fostering the synergies, disclosing the trade-offs', University of Padova; the international workshop 'Catalysing Green Industrialization in Africa', Copenhagen Business School; a faculty seminar hosted by the Global Development Institute, University of Manchester; the 'Regenerate future' debate series, BLOXHUB and Copenhagen Institute for Future Studies, Danish Architecture Centre; a Centre for Business and Development Studies (CBDS) monthly seminar, Copenhagen Business School; a webinar with wine industry actors in South Africa hosted by CCRED, University of Johannesburg; the 2023 conference of the European Association of Development Research and Training Institutes (EADI); the 2023 UNFSS Academic Advisory Council Annual Meeting 2023; the 'Reterritorializing value chains' workshop, organized by the Responsible Value Chains (RVC) initiative, Paris; a faculty seminar at the Department of Cultures, Politics and Society, University of Torino; the research seminar 'Natural wine, labour and migration', Aalborg University; the workshop 'The geography of the twin transition', Department of Economics and Management, University of Padova; the international workshop 'Wine, place and space: Global geographies of wine cultivation, production and consumption', Catholic University of Eichstätt-Ingolstadt; a faculty seminar at the Department of History, Economy and Society, University of Geneva; the international conference 'Power and inequality in global value chains', hosted by CBDS/CBS and

CCRED, University of Johannesburg; and the seminar series 'Économie politique des capitalismes. Perspectives Nord/Sud', LAM-CED, Sciences Po Bordeaux.

I started working on this book at a time when generative artificial intelligence tools had just been released for public use. Given the unclear regulatory situation at my university and in academia at that time, and my own doubts about the uses and abuses of this technology, I decided not to use any of these tools for analysis or writing. What you get in this book is fully human, with all its qualities and limitations. I take full responsibility for any errors or shortcomings.

Funding for fieldwork related to this book project came from the Social Sciences and Humanities Research Council (Canada), Grant number 895-2018-1002: 'The Hidden Costs of Global Supply Chains' (hosted by the University of British Columbia); the University of Johannesburg (as part of my Distinguished Visiting Professor position at the Centre for Competition, Regulation and Economic Development); and the Independent Research Fund Denmark, Project 0133-00046B: 'Power and Inequality in Global Production Systems' (PIPS). As mentioned above, the final writing of the book was made possible by a Carlsberg Foundation Monograph Fellowship, Project CF22-0470.

But ultimately, none of this would have happened without Lisa Ann Richey.

Part I

VALUE(S) AND VALUATION

Chapter 1

INTRODUCTION

Wine is part agriculture, part luxury. You farm at an agriculture scale, but you sell luxury like a Fendi bag.

— South African wine merchant[1]

I prepare some of my vineyard hand by hand with a hoe, or with horses . . . The noise of the earth while you work is amazing, the soil speak

— Italian biodynamic grape farmer and winemaker[2]

[Retailers] always want more sustainability, but they are unwilling to pay for it . . . The tip paid at the restaurant for the wine is higher than the margin for the grape grower!

— Manager of a South African wine cooperative[3]

1.1 THE ALLURE OF BACCHUS: WHY WINE TO UNDERSTAND CONTEMPORARY CAPITALISM?

Bacchus, the god of wine, fertility and pleasure is usually represented in art and literature as joyous and kind by admirers, but also as cruel and mischievous by the enemies of excess (McKinlay 1953).[4] Classical images of Bacchus have been often used by the rich and powerful as an allegory of wealth. Yet historically wine has not been the purview of only the rich and powerful, it has also been a beverage of choice for the working class in many cultures. Today, a wine bottle can be bought as a collector's item by the élite and never be drunk, or as a 'democratic luxury' that can be afforded by most consumers. The bewildering array of wines available for purchase tells us stories of places, nature and people, but also of generic and 'placeless' brands. The first two opening quotes indicate some of the poetry that encapsulates the lifestyles and philosophies of some wine growers and winemakers. How can wine be anything but a vector of joy, conviviality and beauty? But the following three quotes start unfolding a darker side to wine, that of deception and the exploitation of nature and labour.

Image 1 Bacchus (*c.* 1596), oil painting by Michelangelo Merisi da Caravaggio, Galleria degli Uffizi, Florence.

In the wine world, small producers are still seen as being able to escape the most egregious forms of exploitation from more powerful actors, such as large merchants and retailers. They are often portrayed as hard-working and in sometimes heroic terms, toiling the land with family labour and taking care of nature. If there is hope for better ways of organizing economic activity in contemporary capitalism, wine is surely where one should start looking. Yet, the majority of wine sold globally is supplied by industrial and mechanized operations. The valorization of place and the possibility of thoughtfully managing the environment and labour conditions are being codified in standards and certifications that facilitate further capital accumulation by large wine merchants and retailers.

In wine, ideational and performative processes are tightly embedded in the very material actions of growing grapes and making and distributing wine. These processes are also key in valuation processes related to the imaginaries of how place, nature and people shape wine. Physical processes of wine production, manufacturing and logistics are enmeshed in a web of immaterial content creation and connected imaginaries and experiences (such as wine tasting, wine tourism). Physical and symbolic 'winescapes' (Demossier 2020; Peters 1997) are framed by regulatory and institutional practices. They are also often portrayed as 'wine escapes', romantic imaginaries of labour and nature that allow us to ignore the exploitation that may lurk inside the wine bottle or behind the tasting room. As the valuation of wine is increasingly built around intangible features and the forging of identities, the material process of grape production is being obscured and outsourced to indebted farmers at prices below production cost, who then are under pressure to impose even more exploitative conditions on labour.

In this book, I argue that there is no better product than wine to unmask some of the contradictions of contemporary capitalism. Wine is one of the most fragmented and diversified industries, and one that is not yet utterly dominated by large corporate interests. It is also where all sorts of antagonisms to the power of capital are taking place, and where the expansion of uniform and branded offerings is counterbalanced by alternative discourses and practices that attempt to instil appreciation for how place, nature and craft can deliver a large range of different wines. At the same time, viticultural expansion often comes at the cost of biodiversity, while (gendered and racialized) labour is exploited in every producing country. I will show how these tensions and contradictions play out in three sites of 'value struggle' in wine: place, nature and people (along the intersectionality of class, race and gender) and how different combinations of 'worlds of valuation' are leveraged by specific groups of actors to maintain existing power imbalances or to attempt challenging them. Analytically, this entails examining 'value chains' as imbricated in 'chains of value'.[5]

1.2 'VALUE CHAINS' AND 'CHAINS OF VALUES'

If wine is an appropriate sector to identify some of the contradictions of contemporary capitalism, value chains are key to unpacking some of their underlying dynamics. Value chains have become key components of the functioning of the global economy in the past three decades. They are usually defined as the full range of value-adding activities that firms, farmers and workers carry out to bring a product from its conception to its end use, disposal or recycling. Value chains are explicitly governed by one or more groups of 'lead firms' – especially those that exert 'buyer power' by placing large orders, such as retailers or branded food processors. Under some circumstances, value chain actors based in the Global South have been able to upgrade – adding value and extracting more rent, eventually moving up the value chain to more sophisticated and skill-intensive operations (Gereffi 1999, 2014; Humphrey and Schmitz 2002). But in many other cases, they have been delivering more for lower economic returns, and/or in combination with degrading social, labour and environmental conditions of production (see Ponte 2019 for an overview) – what Kaplinsky terms 'immiserizing growth' (Kaplinsky 2005).

Often, the governance of value chains by lead firms is carried out together with (or is contested by) other non-firm actors – such as international NGOs, standard-setting organizations, social movements, governments and labour unions (Cattaneo, Gereffi and Staritz 2010; Gereffi 1994; Gereffi, Humphrey and Sturgeon 2005; Gibbon and Ponte 2005; Milberg and Winkler 2013; Ponte and Gibbon 2005; Ponte 2014). Overall, value chain governance can then be thought of as the combination of 'actions, institutions and norms that shape the conditions for inclusion, exclusion and mode of participation in a value chain, which in turn determine the terms and location of value addition, distribution and capture' (Dallas, Ponte and Sturgeon 2019, 667). Governance dynamics themselves are shaped by different forms of power that include but are not limited to bargaining power among firms as they engage in exchange. The exercise of power in value chains can be understood by unpacking its two main dimensions: the 'transmission mechanisms' (direct and diffuse) and the 'arena of actors' (dyads and collectives) (Dallas, Ponte and Sturgeon 2019). Combining these two dimensions yields four types of power: *bargaining, demonstrative, institutional* and *constitutive* (see more details in Chapter 2). Of these, bargaining power and institutional power have been the focus of much research so far and are well understood – but demonstrative power and constitutive power, which have more prominent normative and discursive features, are still under-researched. This means that we need to better understand the imbrication of 'value' and 'values' in these chains.

Until the mid-1800s, most political economists held an objective theory of value, where value was thought of as residing in a product or service and was often linked to the labour expended for its production. With the advent of neoclassical economics, by the end of that century, the value of things became related to how much a consumer is prepared to pay in the context of relative scarcity, a subjective process. Thus a complete upturn took place, from 'value determining price to price determining value' (Mazzucato 2018, 7). When value is determined by price only, inequality is justified as long as there is a 'market' for the goods and services that generate income. But 'markets . . . are imperfect, so prices and wages are often set by the powerful and paid by the weak' (Mazzucato 2018, 12–13) – as the literature on value chains has clearly demonstrated (see Chapter 2).

While discussions on value have disappeared from most mainstream economics, they have remained one of the main concerns of international political economy, economic sociology and business studies. There has been a proliferation of analytical terms such as shareholder value, shared value, value added and value chains, but only limited theoretical work on what 'value' means. In value chain analysis, much research has focused on the calculation of value added and rents (Havice and Pickles 2019) as a way of highlighting their unequal distribution. We still need a better understanding of what 'value' is beyond the important discussion of rents; what social, economic and institutional conditions allow value to be created by some and captured by others; and what *values* and *valuation* narratives and practices are applied in what contingent situations, industry specificities and historical periods – given that 'values' shape all economic action and regulatory institutions which structure it (Smith 2016).

This book is a contribution in this direction. It draws from the sociology of valuation to enrich the analytical baggage of international political economy. It seeks to unpack value by moving away from an exclusive concern with 'value chains' (and a focus on the distribution of value added and rents along them) and towards understanding their overlap with 'chains of values' – the political, ethical and moral justifications and the techniques and metrics of valuation that contribute to shaping power relations among actors. Ultimately, I seek to explain what kind of normative work is behind *constitutive* power in value chains. In order to do so, I delineate a plurality of 'worlds of valuation' that different groups of actors in a value chain leverage at different sites of struggle.

Who decides what is a sustainable vineyard, a sustainable winery or an empowered owner – and how these create or appropriate value and for/from whom? What is the value of a sustainable, natural or fair wine? To what extent can place be tasted in a wine, and conversely what kinds of value(s) are experienced by tasting wine in a particular place? What does it mean for a region, landscape or vineyard to have heritage value, or to claim to adhere to tradition and authenticity – and what valuation processes underpin these characterizations? When is valuation related to associating certain features to a wine (a geographical appellation, for example) and when is it linked to disassociating it from other features (through, for example, hiding farm labourers from view)?

Value chain analysis can be built upon a critical approach to value (generating reflections on exploitation, struggle and inequality) by engaging not only with value extraction through rent and the appropriation of surplus labour (Neilson and Pritchard 2011) but also through explaining what normative, ethical and political elements underpin a variety of valuation processes. These, when clashing, give rise to 'value struggles'. Therefore, I join a larger group of critical scholars who highlight forms of antagonism (see, inter alia, Alford 2020; Havice and Pickles 2019; Selwyn 2019) that go beyond the significant extraction of surplus labour (and its race and gender dimensions) – to also consider value struggles around place, nature, and the qualification of people as owners of assets. My call is thus *not* one for moving away from a critical analysis of capitalism (and of value chains as one of its important cogs) or to further fetishize labour – quite the contrary. It is to further our understanding of how different 'worlds of valuation' produce different outcomes for different groups of actors in value chains. My exhortation is to examine 'value chains' as imbricated with 'chains of values', and to identify sites of value struggle in view of better understanding the exercise of power in value chains, and especially of constitutive power.

To do so I embrace 'pragmatic structuralism', which brings together 'the systemic approach, which aims to bring processes of broad scope to light, and the pragmatic approach, which aims to shed light on people's actions by analysing the cognitive [and material] structures underlying their exchanges' (Boltanski and Esquerre 2020, 338). I also examine 'context' and 'situated action' to fully leverage the structural conditions and multiple situations that constrain actors and shape the resources and capabilities at their disposal as they engage in valuation processes. I thus build on some of the propositions that Heinich (Heinich 2017, 2020a, b) put forward in her recent work on value and valuation. First, Heinich argues for more focus paid to valuation processes, rather than value per se. For her, 'value is obtained by action, in the processes of qualification and requalification' (Heinich 2020a, 77), and value results from various forms of attribution, it is not the cause of them. Also, she maintains that value is based on several categories of resources, some of which are substantive properties, while others are relational – thus exhorting us to go beyond existing dichotomies. Finally, she suggests that all aspects of valuation should be studied conjointly, not separately: things (usually studied by economists), people (by moral philosophers), actions (by sociologists) and/or states of the world (by political scientists).

In the rest of this book, I examine how different worlds of valuation (market, industrial, domestic, civic, inspired, opinion) operate in three distinct sites of value struggle that are particularly relevant for wine: (1) *place*; (2) *nature*; and (3) *people* (through the intersectionality of class, race and gender). These three sites usually overlap, but an analytical distinction is helpful to better delineate the dynamics and effects of specific struggles.

1.3 EMPIRICAL CASES AND SOURCES OF DATA

The empirical focus of this book is the mutual constitution of value chains and chains of value in South African wine (especially in the Western Cape region) and for Italian wine (especially in the Prosecco and Valpolicella geographical appellations) in the context of broader changes in the global wine industry. South Africa is considered a 'New World' producer country that supplies value-for-money wines, usually sold under a brand and a specified grape variety, and that does not place much emphasis on more specific geographical origins. South Africa provides key insights for understanding the mutual constitution of value chains and chains of values. With the end of *apartheid* and related sanctions, it completely reinvented its wine industry – in relation to the physical operations of vineyard management and winemaking, to the symbolic and normative work of re-branding the country, and to building a very advanced experience economy through wine tourism. It has also been at the forefront of wine sustainability initiatives worldwide and, through legislation and codes of conduct on so-called Black Economic Empowerment (BEE), it had to face (but has far from resolved) the legacy of apartheid in relation to farm labour and the ownership structures of land and the overall economy. Italian wine is structured around a panoply of denominations of geographical origin, which have been traditionally considered more important than brands. In Italy, communicating place and terroir is generally preferred over varietal selection, while ideas and perceptions of tradition, authenticity and heritage battle with technological innovation in vineyard management and winemaking. However, some of these differentiating features are changing in both countries, which are in some ways moving towards each other. For example, in South Africa, more attention is now dedicated to place, while branded wine is making major inroads in Italy.

In the part of the book focused on wine (Chapters 3 to 6), I draw from primary fieldwork material I collected in South Africa and Italy between October 2020 and April 2024, consisting mostly of semi-structured interviews with key informants. Interviews lasted normally 60 minutes but ranged from 30 to 120 minutes. Interviewees were assured anonymity and therefore the primary interview material I use in this book is referred to with a code (SAW for South African Wine interviews, P for Prosecco, V for Valpolicella, IG for Italy General and WG for World General). I conducted most interviews in person, but a few had to be done online due to Covid-19 restrictions. Interviewees were selected through a snowball sampling method, starting from indications suggested by key industry experts and industry associations, and in view of interviewing representatives of as many groups of actors as possible. This process ended when conceptual saturation was achieved. I also utilize information gathered from industry statistical databases and other secondary sources – including firms' websites and other corporate documents, reports published by local or national industry associations and producer consortia, and detailed materials posted on the websites of wine sustainability initiatives and certifications.

In South Africa, between November 2021 and October 2022, I carried out 84 semi-structured interviews (of which 12 online), covering 76 firms/organizations (see details in Appendix Table 1).[6] Interviewees included representatives of government, industry associations, NGOs, research institutions, media, logistics companies, and direct wine value chain actors (private cellars, estates, producer wholesalers, wine cooperatives, wholesalers, distributors and retailers).[7] Most of the fieldwork was undertaken in the Western Cape, the core wine region of South Africa. I also draw from participant observation and the attendance of industry seminars (12 seminars for a total of 33 presentations) and visual inspection of all exhibition stands (over 500) at the CapeWine trade fair (Cape Town, 5–7 October 2022). For issues related to labour and wine tourism, I draw mainly from secondary material and the existing literature. Where relevant, I also use research results from an earlier set of interviews I carried out in the South African wine industry in 2005, which was focused on wine quality (96 interviews in 74 entities; see details in Ponte and Ewert 2007). A sub-set of 22 companies, NGOs and institutions were interviewed in both 2005 and 2022.

In Italy, between October 2020 to July 2022, I conducted 62 semi-structured interviews (of which 3 online), covering 42 entities (see details in Appendix Table 2).[8] These included interviews with private, corporate and cooperative wine producers and marketers, regulatory institutions, consortia for the protection of geographical origin, sustainability certification agencies, suppliers of inputs, research institutions and labour unions. I focused on two of the fastest-growing wine denominations of origin in Italy: Valpolicella (producing mostly red wines) and Prosecco (producing mostly white sparkling wines). Both are located in the Veneto region (Prosecco also extends into another region). All quotes from this part of the fieldwork are translations by the author from the original interview transcripts in Italian. I also had informal conversations, carried out participant observation and attended 14 public seminars (for a total of 45 presentations) at Vinitaly, the main Italian wine fair and expo (Verona, 10–13 April 2022 and 14–17 April 2024) and the Wine2Wine fair (Verona, 13–14 November 2023). I also attended several other industry webinars online. Furthermore, I visually inspected all exposition stands that featured wines from Prosecco and/or Valpolicella at the Vinitaly pavilions dedicated to wines from the Veneto region (a total of 184 stands in 2022 and 179 in 2024). I conducted a similar exercise at the ProWein fair (Dusseldorf, March 2023), which is considered *the* truly global wine trade fair, this time covering South African and Italian wine stands. At ProWein, I also attended seven seminars (or thematic tastings with discussions) for a total of 13 presentations. Finally, I carried out six interviews with international wine industry stakeholders, some online and others at ProWein.

1.4 HOW TO READ THROUGH THE BOOK

In the rest of Part I of the book, I first discuss the mutual constitution of 'value chains' and 'chains of values' (Chapter 2). I briefly review how value has been treated in classical political economy (as price, rent and surplus labour time) and how these discussions have shaped current debates on governance and power in global value chains. I then argue that the insights generated by the sociology of valuation can help us identify different 'worlds of valuation' in view of explaining power relations around specific 'value struggles'. In Chapter 3, I provide essential background on global, South African and Italian wine value chains – highlighting historical trends in production, exports and consumption, value chain configurations and key regulatory features.

In Part II of the book, I examine three sites of value struggle in detail – place, nature and people (class, race and gender) – and their overlaps. The analysis of value struggles around *place* (Chapter 4) is structured around the discussion of mainstream, branded wines ('placeless wines') vis-à-vis wines that are to different degrees attached to specific places and geographical origins ('place wines'). Within the category of place wines, I examine how tradition, authenticity and heritage are leveraged around valuation processes related to geographical origin and terroir, 'fine wines', and wine tourism. In relation to *nature* (Chapter 5), I examine the valuation repertoires that coalesce around issues of regulation and governance of environmental issues; ideas and practices related to ecology, biodiversity conservation and beauty; the varied meanings and contradictions of 'natural wines'; and climate change mitigation and adaptation. I approach value struggles around the qualification of *people* (Chapter 6) through the intersectionality of class, race and gender. I examine valuation struggles in relation to people both as labourers and as owners of tangible and intangible assets.

At the end of each of these three chapters, I interpret the empirical material through the lenses of six worlds of valuation (market, industrial, domestic, civic, inspired and opinion) – drawing from the original formulation of worlds of justification by Boltanski and Thévenot (2006) and extending my previous work in this realm (Ponte and Gibbon 2005; Ponte 2016). These worlds of valuation help us understand how value struggles operate through the overlap of value chains and chains of values – and with what consequences for different groups of actors. In Chapter 7, I continue the discussion of value struggles in wine to further examine the relations between worlds of valuation, power and inequality. I conclude with a reflection on what we can learn by looking at capitalism through the wine glass.

Readers mainly interested in wine may want to prioritize the reading of Chapters 3 to 6. Those interested in new dynamics of accumulation in contemporary capitalism will find Chapters 1 and 7 most relevant. Readers concerned with value chains and production networks, and with the sociology of value and valuation may want to focus on Chapters 2 and 7, in addition to the relevant reflections placed at the end of Chapters 4, 5 and 6. I also hope that many readers will find reading through the whole book fulfilling.

Chapter 2

VALUE CHAINS AND CHAINS OF VALUES

2.1 INTRODUCTION

How value is created, appropriated and distributed has been at the centre of political economy discussions for centuries. Struggles around value remain key for understanding the dynamics of contemporary capitalism. A wide range of interpretations exist on what value is, what actors and activities ascribe it, and how it could be measured. What is the 'value' of things, services and experiences? Who decides what value they have? How is value imbricated with moral, ethical and political 'values'? What valuation processes are employed to assess value? What are the struggles around value creation and appropriation, and how do they change over time? How do we account for the material, immaterial and experiential elements of value? These are all questions that inform the way power is exercised in the pursuit of economic activity, including in value chains.

In Section 2 of this chapter, I briefly discuss how power has been interpreted and operationalized in value chain analysis in the pursuit of explaining governance dynamics and economic, social and environmental outcomes. I highlight how we lack a proper understanding of forms of power that have substantial normative features. In the following section, I examine the direct and indirect influences that key thinkers in classical political economy have had on how 'value' is conceptualized and operationalized in various strands of value chain research. In Section 4, I engage with the sociology of value and valuation and argue that its insights can help us move away from a narrow analysis of value chains and towards that of value chains imbricated with chains of values. I conclude in Section 5 by proposing a typology of six worlds of valuation (market, industrial, domestic, civic, inspiration and opinion). I argue that a specific world of valuation, or a compromise among a plurality, can be stable and dominant at a particular point of a value chain (or throughout it) at a specific time. But some groups of actors can also challenge these dominant valuation ideas, discourses and practices from the standpoint of a different world of valuation or other compromises – through what I call a 'value struggle'. This approach, which I apply to wine in Part II of the book, can help us better understand the normative elements of power in value chains and their distributional effects.

2.2 GOVERNANCE AND POWER IN VALUE CHAINS[1]

Global value chain analysis has been widely used in international political economy, development studies, economic geography and economic sociology to explain the transnational organization of economic activities. It examines discrete 'value chains' (the full range of value-adding activities that firms, farmers and workers carry out to bring a product from its conception to its end use, disposal or recycling) that are explicitly governed by one or more groups of 'lead firms' (such as retailers or branded food processors) (Gereffi 1994). A key aspect of value chain research concerns various forms of *governance* (Cattaneo, Gereffi and Staritz 2010; Gereffi 1994; Gereffi, Humphrey and Sturgeon 2005; Gibbon and Ponte 2005; Milberg and Winkler 2013; Ponte and Gibbon 2005; Ponte and Sturgeon 2014). This literature underscores the role played by powerful corporations, especially those that exert 'buyer power' by placing large orders from their suppliers. These networks are both internal to the (multinational) firm and linked to independent suppliers and customers in increasingly elaborate and spatially extensive systems of sourcing, production, distribution and consumption.

'The idea of governance in value chains rests on the assumption that, while both disintegration of production and its re-integration through inter-firm trade have recognizable dynamics, they do not occur spontaneously, automatically, or even systematically' (Gibbon, Bair and Ponte 2008, 318). Instead, these processes are driven by the strategies and decisions of specific actors. Earlier work in this field focused principally on internal value chain dynamics and thus on lead firms as governing actors, but more recent research has examined the role of other actors, such as governments, social movements and international NGOs. This led to a broader approach to value chain governance defined as 'the actions and norms that shape the conditions for inclusion, exclusion and mode of participation in a value chain, which in turn determine the terms and location of value addition and capture' (Dallas, Ponte and Sturgeon 2019, 667). In this book, rather than returning to various typologies of governance in value chains, I seek to further our understanding of its sources by highlighting how values and valuation processes (subsumed under the concept of 'chains of values') shape power dynamics in relation to specific 'value struggles'.

Up to the 2010s, the value chain literature had focused mostly on *bargaining* power between lead firms and suppliers in view of explaining governance dynamics, when it considered power relations at all. But as value chain analysis expanded, different applications of the concept of power implicitly emerged, ranging from formal to informal. Dallas (2014), for example, highlighted that while socio-economic structures might include elements of cooperation and collective action, they can also be highly contentious, and when fully consolidated, embody and fix power relationships in ways that systematically create winners and losers. In other instances, power can be exerted in even more 'diffuse' ways (e.g. through demonstration effects) and collective outcomes can arise unintendedly. Some of the literature also examined how NGOs and social movements (both transnational and local) normatively contest existing power dynamics in value chains (Bair and Palpacuer 2012; Bartley 2007; Bloomfield 2014, 2017; Schurman and Munro 2009; Levy 2008), for example through different kinds and combinations of activist strategies (protest campaigns, promotion of certification, and the shaping of standards and market facilitation) (Nickow 2015).

Other contributions have drawn attention to how the expansion of capitalist production is necessarily based on the appropriation of nature (Baglioni and Campling 2017; Havice and Campling 2017, 2013). Their research is specifically concerned with how power relations change among value chain actors when environmental issues arise and/or when natural resources are brought to the centre stage of analysis, and often draws from commodity frontier theory (Moore 2015). One of the main arguments in this line of thought is that 'the ability of lead firms to govern . . . cannot be disjointed from the appropriation of nature, strategies to control the labour process and firms' associated ability to capture surplus value' (Baglioni and Campling 2017: 4). This happens not only in relation to resource extraction but also to non-material 'green commodities' such as carbon credits (Buller 2022; Neimark, Mahanty and Dressler 2016). This literature highlights that environmental conditions of production are key to how different kinds of firms reshape or contest power dynamics, and that failures in sustainability governance often arise because the actors that are targets for improvement are constrained by the pressures they are subjected to along the value chain (Ponte 2019).

These reflections led Dallas, Ponte and Sturgeon (2019) to construct a stylized typology of power in value chains that goes beyond bargaining power. Drawing broadly on the literature on different 'faces' of power (e.g. Digeser 1992), and the interactions between the structural power of business and the power of ideas (Fuchs 2007), they argue that power has two broad dimensions: 'transmission mechanisms' and 'arena of actors'. The *transmission mechanisms* of power are anchored by two ideal types: direct and diffuse. On the one end of the spectrum are circumstances where value chain actors (individually or collectively) seek to exert direct forms of influence over other actors or actor groups. This form of power is relatively unambiguous. Actors can clearly identify each other, their actions are intentional and goal-oriented, and specific actors 'possess' power and the tools and methods of exerting it. In such cases, transmission mechanisms tend to be formal and explicit and can be quite specific in their detail (e.g. defined in contracts). The other end of the spectrum consists of more diffuse forms of power in which actors, or collectives of actors, and the objects of power may be less clearly identifiable, and actions less intentional. The transmission mechanisms for diffuse power can be imprecise, such as those emerging from social movements, the propagation of new managerial models, or the emergence of new legitimate ways of doing business.

According to Dallas, Ponte and Sturgeon (2019), the *arena of actors* denotes the specific set of actors or collectives that are directly or indirectly engaged in the processes of value chain governance. There are two ideal types: dyads and collectives. The dyadic arena in the value chain and related literatures (e.g. theories of the firm, strategic management) is well established. This was the arena studied in Gereffi (1994)'s research on 'lead firms' – whether buyer- or producer-driven – and their links to suppliers or intermediaries that managed detailed contracting relationships and translated buyer requirements for factories. The second arena of actors in value chains involves 'collectives' of actors. The locus of power in this case is a function of the collective behaviours of multiple players acting simultaneously (intentionally or not) and/or of more institutionalized collectives such as business associations, multi-stakeholder initiatives or states. Combining the two dimensions of 'transmission mechanisms' and 'arenas of actors' yields a four-category typology that incorporates many of the types of power observed in value chains: *bargaining, demonstrative, institutional* and *constitutive*.

Bargaining power (dyadic and direct) is at play when the arena of actors is dyadic, and the transmission mechanism is direct. It is the most common form of power examined (often implicitly) in the value chain and related literatures (e.g. when referring to buyer, market or competence power). In value chain governance theory (Gereffi, Humphrey and Sturgeon 2005), the intensity of power asymmetry between buyers and suppliers depends on the governance form of the dyadic relationship: internal to the firm in the hierarchical form, strongly dyadic in the captive form, less so in the relational form, weakening in the modular form, and very weak in the market form. Since dyadic power can also be exerted between individual firms and institutions, such as state agencies, it can be used beyond the analysis of inter-firm relationships.

But changes in dyadic value chain relationships (e.g. increasing sustainability requirements) can shape more than the behaviour and choices of those directly involved in exchange. It can also create a demonstration effect among all suppliers or would-be suppliers of a particular good or service, which then can propagate to second-tier suppliers and beyond. This form, *demonstrative power* (dyadic and diffuse), may occur through many mechanisms. For instance, a specific form of upgrading may induce adaptation among competing suppliers, or among suppliers wishing to compete in the future. Demonstration power can also be exerted by non-firm actors, such as NGOs or journalists.

Institutional power (collective and direct) is a form of direct power that is exercised by collectives that are more formally organized (e.g. in business associations, multi-stakeholder initiatives, shared technological platforms or by the state). While power in dyadic relationships stems from resources controlled by a single organization, in collective arenas it is at least partly external, in the sense of being dependent upon the strategic actions of groups of actors, or upon the rules set by formally organized collectives. What distinguishes institutional power from bargaining power is that it derives from the combined engagements of actors that share clear membership in one or more initiatives or organizations and use a particular set of standards or link to shared technology platforms.

Constitutive power (collective and diffuse) is manifested when collective arenas do not exhibit clear or formal common membership and thus power is not embodied in particular actors or has an institutionalized locus, even to the point that the outcome of power may be unintended. Constitutive power is less explicitly codified, is applied through less precise measurement techniques and standards, and requires less direct forms of enforcement. However, actors still know and agree when a general norm or convention has been violated and sanctions may be collectively imposed, though enforcement is decentralized and often subtle and nuanced compared to the pre-ordained arbiters and judges that may be used in institutional power. Examples of constitutive power include the slow diffusion of outsourcing or financialization as general 'best practices' against which firms come to progressively structure themselves, and/or the normative role exerted by social movements on corporate conduct and transparency (Bair and Palpacuer 2015). Many norms, broad conventions and best practices exist in this non-formalized state.

An emerging literature has started to apply, improve upon and/or criticize this way of understanding power in value chains. For example, Ponte (2019) uses it to highlight the role of sustainability in shaping value chain governance – by examining how institutional, demonstrative and constitutive power play a role in enhancing or limiting the exercise of bargaining power in selected agro-food value chains. Lang, Ponte and Vilakazi (2022) explore the links between these forms of power and different aspects of inequality in value chains. Iliopoulos and Wójcik (2024) examine how the Big Four accounting and consultancy firms (KPMG, PwC, EY and Deloitte) use different forms of power to reshape the governance structures of global value chains. A special issue in *Global Networks* includes papers that 'grapple centrally with how to understand the nature, sources, and/or effects of power in GVCs' (Ponte, Bair and Dallas 2023, 3). Among these, Tups and Dannenberg (2023) show how a Norwegian lead firm governs the chemical fertilizer value chain by forging public-private partnerships with government agencies (institutional power), by establishing demonstration farm plots in small farmer communities (demonstrative power) and by proposing synthetic fertilizer practices as reflective of 'modern' farming (constitutive power). These dynamics result in farmers finding themselves squeezed between powerful global buyers of agricultural outputs on the one hand, and a powerful global supplier of agricultural inputs on the other. In this instance, institutional, constitutive and demonstrative power operate in ways that increase the bargaining power of the fertilizer firm.

A different picture emerges from Dallas and Shiu (2023)'s study of the telecommunications value chain. Focusing on constitutive power, they argue that it varies along a continuum between 'encompassing' and 'fractured' – differing in the degree to which actors are self-aware of their own social construction by norms, values and conventions. At the 'encompassing' end of the continuum they place 'governmentality' (Dean 2009), which in extreme cases entails a totalizing situation where 'actors are completely unable to pierce the veil of social construction or attain self-conscious awareness' (Dallas and Shiu 2023, 797). Moving towards more fractured forms of constitutive power, they identify 'hegemonic stability' in a Gramscian sense (Gramsci 1988), which 'combines sufficient material compromises to the dominated, while creating ideological limits on what is possible in society. So, social stability is never assured because it is always potentially contestable, since it sits in limbo between state coercion, material incentive and ideological control' (Dallas and Shiu 2023, 797).[2] At the 'fractured' end of the continuum, they place legitimacy, where constitutive power is less intentional and more partial and inchoate. 'In these circumstances, collective constitution (the norms, values, perceptions, etc.) is more prone to questioning and change because their social construction is not fully taken-for-granted' (Dallas and Shiu 2023, 798). In their contribution, they focus on legitimacy as a fractured form of constitutive power by examining a comprehensive dataset of telecommunications standards. Focusing on an organization called 3GPP that is tasked with setting global mobile telecommunications standards, Dallas and Shiu show that lead firms must cultivate legitimacy by persuading their peer firms to agree to their preferred standards. They argue that the standard-setting process is ultimately driven by legitimacy and constrains the bargaining power of industry leaders.[3]

Bair and Mahutga (2023) and Staricco (2022) instead suggest that value chain analysis would be better served by focusing mainly on bargaining power. Bair and Mahutga examine how value chains generate skew in value capture among participating firms, based on different ratios of buyers to suppliers. They recognize that processes of institutional, demonstrative and constitutive power can shape value chains, but for them, the key question is how these influences affect the skew in value capture. Staricco makes a similar call but draws inspiration from world-systems theory. Through the analysis of the biodiesel value chain, and in particular the struggles of Argentine soy producers in navigating changing regulatory frameworks in the United States and the European Union, Staricco does not see the policy environment as a type of institutional power, but as a factor affecting the value of resources controlled by value chain actors, and thus as a source of bargaining power. For Bair and Mahutga (2023) and Staricco (2023), other forms of power are secondary and lack direct causal impact on value capture. For example, Staricco argues that only value chain actors can wield power, and their actions and relations constitute bargaining power. Other types of power constitute the context and serve to empower the actors.

In contrast, Dallas, Ponte and Sturgeon (2019) consider the four types of power as interactive, layered and combinatory (see also Lang, Ponte and Vilakazi 2022) and

> [blurring] the boundaries between actor and environment such that many of the resources, capabilities and relations of firms derive from, are buttressed by or acquire value from their legal and normative environments . . . [preferring] a tree-soil image in which the roots of the tree are so intertwined with the soil as to make clear-cut distinctions between actor-environment and the four types of power difficult to make in many situations. This, however, does not preclude identifying how, collectively, the four forms of power can shape governance in time, including how other forms of power interactively (re)shape bargaining power.
>
> Ponte, Bair, and Dallas 2023, 5

Whether other forms of power act directly or indirectly through bargaining power, we still need to better understand how demonstrative and constitutive power function in value chains (in this book, given the space limitations, I focus on constitutive power only). Because these kinds of power have important normative and discursive features, I argue that to move this research agenda forward we need to rethink the notion of 'value' in value chains as well. In so doing, I do not seek to directly contribute to current discussions on different types of constitutive power and their degrees of fragmentation or cohesiveness (as in Dallas and Shiu 2023). Rather, I pursue a further understanding of the inner dynamics of constitutive power by unpacking the normative registers that actors draw from when challenging dominant valuation systems.

2.3 ON VALUE IN VALUE CHAINS

Despite featuring prominently in its label, 'value' is not often discussed theoretically in value chain analysis (Havice and Pickles 2019). In this section, I examine the influences that various classical political economy approaches to value (for helpful overviews, see Heilbroner 1983; Mirowski 1990; Pitts 2021) have had on value chain research. In the following section, I delineate what the sociology of value and valuation can contribute to the study of constitutive power in value chains.

Value as price

Two key propositions for the discussion of value arise from the corner of classical political economy that later became the basis for neoclassical economics. One proposition is that things do not hold any value on their own, thus all that is needed to understand value is their price – which is the relation between different things as exchangeable. Another proposition is that value is a set of subjective properties and is linked to the utility that can be gained from these properties in different quantities (Heilbroner 1983, 272). Developing on ideas first introduced by Walras (2014 [1883]) and Jevons (1879), value in neoclassical economics is cast as arising in the act of exchange in the context of subjective desires (Pitts 2021, 53). This is most clearly delineated in the marginal utility theories developed first by Marshall and others (see, inter alia, Marshall 2013 [1890]), for which price is the direct measure of value arising from the balance of supply and demand, with marginal utility (the utility gained from the last increment of the unit of consumption) tending to diminish as the quantity of the good or service consumed increases. From this perspective, a thing cannot embed value irrespectively of quantity and the preferences of consumers, as its price will be different in different market situations and in relation to subjective preferences. This approach delinks value from labour (see below) and provides a moral justification for the unequal returns allocated to workers and capitalists. Human rationality reigns, while political issues, inequality, power relations and social interaction do not shape the value of things. Rent (intended as 'unearned income', see below) is deemed to be only possible in abnormal circumstances or to stimulate innovation (e.g. through time-limited assurance of intellectual property rights), but should disappear once a general equilibrium is restored through perfect competition.

Much of the policy-oriented value chain literature leans on the concept of value as 'what buyers are willing to pay for a product or service ... measured by total revenue' (Porter 1985, 3, 38), essentially equating value with price. Value added is seen as a key component of economic development planning in international institutions, such as UNCTAD, WTO, the World Bank and ILO. By mapping actors and functions in a value chain, this research seeks to assess the 'conditions and consequences of production systems in terms of where gains and losses are made and by whom, measuring national accounts, and planning development interventions accordingly' (Havice and Pickles 2019, 170). These perspectives emphasize participation in value chains in view of creating and distributing value towards targeted groups of actors, often on the basis of analyses of net value added at the national level through input-output matrices and/or measuring its distribution along the value chain, usually as profit, return over capital employed, value added and/or price markups (Gereffi, Humphrey and Kaplinsky 2001). These approaches are often missing a deeper understanding of the power dynamics that shape the distribution of value added (Gradin 2016). To better understand these, we need to turn to the concept of value as rent.

Value as rent

Much global value chain and cognate global production network research (see, e.g. Coe and Yeung 2015) takes an implicit or explicit 'neo-Ricardian' approach to value, seeing it as 'the differential ability to create profits and/or capture monopoly rents from the specific position of a firm in the chain ... with a specific governance form and set of interfirm relations' (Havice and Pickles 2019, 170–1). Neo-Ricardian analyses consider 'value as carried and conserved within things, either inhering within the things themselves or inserted there by the labour that created them' (Pitts 2021, 9). While for the Mercantilists of the seventeenth century, value was equivalent to gold – and all other goods were valued in relation to how much gold would be exchanged for them, many classical political economists from the mid-eighteenth to the end of the nineteenth century claimed that value is ascribed to things during the production process. The French physiocrats, and Quesnay in particular (1894), argued that the value of things derives from the (farm) labour time expended in their production, while for Smith (1977 [1776]), value comprised the costs of (industrial) labour, land and capital.

In the early nineteenth century, Ricardo (1821) critiqued these narrow cost-of-production approaches by questioning how inputs acquire their own value to begin with – and by asking questions about how value is distributed through society. His critique of rentiership as 'unproductive' activity carried out by the landed gentry, merchants and financiers led him to link value to the labour time embedded into a product. Ricardo thus opened the possibility of considering the historical, social and political processes that structure production and the power relations that underpin them (Pitts 2021). He also argued that, like production, consumption can also be productive or unproductive – depending on whether a capitalist invests profits to buy labour to reproduce capital for more profit – and thus contributing to growth ('productive consumption') – or whether a capitalist consumes these profits on luxuries that do nothing to further reproduce capital ('unproductive' consumption) (Mazzucato 2018, 45).

Distinctions between productive and unproductive capital have returned in more recent international political economy debates. Critical scholars argue that, as the platform economy comes to dominate contemporary capitalism through digital monopolies based on network effects, ignoring the issue of rent has become increasingly untenable. As a result, questions about what is value creation and what is value capture, how value and wealth should be distributed in society, what are 'reasonable' rates of profit and rent, and what are productive and parasitic economic activities, have come back to the fore. If value can only be created, then there is no need to understand the antagonistic relations between labour, capital and nature. If rent does not exist (or is considered just a temporary phenomenon as in mainstream economics), there is less justification for looking into the sources of inequality. But if value can also be captured and distributed, then important questions about rents, monopolies and innovation arise (Durand and Milberg 2020; Mazzucato 2018; Quentin and Campling 2018).

Critical political economists remind us that to understand innovation and the value creation (and extraction) dynamics of contemporary capitalism, we should be aware of the heroic assumptions that often characterize the study of entrepreneurship. This is especially the case in business studies, where entrepreneurship is often tied to Schumpeterian notions of creative destruction and waves of innovation (Schumpeter 2013 [1950]). As Mazzucato (2018) argues, innovation is cumulative; it is built on the work of others and related long-term investments; it is also uncertain, with the public sector usually taking the bulk of high risk in the very early stages of technological development when private finance would not enter; and it is collective, as the 'lone entrepreneur' usually benefits from previous work of other entrepreneurs and builds on the benefits of taxpayer-based research funding. Rather than drawing on the brilliance of entrepreneurs, capitalist production is based on the extraction of value from common pools of knowledge (what Hardt and Negri 2017 call 'cooperative social labour') and from natural resources (Moore 2015).

Mazzucato (2018) highlights several ways in which value extraction takes place in the contemporary 'innovation economy'. The first is through venture capital's engagement in financing start-ups just before commercialization, and riding upon the massive investment of 'patient capital' (often from the public sector) in the basic science that precedes it – in other words, through the privatization of gain and the socialization of the higher degree of risk that is typical of early-stage R&D. The second is through the network effects of the so-called platform economy, where networks become more valuable as more people use their services. This amplifies the ability of firms to achieve and maintain monopolistic conditions in their markets and allows them to gain a disproportionate share of value. By posing as providers of free services to their users, these digital platforms actually capture value through users' personal data that is sold to advertisers and other clients (Zuboff 2019).

The third way in which value extraction takes place is the result of a profound transformation of the intellectual property rights regime, which far from stimulating innovation seems to have been transformed into a tool for preventing it. While patents were originally thought of as an instrument of sharing knowledge as well as allowing time-limited monopoly, they have now been transformed into an instrument mainly for defending private rewards (Durand and Milberg 2020). Patents have been expanded from actual products to the knowledge behind the possibility of future innovation. They are now easier to obtain, easier to renew, and can be used strategically to block competition and/or collect royalties. In other words, they offer opportunities for 'unproductive entrepreneurship' that can 'reinforce monopolies and intensify abuse of market power, block the diffusion of knowledge and follow-on innovation, and make it easier to privatize research that is publicly funded and collectively created' (Mazzucato 2018, 206).

In the value chain literature, these debates have often translated into discussions of how different forms of rent shape the distribution of value added, where rent is conceptualized as a particular form of profit that is captured through some form of privileged access. These forms include monopoly rents (e.g. those drawn by first adopters); differential productivity of factors (including entrepreneurship); and barriers to entry (through scarcity or state regulation, for example) (Havice and Pickles 2019, 171). Kaplinsky (2005) in particular highlights the distinct forms of rents that structure global value chains, which can be eroded by competition and innovation.[4] These observations are often included in the large literature on upgrading in value chains (see, inter alia, Humphrey and Schmitz 2002), which is concerned with how the distribution of value (intended as rent) can be reshaped for the benefit of weaker players. Yet, much of this literature does not attempt to explain 'what value is, how it is produced, or how the production of value translates (or does not) into profits and forms of economic organization' (Havice and Pickles 2019, 172). Also, as Quentin and Campling (2018) rightly argue, a focus on value as rent does not per se help understanding of unequal distributions between wages and returns to capital for asset owners, to which I now turn.

Value as surplus labour time

For Marx, the value of commodities is equivalent to the labour time that was used in their production under the command of capital and shaped by its exploitative tendencies. As a corollary, definitions of 'productive' and 'unproductive' activities for Marx depend on historical contexts and the nature of antagonisms between different social classes (1992 [1894]). Marx also highlights the difference between use and exchange value, arguing that a commodity is both a product and a social relation that embodies exchange value (Espeland and Stevens 1998; Pitts 2021). From this perspective, exchange value is thus embedding the value that is already inherent in a commodity, and is built on the commensurability of one commodity with another through the medium of money, measured by price (Mazzucato 2018;

Pitts 2021). Marx argues that production is made possible by 'necessary labour time', during which labourers work for a wage equivalent to assuring their reproduction, and by 'surplus labour time', which is spent to work for the capitalist who then accrues (and tries to maximize) 'surplus value' (Pitts 2021, 18–26). Put differently, workers are exploited because the owners of assets capture the surplus value that workers produce beyond their subsistence needs.

Marx's labour theory of value has been often leveraged in contemporary political economy, political ecology and resource geography debates. These debates have informed work that attempts to unpack the 'value of nature' through examining the articulation of value as '"abstract social labour" that stands in opposition to the "concrete" labour it takes to produce any given commodity, including the concrete engagement with nature, resources and ecosystems' (Huber 2018, 149). This research attempts to unpack the compulsions that are involved in unfettered competition, resulting in labour exploitation and the destruction of ecological systems. It pays particular attention to the roles that biophysical processes and 'material nature play in the process of producing value and enabling expanded capital accumulation' (Kay and Kenney-Lazar 2017, 296). Much of this literature highlights that many ecological impacts are not captured by monetary valuation (they are 'externalities'); that ecosystem services provided by nature are often appropriated for free by capital; that the exploitation of nature is facilitated by specific calculative practices (Robertson 2012); and that the appropriation of value often works through the environment (Havice and Campling 2017).

These debates have also come to shape discussions in the more critical strands of value chain research (Havice and Pickles 2019), including contributions from 'Marxian, feminist, progressive liberal, and labor rights theorists and activists who have criticized the sociological readings of monopoly rents. This grouping turns attention to the centrality of exploitation as the dynamic of underdevelopment and unequal exchange and raising distributional concerns' (Havice and Pickles 2019, 174). This line of research (see, e.g. Bair et al. 2013; Neilson and Pritchard 2011; Selwyn 2014) sees value as a site of social and political struggle and seeks a return of value chain analysis to concerns with distributional issues, class and labour struggle, and gender inequalities (Barrientos 2019). In the following discussion, I build upon these reflections to suggest how a specific take on 'value struggles' can help move forward a research agenda on power and inequality in global value chains.

Value struggles

Havice and Pickles (2019) propose to move value chain analysis forward by examining the form and nature of value as a starting point to explain 'why GVCs have emerged as they have, what drives the incessant search for cost minimization and organizational and technical upgrading, and why GVCs have increasingly become a central feature of contemporary capitalism' (Havice and Pickles 2019, 170). For them, value chain analysis should draw more attention to the 'volatile shifts in the geography of production; the concomitant de/revaluation of labor; iterative, often violent, forms of dispossession; and everyday struggles over value through which subjects navigate their own reproduction as workers, managers, farmers, traders and "surplus-ed" populations' (Havice and Pickles 2019, 175, drawing on Bair et al. 2013).

Pioneering work on value chain struggles by Neilson and Pritchard (2011) took an institutional perspective to chart the restructuring in agri-food value chains in South India. In their take, struggle is triggered when new forms of value chain governance interact with a variety of local institutional environments. They focus on four prisms of struggle in these value chains: over supplier upgrading, over labour and livelihoods, over environmental governance, and over the fate of smallholder farmers more generally. These struggles may result in changes to the politics of inclusion and exclusion, and to forms and scales of chain governance – eventually leading to institutional realignments, the reproduction of territorial differentiation and new forms of mediation by lead actors. These have feedback loops on institutional environments and value chain restructuring, leading to new equilibria and/or new forms of struggle (Neilson and Pritchard 2011). Other research that emphasized the role of value chain struggles includes analyses of appropriation by (larger) capital of surplus value released by (smaller) capital (Starosta 2010), work that highlights antagonistic challenges to value chain governance (Alford 2020), and studies showing that value capture from lead firms often has detrimental or exclusionary impacts on weaker chain participants (Baglioni, Campling and Hanlon 2020; Coveri and Zanfei 2022; Durand and Milberg 2020; Ponte 2019).

These are important contributions, but often missing in these value chain debates is an explicit engagement of the racial and gender dimensions of struggle (see Chapter 6). The relative silence on racial dynamics in value chain analysis is particularly poignant, given the long-standing argument that all kinds of capitalism should be seen as 'racial capitalism' (from Robinson 2000 [1983]; Hall et al. 2019 [1980] onwards) and related calls to adopt 'postcolonial' and 'decolonial' approaches in view of challenging the dominant narratives and traditions emanating from the Global North (Bhambra 2014; Mignolo 2021). More attention is being given to gender issues (see, inter alia, Barrientos 2019), but they are far from being mainstream in value chain analysis. When it comes to 'value', Gradin (2016, 354) suggests that it 'should be understood as a broader philosophical concept concerning the justice and purpose of human productive activity . . . GVC analysis must therefore pay greater attention to political struggles throughout the value chain'. Smith (2016) provides a similar argument, articulating that political struggles are essentially about mobilizing or suppressing values. Finally, recent research on 'ethical value networks' has started to examine the accumulation dynamics operating under the aegis of normative values rooted in ethicality (Murray et al. 2022). In this book, I attempt to move further in this direction by unpacking the normative elements shaping 'value struggles' (including those along the lines of race and gender), and how these operate through constitutive power in value chains – ultimately shaping distributive outcomes. In order to take this step, in the following section I argue that we need to draw inspiration from the sociology of value and valuation.

2.4 THE SOCIOLOGY OF VALUE AND VALUATION

The sociology of value and valuation broadly argues that 'value' arises from a relational sphere, is imbricated in institutions, and is explicitly shaped by political and moral 'values'. Preferences from this perspective are not set before an exchange takes place, as neoclassical economics would have it, but are socially shaped and framed within existing (but dynamic) structures, techniques and metrics of valuation. This branch of sociology focuses specifically on processes of 'valuation'; examines an economic order that is 'good' rather than functional; and seeks a principle of value that 'requires socially acceptable as well as technically sufficient determinations' (Heilbroner 1983, 257). It is based on a view of value that does not only relate to a 'thing' but also to the signification of a person's status (as owner, seller or buyer) in the context of a scheme of valuation dominant in a particular culture (as Veblen 2012 [1899] taught us). Thus, value can be seen 'as continually constructed and reconstructed in the process of market operation' (Mirowski 1990, 708) – and in the context of cultural and moral determinations of taste steeped in class (Bourdieu 1979), race and gender (see Chapter 6). Furthermore, the attributes of a commodity are not only socially constructed in relational terms but also framed and managed by various practices, technologies and institutional frameworks (Pitts 2021, 76–8).

Broadly speaking, work within this field contends that value is not residing *in* the commodity (as in some of the approaches to value in classical political economy discussed above) but is determined through the relations between those who produce, trade and consume things *and* the social practices that frame these encounters. Value is thus a subjective judgement about things (Simmel 1978).

> No objective experiences are possible but only valuations of experiences that create what we perceive as objectively given reality. The subjective attribution of value thus creates the order of social life. Nonetheless, the value of a particular object – although emerging from subjective judgement – is neither arbitrary nor random ... [For Simmel, value is] a socially constructed judgment that nevertheless appears to individuals as natural fact.
>
> Krüger and Reinhart 2017, 269

In short, these approaches seek to go beyond a neat distinction between 'value' (to be studied by economists) and 'values' (to be studied by sociologists), and between the economy and social relations (Stark 2009). 'Value' in the economic sense is linked to what extent people are willing to give up for the objects they desire. 'Values' in a sociological sense is what is 'good, proper, or desirable'. To these distinctions, Graeber (2001) adds a linguistic layer of meaning, that of value as 'meaningful difference'. Ultimately, rather than focusing on the 'static fixtures of value and values' Stark (2009, 7) exhort us to work on the process of valuation.

Much of the sociology of value and valuation revolves around solving the uncertainty of market exchange and the contingency of the value of a product.[5] One of the points of departure in this internally diverse tradition is that 'value and price differ, but markets establish economic value in the form of prices, both as a result of people coming together to trade *and* as an outcome of a specific institutional structure' (Aspers and Beckert 2011, 27, original emphasis; see also Boltanski and Esquerre 2020). This entails that value does not emerge naturally from the market as price. It is socially constructed by the actors involved in exchange – depending on how they assess the material, symbolic and experiential value of a good, the availability and legitimacy of valuation devices, and in the context of varying degrees of competition, regulation and power dynamics (e.g. between buyers and sellers at different points of a value chain).

Another common argument in this literature is that things have 'social lives' themselves. Exchange creates value through the politics that operate throughout different phases in and out of their commodity status – as things acquire multiple meanings and different valuations repertoires are applied in time and space (Appadurai 1988). Methodologically, this implies that 'we have to follow the things themselves, for their meanings are inscribed in their forms, their uses, their trajectories. It is only through the analysis of these trajectories that we can interpret the human transactions and calculations that enliven things' (Appadurai 1988, 5). This approach fits quite naturally with value chain analysis (Ponte, Gereffi and Raj-Reichert 2019), which usually follows a product in 'its *total* trajectory from production, through exchange/distribution, to consumption' (Appadurai 1988, 13, original emphasis).

Aspers and Beckert (2011) suggest distinguishing different (but interrelated) dimensions of value and valuation – moral, economic and symbolic. The moral dimension (whether a good has a better or worse impact on the environment, for example) can and does form the basis of the valuation of goods – as Fourcade (2011) eloquently showed in relation to the valuation of damage from oil spills, and Zelizer (1979) in the context of the emergence of life insurance in the US. The economic dimension 'refers to . . . goods or services in terms of how much money an actor is willing to surrender to obtain property rights to the good in question' (Aspers and Beckert 2011, 8). The symbolic dimension can arise from the positional performance that the good can impart in public on the 'owner within the space of a differentiated social world' (Beckert 2011, 109), but can also stem from the imaginative performance of the good in private, as it can 'evoke fantasies based on symbolic associations with desired events, people . . . and representations of transcendental ideals' (Beckert 2011, 108–9).

Calculation and metrology are at the centre of valuation (Archer 2024) and include devices and assemblages that ensure the operativity of markets and the social conditions and technologies that underpin the qualification of products (Çalışkan and Callon 2009; Callon, Méadel and Rabeharisoa 2002; Callon and Muniesa 2005; Callon, Millo and Muniesa 2007; Muniesa, Millo and Callon 2007). Heinich's recent work (Heinich 2017, 2020a, b) is a further call for more focus paid to valuation processes, rather than value per se. For her, 'value is obtained by action, in the processes of qualification and requalification' (Heinich 2020a, 77). Valuation can relate to different resources, some of which are objective, others are perceptive – and pertains to things, people, actions and states of the world. It can relate to the material properties of the object, the competences of actors (including valuation principles and criteria), and the contexts that frame the interaction between objects and subjects. Valuation can take place through measurement (including but not only in the form of price), attachment (implicit or outwards appreciation through gestures or narratives), and judgement (the actual operation through which value is attributed, e.g. opinion to expert evaluation) (Heinich 2020a).

Finally, relevant to our discussion is work examining the so-called 'enrichment economy', which unpacks 'the way commodities are distributed among several different forms of valuation – that is, according to the way the price attached to a given commodity is justified and critiqued' (Boltanski and Esquerre 2020, 2). In this line of thought, the term 'enrichment economy' is interpreted in a dual sense: first, in the sense of enhancing the value of things or cultural assets that already exist, especially through narratives that shape differences and identities; second, in relation to things that are intended above all for the wealthy, including those that Karpik (2010) considers 'singularities'.[6] For Reckwitz (2020), we actually live in a 'society of singularities', as capitalism moves from industrial to cultural production (more on this in Chapter 4).

Boltanski and Esquerre (2020) focus on moments of exchange, when the prices of things are justified or criticized, and on how different forms of valuation 'generate arguments that serve to mediate, in a sense, between objects and prices' (2020, 74). This occurs in a situation of uncertainty about the persons engaged in the exchange and/or the qualification of the property of the things that are being traded. Given the often-unequal relations between buyer and seller, prices can be contested by either exiting the interaction or by challenging the price – although this rarely happens for everyday items. For Boltanski and Esquerre (2020), the value of material things (they do not examine services) is thus an arrangement for justifying or critiquing their price.[7] Their observation is that the enrichment economy has been growing dramatically in post-industrial societies, and that while the value of industrial products tends to decrease over time, the value of things that are part of the enrichment economy tends to increase. Antiquity objects, works of art, luxury items, and fine wines are some examples of objects that are meant to be kept rather than used or consumed – sometimes they are even stored away and thus are not leveraged for the distinction effects of conspicuous consumption (Boltanski and Esquerre 2020, 42–3). When the logic of acquiring such items is to fill a collection, marginal utility increases instead of decreasing as neoclassical economists would have it.

I will draw from this last set of insights in Chapter 4 when handling 'fine wines' (rare, collection and investment wines), where I also seek to relativize the putative rise of a society of singularities and the enrichment economy in a more global perspective. While these phenomena may have become more common among the upper classes in the Global North (and in more unequal countries of the Global South), I argue that they are framed as constitutive of global capitalism because they mainly arise from the lived experiences of Parisian and other European economic and cultural elites. The broader geographical and class perspective adopted in this book will show that although the society of singularities and the enrichment economy are behind some processes of valuation, they may not be the most significant in contemporary capitalism.

2.5 WORLDS OF VALUATION: AN ANALYTICAL FRAMEWORK

For the purposes of this book, I propose the term 'worlds of valuation' to unpack the discursive, normative and justificatory repertoires that different actors leverage to valorize a product or service in a value chain – in this particular instance, wine and wine tourism experiences. Dewey (1939), in his *Theory of valuation*, holds that

> value emerges only from reflection within a particular situation and can neither be thought of as a fixed objective standard nor as a given subjective feeling nor as intrinsic to certain objects or practices ... Valuation is instead a specific intervention that reorganizes a particular situation by promoting a future course of action based on whether something is good and on how good it is.
>
> Krüger and Reinhart 2017, 271

Stark (2011) observes that, for Dewey, the term valuation can variously refer to 'prizing' (holding precious, a personal and emotional process), 'appraising' (putting a value upon something, a relational and intellectual process), or 'praising' (evoking a sense of amazement, an imaginative process often linked to experience goods, such as the attendance of a concert). But while for Dewey (1939), valuation arises from individual capabilities, in the contemporary sociology of value and valuation (and especially in Boltanski and Thévenot 2006), it takes 'a more structural ... stance by focusing on the interplay between value orders and valuation practices in situations of conflict' – in a society that is in a permanent process of ordering and reconfiguration (Krüger and Reinhart 2017, 273).

In their seminal work, Boltanski and Thévenot (2006, originally published in French in 1991) argue that action, when devised to cope with criticism and justification, is made more legitimate by relying on particular views of the common good (see also Diaz-Bone 2016; Diaz-Bone and de Larquier 2022; Eymard-Duvernay 2006, 1989; Thévenot 1995; Thévenot, Moody and Lafaye 2000). To deal with challenges and critiques, justification processes need to rely on reality tests. These tests involve both people and objects and are related to modes of coordination that are based on historically based 'worlds'. According to Boltanski and Thévenot (2006), these worlds are characterized by variation along a number of elements: a higher common principle; states of worthiness and relations of worth; characterizations of common dignity; lists of 'worthy' subjects, objects and arrangements; investment forms to achieve worthiness; 'natural' relations among beings; harmonious figures of the natural order; model tests; modes of expression of judgment; forms of expression of judgment; and states of deficiency that may lead to decline.

In this line of inquiry, rational calculation is embedded into each world, thus bounded rationality is not a cognitive limit. It is limited by the boundary of the moral order that organizes each world (Stark 2011). At the same time, 'all economic objects are [considered to be] thoroughly cultural, and no moral order could operate without specific material objects' (Stark 2009, 13). The distinction between moral and market economies then disappears, as all economies can only be seen as moral economies. In this book, I adapt Boltanski and Thévenot (2006)'s words to valuation processes, which are ultimately about how actors arrive at a judgement of value (Aspers and Beckert 2011, 14) and are directed by practices and techniques of testing, and by judgement devices and commensuration (Espeland and Stevens 1998).

Some of these reflections have inspired research on the governance of value chains and helped to delineate the differences between 'governance as driving', 'governance as linking', and 'governance as normalizing' (Gibbon, Bair and Ponte 2008). In a nutshell, governance as driving refers to Gereffi (1994)'s original formulation that examines the role played by powerful firm-level actors, or chain 'drivers', in governing whole chains. Governance as linking builds upon Gereffi, Humphrey and Sturgeon (2005)'s theory of governance, which focuses on the characteristics of linkages between firms at individual nodes in the chain. The result is a theory of how and why specific linkages in the chain are governed, rather than a theory of whole chain governance – since firms may form different types of linkages at various times, with different business partners, and at different points in the value chain (Ponte and Sturgeon 2014). Governance as normalizing instead explores the normative, justificatory and discursive dimensions that frame buyer-supplier relations and transmission mechanisms along value chains (Gibbon and Ponte 2005; Gibbon, Bair and Ponte 2008) – a research agenda I continue in this book.

Much of the work on value chain governance as normalizing (Daviron and Ponte 2005; Ouma 2015; Gibbon and Ponte 2005) has sought to explain governance dynamics by examining how quality conventions underpin different forms of coordination that facilitate exchange (Batifoulier 2001; Diaz-Bone and de Larquier 2022; Eymard-Duvernay 2006). Variations of this approach can also be found in work on 'worlds of production' (Salais and Storper 1992; Storper and Salais 1997) and 'worlds of food' (Morgan, Marsden and Murdoch 2006). From these vantage points, value chains are organized along the lines of product qualification, with the valuation of quality as key to understanding how competitive strategies emerge, consolidate and/or dissolve (Allaire and Boyer 1995; Allaire and Daviron 2018; Ponte 2016). Often, this entails examining whether and how dominant quality conventions are transmitted along value chains, what makes them travel, and which actors have the normative power to impose one convention over another beyond a single value chain node (Gibbon and Ponte 2005). Collectively, this body of work seeks to explain how certain strategies are employed to align a firm to a general perception of what is believed to be 'best practice' at a particular time (Gibbon and Riisgaard 2014; Karlsen 2018; Ponte and Gibbon 2005). It also shows that, while conventions typically overlap, one or a specific combination often form a dominant underpinning for certain forms of coordination in a value chain node at a particular time (Coq-Huelva, Sanz-Cañada and Sánchez-Escobar 2014). But plural conventions can also overlap; the same firm may rely on different ones with different clients; and distinct quality conventions can be applied simultaneously in the same supplier-buyer transaction (Kanamaru 2020; Kumar and Beerepoot 2019).[8]

The concept of convention has been often leveraged to understand different registers of quality at the moment of exchange of a good or service along a value chain. Through the delineation of broader 'worlds of valuation', in this book, I seek to operationalize the multiple meanings of value as 'prizing' (holding precious), 'appraising' (putting a value upon something) and 'praising' (evoking a sense of amazement) (Dewey 1939). This way, I contribute to further understanding how constitutive power can drive 'governance through normalization' in value chains. For this purpose, I adapt the six worlds of justification in Boltanski and Thévenot (2006)[9] to processes of valuation in view of unpacking the mutual constitution of value chains and chains of values (see Table 1):

- In the *market world*, the common principle is market competition, and valuation is based on the market price for goods and services, including labour.
- In the *industrial world*, the common principle is efficiency, and valuation is linked to the ability to achieve scalability and proper functionality.
- In the *domestic world*, the common principle is related to traditional benevolence – often extending the chains of hierarchical and personal dependency through generations. Valuation is related to trust, authenticity and history.
- In the *civic world*, the common principle is collective solidarity, and valuation is associated with the collective impacts on social, labour and/or environmental conditions.
- In the *inspired world*, the common principle is spiritual or creative enhancement, and valuation is linked to the creative or adventurous aspects of an experience, and/or a unique set of practices or personality.
- In the *world of opinion*, the common principle is fame, and valuation is linked to renown and visibility.

These worlds of valuation do not have a hierarchical structure, nor do I portray any of them as historical inevitabilities – although the empirical analysis will show that market/industrial valuation compromises tend to be dominant in wine value chains and in contemporary capitalism more generally. But even when one world of valuation or a combination of worlds may be dominant at a specific place and time, it may be challenged – thus leading to processes of clarification, change, compromise or demise, as I examine in Part II of the book. I will also show that worlds of valuation are not purely representational – they actually shape power structures in value chains. Different worlds actually entail specific cognitive barriers and asymmetries in power relations among actors. They privilege some

Table 1 Key features of different worlds of valuation

Worlds of valuation

	Market	Industrial	Domestic	Civic	Inspired	Opinion
Common principle	Competition	Efficiency	Traditional benevolence	Collective solidarity	Spiritual or creative enhancement	Fame
Units of valuation	Product units	Plans, systems, controls, forecasts	Specific assets	Negotiation, consultation, distributional arrangements	Innovation, creation	Public relations, brand names, social media recognition
Questions underpinning valuation processes	Is it economic?	Is it technically efficient, scalable, functional?	Does it follow tradition? Can it be trusted?	Is it collectively safe, healthy, environmentally sound?	Is it new or unique? Is it a breakthrough?	Is it accepted by the public / consumers?
Valuation focus	Price	Scalability, and proper functionality	Trust, history, repetition	Social, labour, environmental, collective impacts	Creativity, novelty, personality	Renown, visibility

Source: Adapted and expanded from Boltanski and Thévenot (2006), Gibbon and Riisgaard (2014, 101), Ponte (2009, 240), and Ponte and Sturgeon (2014, 208).

actors and activities over others in the power struggles over value creation, capture and distribution. Therefore, disadvantaged actors, seeking to change the status quo, can create venues of value capture or at least avoid value predation by others by applying different leverage points in different situations. To do so, they need to challenge the justifications that underpin the dominant world(s) of valuation and question their injustices.

In the rest of this book, I examine how these six worlds of valuation (market, industrial, domestic, civic, inspired, opinion) operate in three distinct sites of value struggle that are particularly relevant for the study of wine: (1) *place*; (2) *nature*; and (3) *people* (through the intersectionality of class, race and gender). These three sites are not exclusive – in other empirical settings, different sites may be relevant while some of the ones I delineate here may not be (e.g. place). These sites also partly overlap, but an analytical distinction is helpful to better delineate the dynamics and effects of specific struggles. This approach will ultimately inform a reflection of the nature and dynamics of constitutive power in global value chains.

Chapter 3

THE GLOBAL, SOUTH AFRICAN AND ITALIAN VALUE CHAINS FOR WINE

3.1 INTRODUCTION

In this chapter, I provide the essential background information on value chain configurations for wine, material and intangible assets and flows, and various forms of regulation – the structural framework around, within and through which overlapping 'chains of values' operate. These chains of value bring together a plurality of worlds of valuation that are leveraged by various groups of actors at different sites of value struggle (the focus of Part II of the book). Valuation processes in wine have material, symbolic and experiential aspects. The tangible base is linked first and foremost to the intrinsic quality of wine in its material characteristics (such as alcohol level, colour, acidity, body, effervescence, sweetness, grape variety or blend) and the processes that are needed to deliver them (such as viticulture practices and vinification style). The intangible dimensions relate to brand, geographical origin, and various environmental and labour/social sustainability attributes, among others. The valuation signifiers that are behind these different dimensions are usually embedded in packaging (label, bottle design, etchings, medals, certification seals) and are shaped by reputation and storytelling, including those related to tradition, heritage and authenticity. Furthermore, wine can be valued for its exclusivity or affordability (indicating availability and scale of production) and/or for its typicality or uniqueness (indicating the degree of differentiation vis-à-vis other wines). Very rarely, however, there is appreciation for the (often unseen) manual work that (gendered and racialized) farmworkers provide in tending both grape/wine production and the touristic sites where wine can be experienced in situ. As a matter of fact, they are often hidden from view, thus operating a process of labour fetishization.

Different sources of information are available to consumers for valuing wine. They can gather this information directly from the seller/producer, at the cellar or tasting room, and/or as part of wine tourism experiences. Often valuation is mediated through online sources (websites, social media, videos/podcasts), traditional media (general audience printed media, television, specialist magazines) – in the context of broader infrastructures of taste and opinion, including competitions, scores, medals and awards. Specific pedagogies of tasting will lead consumers to appreciate some wine traits rather than others. Taste is formed through exposure to trends, fashions and dominant (but also changing) discourses, and can be trained through wine appreciation courses.

The opinion of 'experts' (journalists, judges in competitions, celebrities and influencers and peers on social media) is key in shaping wine valuation. Critics and specialized media provide three kinds of services: gatekeeping (sorting through thousands of different wines to provide information that consumers could not assess for each wine); decoding the symbolic features and socio-cultural context of each wine (just like art critics do); and judging quality through rankings or scores (Negro and Hannan 2022). The taste of wine is indeed 'not only about how it registers on the palate; it is also bound up with social conventions of legitimacy and value' (Smith Maguire 2019, 171). Value struggles then also play out in relation to the reputation and perceived impartiality of critics, competition around their different preferences and aesthetic leanings, and the specific valuation features and metrics that each critic or media outlet selects.

Situations of purchase and consumption provide key moments of valuation. In specialist wine shops, customers are more likely to socially interact with sellers and receive advice, but the majority of wine purchases are actually made in supermarkets without such interaction. Wine is also being increasingly purchased online, through websites or apps, or as part of wine club memberships or subscription systems. Wine purchases directly at the winery are an important part of experiential valuations, and in shaping lingering memories afterwards. These purchases can be part of a tourist experience, but also of local, zero-Km and consumer-to-producer direct relations. Consumption experiences vary as well – they can take place at home, in restaurants, hotels and bars/wine bars. If stored, wine can be cellared at home (by hobbyists), in cellars (by elites) and/or in dedicated storage spaces for collecting or investing purposes (by the super elite). Given this complexity of valuation moments, situations and dynamics, approaching the 'value' of wine only in relation to its price would be obviously reductive.

Covering all these facets in detail would be an encyclopaedic exercise and require much more than the available space here. In this book, I focus more on valuation processes behind wine production and trade, and less on retail and consumption (with the partial exception of wine tourism), given the existence of large specialist literatures and even whole journals dedicated to the latter aspects.[1] In the rest of this chapter, I focus on the physical flows and organizational and regulatory features of the global value chain for wine, followed by the analysis of the value chains for South African wine (with focus on the Western Cape) and Italian wine (with focus on Prosecco and Valpolicella). For each, I highlight key trends and trace the emerging parallel dynamics of globalization and localization, and of commodification and differentiation. In Part II of the book, I will then delineate how different worlds of valuation are leveraged in three main sites of value struggle in wine: place, nature and people.

3.2 THE GLOBAL VALUE CHAIN FOR WINE

Key trends in production and exports

The global value chain for wine has been going through major processes of restructuring in the past few decades. Detailed analyses of trends in the geography of wine production, trade and consumption, as well as historical changes in the quality composition of supply and demand, have been well documented elsewhere (Anderson 2004; Anderson and Nelgen 2011; Anderson, Nelgen and Pinilla 2017; Anderson and Pinilla 2018; Gilinsky et al. 2015; Hira 2013; Unwin 1991). In short, these have included a dramatic fall in production volumes and per capita consumption in traditional (so-called 'Old World') wine-making and -consuming countries, such as Portugal, Spain, France and Italy in the past few decades – partly compensated by growing production and exports in so-called New World producing countries (such as Argentina, Chile, South Africa, New Zealand, Australia and the USA) and by increasing consumption in the UK, the USA and in some Asian countries (for a critique of the distinction between Old and New World producing countries in wine, see Banks and Overton 2010). Exports as a share of total production went from 5 to 15 per cent between 1960 and 1990 and increased to over 40 per cent from 2012 onwards. This means that wine went from being one of the least traded agricultural products into one of the most traded in a half century (Anderson and Pinilla 2018).[2]

Table 2 shows the top ten wine-producing countries in the world by volume from 2014 to 2023, ranked according to their position in 2023. As we can see, the top four wine-producing countries have been the same for the whole period (with differing ranks): France, Italy, Spain and the USA – with Italy and France alternating in first and second place, Spain retaining third place and the USA in fourth. The fifth position has been alternately occupied by Australia or Chile. South Africa is generally placed seventh or eighth. The world share of wine production by volume of the top five countries has been relatively stable over the years, in the range of 61–65 per cent (except in 2017). Similarly, the world share of wine production of the top ten countries has remained relatively steady in the range of 79–83 per cent. Italy and France together usually account for around one-third of total annual wine production by volume.

When it comes to the top performers in terms of exports by value (see Table 3), we can observe that the top ten countries have been the same throughout the period – with France, Italy and Spain ranking as the top three for the 2014–2023 period, but with a significant gap between the first two (around 10 per cent). The world share of the top five countries has been relatively steady in the range of 68–71 per cent, while the share of the top ten ranges in the 84–87 per cent band. France and Italy combined account for around half of world wine exports by value. By export volume, however, France ranks only third, with Spain and Italy ranking first and second. This is because the average export price is much higher in France than in Italy and Spain (in 2023, it was 9,40€/l, compared to 3,61€/l for Italy and 1,40€/l for Spain).[4]

Table 2 World top ten wine-producing countries by volume (2014–2023)

Rank (2023)		2014		2015		2016		2017		2018		PRODUCTION 2019		2020		2021		2022		2023*	
		mhl	World share	mhl	World share	mhl	World share	mhl	World share	mhl	World share	mhl	World share	mhl	World share	mhl	World share	mhl	World share	mhl	World share
1	France	46,5	17,3%	47	17,1%	45,3	16,8%	36,3	14,6%	48,6	16,5%	42,2	16,4%	46,7	17,8%	37,6	14,5%	46,0	17,5%	48,0	20,2%
2	Italy	44,2	16,4%	50	18,2%	50,9	18,9%	42,5	17,1%	54,8	18,6%	47,5	18,4%	49,1	18,7%	50,2	19,3%	49,8	19,0%	38,3	16,1%
3	Spain	39,5	14,7%	37,7	13,7%	39,7	14,8%	32,5	13,1%	44,4	15,1%	33,7	13,1%	40,9	15,6%	35,3	13,6%	35,8	13,6%	28,3	11,9%
4	USA	23,1	8,6%	21,7	7,9%	23,7	8,8%	23,3	9,4%	23,9	8,1%	25,6	9,9%	22,8	8,7%	24,1	9,3%	22,4	8,5%	24,3	10,2%
5	Chile	9,9	3,7%	12,9	4,8%	10,1	3,8%	9,5	3,5%	12,9	4,8%	11,9	4,6%	10,3	3,9%	13,4	5,2%	12,4	4,7%	11,0	4,6%
Top 5		163,2	60,7%	169,3	61,6%	169,7	63,1%	144,1	58,1%	184,6	62,8%	160,9	62,4%	169,8	64,8%	160,6	61,8%	166,4	63,4%	149,9	63,2%
6	Australia	11,9	4,4%	11,9	4,3%	13,1	4,9%	13,7	5,5%	12,9	4,4%	12,0	4,7%	10,9	4,2%	14,8	5,7%	13,1	5,0%	9,6	4,0%
7	South Africa	11,5	4,3%	11,2	4,1%	10,5	3,9%	10,8	4,4%	9,5	3,2%	9,7	3,8%	10,4	4,0%	10,8	4,2%	10,3	3,9%	9,3	3,9%
8	Argentina	15,2	5,7%	13,4	4,9%	9,4	3,5%	11,8	4,8%	14,5	4,9%	13,0	5,0%	10,8	4,1%	12,5	4,8%	11,5	4,4%	8,8	3,7%
9	Germany	9,2	3,4%	8,8	3,2%	9,0	3,3%	7,5	3,0%	10,3	3,5%	8,2	3,2%	8,4	3,2%	8,4	3,2%	8,9	3,4%	8,6	3,6%
10	Portugal	6,2	2,3%	7,0	2,5%	6,0	2,2%	6,7	2,7%	6,1	2,1%	6,5	2,5%	6,4	2,4%	7,4	2,8%	6,8	2,6%	7,5	3,2%
Top 10		217,2	80,7%	221,6	80,6%	217,7	80,9%	194,6	78,5%	237,9	80,9%	210,3	81,5%	216,7	82,6%	214,5	82,6%	217	82,6%	193,7	81,6%
	World	269,0		275,0		269,0		248,0		294,0		257,9		262,2		259,7		262,6		237,3	

*Data for 2023 is preliminary.

Sources: Elaborated from data in 'OIV – State of the world vine and wine sector', various issues.[3]

Table 3 World top ten wine-exporting countries by value (2014–2023)

EXPORT BY VALUE

Rank (2023)		2014 €bn	2014 World share	2015 €bn	2015 World share	2016 €bn	2016 World share	2017 €bn	2017 World share	2018 €bn	2018 World share	2019 €bn	2019 World share	2020 €bn	2020 World share	2021 €bn	2021 World share	2022* €bn	2022* World share	2023* €bn	2023* World share
1	France	7,7	29,6%	8,3	29,6%	8,3	28,6%	9,1	29,4%	9,3	30,0%	9,8	30,9%	8,7	29,4%	11,1	32,2%	12,3	32,5%	11,9	33,2%
2	Italy	5,1	19,6%	5,4	19,3%	5,6	19,3%	6,0	19,4%	6,1	19,7%	6,4	20,2%	6,3	21,1%	7,1	20,7%	7,8	20,6%	7,7	21,5%
3	Spain	2,5	9,6%	2,6	9,3%	2,6	9,0%	2,9	9,4%	2,9	9,4%	2,7	8,6%	2,6	8,9%	2,9	8,4%	3,0	8,0%	2,9	8,1%
4	Chile	1,4	5,4%	1,6	5,7%	1,7	5,9%	1,8	5,8%	1,7	5,5%	1,7	5,4%	1,6	5,4%	1,7	4,9%	1,8	4,8%	1,3	3,6%
5	Australia	1,3	5,0%	1,5	5,4%	1,5	5,2%	1,8	5,8%	1,8	5,8%	1,8	5,8%	1,8	6,0%	1,4	3,9%	1,4	3,7%	1,2	3,4%
Top 5		18,0	69,2%	19,4	69,3%	19,7	67,9%	21,6	69,7%	21,8	70,3%	22,5	70,8%	21,0	70,8%	24,1	70,1%	26,3	69,6%	25,1	69,8%
6	New Zeland	0,8	1,0%	1,0	1,1%	1,0	3,4%	0,6	1,9%	0,7	2,3%	1,1	3,5%	1,2	3,9%	1,2	3,4%	1,4	3,6%	1,2	3,3%
7	USA	1,1	4,2%	1,4	5,0%	1,4	4,8%	1,3	4,2%	1,2	3,9%	1,3	3,9%	1,2	3,9%	1,3	3,6%	1,4	3,7%	1,1	3,1%
8	Germany	1,0	3,8%	1,0	3,6%	0,9	3,1%	1,0	3,2%	1,0	3,2%	1,0	3,3%	0,9	3,1%	1,0	2,9%	1,0	2,8%	1,1	2,9%
9	Portugal	0,7	2,7%	0,7	2,5%	0,7	2,4%	0,8	2,6%	0,8	2,6%	0,8	2,6%	0,9	2,9%	0,9	2,7%	0,9	2,5%	0,9	2,6%
10	Argentina	0,6	2,3%	0,7	2,5%	0,7	2,4%	0,7	2,3%	0,7	2,3%	0,7	2,1%	0,7	2,2%	0,7	2,0%	0,8	2,0%	0,6	1,7%
Top 10		22,2	85,4%	24,2	86,4%	24,4	84,1%	26	83,9%	26,2	84,5%	27,34	86,2%	25,76	86,7%	29,17	84,8%	31,77	84,0%	30,06	83,5%
World		26,0		28,0		29,0		31,0		31,0		31,7		29,7		34,4		37,8		36,0	

* Data for 2023 is preliminary.

Source: Elaborated from data in 'OIV – state of the world vine and wine sector', various issues.[5]

Table 4 World top ten wine-consuming countries by volume (2014–2023)

CONSUMPTION

Rank (2023)		2014 mhl	World share	2015 mhl	World share	2016 mhl	World share	2017 mhl	World share	2018 mhl	World share	2019 mhl	World share	2020 mhl	World share	2021 mhl	World share	2022* mhl	World share	2023* mhl	World share
1	USA	30,6	12,7%	30,9	12,7%	31,7	13,0%	32,6	13,3%	33,0	13,4%	34,3	14,5%	32,9	14,2%	33,1	14,1%	34,3	15,1%	33,3	15,1%
2	France	27,5	11,4%	27,3	11,2%	27,1	11,1%	27,0	11,0%	26,8	10,9%	24,7	10,4%	23,2	10,0%	24,9	10,6%	25,0	11,0%	24,4	11,0%
3	Italy	19,5	8,1%	21,4	8,8%	22,4	9,2%	22,6	9,2%	22,4	9,1%	22,6	9,5%	24,2	10,4%	24,2	10,3%	22,4	9,8%	21,8	9,9%
4	Germany	20,3	8,4%	20,5	8,4%	20,2	8,3%	19,7	8,0%	20,0	8,1%	19,5	8,2%	19,8	8,5%	19,9	8,5%	19,4	8,5%	19,1	8,6%
5	UK	12,6	5,2%	12,7	5,2%	12,9	5,3%	12,7	5,2%	12,4	5,0%	12,6	5,3%	13,7	5,9%	13,9	5,9%	13,1	5,7%	12,8	5,8%
Top 5		110,5	45,9%	112,8	46,4%	114,3	46,8%	114,6	46,6%	114,6	46,6%	113,7	48,1%	113,8	49,2%	116,0	49,5%	114,2	50,3%	111,4	50,4%
6	Spain	9,8	1,0%	9,8	1,1%	9,9	4,1%	10,5	4,3%	10,5	4,3%	10,2	4,3%	9,2	3,9%	10,3	4,4%	9,6	4,2%	9,8	4,4%
7	Russia	11,1	4,6%	10,8	4,4%	10,5	4,3%	11,1	4,5%	11,9	4,8%	8,7	3,6%	8,5	3,6%	8,1	3,4%	8,4	3,7%	8,6	3,9%
8	Argentina	9,9	4,1%	10,3	4,2%	9,4	3,9%	8,9	3,6%	8,4	3,4%	8,5	3,6%	9,4	4,0%	8,4	3,5%	8,3	3,6%	7,8	3,5%
9	China	17,4	7,2%	18,1	7,4%	19,2	7,9%	19,3	7,8%	17,6	7,2%	15,0	6,3%	12,4	5,3%	10,5	4,4%	9,1	4,0%	6,8	3,1%
10	Australia	5,4	2,2%	5,5	2,3%	5,4	2,2%	5,9	2,4%	6,0	2,4%	5,8	2,4%	6,0	2,6%	5,6	2,3%	5,4	2,3%	5,4	2,4%
Top 10		164,1	68,1%	167,3	68,8%	168,7	69,1%	170,3	69,2%	169,0	68,7%	161,9	68,6%	159,3	68,9%	158,9	67,9%	155,0	68,2%	149,8	67,8%
World		241,0		243,0		244,0		246,0		246,0		236,0		231,0		234,0		227,0		221,0	

*Data for 2023 is preliminary.

Sources: Elaborated from data in 'OIV – state of the world vine and wine sector', various issues.[6]

Global consumption of wine by volume remained relatively stable in the 2010s but then exhibited a significant drop in the early 2020s (see Table 4). Consumption is decreasing particularly among younger people, whose interest in lower- and no-alcohol wines is growing.[7] The USA remains the largest wine consumer country by volume, followed by France, Italy, Germany and the UK. This ranking has remained stable throughout the decade 2014–2023. In fifth to tenth place in 2023, we find Spain, Russia, Argentina, China and Australia. Wine retail, which was traditionally the domain of small specialist shops, is now in the hands of supermarket chains, especially in northern Europe, the UK and the US, but increasingly in southern Europe as well (Gwynne 2008).

Value chain configurations

What for centuries was considered a cottage industry is now characterized by the presence of large multinational companies (Anderson 2004; Outreville and Hanni 2013). A surge of foreign direct investment and mergers and acquisitions is taking place (Anderson and Pinilla 2018), in view of achieving not only economies of scale but also economies of scope. Some of the main international groups are seeking to build a global portfolio of wines that include different origins, varieties, styles and price points (Outreville and Hanni 2013; Overton and Murray 2016). In the early 2000s, institutional investors started setting up specialized wine funds, and some of the main international wine groups increased their focus on core business competences and moved towards more explicit financialization strategies (including share repurchases by listed companies) to maximize shareholder value. Other groups, however, did not follow the path of 'deep financialization' and founding family members still retain a significant level of control (Coelho and Rastoin 2006).

Corporate capital has avoided large-scale land acquisition (with some exceptions, such as in Champagne and Bordeaux), tends to be linked to ownership of local brands, and usually invests in faster-return and lower-risk activities, such as marketing and brand development (Overton and Murray 2016). 'In these circumstances, corporate capital will happily seek contract arrangements with other forms so that they can gain access to a reliable source of grapes without having to sink their capital into expensive land holding' (Overton and Murray 2013, 13; 2016). Therefore, we can observe a variety of capital engagements in the wine industry: investment focused on short-term profit maximization; longer-term engagement targeted towards possible asset appreciation (including land); forms of investment seeking status enhancement, such as celebrity wineries; investment of gains made in other industries to seek rural idyll and/or social recognition; investment that, in combination with other non-wine assets, achieves tax optimization objectives; and lifestyle property development, such as hybrid housing and winery complexes (Overton and Murray 2016). The market and financial value of rare wines, collection pieces and investment wines (see also Chapter 4) has been growing (Donzé and Katsumata 2022), with transactions going through brokers, intermediary agencies or online platforms, and with the top end of fine wines often being sold at auctions (Garcia-Parpet 2011). Mutual funds specializing in wine, which are managed like hedge funds, have also emerged (Sanning, Shaffer and Sharratt 2008).

Value chains for wine are organized in four main phases: grape production, winemaking and bottling, distribution and retail through various channels. Grape producers at the primary level grow and sell wine grapes to wine cellars. Grape growers can also be vertically integrated through ownership into wine production, including through membership or shareholding in a cooperative. At this level, wine cellars produce or blend wine which they sell domestically or to international markets, through traders, importers, agents or distributors, or directly to retailers. Consumers access wine at the cellar door, on-trade (on-premises consumption such as in bars, restaurants, hotels, nightclubs), and off-trade (sales for off-premises consumption through supermarkets, wholesalers, retail liquor stores and online). In many countries, the value chains for wine are characterized by a large number of actors at the grape production level. Figure 1 shows the organization of the domestic segment of the value chain for Italian wine for illustrative purposes.

All in all, compared to other beverages, such as beer or spirits, the wine industry remains relatively fragmented (Coelho and Rastoin 2006). Although there have been fears of massive homogenization of styles and offerings in the wine market, this is still an industry that produces a phenomenal array of different products, which are sold under a combination of brand names, grape variety, sustainability labels and/or geographical indications of origin. At the same time, around 40 per cent of globally traded wine is currently traded in bulk – shipped in 'flexitank' bladders that fit into 20 ft containers (Rainer, Steiner and Pütz 2023). This allows specialist bulk wine bottlers to blend wine from very different regions of the world to be sold under private labels (their own or those of retailers) at very competitive prices. These blends may contain wines from different countries in different years but strive to provide exactly the same drinking experience to the consumer year in, year out. Some blends indicate the grape varieties used, while others are simply labelled as a generic red or white (Rainer, Steiner and Pütz 2023).

While a general process of globalization of the wine industry has taken place in the past few decades, it has not been unidirectional – often bifurcating into parallel trends of globalization and localization, and of commodification and differentiation (Inglis and Almila 2019; Overton and Murray 2013). In relation to *production*, we observe a mutual influence between the so-called Old World and New World styles of production (both in the vineyard and the cellar) rather than a univocal movement towards New World styles; the presence of massive companies/global brands as well as of smaller, local operations that are more attached to specific places; the use of fertile/flat land suitable for irrigation and mechanization for the production of low cost wines as well as of marginal land where vines struggle to find nutrients and water and thus produce fruit with concentrated flavours for higher quality wines; the coexistence of bulk, undifferentiated wine and of wine as singularized, elite object of desire; the presence of industrial-size production facilities hidden from the tourist eye as well as the increasing integration of (smaller, sometimes token) viticultural and winemaking facilities into the tourist and leisure economies;

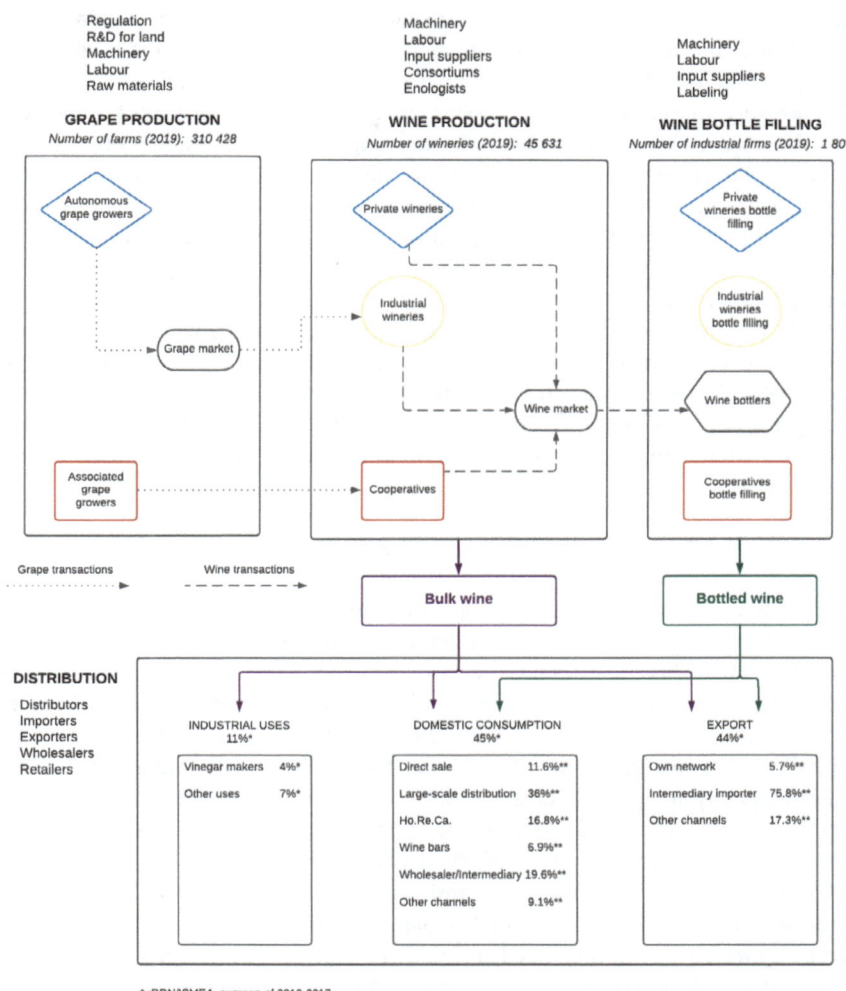

Figure 1 Example of a value chain for wine (Italy). Source: Own elaboration, drawing from Ismea data found at https://www.ismeamercati.it/vino.

and the coexistence of technological innovation and of more natural ways of making wine (Inglis and Almila 2019, 2–3; Overton and Murray 2016).

When it comes to *consumption*, some of the key trends include: a decline in volumes of consumption in traditional wine markets but also the emergence and consolidation of transnational, cosmopolitan drinking cultures; a democratization of wine drinking, with easier-to-recognize brands and varietals, but also 'new forms of social division, elite arrogance and snobbery' (Inglis and Almila 2019, 3); the increasing importance of low- and no-alcohol wine consumption especially among younger generations; wine purchasing for immediate consumption, but also as a form of investment and financial speculation; and the growth of global wine brands at the entry quality level, but also of global luxury wine brands (especially of Champagne, but not only) marketed along other items, such as designer perfumes or fashion items.

These trends are accompanied by a wide range of discourses and representations where value struggles play out: different reference models on how to appreciate wine, with multiple and localized adaptations – including what stock words are used to describe the various qualities of wine; competing aesthetic models and ideas of quality developed by wine critics, sommeliers, chefs, celebrities and influencers (Inglis and Almila 2019); constant reconfigurations of the meanings of terroir, tradition, typicality, authenticity, origin, and 'naturalness' (see Chapter 4); disputes over interpretations of environmental sustainability (see Chapter 5) and acceptable labour conditions and ownership patterns (see Chapter 6). These struggles play out along the value chain but also within institutions (producer consortia, for example) and through regulatory action, especially in the EU.

Wine regulation and reform in the EU

Value chains for wine are heavily regulated, and collective action by producers is more developed than for many other agro-food products – both are also in constant flux. This is especially the case in Europe, while New World producing countries are characterized by a generally lighter regulatory approach. France is where regulating quality in the wine industry started. The 1855 Bordeaux wine classifications are generally regarded as the first institutionalized instance of linking quality and place of origin.[8] These classifications were developed internally by the wine industry, and especially by wine *negotiants* (merchants), in Bordeaux so they could be used at the 1855 Paris Exposition (Trubek 2008). This story is not entirely one of bottom-up dynamics though. The request for some form of classification actually came from Napoleon III, who instructed the industry to come up with a system organized around five 'growths'. The first growths, being the most esteemed, ended up being assigned to elite and noble estates – with properties run by growers without aristocratic roots placed in lower growths (Ulin 2013). Therefore, the classification was class based, but became institutionalized in time as if it were an objective reality linked to terroir (Fourcade 2012).

The Bordeaux classification, although not yet involving the state, provided the kickstart for a more general process aimed at protecting French agricultural products, and wine in particular. Champagne wine was the first product for which a legal system of protection of origin was developed in 1905 – originally to protect against fraud (that is, sparkling wines that were sold as 'Champagne' but were not produced in that area of France). In the 1908 amendments to this regulation, we find the first elaboration of what makes a certain wine unique (as opposed to just coming from a particular location), as they state that a wine has to display a 'local, loyal, and constant' association to a place (Trubek 2008). Champagne producers created 'aristocratic genealogies and myths' that sought to link their wine not only to its place of production but also to stories of the past – and facilitated the staking of claims by consumers to a 'civilized life' during the *belle epoque* of the late nineteenth and early twentieth centuries (Guy 2003; Trubek 2008). These regulations were also the result of an effort by grape growers to capture more value from their product, given that Champagne production was (and still is) dominated by large companies that purchase and blend grapes from many different locations within the region.

The Champagne legislation did not set specific parameters on how viticulture had to be carried out or wine made, nor did it define caps to production or sales volumes. Yet, it sparked a process that eventually led in the 1930s to the founding of the Institut National des Appellations d'Origine (INAO) and the regulatory instruments that made up the Appellations d'Origine Contrôlées (AOC) system.[9] This system was based on uniqueness and quality, not simply geographical origin, as foundational elements (Trubek 2008; Unwin 1991). Essentially, the AOC system resulted from the combined role of the state, in its attempt to control quality, and a series of grassroots movements, led by the wealthiest producers, to snatch power away from merchants (Fourcade 2012).

The 1935 AOC law and the creation of INAO were not the only noteworthy collective features that came to define the appellation system. Equally important was the requirement that, in order to have an AOC approved, a local committee of producers had to apply. This is where 'authenticity', and its explicit link to quality, comes into play. The application to obtain a geographical appellation has to include a document called *cahier des charges*, which sets the boundaries of the area and its geographical links to the appellation name. It usually identifies allowed grape varieties, maximum yields, residual sugar and alcohol levels, and any special techniques that need to be used in viticulture and winemaking. These have to be combined in ways that stylistically construct the appellation wine as having internally shared, but externally unique, characteristics linked to that place. Therefore, the smaller the appellation, the greater tends to be the internal consistency of terroir (Farmer 2013). Also key in this system is that geographical appellation processes are heavily subsidized by governments – in France, INAO's mission actually includes being a 'steward of the relationship between locale and flavour, and to encourage everyone to agree that they can taste place' (Trubek 2008, 31) (see Chapter 4).

When granted, geographical appellations are protected as the collective property of all producers in that area and are managed through a producer-led consortium. Tasting panels are organized to maintain whether any wine wanting to be sold as AOC conforms to a 'typicality' test (a bone of contention for more innovative winemakers). Although some flexibility is allowed around what typicality means, a general family resemblance must be assured. Therefore, these panels test the 'true' taste of place through a bureaucratic process at the local level (Kaplonski 2019). If a wine fails a test of typicality, it can only be sold as a generic 'table wine' and cannot carry the AOC label. This aspect highlights a paradox – on the one hand, geographical appellation is based on uniqueness and a link between place and quality; on the other hand, the internal process of ensuring typicality pushes towards the relative homogenization of wines within the boundaries of an appellation (Kaplonski 2019; Teil 2014).

The state in Europe played a key role in the construction of supply and demand in the wine market – leading to the coexistence of two systems based on distinct logics in the post–World War II period: (1) a state-organized mass market, often plagued by oversupply and regulated through limited supply and obligatory stockpiling and distilling; and (2) an appellation system, which 'turned terroir names into guaranteed income for reputable vineyards, a form of corporatism in which professionals came to control the conditions of access to the labels' (Garcia-Parpet 2011, 135). This dual system was framed by the EU Common Agricultural Policy (CAP), established in 1962 officially in view of safeguarding both producers and consumers. The original objectives of CAP related to increasing productivity, stabilizing markets and ensuring supply, and maintaining a fair standard of living for farmers, while at the same time supplying consumers at reasonable prices. However, the objectives of CAP have both expanded and re-focused in time – and now include, inter alia, environmental protection, sustainable development, animal welfare, food quality and safety, and economic, social and territorial cohesion (Pomarici and Sardone 2020).

EU wine policy started in 1962 with the issuance of a regulation aimed at collecting information and starting the process of homogenizing some aspects of legislation in member states. New regulatory aspects were added in the 1970s – including specific rules on viticulture and wine production and labelling, the definition of different types of wines, and the introduction of reference prices for market intervention. Differently from the bulk of CAP support, however, wine regulation included a ban on new vineyard planting, subsidies for abandoning viticultured areas and financial support for the restructuring and conversion of vineyards (Meloni and Swinnen 2013).

The EU rules for geographical indications are also embedded into an international regulatory framework under the WTO. Geographical indication is a general term that includes various regulatory mechanisms to protect the geographical origin of a product, which ultimately provide an exclusive right to use such denomination to producers residing in that area. According to the 'Agreement on Trade-Related Aspects of Intellectual Property Rights' (TRIPS),[10] geographical indications can be claimed when even a single quality feature of a product (or even just its reputation) can be linked to its geographical origin. To ensure stricter protection under an 'appellation of origin', however, the quality of a product needs to result exclusively or essentially from its geographical origin, including natural and human factors, as defined in Article 2 of the 'Lisbon Agreement for the Protection of Appellations of Origin and their International Registration'.[11]

In the 2000s, the EU started a process that led to a comprehensive reform of wine regulation in 2008. Following the broader 2013 CAP reform, the new wine policy was then folded into the Single Common Market Organization, which is currently in force under Regulation (EU) 1308/2013. The following key features of this regulation should be kept in mind for the purposes of this book:

1. winemaking can only take place by using permitted practices and technologies, as applied to specific grape varieties that are allowed for wine production in member states;
2. continuing previous practice, the EU protects all registered geographical names and recognizes the intellectual property rights of producers in these

areas; these origins are communicated to consumers either as Protected Designation of Origin (PDO) or Protected Geographical Indication (PGI);
3. producer organizations and their interbranch organizations and their associations are recognized as strategic actors and are allowed to establish marketing rules to regulate supply; and
4. a (revised) system of planting authorization is maintained (control mechanisms of this sort are no longer used for other sectors regulated by the CAP), allowing a one per cent maximum annual increase in the area under vine planting, according to the national inventories.

In terms of expenditure measures, the single CMO allows five structural measures that seek to strengthen the competitiveness of the wine sector in member states: promotion, restructuring and conversion of vineyards, infrastructural investments, innovation and by-product distillation. These measures can be differently targeted to various actors in the value chain, not just farmers. Three conjunctural measures are also allowed, which aim at preventing major falls in farmers' revenue: setting up of mutual funds, harvest insurance contracts, and removal of grapes before maturation (Itçaina, Roger and Smith 2016).

Itçaina, Roger and Smith (2016) provide a detailed and fascinating examination of the processes that shaped the 2008 EU wine reform. They delineate how the ideational creation of the 'new wine consumer' was key in preparing the ground for reform. This new consumer was portrayed as demanding more standardized and predictable wines, year after year. Paradoxically, these are wines that New World producers are better equipped to deliver given their less regulated wine value chains, thus threatening European producers. Furthermore, changes in the scientific field – driven by emerging networks of biochemistry, economics and marketing scholars in the US, Australia and South Africa – coincided in structured but also contingent ways with the interests of specific segments of the wine industry (see also Giuliani et al. 2010; Giuliani, Morrison and Rabellotti 2011). The political work of wine merchants (and certain groups of grape growers) made it possible to transfer innovations from the scientific field to the economic field. This process was facilitated by a revolution in wine retailing in Europe (with much of it moving from specialized retailers to supermarkets), the increasing importance of branding in wine marketing (vis-à-vis or alongside geographical appellations), and increased concentration in wine trading and to some extent grape growing (Itçaina, Roger and Smith 2016).

Once passed, the process of implementation of the EU wine reform was built around key processes of legitimation. Old policy instruments (distillation subsidies, grants for grubbing out vines) were delegitimized, leading to their abandonment or only partial retaining (as in the case of the regulation of planting rights) (Itçaina, Roger and Smith 2016). The categories for geographical indication wines were also simplified (into geographical indication and non-geographical indication wines), while 'table wines' were reinvented to be sold with the indication of brand names and grape varietals. New support measures included subsidies for marketing in third countries and intrafirm investment support – which were appropriated by individual, powerful actors at the expense of collective action. Itçaina, Roger and

Smith (2016) conclude that EU wine reform cannot be attributed to a simple neoliberal logic. While it led to the demise of some old instruments, it also allowed the reiteration of others and the launch of new forms of support. Reform was shaped by a main shift from an institutionalized order based on supply to one based on demand. It was preconditioned by displacements in scientific, economic and bureaucratic fields that were structured but also moulded by coincidental resonances. And it was delivered through political work applied to problematization, instrumentalization and legitimation processes.

Value struggles around wine classifications are thus playing out in and out of regulatory processes – fuelled by cultural and economic wars over criteria of excellence and the selection of expert juries (Garcia-Parpet 2011) and through political manoeuvring (Carter 2018; Colman 2008). Despite the recent EU reform, critical voices argue that appellation systems are still too rigid in comparison with the constantly evolving material and discursive features of winemaking (Howland and Dutton 2020). As a result, some of the most innovative winemakers in France and Italy choose to not sell their wines under the appellation labels, as they seek more flexibility and space for experimentation (more on this in Chapter 4).

3.3 SOUTH AFRICAN WINE[12]

Brief history and recent trends

Despite its classification as a 'New World' producing country, South Africa is *not* a new player in the global wine trade. The first vineyards were planted in the Cape peninsula by Dutch settlers as early as 1655. Constantia wine was very popular in Europe at the time, and apparently a favourite of Napoleon. At the beginning of the nineteenth century, wine represented almost 90 per cent of exports from the colony (Vink, Williams and Kirsten 2004, 229). But by the end of the century, exports had almost collapsed. In 1861, the UK – the main importer of South African wine at that time and still currently – and France signed a trade agreement that made French wines cheaper to import (Nugent 2024a). The spread of phylloxera in the late nineteenth century destroyed most of the vineyards in the Cape.

Throughout much of the twentieth century, the South African wine industry was centred around cooperative wine cellars, which were responsible for a large share of total wine production, and supplied bulk wine of lower quality, with farmers dependent on cheap Black labour. In the early twentieth century, a giant cooperative, the Ko-öperatieve Wijnbouwers Vereniging van Zuid-Afrika (KWV), was granted the statutory powers to regulate the industry. KWV controlled sales and stabilized prices, and later managed a quota system that regulated new plantings, varietal choices and vine material imports. This period was characterized by a focus on high yields and volume over quality, and an overall orientation towards the production of brandy and fortified wine (Nugent 2024a). These characteristics, and the imposition of international trade sanctions against apartheid in the 1980s, brought the industry almost to a halt. Between 1964 and

1989, official exports fell by two-thirds, and the industry survived through domestic consumption and some exports of low-quality wine to Eastern Europe (Ewert and Du Toit 2005; Nugent 2024b, a; Vink 2018; Williams 2005).

Following the end of apartheid and the political transition of the mid-1990s, the wine value chain went through a major restructuring – resulting from deregulation, the opening of export markets, and the regulation of labour (Nugent 2024a). Investment flowed in, new farms and cellars were established, wine quality improved, cooperatives were modernized in terms of management and infrastructure, and export volumes increased dramatically. South African wine styles started matching those required in its main export markets (fruit-forward, easy-to-drink, full colour). In the 1990s and early 2000s, this reflected a search for riper, more concentrated wines with higher alcohols to appease, depending on the wine segment, wine judges or the perceived preferences of Anglo-Saxon consumers (Ponte and Ewert 2009). These transitions led to a double divide. The first divide entailed winners and losers among cellars and farmers, depending on how positioned they were to make use of new export opportunities. The second divide took place among the workers who remained in the permanent workforce (the more skilled ones) and those who were casualized, externalized and (re)hired through labour contractors (Du Toit, Kruger and Ponte 2008). Ownership of land and wineries, however, remained by and large in white hands (see Chapter 6).

South Africa has over the past fifteen years struggled to grow its wine export volumes and to shake off its image as a low-value, bulk wine producer. This situation persists despite substantial investments by South African grape and wine producers in environmental management and some efforts aimed at addressing social and labour conditions of production – in the context of the enduring heritage of apartheid in the country. Some of these initiatives have been stimulated through the development of domestic standards (Hamann et al. 2017; Herman 2018; Howson 2022; Howson, Murray and Overton 2020). Others have been driven by the general requirements of major buyers in the Global North, particularly in Europe, but also of large domestic retailers (Das Nair 2018, 2019; Das Nair, Chisoro and Ziba 2018). Alcohol monopoly buyers, like Sweden's state-controlled Systembolaget, and other retailers require adherence to specific social and environmental standards, motivated in part by South Africa's troubled history around the treatment of farm and cellar workers.

The continuing domination of white (and male) ownership in the industry is a persisting issue – driven by (the largely failing) government transformation initiatives under the umbrella of 'Black Economic Empowerment' (BEE) legislation and related scorecards (Du Toit, Kruger and Ponte 2008; Herman 2012, 2018; Ponte, Roberts and Van Sittert 2007; Vilakazi and Bosiu 2022; Williams 2005). Labour conditions on farms remain problematic. Environmental issues are becoming important for international and domestic retailers and are translating into new requirements or information requests – such as those on water and energy consumption, for the use of lighter glass bottles and more sustainable packaging materials, and the promotion of less harmful methods of pest and disease control.

The existence of these initiatives does not necessarily entail that they are easing the local environmental impacts of viticulture and winemaking, or that working conditions are necessarily improving. On the former, very little is known. On the latter, a rich literature in the 2000s showed how ownership patterns and working conditions remained very problematic even after the end of apartheid (Bek, McEwan and Bek 2007; Du Toit 2002; Du Toit, Kruger and Ponte 2008; McEwan and Bek 2009a, b; Moseley and McCusker 2008; Williams 2005) – a situation that to a large extent still persists (Alford, Visser and Barrientos 2021; Howson 2022). At the same time, some scholars highlight the potential for improving social and labour conditions (Herman 2012, 2018). In particular, Hastings (2019) has shown how transnational networks of unions in South Africa and in the Nordic countries have been able to campaign for change in labour processes and to push for stronger public and private regulation in monitoring working conditions – by building on existing domestic coalitions (McEwan and Bek 2009a) and by targeting Nordic alcohol monopolies through media exposure.[13] Yet, Hastings (2019) concludes that producers are still footing much of the bill for more onerous labour standards adherence, a situation that puts downward pressure on pay and work conditions and leads to the increased casualization of labour – extending a well-known post-apartheid trajectory (Ewert and Du Toit 2005).

Value chain characteristics

As of 2021, at the primary grape-growing level, there were around 2,613 *farmers* producing grapes for wine in South Africa (see details in Table 5). This number has decreased substantially from 4,185 producers in 2006,[14] illustrating consolidation at the grower level of the value chain. Small farmers have either exited completely, their farms have been bought up by larger players, or they have started growing other crops that are more profitable.[15] Of these farmers, 85 per cent produce 1,000 tons of grapes or less.[16] Only seven large grape growers produce more than 10,000 tons. The largest decline has been in the number of smaller growers that produce under 500 tons of grapes, while there has been some growth in the number of larger growers (over 1,000 tons).

Grapes are then processed into wine at wine cellars through different organizational models:[17]

- *Producer cellars* (also known as wine cooperatives) receive and process grapes on a communal basis on behalf of their members and market wine in packaged or bulk form. Around 80 per cent of South Africa's total harvest is pressed at producer cellars, which have invested significantly in equipment.
- *Private cellars* are owned by individuals or groups to produce wine at their own cellars by using their own grapes (when vertically integrated) or by buying in grapes from other growers. The wine produced is usually sold under their own brand name or sold to others in bulk or packaged form. Some private cellars may also buy ready-made wine from other cellars for bottling or blending.

- *Wine estates* are farms and cellars demarcated as a unit approved by the South Africa Wine and Spirits Board. To sell 'estate wine', the producer has to be certified as an estate. However, the term 'estate' can also be used on the bottle to identify a producer even though it is not registered for the production of an 'estate wine'. A dispensation in 2004 allowed for estate wine to be produced in contiguous/adjacent vineyards farmed as single units.
- *Producing wholesalers* do not necessarily have their own wine production premises. They may buy grapes for their own wine production but also buy wine in bulk or packaged form from other wineries.

The number of wine producers in South Africa has declined from 576 in 2006 to 536 in 2021, indicating a small degree of consolidation.[18] Of these, seven large companies dominate exports.[19] Next in the value chain we find *wholesalers*, which buy wine in bulk and resell either in bulk or in packaged form. In 2021, there were around ninety-two registered wholesalers (excluding producing wholesalers) in the country. This number has increased from around eighty-seven in 2006.[20] Finally, two large distributors play an important role in aggregating bottled wine and selling it throughout the country and to other African countries. There is also a degree of cross-ownership and vertical integration with other players in the value chain (SAW31).

The value chain for wine is supported by an ecosystem of key organizations that aim to promote research and development, market access and transformation (for more details, see Das Nair, Chisoro and Ponte 2023). A statutory levy is paid by wine producers, wine traders, wine spirit producers and wine exporters.[21] Organizations whose activities are funded through the statutory levy pay an estimated 20 per cent of each business unit's funds towards the Transformation Unit (SAW1, SAW2) (see Chapter 6).[22] To promote greater cohesion and for the industry body to speak in one voice to promote growth, development and innovation, the industry has recently formed a new organization, SA Wine.[23]

Table 5 Number of players at each node of the value chain for South African wine

	Tons	Number
Number of primary grape producers		2,613
	1-100	983
	>100-500	886
	>500-1,000	344
	>1,000-5,000	377
	>5,000-10,000	16
	>10,000	7
Number of wine cellars		536
	Producer cellars	43
	Private wine cellars	471
	Producing wholesalers	22
Number of wholesalers	(including producer wholesalers)	**114**

Source: Compiled from data in 'SAWIS Statistical Booklet, 2021'.

Production and exports

South Africa is the eighth largest wine producer globally.[24] Wine production grew rapidly from 2006 to 2015, but has remained stable since then, with noticeable drops in 2018 and 2019 (Figure 2). The vineyard area has decreased from 101,607 ha of land under wine-grape vines in 2005 to around 89,384 ha in 2022.[25] As a South African wine journalist told me, 'this means that grape farmers are working the vineyards harder, do less replanting, and apply more chemicals, with implications for the sustainability of the industry' (SAW30). South Africa produces mainly white wine, accounting for around two-thirds of total production. This trend has been fairly consistent historically (Figure 3).

The share of exports in total wine production has been declining since its peak at 57 per cent in 2013 to 40 per cent in 2022 (Figure 4). The value of exports increased steadily between 2001 and 2013, after which values have been relatively stagnant or declining (Figure 5). Still wine constitutes the bulk of South Africa's wine exports alongside very small quantities of fortified wine, sparkling wine and Cap Classique. In 2023/24, the UK, Germany, France, Belgium and Canada were the largest five export destinations for South African wine by volume (Figure 6), but the aggregate export values to Europe decreased from 2013 onwards (Figure 7). Sales to Asia grew from around 2000 but declined from 2018 onwards. Sales to US markets have been steady since the early 2000s. The profile of exports has changed dramatically between 2005 and 2021 (see Table 6). In 2005, 68 per cent of exports were packaged, while the remaining 32 per cent were in bulk form. By 2021, we can see the opposite situation: 38 per cent of exports were packaged, and 62 per cent in bulk. This has key implications for South Africa's premiumization objectives.

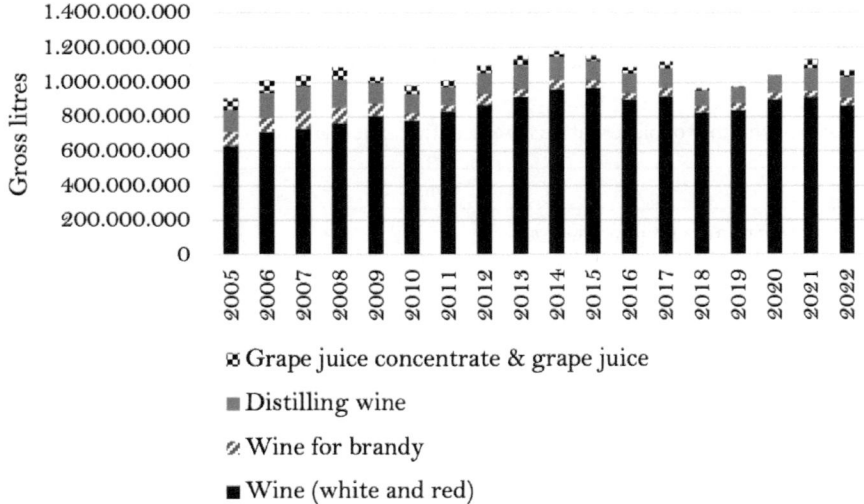

Figure 2 South African wine production by volume (2005–2022). Source: Compiled from data in 'SAWIS Statistical Booklets', 2006 to 2022.

In view of further growing the domestic market, niche products are also being developed for the young, trendy, emerging Black middle-class consumer in South Africa. Many of my interviewees framed the search for new market demographics in terms of 'us' versus 'them' in racial terms, denoting the continued legacy of apartheid. The chief winemaker of a large winery told me how they have tailored their Methode Cape Classique range to create a demi-sec offering to attract young consumers, especially women. 'The branding, bottling and labelling need to be

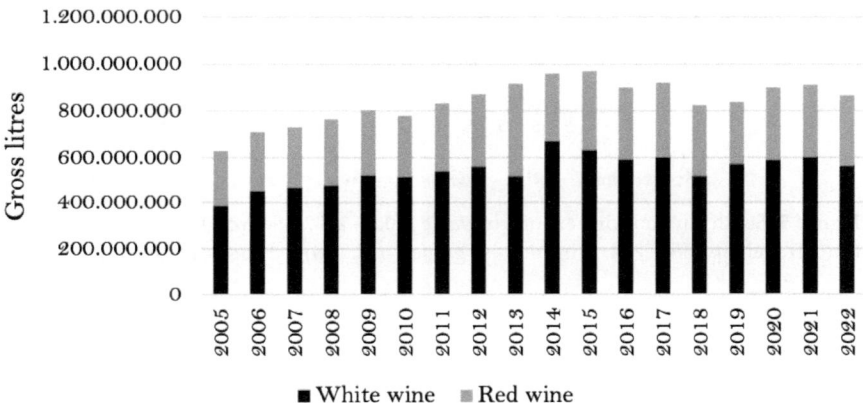

Figure 3 South African wine production of red and white wines by volume (2005–2022). Source: Compiled from data in 'SAWIS Statistical Booklets', 2006 to 2022.

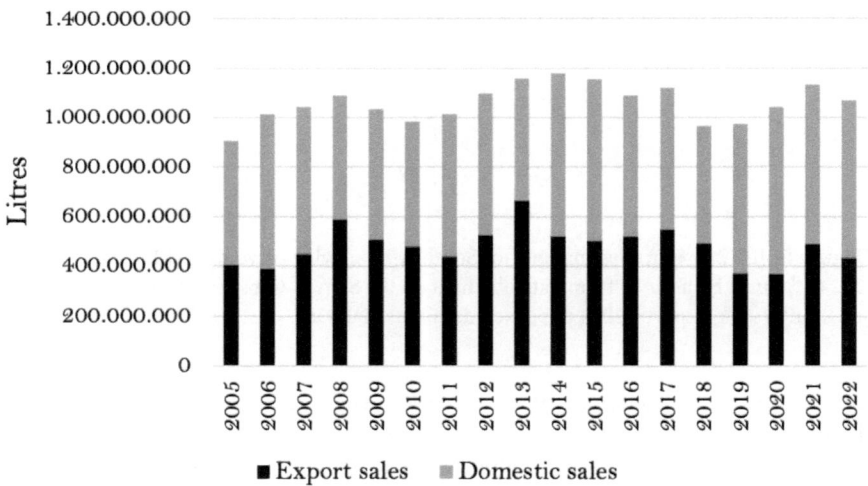

Figure 4 Domestic and export sales of South African wine (2005–2022). Source: Compiled from data in 'SAWIS Statistical Booklets', 2006 to 2022 (excl. industrial wine).

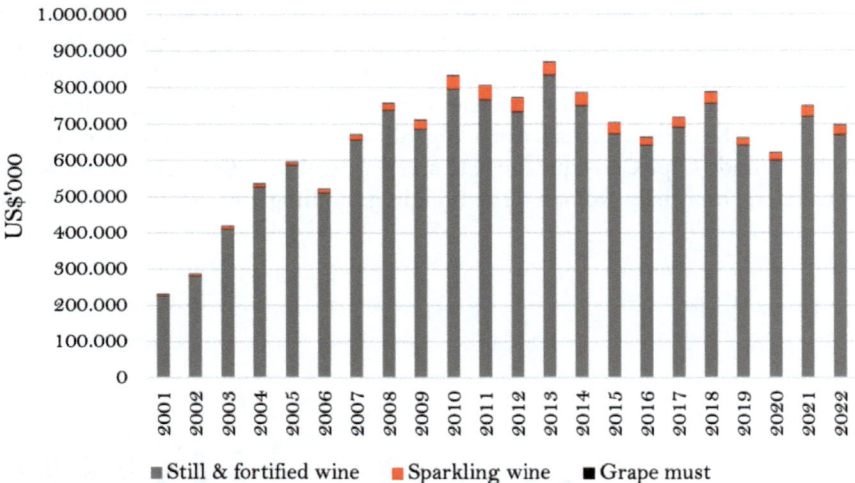

Figure 5 South African wine exports by value (2001–2022). Source: Elaboration of data from TradeMap. HST2204. Wine of fresh grapes, incl. fortified wines, grape must.

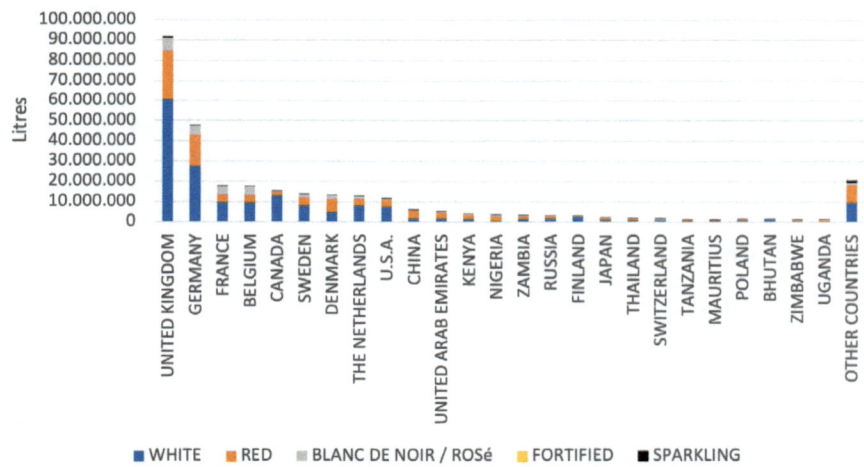

Figure 6 Top 25 export destinations for South African wine by volume (May 2023–April 2024). Source: Elaborated from data obtained on the SAWIS website: https://www.sawis.co.za/info/stats_exports_2024.php; excludes industrial wine.

opulent to attract this demographic' (SAW51). The young, Black urban population is considered image- and brand-conscious, and attracting this relatively untapped market is seen as presenting an opportunity for growth. One interviewee gave an estimate that only 3 per cent of this market has been captured so far (SAW31). A common approach is to attract new Black consumers in successive steps. As the general manager of a private cellar told me, one specific company 'has changed the

3. Global, South African and Italian Value Chains for Wine

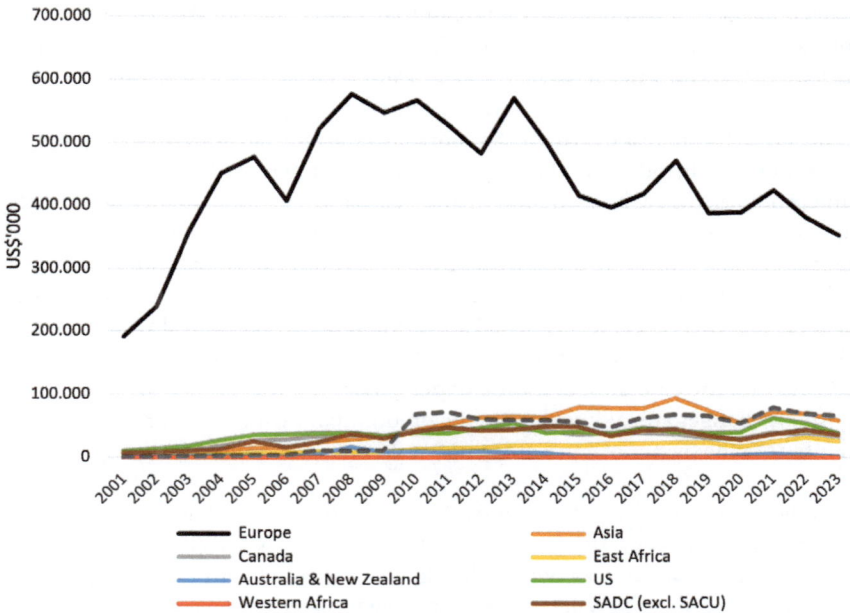

Figure 7 South African wine exports by destination, by value (2001–2023). Source: Elaboration of SARS data obtained from Quantec (HST2204: Wine of fresh grapes, including fortified wines; grape must other than that of heading 20.09).

Table 6 Packaged and bulk South African wine exports by volume (2005, 2021)

	2005	2005 (%)	2021	2021 (%)
Packaged	189,350,030	68	145,567,547	38
Bulk	89,767,167	32	242,565,602	62
Total exports	**279,117,197**		**388,133,149**	

Source: Compiled from data in 'SAWIS Statistical Booklet', 2021.

wine industry in South Africa. They put sweet wine in a magnum bottle at a very low price. It has been a big success . . . you start sweet and cheap and then move up and onwards' (SAW4). Yet, as the sales manager of a large producer wholesaler stated in an interview, the industry

> still has a long journey to bring a big part of the population into wine drinking. If you look at what is selling now is sweet rosé . . . it doesn't come from old vines, it doesn't come from varietal . . . It's a gateway into wine and hopefully we grow them with us and then get to a point where they . . . will want something less sweet and move into medium-dry into dry and then you can start getting interested in what is [real] wine.
>
> SAW17

Seeking new consumers is a strategy that has been applied not only in the domestic market, as seen above but also in other African countries as well. Notably, sales to SADC countries have seen a significant increase since 2009 (albeit from a low base). The owner of a large wine-exporting company explained to me that selling wine to the rest of Africa is a more attractive proposition than attempting to premiumize in other markets and trying to compete with other New World wine producers like Chile, Argentina and Australia. He highlighted that growing exports into Africa requires innovation: 'you can't copy your EU wine export business model and make it work for Africa; you need to do something dedicated and unique' (SAW45). Countries where potential for growth was reported include those in the SADC region for boxed wine and other lower-priced wine (SAW34, SAW31), and in Kenya, Tanzania, Uganda, Ghana and Nigeria for the tourism industry and the emerging domestic upper classes (SAW2, SAW5, SAW31).

Major changes are taking place in the predominant wine styles produced in the country. As the owner of a private winery told me:

> In the 2000s, wines were fruit-forward, with lots of wood . . . but now styles are more suited to South Africa's characteristics – with wines that are less powerful, more restrained, less alcoholic, fresher, lighter, easier but with personality. This emerging trend is especially important among younger winemakers coming out of the *garagiste* movement. There is a second renaissance of South African wine linked to Chenin Blanc as a unique offering that is suited to different terroirs and thus can offer styles from fresh all the way to wooded and fruity.
>
> SAW80

Some key observers of South African wine say that confidence is increasing in the country: (1) more styles that are characteristic of different places are emerging; (2) certified 'old vineyards' are bringing to the fore the expression of a sense of place; (3) the Western Cape is increasingly seen as unique, a region that can produce very different styles because of a multitude of climatic conditions; (4) new pruning techniques are being introduced, which can lead to massive savings because they lengthen the lifespan of vines and spread out the replanting schedules (SAW17); (5) oak use has drastically decreased, helping express place in the wine (SAW56); and (6) some winemakers are also starting to make wine in ceramic amphoras (SAW4).[26]

A South African winemaker of a wine estate argued that 'the South African wine industry is one of the most exciting in the world right now' (SAW56). Another stated that 'South African wine is winning big awards and the quality is considered to be very high. It is an industry with knowledgeable innovative people, but we are not yet moving from the bottom price points . . . South Africa needs big brands that demand higher prices, so others can piggyback on them' (SAW64). This set of views suggests that South Africa should be able to sell wines for higher prices in general. Some also think that the industry needs bigger brand leaders in the international market at the right price points, like Australians and Chileans have done (SAW57). Others also suggest that premiumization should be built upon the strength of the very well-developed and sophisticated wine tourism industry, but that producers also need to be better at selling stories – including those linked to terroir, different microclimates, and biodynamic and regenerative viticulture (SAW71).

Profitability

Given that quality is improving and the styles of wine produced in South Africa meet current demand, one would expect a healthy profitability environment in the industry. But this is not the case. Wine operators in South Africa, particularly at the grape-grower level, have faced increasing pressure from rising input costs which have affected their profitability (Figure 8). The South African wine industry uses Net Farm Income (NFI) as a proxy for profitability. NFI is calculated as gross income for a specific vintage less total production cost.[27] Gross income is shown in the dark grey bars. The gross margin, which is described as the cash-flow effect per hectare (gross income less production costs but before provisions are made for renewal or reinvestment) is depicted by the light grey bars. After provisions for renewal are accounted for, the green bars map the industry average NFI. Of interest to the industry is the comparison between the 'suggested NFI' per ha (the horizontal line) and the actual industry average NFI (bars to the right). The suggested NFI is a guideline of what is required for financially sustainable production for grape growers.

Furthermore, Figure 9 shows that the gap between suggested NFI and actual NFI has been widening since 2013.[28] For the 2022 vintage, an actual NFI of R17,247 per hectare was realized compared to a suggested NFI of R41,425. In 2022, data

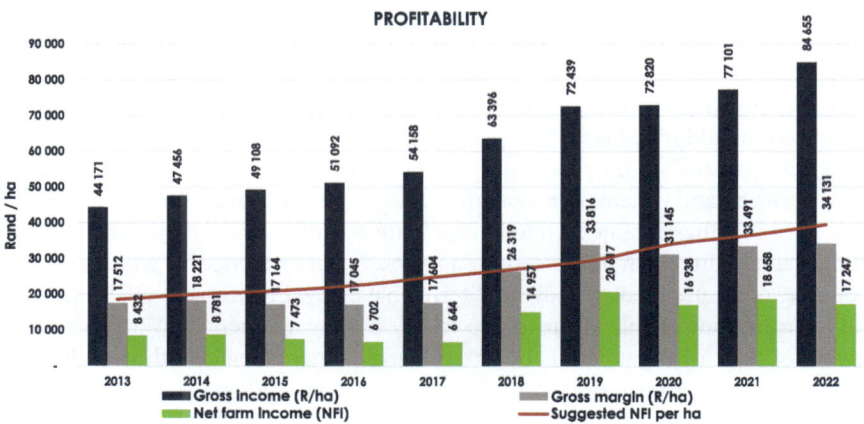

Figure 8 Wine grape farming profitability in South Africa (2013–2022). Source: Vinpro Production Plan Survey (2022), reproduced with permission.

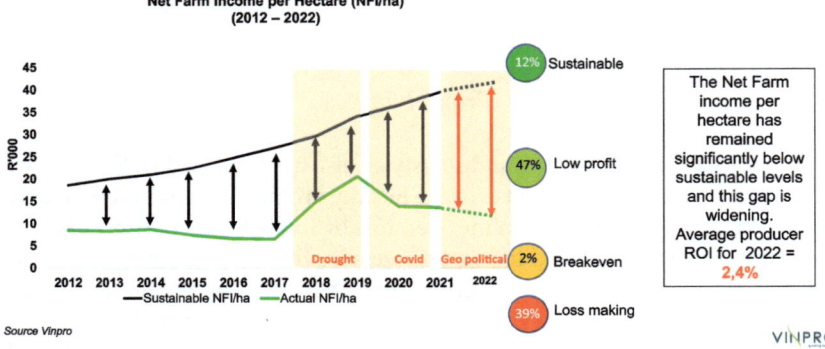

Figure 9 Continued profitability decline at farm level, South Africa (2012–2022). Source: Presentation by Rico Basson at #Vinproday, 19 January 2023, reproduced with permission.

presented by Vinpro showed that only 9 per cent of growers were sustainable (above suggested NFI), 50 per cent made low profits (but not sufficient to effectively reinvest), 3 per cent broke even and 38 per cent made losses (below suggested NFI).[29] Increasing financial pressure and declining profitability at the grape-farming node of the value chain have serious implications directly for farmers and indirectly for farmworkers.

On the distribution of value added along the wine value chain, Figure 10 highlights the cost breakdown of a bottle of wine sold domestically at 45 ZAR (around 3 USD). At the grape producer level, the net farm income is very low (0.77 ZAR, or around 0.05 USD), less than 2 per cent of the sales price of the bottle. Total production costs and margins for farming and winemaking combined account for only 12.5 per cent of the total. The largest component of value added (65.2 per cent) is in downstream functions (packaging, distribution and retail), with the rest being accounted for by taxes (22.3 per cent).

While similar data on profitability at the winemaking level or for integrated grape growing and winemaking operations are not publicly available, interviewees suggested that these rising production costs are also directly affecting other actors in the value chain. Cash flow is reported to be a major challenge for wineries – for example, domestic retailers' payment terms have now grown from 60–90 to 120 days. Furthermore, it takes time to ship and clear a consignment (SAW6). With the advent of the Covid pandemic, buyers also moved to consolidate the number of suppliers they buy from (contrary to the general discourse of supplier diversification to manage supply chain failure), and these fewer suppliers need to maintain higher levels of stocks. The manager of a wine wholesaler told me that 'in the past, a buyer may purchase eight wines from you, now they buy only four but ask you to stock

Figure 10 Vinpro cost breakdown of a bottle of wine, South Africa (2021). Source: 'Liquor sales open, but wine industry hit with other setbacks', Jana Loots, 2 March 2021,[30] reproduced with permission.

more because they are afraid of running out of them because of logistics problems' (SAW6).

A representative of one of the large producer wholesalers also reported that producers are

> making very little or no money. With profits of R10,000/ha in grape farming, you make a 2 per cent margin, but you need 10 per cent to survive. Farmers are looking at alternative crops. And if climate change makes yields drop by 10 per cent then there will be no profit at all – it is a very fragile situation. The only businesses that have the chance to survive are those in high-yield areas (30-40 tons/ha) that produce basic quality wine and those that are at the top end of the market. Those producing middle-range wines have no survival prospects.
>
> SAW49

These pressures are also leading to a significant number of properties and wineries being sold to foreign investors.

Regulation

In 'New World' countries, deep regulation of supply and demand in the wine sector never took off, but South Africa in the second part of the twentieth century, before the end of apartheid, is a clear exception (Nugent 2024a). Geographical appellations have been much less powerful in these countries, including in South Africa. Designation areas tend to be larger and rarely include quality distinctions or checks. They are often based on administrative boundaries (a county or province, for example), rather than on local links of quality and terroir, and rely mainly on the specification of grape varieties and/or a generic wine style.[31]

The Wine of Origin scheme

The Wine of Origin (WO) scheme in South Africa is a set of regulations that guarantees the origin, cultivar and vintage of wines. It was first introduced in 1973. Currently, all wines for export need to be certified under the WO scheme (see Image 2), while wines for domestic consumption are only subject to these regulations if the producer wants to specify the origin, cultivar and/or vintage on the label. The WO scheme is administered by the Wine and Spirits Board, which performs control functions and carries out sensory analysis of all batches of wine submitted for certification. WSB also administers a voluntary sustainability seal that can be affixed to the bottle (see Chapter 5).

There are several layers of geographical indication, from broad regions to individual vineyards, but no specific limitations on cultivar, grape quality, and viticulture and winemaking techniques are imposed. Legislation also allows for blending wines and grapes from different wine of origin areas, and for indicating all the areas on the label (e.g. Wine of Origin Stellenbosch and Paarl; previously, it would have been labelled 'Coastal', a larger unit).

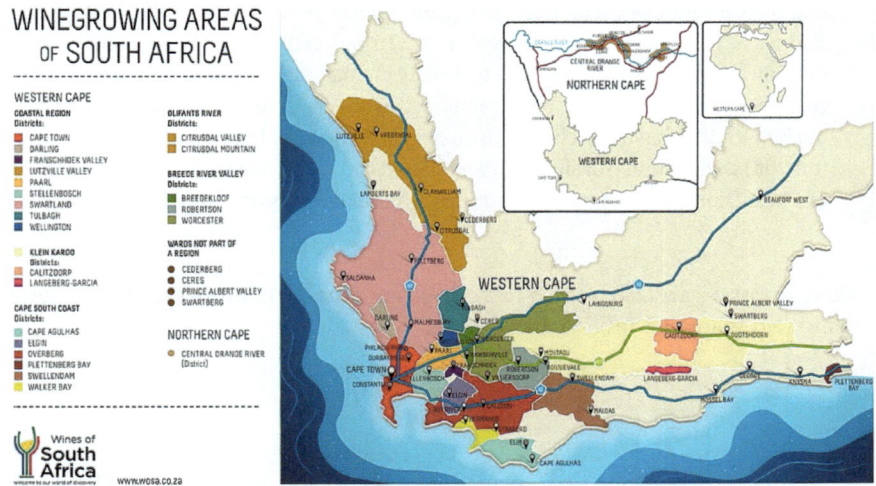

Image 2 Winegrowing areas of South Africa. Source: WOSA, reproduced with permission.[32]

The smallest production unit that can be certified under the Wine of Origin scheme is *single vineyard* wine, made with grapes coming from a single cultivar and a single vineyard not exceeding five hectares. This system (operational since 2005) has not had many takers even among high-quality producers. It is specifically inspired by the French idea of the *clos* (a specific vineyard with unique characteristics that was historically enclosed by a wall). But in the South African system, differently from the French, there is no requirement for the soil characteristics and structure in the vineyard to be uniform. Recently, a certification system for *Terroir Specific Wines* has also been developed. These wines must show identifiable and homogeneous characteristics with respect to topographical, climatic, soil and geological patterns (as in the French definition of terroir; see Chapter 4). This is a further step in South Africa towards the demarcation of geographical origin according to the European model, but it is not backed up by strict rules on quality, cultivar choice and specific viticultural techniques.

The 'Porto Agreement'

Wine trade between the EU and South Africa is regulated by the 2002 'Agreement on trade in wine' (also known as the 'Porto Agreement'). This is part of the overall 'Trade, Development and Cooperation Agreement' (TDCA), which was finalized in 1999. The genesis and politics of the wine agreement has been covered extensively elsewhere (Craven and Mather 2001). What is important to highlight here is that discussions on the use of geographical origin names (such as 'Port' and 'Sherry') almost derailed the whole TDCA. Only by signing separate agreements on wine and spirits was South Africa able to conclude it.

During the TDCA negotiation process, the EU (under pressure from Spain and Portugal) made the case that South African producers should stop using the names 'Port' and 'Sherry' for wines of these styles that are produced locally. To conclude a draft TDCA agreement, South Africa agreed to phase these names out over a period of five years in export markets and twelve years in the domestic market. In exchange, the EU committed to provide a duty-free quota of 32 million litres of wine and a grant of €15 million to assist South African producers in designing new names for their products. Under this agreement, exports are required to comply with sanitary, phytosanitary and other technical requirements and the rules of origin stipulated by the TDCA. Eighty per cent of the first allocation of permits was divided up in proportion to the historical market share of exporters, and the rest allocated to small and medium enterprises.

Interestingly, when the tariff quota was first applied, it was used mostly for exports to the UK. In general, retailers in Europe refused to pass on the import tariff cut to exporters and instead pocketed the difference (Ponte and Ewert 2007). Subsequently, under pressure from WOSA, UK retailers agreed to deposit tariff quota savings into a WOSA fund for the generic promotion of South African wine in the UK. Retailers in the Netherlands refused to do so, and thus exporters in practice have used licenses for tariff quota exports primarily destined for the UK. In other words, the Porto Agreement could have led to higher profitability for the qualifying South African producers. In practice, it only lowered the price offered to European buyers and introduced pressures on exporters to sell non-quota wine at a lower price too (SAW18, SAW26).

Wine tourism

South Africa, and especially the Western Cape province, are considered among the best-developed wine tourism destinations in the world (Ferreira and Hunter 2017). The winemaker of a private cellar told me that 'the wine landscape in the Western Cape is itself a destination of choice. It is affordable and beautiful' (SAW66). WOSA lists twenty-three wine routes in the country.[33] The first one to be established was the Stellenbosch wine route in 1971 (Bruwer 2003), on the back of three pioneer wineries that had just started to organize tastings at their cellars (Ferreira and Hunter 2017). Many wineries are open to the public any day of the week all year round, without the need for booking a tasting. Most offer free tastings of wines (except for their most expensive ones) and organize wine-centred events – often combined with music, art, outdoor adventure and food pairings (Joy et al. 2018).

Wine tourism is not a niche economic sector, it is a core visit experience in South Africa (SAW32). The Western Cape provincial government aims to position the region as a leading global wine tourism destination (SAW32). In 2020, it rejoined the 'wine capitals network' (the city of Cape Town was previously in it, but then left) to promote the Western Cape at a global scale. Wine tourism is an important income earner for wineries domestically. Some wineries would not actually be able to survive without it (SAW61, SAW64). Wine tourism facilities are key to introducing brands that are not well known to potential wine drinkers. As stated by the winemaker of a private cellar, the idea is that 'foreign tourists then can go back to their countries and want to buy more South African wine' (SAW66).

In 2022, wine tourism is estimated to have contributed R3 bn ($184 m) directly and R9.3 bn in total ($570 m; including direct, indirect and induced impacts) to the South African economy. It accounted for 14.3 per cent of wine cellar turnover on average, and for 36 per cent of micro wine cellars (with a total turnover of less than R10 million). It supported directly over 6,000 permanent jobs and a range of between 2,800 and 4,800 casual jobs (depending on the season). With direct and induced impacts, the employment figure goes up to 40,000 jobs. Wine tourism brings in revenue through wine tastings (36 per cent of total turnover from wine tourism), overnight accommodation (18 per cent), food and beverage sales (26 per cent), conferences (12 per cent) and events (5 per cent). About half of overnight visitors are foreign tourists and non-South African residents.[34]

In some wineries, tourism accounts for a significant proportion of sales. Two interviewees highlighted that it accounted for 30 per cent of their sales, with one noting that it has a substantial impact on international sales (SAW84; SAW4). Others stated that it counted for between 10 per cent and 25 per cent of their sales (SAW80; SAW28), with margins on cellar door sales being higher than sales through other routes (SAW28, SAW26; SAW31). Several highlighted the importance of wine tourism for their businesses, and the value of diversifying into wine tourism to avoid being reliant solely on wine production (SAW61, SAW64, SAW65).

For the international market, wine tourism offers an opportunity to promote South Africa as a destination of choice which could then translate into wine sales (SAW66). Conservation initiatives also spill over into tourism opportunities by offering walking, mountain biking and hiking experiences on wine farms (SAW52, SAW61, SAW75, SAW76, SAW84), as well as wildlife experiences (SAW9 and SAW51). There is recognition however that there is greater scope to create stronger links between conservation and tourism (SAW7). Many interviewees stated that, especially for smaller producers, the key to value addition is embedded in wine tourism, and in leveraging beauty, terroir and location. The head of sales of a wine estate told me that 'it's all about aesthetics, restaurants ... When somebody visits, they feel history, tradition and a visual connection of the vineyard with the actual wine. Visitors want authenticity and spend more for that. Wine in the property tastes different than when you drink anywhere else' (SAW70).

3.4 ITALIAN WINE

Brief history and recent trends

The history of Italian wine in the post-war period can be summarized in four broad phases (Corsi, Pomarici and Sardone 2018). A first phase (from 1946 to 1970) saw the expansion of yields and wine production of low quality (with a small proportion of exports, mostly relegated to low price segments), the gradual abandonment of intercropping, major technical and agronomic changes, the movement from production for self-consumption towards commercialization, the increasing importance of wine cooperatives, and a major increase in domestic consumption per capita. A second phase (from 1970 to 1986) was characterized by a switch in focus from domestic sales to exports, more moderate growth in yields (but not enough to address overproduction), decreasing domestic consumption per capita (which has continued to this day), and booming exports (mostly at the low end of the price range, but with an increasing share of premium wines). This period ended in 1986, when the so-called methanol scandal led to a turning point in the Italian wine industry (see Chapter 4).

The third phase (1960-2000) was one marked by a 'quality turn' – a stabilization of yields (as appellation wines became more important, and rules were established to limit yields) and, for the first time since World War II, decreasing production volumes. These trends were accompanied by innovation, consolidation (especially among cooperatives), better management and increasing vertical integration among wine value chain operators – leading to a continued growth of export volumes and increasing unit prices. A fourth phase (2000-2014) was marked by an actual decline in yields and production volumes, and continued growth of exports and unit prices (with geographical origin wines becoming increasingly important), as the industry continued to consolidate and vertically integrate.

Some key trends from the past decade or so are also worth highlighting here. Wine production in Italy started to increase noticeably from the mid-2010s onwards (Table 7). This was driven by a substantial increase in the total area planted with vineyards for wine grape production from 2017 onwards, following a period of falling area planted in 2009–2016 (see Figure 11). Much of this growth is attributable to the expansion of production of geographical appellation wines, a sign of the growing valorization of 'place' (see Figure 12). The Veneto region has been a major source of this growth, and within Veneto, we can notice the same in the provinces of Treviso (the core area of Prosecco wines) and to a lesser extent Verona (the exclusive area of production of Valpolicella) (see Table 8). Total Italian wine exports reached a value of almost €8 bn in 2022 and 2023 (Figure 13), almost double the value of exports in 2010. The main country destinations for Italian bottled wine are the USA, Germany and the UK, which together in 2023 accounted for almost 50 per cent of the value of total exports.

According to Malorgio et al. (2011), the value chain for Italian wine is a combination of different systems that have different levels of market integration,

Table 7 Italian wine production (2009–2023)

Year	Total production (million hl)	of which DOP	of which IGP	of which table wines
2009	43.4	15.3	12.3	15.9
2010	44.7	15.7	14.0	15.0
2011	40.6	15.1	13.6	12.0
2012	38.3	16.0	12.5	9.7
2013	45.0	17.3	15.8	11.9
2014	39.7	16.4	13.5	9.9
2015	48.6	19.0	15.4	14.3
2016	51.6	19.5	15.3	16.8
2017	43.8	17.4	11.8	14.6
2018	54.1	22.9	13.5	17.8
2019	49.9	22.0	11.8	16.0
2020	51.9	22.5	12.7	16.7
2021	50.9	23.1	12.3	15.5
2022	54.0	24.6	13.9	15.5
2023	42.5	20.3	11.5	10.7
Average 2009–2023	*46.6*	*19.1*	*13.3*	*14.2*
Average 2014–2023	*48.7*	*20.8*	*13.2*	*14.8*
Average 2019–2023	*49.8*	*22.5*	*12.4*	*14.9*

Source: Elaboration from ISTAT data.[35]

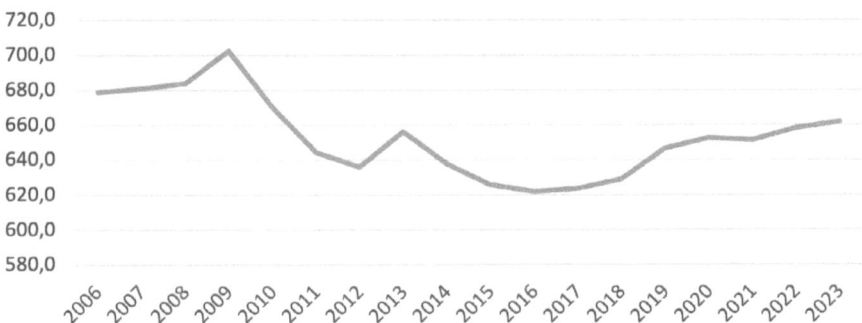

Figure 11 Total area under vineyard cultivation for wine grapes in Italy (2006–2023). Source: Elaboration from ISTAT data.[36]

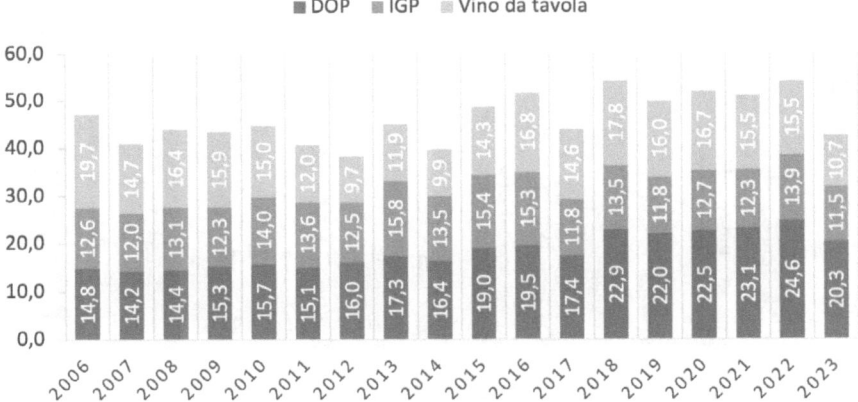

Figure 12 Italian wine production by type of denomination (2006-2023). Source: Elaboration from ISTAT data.[37]

models of vertical integration and productive philosophies. Upstream, the value chain is very fragmented, with over 240,000 registered farms as of 2023. There are also over 33,000 winemaking firms, which can be divided up into three main types: (i) wine cellars that make wine from own grapes, which can also buy grapes in the open market as needed; (ii) industrial winemakers, which make wine exclusively from grapes purchased from contract farmers or in the open market; and (iii) consortium or cooperative winemakers, which make wine from grapes sourced from their members and from the open market; about half of total

Table 8 Wine production in Italy, the Veneto region and by province in Veneto (2014–2023)

(hl/1000)	2014	2015	2016	2017	2018	2019	2020	2021	2022	2023
ITALY	39741	48635	51615	43829	54150	49859	51916	50885	54005	42449
Veneto	8177	9733	10145	8473	12866	11333	11038	10927	11870	10624
Verona	2759	3106	3493	2791	4155	3354	3472	2959	3144	3015
Vicenza	669	901	985	895	1071	926	929	772	876	832
Belluno	3	6	9	16	21	25	18	23	22	22
Treviso	3529	4291	4252	4358	5645	5296	4728	5174	5617	4863
Venezia	774	799	748	851	1108	914	1060	1190	1221	1002
Padova	537	620	646	793	849	798	812	793	968	870
Rovigo	10	10	13	18	17	20	20	17	22	19

Source: Elaboration from www.inumeridelvino.it based on data from ISTAT.

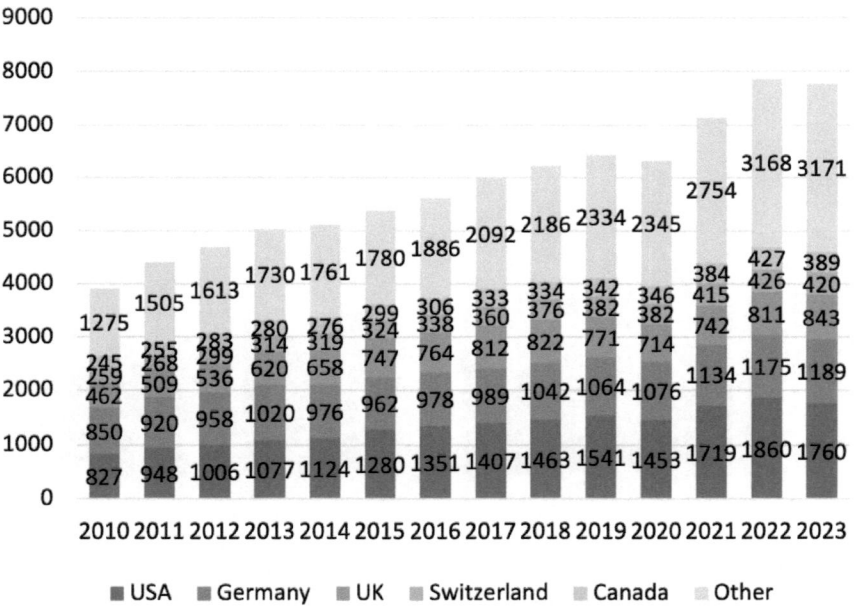

Figure 13 Italian wine exports by value (2010–2023). Source: Elaboration from www.inumeridelvino.it based on data from ISTAT.[38]

production of grapes for wine are sourced by these cooperatives (Malorgio et al. 2011). Three-quarters of winemaker firms produce less than 10,000 litres of wine, while less than 1 per cent of firms produce more than 10 million litres and contribute to 43 per cent of total production.[40] The top ten winemaking firms in Italy include four cooperatives, four family-owned firms and only two firms that have a more corporate structure (see Table 9).

Table 9 Top 10 Italian winemaking firms (2021–2022)

Firm	Turnover in 2022* (€ m)	Turnover in 2021 (€ m)	Ownership type	% variation 2021–2022*
CANTINE RIUNITE & CIV	698,5	634,2	Cooperative	+10,1
ARGEA	455,1	415,0	Corporate	+9,6
ITALIAN WINE BRANDS	430,3	408,9	Corporate	+5,2
CAVIRO	417,4	389,9	Cooperative	+7,1
CAVIT CANTINA VITICOLTORI	264,8	271,0	Cooperative	−2,3
SANTA MARGHERITA	260,7	220,6	Family-owned	+18,2
FRATELLI MARTINI SEC. LUIGI	237,6	219,6	Family-owned	+8,2
MARCHESI ANTINORI	245,4	213,5	Family-owned	+14,9
CASA VINICOLA ZONIN	200,1	198,5	Family-owned	+0,8
MEZZACORONA	213,4	196,5	Cooperative	+8,6

* Data for 2022 is provisional. Elaboration of data from 'Area Studi Mediobanca: Il settore vinicolo in Italia – sintesi 2023'.[39]

Regulation

The value chain for Italian wine is regulated at the EU level under the EU Common Agricultural Policy and a series of EU wine-specific regulations (see above). This set of regulations is complemented by a layer of applicative Italian legislation that includes a 'unified wine text' (Testo Unico Vino, TUV, legge 238/2016), ministerial implementation regulations and applicative circulars. The TUV is mostly a collection of already existing wine laws that are organized into a single text, plus applicative regulations of new reforms. Italy's system of geographical designations has been operating since 1963, when very strict rules on the production and marketing of wines were introduced – including product specifications defined for each designation, special registers for recording viticulture areas, and a system of reporting the quantity of grapes produced within a particular designation. In 1992, the system was partially revised with the introduction of IGT wines, the possibility of harvesting the same vineyard for different designations of origin, and the possibility of setting up more restricted areas within existing designations. Finally, following the adoption of the 2008 EU wine reform, the Italian state revised its pyramidal construction of quality wines, now defined (in descending order of quality) as: Denominazione d'Origine Controllata e Garantita (DOCG), Denominazione d'Origine Controllata DOC, Indicazione Geografica Tipica (IGT) and Vino da Tavola (VDT). The first two pertain to the EU definition of PDO wines, while the third pertains to PGI wines. The fourth is part of what the EU defines as 'varietal wines' and/or 'generic wines'.

The latest adjustments of the TUV took place with Laws 77/2020 and 120/2020. These have introduced stricter rules for the recognition of DOCG areas, including the rule stating that only an entire DOC area can apply for DOCG status. This is of particular interest because it was enacted explicitly to avoid what happened when Prosecco was split into a DOC area and two separate DOCG areas in the late 2000s (see details in Chapter 4). Under this regulatory framework, producer consortia are repositories of important regulatory functions that go beyond safeguarding their geographical indications. They have been formally recognized as strategic actors and are allowed to establish marketing rules to regulate supply. This means that collective consortia can take action to maintain an equilibrium between supply and demand and to avoid market failure. There are currently 527 geographical denominations in Italy, of which 332 are DOC, 77 DOCG and 119 IGT – accounting for over 70 per cent of total wine production in 2022 (see Figure 12) (P3).[41]

Wine tourism

Wine tourism in Italy is a relatively new phenomenon. According to Colombini (2015), when the first edition of 'Cantine Aperte' (Open Cellars) took place in 1993, there were only twenty wineries in the whole country that were open to tourists. Therefore, when 100 wineries opened their doors to tourists in Toscana, the event was considered revolutionary. As wineries started to understand the benefits of wine tourism in terms of income, visibility and media attention, it became progressively more widespread. An initial phase of development, when wineries started adapting their operations to a growing number of visitors, was followed by the setting up of special areas for tourism purposes (Colombini 2015). Wine routes have played an important role in this development (Festa et al. 2020).

Colombini (2015) classifies Italian wineries that cater for tourists into three main types: 'functional wineries', which are focused on efficiency and where 'everything works but nothing excites' (Colombini 2015, 33); 'monumental', which tend to be renovated historical buildings that seek to be grandiose; and 'modern starchitecture' designs by famous architects, where aesthetics is the key attraction. Within the last two categories, we can also find properties that are strongly linked to the identity of the owner or winemaker. In the mid-2010s, around 16 per cent of the €73 billion spent by tourists annually in Italy related to wine and food. Direct sales in wineries accounted for 10–20 per cent of total income on average (with a higher proportion in smaller properties) (Colombini 2015). Wine tourists in Italy generally seek an 'authentic experience' of place, with participatory farm experiences helping tourists escape the stress of urban/daily life (Esau and Senese 2022).

Prosecco and Valpolicella: A brief introduction

Prosecco sparkling wine is produced in northeast Italy from grapes of the glera vine. The classic area of production is located on steep hills around Valdobbiadene and on gentler slopes and flatland close to Conegliano (see Image 3). The first consortium charged with protecting the Prosecco geographical denomination was established in 1962 (Prosecco DOC). But as the 2008 EU wine reform (Itçaina et al., 2016; Pomarici and Sardone, 2020) deepened the regulation of indications of geographical origin, the DOC area became under threat of losing its exclusive claim because the denomination Prosecco was related to a grape variety at that time, not a territorial place. This meant that Prosecco, under new EU legislation, potentially could be produced anywhere. In reaction to this threat, the consortium managed to construct a historical heritage story to apply for a reform of the geographical indication system for Prosecco. The reform process expanded the overall Prosecco DOC from a relatively small area within the province of Treviso to other four provinces in Veneto and the whole of the Friuli-Venezia Giulia region (see Image 3). In parallel to this, the original Conegliano and Valdobbiadene area was upgraded to DOCG, which denotes higher quality – along with the establishment of the DOCG of Asolo Prosecco and the sub-denomination Prosecco DOC Treviso e Trieste (see details in Chapter 4).

Following these reforms, and in conjunction with a quick uptake in demand, the total planted area of Prosecco DOC grew dramatically, from 8,700 hectares in 2010 to almost three times as much (24,450 hectares) in 2020. Production volumes followed suit, going from 141 million bottles in 2010 to 616 million in 2023, for a sales value of over €3 billion – to these, we need to add a production of around 100 million bottles of DOCG Conegliano Valdobbiadene Prosecco and 24 million bottles of Asolo Prosecco Superiore DOCG. In 2015, exports of Prosecco were valued at €668 million – in 2023, this figure was over € 2.2 billion.[42] The Prosecco DOC area alone currently counts around 10,400 registered viticulturists, 1,173 makers of the base wine, and 364 bottlers of sparkling wine.[43]

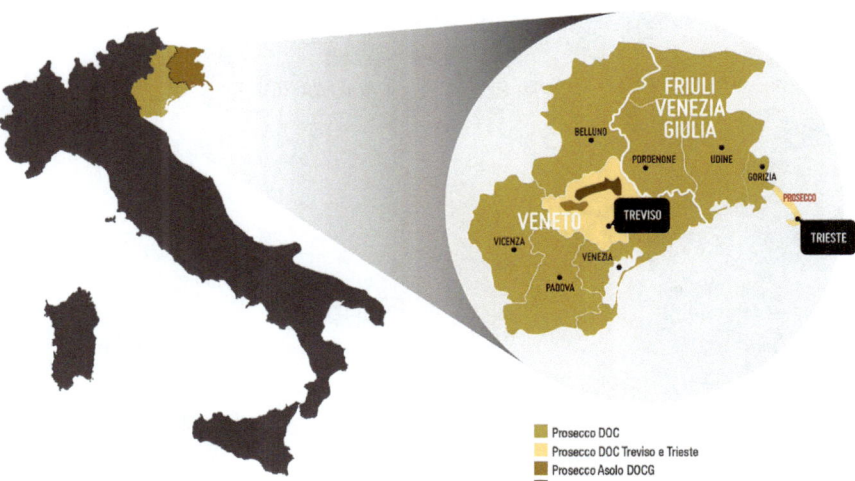

Image 3 Map of the Prosecco area of production, Italy. Source: https://www.prosecco.wine, reproduced with permission.

Although the rest of the Italian wine industry has also innovated and adapted in the past two–three decades (Cusmano, Morrison and Rabellotti 2010), the performance of Prosecco has been particularly impressive (Checchinato et al. 2024). Prosecco accounts for about one-third of global exports of sparkling wine in terms of volume, while its main competitors (Cava and Champagne) together account for one-third.[44] It should be noted that Champagne attracts much higher unit prices than Cava or Prosecco. Data on the total value of sparkling wine exports (a proxy for these three origins) indicate that France accounted for 52 per cent of global exports by value in 2018 (down from 70 per cent in 2003), followed by Italy (25 per cent) and Spain (7 per cent).[45]

The Valpolicella geographical appellation is organized around a consortium of producers (*Consorzio per la Tutela Vini Valpolicella*), which was first established in 1924/25 but took its current form in 1970. The geographical appellation is located within a set of municipalities within the province of Verona, Veneto region (see Image 4). Differently from Prosecco, the four main denominations of Valpolicella are based on different types of wine, rather than referring to separate geographical areas: Valpolicella DOC, Valpolicella Ripasso DOC, Amarone della Valpolicella DOCG and Recioto della Valpolicella DOCG. Since 2010, the Valpolicella consortium (like all DOC/DOCG consortia in Italy) has been allowed to play the functions of wine promotion and valorization. In the same year, it set up the DOCG denomination for its top-quality wines (the iconic Amarone and its sweet version Recioto). Like in the case of Prosecco, Amarone became known beyond the local and regional markets only in the 1990s (see Chapter 4), with fast growth in exports from the 2000s onwards (V1). There are currently 2,251 registered grape farmers in Valpolicella, 344 private wineries and six cooperative wineries. The area

Image 4 Map of the Valpolicella areas of production, Italy. Source: https://www.bookyourwineguide.com/valpolicella-amarone-tour/, reproduced with permission.

under production has seen a major growth since the turn of the century – from 5,719 ha in 2005 to 8,586 ha in 2023 – reversing a declining trend in the 1980s and 1990s. Production has also increased, from about 49.5 million bottles in 2005 to 67.5 million in 2022. Total Valpolicella sales amounted to about €600 million in 2022, 60 per cent of which were exported to eighty-seven markets.[46]

3.5 WHAT'S NEXT

On the basis of the background provided in this chapter on the global, South African and Italian value chains for wine, Part II of the book examines how different worlds of valuation are leveraged by different groups of actors in three key sites of value struggle in wine: the first site coalesces around *place*, and specifically the tensions between 'placeless' and 'place' wines that are linked to terroir and geographical origin; this is explored both in terms of tasting 'place in wine' and in relation to the consumption of 'wine in place' (wine tourism destinations and the articulation of attached imaginaries and subsequent memories); the second site relates to multiple processes of qualification of *nature*, the environment and climate change, in the context of broader discourses and practices of sustainability; the third site concerns *people*, and the value struggles that take place around class, race and gender in relation to labour processes and ownership patterns.

At the same time, we should also remember that 'ephemerality is wine's, and especially good or fine wine's, default mode of being' (Howland and Dutton 2020, 3). Grape wine is effectively an arrested by-product of ripening grapes that ferment into vinegar and compost (Howland 2019a, 166). Given the tendency of vines to vary genetically, and the multitude of factors involved in viticulture and winemaking, perpetual change is perhaps one of the main characteristics of wine unless it is tamed by human intervention and technology (Howland and Dutton 2020). This means that valuation practices are constantly changing. Different worlds of valuation often overlap, their configurations change over time, and can be contested (Isla 2017; Sánchez-Hernández 2023). Also, the three sites of value struggle indicated here should not be taken as mutually exclusive. They are tightly interwoven and thus any categorization involves a degree of simplification. For example, conservation, landscape and heritage issues are examined in Chapter 4 on place, even though they also underpin value struggles related to nature. The value struggles around nature discussed in Chapter 5 are also tightly linked to the labour and social sustainability issues discussed in Chapter 6 on people (in relation to class, race and gender). To ensure an easier flow for readers interested mainly in wine, I interpret the empirics theoretically through the six worlds of valuation delineated in Chapter 2 only at the end of each empirical chapter. In Chapter 7, I will then bring these analytical reflections together to reflect on what they can tell us about power dynamics in value chains and in contemporary capitalism more generally.

Part II

THREE SITES OF VALUE STRUGGLE

Chapter 4

PLACE

4.1 INTRODUCTION

Viticulture can be seen as the violent commodification and homogenization of environmental and genetic variety to make wine work for the (mainstream) market under the mantle of predictable variation. On the one hand, grapes for winemaking have 'nature capital' that transcends the mediation of humanity – not only in genetic terms but also in their innate capacity to ferment sugars into alcohol through the natural yeasts contained in their skins, and in their capacity to produce immense chemical component variations – depending on climate, soil conditions, water availability and altitude (Howland 2019a). On the other hand, wine also has 'material capital' that is linked to human endeavour – if winemakers fail to achieve minimal fermentation, they get unpalatable juice; if they exceed the maximum, they get vinegar (Howland 2019a, 154). Within these parameters, humans can still choose to 'let the vines speak' and express place, or to suppress these nuances by manufacturing wines that yield predictable results across space and over time (Howland and Dutton 2020). Place-based differentiation can unfold horizontally, in the sense that a wine from one place can taste different to a wine from another place. But it can also be developed vertically, as different wines from the same place can taste differently depending on their quality levels (Fourcade 2012).

In this chapter, I examine various aspects of place as a site of value struggle in wine. First, I identify key tensions and overlaps between key processes of differentiation/uniqueness and homogenization/commodification – in other words, between valuation processes related to mainstream, branded wines vis-à-vis wines that are to different degrees attached to specific places and geographical origins. The former tend to be 'placeless' and have minor or no attachment to specific locations and producers (Colman 2008); the latter are generally sold with more explicit reference to more or less specific places.[1] The markers of identity in 'place wines' can be a combination of geographical origin (e.g. Valpolicella, Stellenbosch), the name of a winery, often but not always a family name (e.g. Tommasi, Paul Clüver), a particular style of making wine that is specific to that place (e.g. Ripasso, Cape Classic) and/or the specific plot where the grapes come from (e.g. Monte dei Ragni, the Chocolate Block). Valuation discourses and practices for place wines can refer to a particular vineyard and/or winery located in a specific place but are often embedded in geographical indications that are to a significant extent controlled collectively by local institutions and producers.

Second, within the broad category of place wines, I provide a detailed examination of the value struggles that occur in relation to terroir and geographical origin. These take place through different repertoires of valuation related to *tradition* (a set of viticultural and winemaking practices that have become historically prevalent in a specific geographical area); *authenticity* (a wine as the 'true' or 'typical' expression of a particular place); and *heritage* (the inherent characteristics of a place that need to be preserved and transmitted to future generations). Third, I analyse 'fine wines' and the valuation of place as articulated in issues of taste, uniqueness, rarity and investment. The extensive coverage of fine wines in the literature is a fascinating aspect on its own. I suspect that the disproportional attention to this tiny portion of the wine market happens partly because of our fascination with the rich and powerful, and partly because of the prominence of wine as an empirical example in discussions of distinction (Bourdieu 1979) and taste (see below), and in classical political economy more generally (Martineau 1832; Ricardo 1821; Smith 1977 [1776]). But examining elitism and luxury (and their place-based dimensions) is also a way to show how the value enhancement processes typical of the enrichment economy (Boltanski and Esquerre 2020) are built upon the original value extraction from nature (see Chapter 5) and from racialized and gendered labour exploitation and dehumanization (see Chapter 6). Fourth, I examine how producers, marketers and institutions draw from these repertoires of valuation to sell the ideas of not only tasting place in wine but also tasting wine in place through tourism. Finally, I return more explicitly to the analytical framework of worlds of valuation to highlight the multifaceted role of place in shaping value struggles in wine.

4.2 'PLACELESS WINES'

For 'placeless wines', price and brand are the two most important features of wine valuation (Negro and Hannan 2022). At the lower end of the quality scale, wine is sold as a commodity like many others, where distinctions are made only at the very generic level – whether the wine is white or red, sweet or dry, and still or sparkling. Much of this wine is the result of blending a number of wine varieties and areas of production, even different countries, mostly traded in bulk – to provide the cheapest wine that does not present obvious taints (Rainer, Steiner and Pütz 2023). These wines can be sold under brands owned by merchants or retailers, but price is paramount as a valuation device.

Placeless wines one step up in the quality scale can also indicate a reference to 'place' (e.g. Western Cape, Prosecco) at a very generic level – but this is more akin to signalling a broad regional origin or a wine style than the specific place where the wine was made. In this segment, brands become more important as a value signifier in combination with the indication of a single varietal or a combination of two–three varietals. Globally known brands such as Yellow Tail and Barefoot are examples of how the wine industry is trying to lure new consumers into buying wine by reducing complexity and referring to lifestyle signifiers instead of place. Modern production processes and careful blending reduce variation in time, so that each vintage tastes the same as the previous one, therefore assuring homogeneity within a broad area/region and in time (Colman 2008; Negro and Hannan 2022). Placeless wines provide much flexibility to large-scale blenders and marketers to source wine from the cheapest origins, and through buyer power to squeeze margins from grape farmers and bulk wineries (Ponte 2019). Both Italy and South Africa have for decades catered to the lower end of the wine market, and even if they have been successful in producing higher quality wines, they are still perceived (as general national origins) as cheap and cheerful. In Italy, this creates chagrin at the industry level in relation to the embarrassing gap between Italian export unit prices (€3.6/litre in 2023) and those of France (€9.4), and endless discussions about how to lower yields and improve quality.[2]

In South Africa, this debate is at the very centre of strategic and policy discussion, framed around the role of bulk wine exports and the perceived need to 'premiumize' South African wines (see Chapter 3). As an alternative to bottled wine, some importers and retailers (especially in Germany, Denmark and the UK) prefer to buy wine in bulk from South Africa, which they then bottle in the EU, often for their own private labels. Bulk exports have lower unit-level carbon emissions (SAW1) – twenty-foot containers are fitted with a flexibag that can contain 24,000 litres of wine. In 75 cl bottles, one can only fit the equivalent of 10,000 litres in these containers. They are also heavier because of the weight of the glass and pallets (SAW73). With bulk shipments, however, exporters usually lose control of their wine, unless they maintain ownership and a branded offering on the import side by bottling it themselves in Europe (SAW1). Bulk wine exports are not yet allowed to receive the South African Sustainability & Integrity logo once they are bottled-at-destination wine (see Chapter 5). This is technically possible and would give South Africa a unique selling point in the bulk market where it competes with Chile, Australia and Argentina. Another aspect much debated in the South African industry is that, when you export wine in bulk, you also implicitly export jobs in the sense that the employment entailed in bottling and packaging is lost to the local economy (SAW6, SAW49). This is a highly contentious political issue in a country with very high unemployment rates.

Another angle to the debates on premiumization is that South Africa should be playing mainly a niche market role, based on quality, site and regional specificity instead of selling cheap wine at volume and in bulk – given the low profitability of grape farming (SAW64, SAW72). A third perspective is that bulk wine of clean minimum quality is in demand anyway, and it allows operators to manage cash flows. Therefore, whatever happens at the top end of quality, there is space for cheap bulk wine and other producing countries that sell cheap wine are also able to sell very expensive wines. This is especially the case among cooperatives (SAW5). At the same time, the owner of a wine wholesaler argued against the constant flow of complaints from wine industry operators regarding the lack of premiumization. He told me that you have to understand the luxury side of wine and the agricultural side of production. You need to add value to the product and thus take a knock on the yield. I understand the gripe from farmers: the cost of audits etcetera, but you need to be better at increasing your price. Yet, it is a competitive industry. So, stop complaining and find ways of doing it better, or get out . . . If the consumer is not paying more, then you need to be more efficient and creative. Look at Concha Y Toro in Chile: they are efficient at scale, deliver high quality at reasonable price. They are a gold standard for many, a very clever model.

SAW63

Whether better prices are being paid for higher quality wine or not, the general view in the South African industry is that quality has increased dramatically in the past decade or so, together with a diversification of styles. In particular, old vine wines are transcending regions and styles (see below). Journalists are very interested in them and they attract substantial premia, especially for Chenin Blanc. In terms of styles, a prominent South African wine journalist told me that

> although in South Africa we are still making icon wines with lots of power and traction, lots of oak . . . we are also making more elegant wines, with older oak and less extraction. We are letting the vineyard talk. These are exciting wines from a newer generation of winemakers who want a light imprint on the wine. This is an expanding segment of the portfolio.
>
> SAW23

An indicator of the upward trajectory of quality is that Platter (the most influential guide for South African wines), only awarded twenty-six wines with a 5-star rating back in 2007. Now there are more than 200. This also shows in the results of competitions. The same journalist argued that

> in the past, 30 per cent of South African entries were not even tasted in competitions as they were not good enough, now they all tend to be tasted . . . At the same time, the Master of Wine examiners still think that there is not enough regionality within South Africa to make wines recognizable in blind tastings (such as Paarl or Stellenbosch). The industry should also work with a new generation of social media influencers, both domestically and internationally, instead of scoffing at their apparent lack of knowledge or palate . . . Reaching a new generation of consumers is tied to being able to influence the influencers.
>
> SAW23

These reflections suggest that much of the debate in South Africa revolves around wine styles, intrinsic quality and the stories that are told around wine, but not so much about the valorization of place yet. Where place is used for storytelling it refers to a specific vineyard or property, a private reference rather than a link to collective geographical origins. Lacking a geographical appellation system that ensures an exclusive or essential link between product quality and place of origin, these scattered efforts do not yet create collective place rents and have a much weaker impact on the perception of place by wine buyers and ultimately consumers.³

4.3 TASTING PLACE IN WINE: TRADITION AND AUTHENTICITY

Terroir

The French term *terroir* derives from the Latin *territorium* – a domain, district, or territory that combines 'the social construction of space (town, district, etc.) with the agricultural role of the land' (Parker 2015, 5). Both aspects were progressively incorporated by the French in their development of the concept – from conceiving cuisine as part of (local and national) cultural identity-making during the Renaissance to the emergence of the cult of connoisseurship (Howland 2013) – eventually becoming a distinction based on class and political identity (Parker 2015). Terroir is then both an ideal and a set of practices, a marker of identity and the source of exclusion and inequality. It is a signifier of quality, but also a symbolic connection to a place and the people who live there (Swinburn 2019). It is where people and place, cultural traditions and landscape ecology come together in mutually constitutive ways over time (Demossier 2020).

A *narrow* definition of terroir relates to the precise characteristics of the natural environment in a specific location where grapes are grown to make a specific wine. A *broad* definition also considers 'place', intended as 'space imbued with meaning' (Swinburn 2019, 227). This broader definition combines nature with the 'ensemble of knowledge' particular to a location (Daynes 2013), including the human agency of viticulturists and winemakers who live there (workers are unfortunately rarely mentioned) and their local crafting traditions. Terroir can then be seen as a 'latent possibility of the environment . . . a sensitivity with which one looks at the world of wine . . . com[ing] to life not just in the interaction between farmer and environment, but also in the stories told about it' (Cisterna 2013, 55). 'To use *terroir* as a category of analysis thus entails paying attention to the interplay between the latent physical potential of a location, the farming techniques deployed, the kind of economic system in which these products will circulate, and the contested stories told of this process' (Cisterna 2013, 56). As argued in the flagship publication on the terroirs of Conegliano and Valdobbiadene Prosecco DOCG, 'a wine to become famous needs places and stories and Conegliano Valdobbiadene Prosecco is one of the most beautiful stories of world viticulture'.⁴

Terroir as a set of discourses is often examined through the dichotomies of tradition vs modernity, Old World vs New World, and local vs global – but as a set of practices it usually combines both elements in these dyads (Daynes 2013; Demossier 2020). Winemakers also use terroir 'to explore science, technique, and art' (Black and Ulin 2013, 12, referring to Daynes 2013) and to leverage uniqueness (a specific wine that can only be made in a particular place) and variability (weather conditions imparting possibly different characteristics to each vintage). A wine that is the expression of broadly conceived terroir brings together nature – specific topographies, soil structures and microclimates that shape viticulture in a particular location – and craft, the human activities in the vineyard and winery that translate these natural elements into a specific wine. Terroir in this sense relates to both space – wine coming from grapes grown in a delimited location – and place, wine as the expression of locally bound identities and imaginaries, as well as a contributor to their formation. It is an expression of materiality – specific soils, vines, techniques – but also of symbolism through varied aesthetic, spiritual and philosophical attachments.

One of the key issues around the heated debates on terroir is whether one can actually discern an authentic 'taste of place' – through gustatory pleasure and/or evocative possibilities (Trubek 2008). On the one hand, supporters of terroir argue that social practices mediate the relation between the physical conditions of production and the quality of wine. Techniques, practices and aesthetic preferences are specific to a place and thus impossible to reproduce anywhere else. On the other hand, detractors of terroir contend that it does not matter and that through the employment of science and technique a wine produced in one place can actually be reproduced elsewhere (Daynes 2013). As argued by Benjamin (1935), the ability to make reproductions (of artworks in his case) challenges at the core the idea of authenticity. For critical observers like Matthews (2016), terroir is not actually important in the contemporary and globalized wine industry. For Teil (2012), it simply does not exist.

However, a debate framed along these binomial traits is too narrow – as terroir should be seen as aspirational, a way of seeing the world, and thus has merit as a value proposition per se (Charters, Spielmann and Babin 2017). Whether it objectively exists or not, 'it is something that many winemakers purpose, and to this end, it exists as a goal and a social fact' (Kaplonski 2019, 200). Terroir is thus performative, a set of valuation narratives that seek to transform local realities so that they align with idealizations of place and wine. These narratives sell unique terroir to consumers of wine (and wine tourists), together with invented or idealized vernacular histories and traditions of production (Fournier 2019).

Finally, tasting place is not conjured only through the physiological experience of drinking wine but also through locational experiences, memories and imaginations. Wine as a material product ends up being drunk or stored for future consumption and investment purposes, but once consumed corporeal experience gives way to memory and nostalgia (Howland and Dutton 2020). Terroir can therefore be experienced as a landscape (e.g. through wine tourism) but also through the evocation of past experience, exposure to a place, and/or through imaginaries and identities (more on these aspects below).

Geographical indications and appellations

Terroir can be valorized by individual wineries but is often part of collective claims at various geographical scales. The global wine industry is replete with initiatives seeking to redefine, reconstitute, promote and differentiate place through geographical origin (Barham 2003; Overton and Heitger 2008; Overton and Murray 2011), including efforts to shape the spatial contours of production (Neilson, Wright and Aklimawati 2018) and to reallocate accumulated value (Ponte 2019). These processes are often led or supported by specific regulatory agencies and institutions (Brunori and Rossi 2007). The institutional incorporation of terroir in geographical indications is thus key to understanding value struggles that occur around place (see Chapter 3). For the purposes of our discussion, geographical indications and appellations can be seen as the institutionalization of terroir (at various scales and with varying degrees of proof) that provides intellectual property rents to all producers in a designated area (Bonanno, Sekine and Feuer 2020; Lubinga et al. 2021).

Much of the discussion on geographical indications and appellations has been framed in dual terms. On the one hand, we are told that Old World countries tend to have sophisticated geographical appellation systems, which include specific limitations on what cultivars can be planted within certain areas, which viticultural techniques can be used, when the harvest can take place, what the character of grapes needs to be for specific labels, and what winemaking techniques can be used. In appellation systems, each activity related to the production, processing and preparation of a product must be carried out within its geographical demarcation, while for indications at least one of these functions can be operated elsewhere (Lubinga et al. 2021). As indicated in Chapter 3, Italy has developed many geographical indications and appellations in the wine industry (529 wines were registered as such in 2022, managed by 133 producer consorzia), including those in Valpolicella and Prosecco.[5]

But the argument that place can be tasted in a wine, and that rules defining various practices in geographical appellations are there to ensure authenticity, can clash with the fact that even the most prestigious wines can be corrected through various chemical and mechanical interventions in the cellar. These are completely legal, although rules vary from one appellation to another. They range from adding 'rectified concentrated must' to increase sugar levels before fermentation (a practice that in Italy should be limited to years of particular climatic adversity but is routinely allowed instead) to the use of additives that increase acidity, tannins that improve the body of a wine and avoid discolouration in time, selected yeasts that can help a wine develop specific aroma characteristics, and animal gelatine or albumin for clarification (these wines are not vegetarian or vegan) – all the way to the mixing of wood chips in metal tanks instead of using barriques.[6] These are common operations that are carried out to improve or adjust the basic quality of placeless wines but are also often applied fully legally to place wines in some appellations. Because wine producers until recently were not obliged to communicate the use of these additives and techniques on the label, consumers were normally kept in the dark – thus reiterating the fantasy that wine is a 'natural' product.[7] In addition to these legal operations, we should also reflect upon the long string of scandals that have involved illegal manoeuvres, such as adding methanol, vinifying table grapes, adding artificial flavours or using cheaper wines from southern Italy to be blended into more expensive appellation wines in northern Italy.[8] These practices, legal or otherwise, generally undermine claims that one can taste place in wine.

On the other hand, there is a general understanding that New World countries have until recently relied mostly on brands, cultivar names and general references to place for consumer recognition. Where they have developed geographical indications, they tend to link to broader areas and/or follow administrative boundaries, rather than terroir per se. South Africa, for example, does not have specific legislation protecting geographical origin *sui generis*, so specific legislation is in place for that purpose (Sibanda 2016). Instead, South Africa operates a Wine of Origin system through the Wine and Spirits Board, with several layers of geographical indication (including seven regions, twenty-eight districts and ninety-eight wards) but has no appellation system (see details in Chapter 3).[9] This means that there are no specific limitations on cultivar, grape quality, and viticulture and winemaking techniques within these demarcations, only that all grapes used for a wine claiming origin have to be sourced within that area – with some exceptions (Engelbrecht, Herbst and Bruwer 2014; Nugent 2024a).

These dichotomies on the role of place in Old vs New World wine-producing countries are often used to argue that only European winemakers can truly articulate terroir in their wines (Trubek 2008), as they have had centuries to tinker with space and place – despite the fact that, for example, South Africa has been making wine since 1659. But even though terroir may not be as formalized into appellations of geographical origin as in France or Italy, it is leveraged everywhere to evoke philosophic and spiritual belonging or reverence to a place (Swinburn 2013). Narratives of terroir and geographical origin are starting to be articulated in New World wine-producing countries as well (Demossier 2020). This has led some critics to argue that the extension of terroir in these new(er) wine-producing regions leads to more detached and less anchored signifiers that are leveraged for commercial purposes and/or for capital extraction through increasing land values (Charters, Spielmann and Babin 2017; Cross, Plantinga and Stavins 2017). But these processes are in place in Old World wine countries as well. What we are observing is actually a combination of several processes of hybridization of terroir. The adaptation of French-style terroir in New World producing countries is actually feeding back into Old World countries' practices (Morrison and Rabellotti 2017). In the so-called 'New-New World' – novel places where wine production is expanding as a result of climate change (e.g. in England and Denmark) and/or increasing local demand for locally made wine (e.g. in Japan) (Feuer 2019) – adaptation can also lead to some degree of disarticulation from the original model of terroir.[10] And practices from the 'Old-Old World' of winemaking (ancient wine production areas that are returning to quality production, such as Georgia), such as the use of amphoras, are being reappropriated by everyone else.

The result of these processes is a hybridization of terroir at a global scale. Demossier (2020), for example, argues how Burgundy terroir should not be seen as authentic, stable and reliable – it is constantly rearticulated to fit changing markets and repositioned to maintain differentiation. In Burgundy, the reaffirmation of its unique status vis-à-vis changing markets, increasing competition and globalization has entailed 're-enacting some of the global references linking place to taste by fossilizing and historicizing the site of production, which is presented as a stable, trustworthy and reliable place. Yet it has also been about transforming that place by creating new images, norms and connections and adding a veneer to an old mythology' (Demossier 2020, 53). This constitutes a 'reflexive imbrication' with globalization through the management of place-making, authenticity[11] and scale. Place then is not simply the articulation of a superior local endowment, and it can go well beyond locality to become a global story. The story of Burgundy suggests that valorizing discourses of origin and authenticity is essential in view of mastering the forces of globalization and homogenization that work against terroir. Climate change is also challenging terroir as a story of constancy and tradition, given the impact of changing rainfall patterns and higher temperatures on grape-growing conditions (see Chapter 5). The key to terroir success is then adapting to new situations while continuing to construct and reconstruct a valorization story controlled by (usually smaller) producers.

The (re)invention of Prosecco

Although the earliest records referring to the production of white wines on and around the hills of Valdobbiadene date back to 1282,[12] it was only in the late nineteenth century that Prosecco was further developed in this area, following the establishment of the Treviso Oenological Society in Conegliano – later transformed in the School of Oenology and Viticulture. In the nineteenth century, viticulture was still a secondary activity in this area, and small-scale production was mainly aimed at self-consumption. This situation remained relatively unchanged until the 1960s (Visentin and Vallerani 2018). The first recorded attempts at developing a sparkling wine through a second fermentation were made by Antonio Carpené in the nineteenth century, and then perfected by his nephew in the early twentieth century. The first bottle of sparkling Prosecco is thought to have been produced by the firm Carpené & Malvolti in 1924.[13]

A professor at a key wine institution in the Prosecco region stated that

> before World War II, Valdobbiadene was an area of net emigration. People here were starving. Wine production for sale is actually a relatively recent activity ... Commercial production of Prosecco in Valdobbiadene developed mostly from the 1960s onwards, but until the 1980s, this wine was still considered a local product, a wine that was served during the weekend when farms opened to guests and served their own rustic food and wine.
>
> P4

Up to the 1980s, the Prosecco wine industry lived through a period of mere survival, as market demand at that time was for white wines with higher alcohol content. Prosecco producers mainly supplied 'base wines' for the large winemakers of Emilia Romagna and Piemonte. This tendency started to shift following the methanol scandal of 1986, when twenty-three people died and over ninety were hospitalized after being poisoned with methanol that had been mixed with wine by several producers (mostly in Piemonte) to increase its alcohol content (Barbera and Audifredi 2012; Giuliani, Lorenzoni and Visentin 2015). Three hundred labels were listed as suspect, and twelve growers were arrested on charges of manslaughter, grievous bodily harm or illegal adulteration of food. Large quantities of Italian wine were seized in France and Germany, while Denmark enforced a ban on all Italian-made drinks for a period.[14] In response to this scandal, many Italian producers invested in new technology and improved vineyard and winemaking practices to upgrade quality and efficiency (Bell and Giuliani 2007; Cusmano, Morrison and Rabellotti 2010; Giuliani, Morrison and Rabellotti 2011; Morrison and Rabellotti 2009).

The 1990s witnessed a slow movement towards less focus on quantity and more on quality in the Italian wine industry more broadly (see Chapter 3), as lifestyles changed and drinking an *aperitivo* at a bar or café before lunch or dinner became more popular. In the 2000s, consumer appreciation started to increase for Prosecco's fruity and floral tones and mild scent – together with rising interest in sparkling wines that are drier than the traditional Muscat-based sparkling wines but sweeter than Champagne.[15] Also, the 'democratic price' of Prosecco made it more affordable for everyday use than Champagne (P4; see also Checchinato et al. 2024).

The first consortium for the protection of a geographical denomination attached to Prosecco was established in 1962 (Prosecco DOC, *Denominazione d'Origine Controllata*), followed in 1966 by the establishment of the Conegliano Valdobbiadene 'white wine route' and the formal registration of the DOC in 1969. Until 2009, only areas in Conegliano, Valdobbiadene and Asolo were allowed to produce Prosecco DOC under the existing legislation that protected the denomination of origin (P4, P12). From the mid-1970s, however, Prosecco produced in the surrounding plains was allowed to be sold as an IGT wine, 'one that did not possess the quality sanctioned by the [DOC] . . . product regulations but allowed to consolidate the familiarity of the Italian market' with this geographical indication (Checchinato et al. 2024, 7). As the 2008 EU wine reform more tightly regulated the indications of geographical origin, the DOC had become in danger of losing its exclusive claim to the denomination because it was related to a grape variety known as Prosecco (and its variations Prosecco lungo and Prosecco tondo *in primis*),[16] not to a distinctive territorial place named Prosecco.[17] The risk at that point was that Prosecco could be produced anywhere in Italy or even abroad.

Although the first efforts in this direction had started in the 1990s already, what brought urgency for reform was a 2006 marketing plan from a British drinks business that would have involved celebrity Paris Hilton arriving in Veneto by helicopter to promote a version of 'Prosecco' packaged in a gold-coloured can called 'Rich'. Prosecco, under Italian law 'can be sold only in bottles, but producers of the canned prosecco sell to countries such as Britain, Germany, Austria and Switzerland'.[18] The consortium realized that they were losing control of the name and thus of the territorial elements that may define it. The approach the consortium and the regional political elite took to solve this problem was quite inventive. They realized that a village named 'Prosecco' is located close to Trieste (see Image 3), quite far (about 150 Km) from the then core area of Prosecco wine production in Conegliano and Valdobbiadene. They dug out historical records showing that in the late sixteenth century, the Carsic hills around Prosecco village were already known for the cultivation of local grape varieties and the production of a wine called in the local dialect *Prosekar*, a term derived from the Slovenian word *Prošek*, meaning 'deforested area' (Visentin and Vallerani 2018). However, this wine was not based on the Prosecco grape. It was made with a blend of Vitozza, Malvasia and Terrano grapes and, most importantly, it was a flat white wine, not a sparkling wine.[19]

Yet, the consortium managed to construct a historical heritage story related to *Prosekar* to apply for a reform of the geographical indication system for Prosecco, seeking that grape growers and winemakers in other areas growing this grape could no longer call the wine they make from it 'Prosecco'. In the process, the grape variety was officially renamed 'glera' to distinguish the term from the now location-embedded Prosecco wine. This way, wine made from glera grapes grown outside of the Prosecco appellations would only be allowed to be sold as 'glera', not 'Prosecco'. This strategic move was supported and eventually embedded into regulation by the then Minister of Agriculture, Luca Zaia – whose home constituency is Treviso and where he had previously been the president of the province (which includes the areas of Conegliano and Valdobbiadene). Zaia, a prominent member of the Lega party, has been the governor of the Veneto region since 2010. He was re-elected for a third consecutive term in 2020 with an astounding 77 per cent of the popular vote.

This saga was featured in a November 2016 episode of the popular investigative journalism programme *Report*, produced by the public broadcaster RAI3.[20] In the documentary, it is claimed that in exchange for the use of the name 'Prosecco' for the larger geographical indication, a local committee in the village of Prosecco had asked for funding from the Ministry of Agriculture to transform a 100 hectare Carsic hilly area overlooking the Adriatic sea to make it suitable for glera vineyards. By the time the request had gone through the ministerial system Luca Zaia was no longer the minister – and was eventually denied. In other words, the village 'sold its soul' without getting anything in exchange. The RAI documentary features members of the committee now claiming that they should at least get a small contribution from each Prosecco bottle sold, so they can go ahead and valorize the Carsic hills to produce glera grapes. In a follow-up episode,[21] Luca Zaia, now the president of Veneto region, says that this is now a matter for the Ministry of Agriculture, not the region. There is no Prosecco wine produced in Prosecco village for the time being, but in the meanwhile, Prosecco producers elsewhere in Veneto and Friuli-Venezia Giulia have fought off the challenge brought by the EU wine reform and continue to dramatically grow their business.

The reform process resulted in a dramatic expansion of the overall Prosecco DOC from a relatively small area within the province of Treviso to four other provinces in Veneto (Belluno, Padova, Venezia and Vicenza) and four provinces in the Friuli-Venezia Giulia region (Gorizia, Pordenone, Trieste and Udine) (see Image 3). The original Conegliano and Valdobbiadene area (which also includes the top-quality sub-zones of Cartizze and Rive) has been upgraded to a Controlled and Guaranteed Denomination of Origin (*Denominazione d'Origine Controllata e Garantita*, DOCG), which denotes higher quality – along with the establishment of the new DOCG of Asolo Prosecco (P4, P5, P12).

In a further twist of this story, the Italian wine industry subsequently went up in arms when Croatia attempted to regain approval from the EU for their own *Prošek* (a sweet flat wine). The EU had banned the use of the name Prošek in 2013; but Croatia subsequently filed a complaint, that the European Commission agreed to consider in 2021. In 2022, Luca Zaia, commenting on the Prošek affair, stated that

> Prosecco is ours, it is a symbol of our heroic viticulture, a flag of our land that cannot be imitated ... Our commitment will always be alongside those who fight to defend a product that is as unique as the terroir where its vineyards grow. We need to defend our history and identity. To those who think of using the name Prosek casually, we remind you that our Prosecco is not a wine created a few days ago ... [It is] part of our culture, our work and our territories.[22]

Eventually, in 2023, during the process of reforming the EU's system of geographical indications, the Italian wine lobby was able include a clause clarifying that variations of traditional geographical mentions (such as Prošek, evoking Prosecco) cannot be registered.[23] The two Prosecco consortia continue to take aggressive lobbying and legal actions against anyone trying to 'usurp' their name – inside and outside the EU.[24] A new company called 'Sistema Prosecco' seeks to protect all the DOC and DOCG Prosecco denominations 'against misappropriation of the name, not only in wines but also in alcoholic mixes and other products. It has been used in marketing cosmetics, nail polish and even sex toys!' (P5). The reinvention of Prosecco and defence against its value 'usurpation' are a clear example of what Monterescu (2017) calls 'the territorialization of terroir', a nationalist political project that is quite common in terroirs across (contested) borders.[25]

Geographical indications in South Africa

The story of Prosecco provided an illustration of the power leveraged through geographical appellation but also of the large degree of flexibility in the interpretation of rules. It shows that institutional, political and collective efforts are key in valuation processes based on place. This is a burning issue in South Africa, where despite a recent embrace of terroir among premium wine producers (Nugent 2024b, a), the wine industry has not yet developed a regulatory framework that facilitates the setting up of appellation systems (rather than more generic geographical indications; see Chapter 3) and has not developed strong collective initiatives in this realm, (Steyn 2021).

But there are exceptions. Cape Site Specific, for example, was recently launched to further facilitate the recognition of different wine regions and terroirs within the Western Cape, in view of addressing the lack of knowledge, both domestically and internationally, of the wide diversity of sites within that region. One of the main drivers behind this initiative told me that it is a marketing collaboration – when it comes to sales each winery and brand has its own team – but they use events to inform buyers and consumers and to seek change in the current perception of South African wine as cheap and cheerful. This is also used as a strategy to find financial viability options to avoid losing 'properties that are being snapped up by corporate and foreign investors' (SAW70).

One of the problems they face relates to South African wine regulations, which were amended in 2006 so that wineries can use the name 'estate' in their brand/ name of the property even though these wines are not technically 'estate wines' (see detailed discussion in Nugent 2024a). 'Estate wine' can be 'produced solely from grapes harvested on the estate concerned'.[26] But the head of marketing of a wine estate told me that 'consumers do not know the difference; in South Africa they think that all are estates in equal measure . . . This is an example of commercial branding competing directly with "real" estates' (SAW70).

South African regulation also allows for the labelling of 'single vineyard' wine, which is made from a registered unit producing grapes of only one variety in an area not exceeding six hectares.[27] But the absence of a proper appellation system makes single vineyard wine a scattered effort with weak collective identity and organizational backing. While there is now 'bigger focus on the immediate surroundings by smaller producers, more attention to terroir and more so if farms are linked to a popular geographical area' (SAW70) there is also a perception of lack of regionality:

> Masters of Wine say that there is differentiated regional typicality only for Sauvignon Blanc in South Africa. But if you buy grapes from different regions and blend it all together, you lose the typicality of different areas, you lose stylistic identity this way. Also, the fact that big companies sell wine that is coming from Stellenbosch WOO all the way to Coastal or even Western Cape is not good, it works against differentiation . . . Corporate and foreign owners will not help in the quest of building terroir in South Africa: Will they continue to tell the story of it properly? Yes, they will use locals to sell at trade fairs to be seen as embedded, but it is not quite the same thing.
>
> SAW70

Immutable tradition or flexible bricolage?

In view of maintaining diversity and uniqueness, terroir is one of wine producers' key instruments in value struggles related to place – in response to the ongoing globalization of wine styles and its compounding homogenization (Barham 2003). On the one hand, terroir is leveraged in valuation repertoires attempting to preserve the link between place and quality, and the role of producers in shaping both. On the other hand, terroir can also be a source of historical determinism – used to romanticize social relations and provide nostalgic justifications that can hamper innovation. When tradition 'becomes a fixed institutionalized fact . . . any organic relationship with the past is lost' (Trubek 2008, 247). Yet, claims ascribed to terroir are not frozen in time – they can be (re)constructed and new markets created around it through collective efforts (Demossier 2020; Steyn 2021). Valuation discourses related to innovation and tradition are often navigated flexibly. Some winemakers, for example, are returning to 'old ways' of doing things (e.g. using amphoras, weeding mechanically), which may actually not be simply nostalgic but also innovative (Ulin 2013). This way, winemaking can become playful, inspirational and personalized, driven by innovation that is 'ascribed within tradition', rather than opposed to it. This is often portrayed as a desire to go back to simpler ways of doing things, for example harking to past practices that were actually present *before* the formalization of geographical appellation rules – such as the use of concrete vats or ceramic amphoras instead of oak barrels (Daynes 2013).

Amphoras, used since time immemorial in Georgia to make wine, have been rediscovered in the past few years (see Image 5), as winemaking styles that are less interventionist and aggressive are becoming more popular. One of the top-end Italian producers of amphoras for winemaking I interviewed went from a turnover of €100,000 in 2016 to over 3.5 million in 2020 and had a full book of orders for the following several years, including from the top Bordeaux chateaux. He has moved to bigger premises and installed precision ovens that allow him to produce amphoras with great precision and different specifications – for example, if they are used for

Image 5 Modern wine amphoras. Source: Author.

maceration, thus needing higher oxygenation needs, or for ageing; and depending on the kind of style winemakers are seeking. In 2020, there were eighteen producers of amphoras in Italy and thirty in the rest of the world, including in China (IG2).

> They are all the rage in the wine sector because they are inert and let the wine do what it needs; they allow micro-oxygenation and the softening of tannins without releasing the flavour of wood; they eliminate interactions that make the wine 'unnatural'; they produce wines that are more evolved, fresher and more pleasurable . . . Cement is not porous and needs to be treated, plus it is alkaline; wood is porous so it's ok for oxygenation but releases its own organoleptic characteristics so it shapes the wine; stainless steel is clean but wine needs to breathe or it stays too 'restricted' and accumulates an electrostatic charge; steel also has high thermal conduction that can ruin the wine if not controlled properly.
>
> IG2

A Valpolicella wine producer told me that 'the effect of amphoras on the wine is similar to that of wood barrels, but ceramic opens up the wine nicely . . . Wine ages more quickly in steel containers than in ceramic, and amphoras give it nice spicy notes, a bit like Pinot Noir in Bourgogne' (V5).

In Valpolicella, other examples of 'rediscovery' and of older traditions, followed by adaptation, are the current attention towards autochthonous grape varieties that were commercially abandoned and are now being revalorized; and the push from smaller producers to go back to the traditional *pergola veronese* training system for vineyards instead of the more 'modern' *Guyot* style (see Chapter 5). These examples suggest that, rather than an assemblage of unchanging ideals and practices, terroir is being constantly reinvented.

Another way of unpacking tradition is to look at valuation processes in wine that are tied to collective understandings of what is 'typical' in a wine genre or style, and whether the reference framework for typicality is clearcut or more ambiguous. This applies both to typicality as regulated by geographical appellation systems but also to other, less regulated but still collective, understandings of a genre or style of a wine (Negro and Hannan 2022). These general understandings are shaped through iterative interactions between producers (and their associations), critics, retailers, consumers and regulators (Colman 2008). Overall, the 'local, loyal and constant' framing of appellations systems (especially in France, but also elsewhere) is linked to three fundamental valuation questions: whether the wine is linked to a place; whether there is a tradition of practice linking place and the wine that is recognized internally and externally; and whether there is historical consistency of such practice in time. But there is always internal strife and constant accommodation, reinvention and adaptation of both tradition and typicality. Appellation rules set 'necessary but not sufficient conditions that together constitute a synergistic marker that stands as a proxy for socially constructed meanings . . . that often remain purposely vague or undefined' (Farmer 2013, 146).

One excellent example of value struggle related to typicality is recounted in detail in Negro and Hannan (2022), who show us how the typicality of Barolo and

Barbaresco wines from Piemonte (northwest Italy) was developed throughout a long process that included state regulation specifying rules for 'typical wines' in 1924 (a top-down process) and the codification of these rules through the actions of voluntary producer consortia from 1934 onwards (a bottom-up process). The legal rules that were included in the establishment of the overall DOC appellation system generated a process of *horizontal* differentiation (for example, a wine from Barolo is different to a wine from Valpolicella); but in more recent times, Italian and EU regulations have also allowed the delineation of different levels of quality within these appellations, opening up spaces for *vertical* differentiation (for example, an *Amarone della Valpolicella* DOCG is considered of higher quality than a *Ripasso della Valpolicella* DOC).

However, 'typical styles' are not set in stone. Negro and Hannan (2022) chronicle how established ways of making Barolo and Barbaresco wines came under attack in the 1980s and 1990s, partly as a result of the 'methanol scandal' that rocked the Italian wine industry in 1986 (see also Barbera and Audifredi 2012). This led to what have become known as the 'Barolo wars' between 'traditionalist' and 'modernist' winemakers. One of the bones of contention is whether Barolo is aged in larger wooden barrels (the traditional way of slowly ageing the wine) or in French barriques (smaller barrels). Although some modernist winemakers had to declassify their wines as they failed the test of typicality, wine markets actually reacted positively to these new styles (characterized by softer tannins, a more fruit-forward profile and lacking some of the more unpleasant smells you could find in traditional Barolo). These wines started to receive higher scores from wine critics and higher prices than the more traditional styles (Negro and Hannan 2022).

The following counter-response from traditionalists emphasized the uniqueness of their wines. But as modernists started to retreat from some more extreme practices (decreasing the use of new barriques, for example), some traditionalists embraced a more pragmatist and less ideological approach to wine traditions. The range of Barolo styles thus started to converge since the late 1990s, with prices of more traditional style Barolos increasing sharply relative to their counterparts in the past two decades (Negro and Hannan 2022). Thus, a range of valuation challenges actually came from within the industry in the context of a relatively clear (but somewhat flexible) frame of reference (the DOC and DOCG rules) – with a group of winemakers challenging the status quo and a strong reaction by more traditionalists, ending up in a process of hybridization of styles.[28]

Is Amarone della Valpolicella 'traditional'?

Although tradition is often used to valorize a unique profile for a wine, place as flexible reference and tradition may not have such a long historical pedigree. It is also constantly reinvented. The wine now known as *Amarone della Valpolicella* (usually referred to simply as 'Amarone') is a good illustration of these dynamics. Amarone was not well known until relatively recently, and rumour has it that it was born by mistake. The sweet wine 'Passito Recioto' had been produced in

Valpolicella for a very long time. But what came to be known as 'Amarone' started to be produced only in the 1900s, essentially because of an accidental discovery from a batch of sweet Recioto that was forgotten in a barrel and fermented until it became a dry, high-alcohol wine. The first commercial sales took place in the 1930s, but Amarone became known beyond the local and regional markets only relatively recently. It was bottled with that name for the first time in 1952 and mentioned as a dry variant of Recioto (V1). It was recognized as a separate DOC denomination in 1968 and upgraded to a DOCG in 2009 when the overall Valpolicella DOC was divided into four denominations (Valpolicella DOC, Ripasso DOC, Recioto DOCG and Amarone DOCG).

The director of production of one of the largest wine wholesalers in the country told me that

> Italy in the 1980s was a country of autochthonous wines, light wines with a low alcoholic level (10-12 degrees) – these were wines to quench thirst, and to be drunk with your meals. Southern Italian wines were practically unknown. But in other parts of the world people started making so-called Parker wines, powerful, dark-coloured wines that spent a lot of time in barrique and went up to 14.5 degrees of alcohol. Consumers started to look for these kinds of wine, which were not common in Italy. Amarone happened to be the closest available wine that fit that profile. So, particularly from the early 2000s, it started to be known abroad. It attracted a lot of curiosity because it was produced with local varieties, it had a unique and recognizable taste, and there was a fascination with the process of *appassimento*.
>
> V4

Until then, there had been no iconic reference wine in Veneto, while Toscana had Brunello di Montalcino and Piemonte had Barolo. Amarone is not sweet, but its soft palate and high alcohol levels provide an illusion of sweetness. As the general manager of a large Valpolicella wine producer told me, 'it is a unique wine in the world. It is linked to a very special area of production that is unique in its natural and cultural features. It is made with autochthonous wine grapes. It is made with a unique technique that ensures longevity' (V2).

The key features of the current version of tradition are codified in specific rules and regulations set by producer-led consortia. For Amarone, the rulebook (*disciplinare*) states the following:[29]

- Amarone can be made only from Corvina Veronese and/or Corvinone grapes (for a proportion of 45 per cent to 95 per cent); and Rondinella (5 per cent to 30 per cent); a maximum of 25 per cent can contain grapes from other varieties included in the provincial register.
- The maximum yield is 12 tons/hectare and grapes must be harvested by hand.
- Up to 65 per cent of harvested grapes are allowed to be used for the production of Amarone (the rest can be used for other types of Valpolicella wine).

- Grapes need to go through an *appassimento* process for 100/110 days: grapes are left to partially dry out in single layers on plastic trays in specially designed aerated warehouses; once pressed to make Amarone, the leftover grape skins can be used again to macerate with regular Valpolicella wine for 15–20 days to make Ripasso.
- The wine has to age for a minimum of two years in wood barrels (four years if labelled 'Riserva').
- Harvest, winemaking and bottling need to take place within the boundaries of the DOCG area; Amarone can only be sold in bottles and screw caps are not allowed for bottles bigger than 250 ml.

But tradition is constantly (re)negotiated and adapted to changing commercial imperatives. Viticulture expansion in Valpolicella since the early 2000s (see Chapter 3) led to regular supply gluts and downward pressure on prices (and to environmental challenges, see Chapter 5). A large Valpolicella producer explained to me that

> in 2001, there were 5,400 ha of Valpolicella vineyards; in 2020 they are 8,200! This expansion is without clear criteria – it was ok up to a certain point as demand was increasing, but volume increased too much, and thus now grape prices have been decreasing. The consortium then lowered the allowed yields and the percentage of grapes allowed for appassimento.
>
> V2

This is a clear instance of readjustment of 'tradition'.

Furthermore, from 2020 onwards, the *consorzio* has allowed the use of up to 10 per cent of dried grapes set aside for vinifying Amarone to make Ripasso directly. Ripasso is usually made by re-pressing the leftover skins after the making of Amarone. Essentially, the *consorzio* is attempting to reduce the production of Amarone to make more Ripasso. A small wine producer in Valpolicella argued that this is

> because there was too much production of Amarone at that point and the market was saturated. Part of this was due to the Covid pandemic but also because of the growth in vineyard areas. It is in the *consorzio*'s interest to increase production as their income is linked to volume of wine produced. Vineyard expansion has now been stopped. But it is not only the area that counts: the *consorzio* has allowed a decrease in the minimum space between stumps from 100 cm to 60 cm. But this brings more disease because of lower air flow, and so we need to increase agro-chemical applications.
>
> V1

As confirmed by another producer,

> the problem is that there is too much production in Valpolicella now, also in places that are not suitable for it; the market is saturated and all Amarone is

being sold under one geographical origin, although it can be very different depending on where and how it has been produced. It is important to valorize the areas that are best suited for it.

V13

The preferred style of Amarone is also changing, thus challenging established arguments of typicality. Historically, Amarone is a dry wine, woody on the palate, but its profile has been changing in the past decade because some export markets (especially Germany and Nordic countries) like it sweeter (with higher residual sugars) and rounder on the palate. The enologist of one of the large cooperatives in Valpolicella told me that 'some of the large producers now tend to stop the fermentation process a bit earlier and do more filtration and use older barrels; they also release the wine earlier than in the past' (V8). It is increasingly produced on demand within the limits allowed by the (changing rules of the) *disciplinare*. 'Amarone is left in the barrel for less than a year when we use a new barrel; then, we take it out and store it in cement vats. It is only bottled when an order is confirmed, and a specific blend of various batches is used to meet the characteristics asked by the individual buyer' (V8). Another producer confirmed that 'young Amarone is rounder and sweeter. We are shaping the wine to meet what the market wants' (V13). The story of Amarone ultimately suggests that defending the uniqueness of a wine entails value struggles over changing ideas of typicality and tradition. This is important because craft and artisanship are at the core of wine identities seeking to preserve differentiation based on place as a producer-driven valuation strategy – against the onslaught of wine globalization and related uniformity.

4.4 HERITAGE

'Heritage' can be thought of as something 'rooted in the past and existing in the present, [which] people would like to preserve for future generations' (Harvey, Frost and White 2014, 4). Wine heritage can relate to tangible immovables, such as wineries, tasting rooms, houses within a farm, and to some extent landscapes, vineyards and grapevines. It can also refer to tangible movables, like wine in barrels or bottles, and equipment. Finally, it can link to intangible assets, such as brands or family names, stories, images, styles, customs, and/or festivals (Harvey, Frost and White 2014). Value struggles around heritage relate to who determines what aspects of heritage need to be preserved and for what reasons. Heritage is thus a 'negotiated and contested social construct rather than an immutable truth' (Harvey, Frost and White 2014, 4). It is something that can be embedded in brand identity and positioning and valorized by leveraging mythologies through storytelling. Events, such as regional festivals, can also be part of heritage building (see below on wine tourism).

I explore three main instances of value struggle through heritage in this section. The first instance is linked to the efforts by the United Nations Educational, Scientific and Cultural Organization (UNESCO) to preserve 'cultural landscapes', and especially the recognition of 'The Prosecco Hills of Conegliano and

Valdobbiadene'.[30] The second concerns heritage claims that are linked to the historical presence of specific winemaking families in Valpolicella. The third is about 'heritage wines' that are made from certified old vines. Although at first sight this form of heritage does not seem to relate to place, a deeper look into these dynamics reveals that it is the literal rootedness of these old vines in particular places that is sold as a premium, packaged in ideas of 'higher quality in place'. This has been an important movement in South Africa.[31]

UNESCO recognition of 'The Prosecco Hills of Conegliano and Valdobbiadene'

One of the instruments for valorizing terroir through heritage is the possibility of obtaining UNESCO World Heritage status, which since 1992 has been extended to 'cultural landscapes'. Ten vineyard-centred cultural landscape sites have been recognized by UNESCO so far: Champagne and Burgundy in France; Tokaj in Hungary; Alto Douro and Pico Island in Portugal, Piemonte (Langhe-Roero and Monferrato) and Prosecco in Italy; Wachau in Austria; Middle Rhine Valley in Germany; and Lavaux in Switzerland. For several other sites, vineyards are not the core of the heritage recognition but also play a role. In total, thirty-two UNESCO sites mention wine or vineyards in their description.[32] UNESCO heritage recognition helps the process of 'transforming local places into objects of international interest, bringing local, national and international politics into the arena' (Demossier 2020, 219).

In 2019, the 'Prosecco Hills of Conegliano and Valdobbiadene' was inscribed as a UNESCO heritage site. The dossier for the candidacy was developed by an ad hoc association that was originally formed in 2008 by the DOCG consortium, the province of Treviso and the local chamber of commerce. It was curated by three consultants and politically supported by the president of the Veneto region, Luca Zaia (the same politician who had facilitated the expansion of the Prosecco DOC area in the late 2000s when he was the Minister of Agriculture; see above). Zaia, on the occasion of the award of the UNESCO site, declared that this recognition would 'promote at the international level a microcosm of nature and culture, of rural activities and historical sites that have shaped these hills in ways that are original and unmistakable'.[33]

The main features highlighted in the application dossier for UNESCO refer to three landscape elements that are worthy of preservation: (1) a 'mosaic of small vineyards interspersed between wooded areas'; (2) a specific geomorphological formation called hogback; and (3) peculiar grass edges (*ciglioni* in Italian) that climb the very steep hills (slopes of between 15 and 60 degrees), which are thought to have been used since the seventeenth century.[34] The UNESCO site is divided into three zones: a core zone that delimits the actual site; a buffer zone that is also characterized by hills and vineyards, but with lower inclines; and a commitment zone, which is not hilly but where the same regulations as in the other two areas are used to safeguard the landscape, especially that related to viticulture (see Image 6 and Image 7).[35] As part of UNESCO recognition, by 2026 all wine producers will

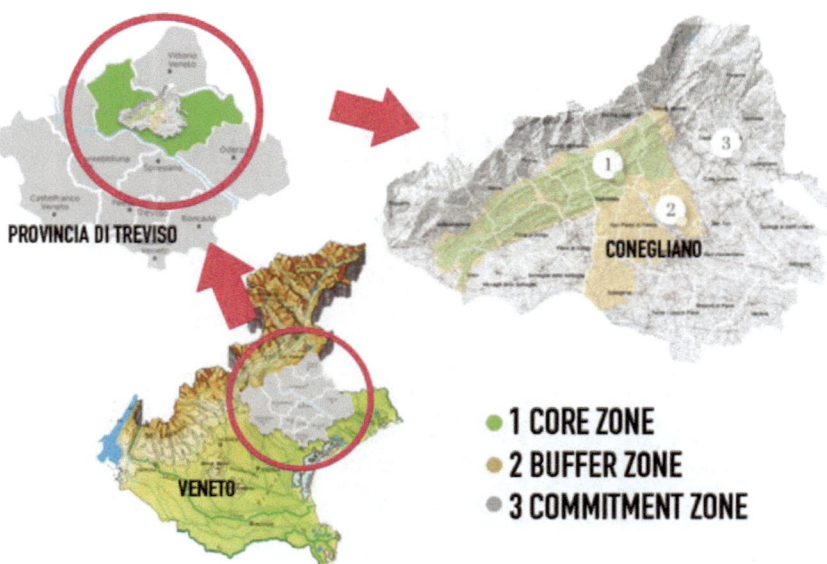

Image 6 Map of the UNESCO site 'Prosecco Hills of Conegliano and Valdobbiadene', Italy. Source: https://www.italiaatavola.net/tendenze-mercato/vino-beverage/2019/7/7/colline-del-prosecco-sono-patrimonio-unesco/61729/, reproduced with permission.

need to be SQNPI certified (a sustainability certification mainly based on integrated production standards and related code of conduct; see Chapter 5) (P2). The text of the UNESCO final decision on the inscription of the site is based on three principles: (1) the *authenticity* of claims that these practices have been developed over time in the area; (2) the *integrity* of the landscape that viticultural techniques have been able to maintain (including manual harvesting) – this integrity is seen to be in need of further safeguarding because of novel pressures arising from increasing demand for Prosecco wine; and (3) the adequate *regulatory framework* that ensures the safeguarding of the rural landscape, especially those embedded in the wine and viticulture protocols of the DOCG consortium; these rules seek to maintain vineyards and hedges to ensure the continuation of local traditions and to safeguard biodiversity and associated ecosystem services.[36]

Heritage recognition is one of the activities in the wine sector seeking to functionally leverage 'traditional cultural landscapes' (Torquati, Giacchè and Venanzi 2015) in view of creating and distributing value. Although some of the principles listed above sit quite uneasily vis-à-vis the expansion of viticulture in the DOCG Prosecco area, the inscription of the UNESCO heritage site could be seen as an attempt to address existing conflicts. The marketing manager of a large Prosecco-producing company told me that 'viticulturists are seen as serial polluters by local communities . . . There is envy in the local community because Prosecco producers have made a lot of money, therefore the perception is that they are usurpers and exploiters' (P2). A professor at a local research institution argued that

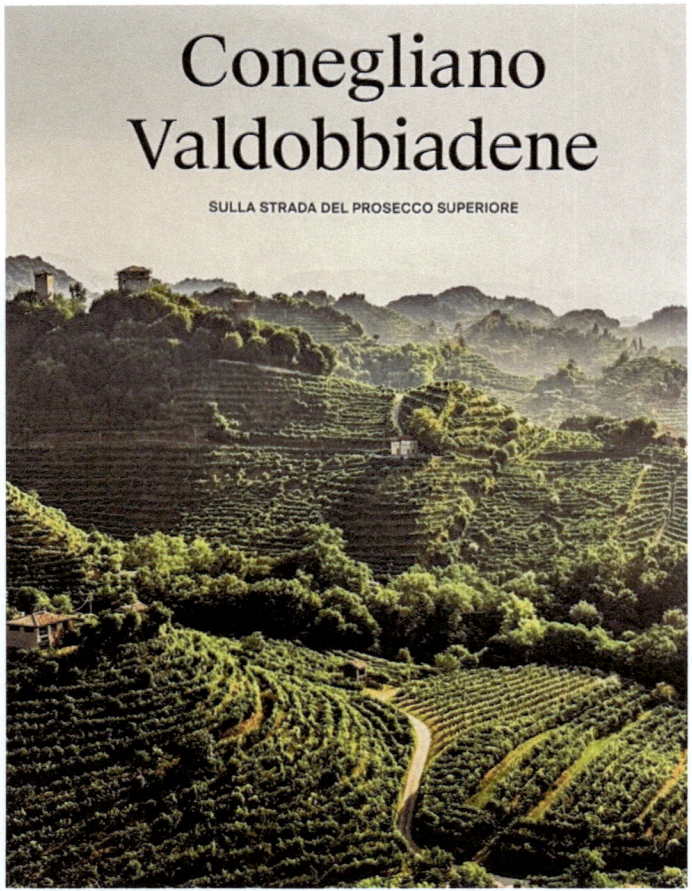

Image 7 Typical vineyard landscape in Valdobbiadene, Italy. Source: Photo of the cover of the magazine *Visit Conegliano Valdobbiadene*, issue 01/2020, published by the Consorzio di tutela del vino Conegliano Valdobbiadene Prosecco and the Strada del Prosecco e vini dei colli Conegliano Valdobbiadene.

the UNESCO initiative 'is part of a social sustainability effort, in view of attracting wine tourists and promote a larger portfolio of products and services in the area, so that instead of just wine industry operators making money, the beneficiary base can be broadened ... There is a lot of envy around, and there have been protests against agro-chemical application' (P4).

The UNESCO inscription should then be seen as promoting alternative ideas of how Prosecco creates value beyond the social realm of producers and industry actors – through a remodulation of landscape and territory. But because heritage adds other elements to value creation processes (other types of products, wine tourism, ecotourism) without substantially altering the core sources of existing conflicts, it allows a disregard for their key drivers – such as viticultural sprawl, the consumption of nature, soil erosion and the reshaping of property prices. The romanticization of vineyards to defend the authenticity and integrity of traditional cultural landscapes also clashes with the dominant monoculture approach to viticulture and its progressive domination of land use (Basso and Vettoretto 2020). In other words, the UNESCO inscription is an instance of territorial marketing that seeks to widen the putative beneficiary groups of the explosive growth of Prosecco sales and exports.

As local repositioning of the expression of terroir, heritage recognition offers new readings of place in view of reframing cultural and regional identities. It allows to valorize place as heritage of humanity but at the same time delineates it as an object of consumption (Demossier 2020, 240) and allows what Gade (2004) calls the 'patrimonialization of wine'. The actual effects of heritage recognition depend on the local political economy. In Champagne, for example, where large branded operators are dominant, grapes are blended from many different localities without distinguishing differences in style – and only a single appellation is in place (Charters 2019). In Burgundy, small-scale wine farming is the norm, and terroir is related to a very specific plot of land, site or village – formalized in around 100 geographical appellations of origin. So while terroir was used distinctively by Burgundy in the application for UNESCO World Heritage Designation for the vineyards of its Côte d'Or region ('The Climats, Terroirs of Burgundy'), Champagne obtained its own designation for the 'Champagne Hillsides, Houses and Cellars', with little focus on terroir in the supporting application (Charters 2019). Prosecco sits somewhere in between, given that it has some degree of differentiation between a few geographical sub-appellations, and its application for UNESCO recognition mentioned its vineyards as one of three main principles.

Amarone and the 'famiglie storiche'

In Valpolicella, a particular value struggle related to heritage is about which actors or groups can speak for tradition and quality production. The 'Consorzio Tutela Vini della Valpolicella'[37] is considered to be controlled by smaller wineries in coordination with the main large cooperatives. Following some major internal conflicts, a group of family-controlled wineries (some of which are actually quite large and have a corporate structure) splintered from the *consorzio* to set up in 2009 a separate association – originally called *Amarone Families – Famiglie dell'Amarone d'Arte*.[38] The thirteen members of this association that left the consortium own about 800–900 hectares of vineyards in Valpolicella, about 10 per cent of the total. They lamented a continuous process of decreasing standards. A representative of one of their members stated that

> everyone makes wine, but many are essentially grape growers that make some wine. Being a serious winemaker is a different story; the quality standards cannot be going down. But this is what has been happening. For example, for Amarone, the consortium reduced the time of *appassimento* to a lower standard starting in 2002 … Ourselves, we do not bottle Amarone every year, but only when the quality is good. If it is not good enough, it is sold as Valpolicella.
>
> V2

The *consorzio* then started a legal proceeding against the use of 'Amarone' in the title of the association, given that one of its main functions is to safeguard the name of the wine on behalf of all producers in Valpolicella. The *consorzio* won the legal case in Italy, and the association was subsequently renamed simply *Famiglie storiche*.[39] A former chairperson of the association argued that their intention was 'to put Amarone at the centre of attention, so that it can pull Valpolicella, Verona and Veneto, along with it. We want to valorize both the wine and the area ... We are against the massification of Amarone production that is taking place, where volume has taken over quality. We want Amarone to be iconic and expensive' (V11). Even from outside the consortium, the *Famiglie storiche* have been able to lobby and work to improve the positioning of Amarone anyway. They indirectly shaped some recent changes in the *disciplinare*: for example, 'in the past the ratio of Amarone/Ripasso was a free-for-all situation, now it is set at one to two. Maximum yields were also lowered in 2022. As a result, the prices of Amarone and Ripasso are increasing' (V11). The association also wants to push through a rule that would see Amarone production taking place only on hilly areas, but this has been difficult to implement (V11).

Heritage vineyards in South Africa

South Africa's Certified Heritage Vineyards project started operating in 2016 and certifies old vine vineyards that are thirty-five years of age and above (SAW23) (Mafata et al. 2020). From 2019 onwards, producers have been able to obtain a 'Certified Heritage Vineyard' seal that can be placed on the bottles of wine produced from these vineyards (SAW35). The seal identifies the planting date of the vineyard, which is verified by the South African Wine Industry Information System (SAWIS) through a database tracing all plantings from 1900 onwards. According to the project personnel, South Africa is the only wine-producing country with an organized old vine initiative that can verify these claims this far back (they claim that Chile can only go back to 1986) (SAW23, SAW29, SAW35).[40] South Africa has 4,000 ha of vineyards that are thirty-five years or older, around 4.5 per cent of the total planted vineyard area in the country. Most are white varieties, with Chenin Blanc accounting for about 50 per cent of the total. Bush vines are about 46 per cent of the total, the rest are trellised. The majority are located in Stellenbosch, Swartland, Paarl and Wellington – in warmer climates, given that old vines do not like cold winters (SAW29, SAW38).

The Certified Heritage Vineyard initiative is based on the argument, as posed by one of its representatives, that

> after thirty years, the vine stabilizes. It sends juice to the cellar that is almost perfect ... Vines 'read' the vintage and adapt. Young vines live like there is no tomorrow. Old vines are more thoughtful, so to speak, they invest more in their root system in the place they have been growing for a long time, they are looking for survival ... Old vines make themselves as attractive as possible to spread

their seeds around – they know they are about to die. They have a more concentrated production . . . and thus quality is higher.

SAW29

The head of sales of a wine cooperative that has obtained this certification stated that

old vines are definitely an advantage to our industry . . . The quality of grapes is good as the root system is quite deep in the soil and gives nutrients that have not been washed out in the top half metre over thousands of years. You really get into a different cell structure and different nutrient levels in the lower soils and that's what old vines can do, they can go into the deepest soil because of their age. They also have thicker skins and are more heat tolerant, so there are a lot of advantages.

SAW20

However, as vineyards get older, yields decline (SAW9) and in normal market conditions, they become uneconomical for the grower. 'When you go under five tons per hectare it does not pay to continue tending the vine, unless you get a premium for the grapes you harvest' (SAW29). The Certified Heritage Vineyards project has developed a business model where brand owners are willing to pay a premium for these grapes (Priilaid and Steyn 2020). Farmers are actually receiving a high premium for old vine grapes (from 200 per cent up to 400 per cent of the price for the same grapes obtained in the regular market). Wine made from old vines is therefore a premium category (SAW35). This is particularly encouraging in an environment where many farmers are selling their land or switching to other crops due to high costs and low grape prices (SAW38, SAW83).

The main challenge has been to convince farmers who are members of cooperatives (85 per cent of old vines in South Africa are planted in the cooperative system) to save these old vines, and to convince the cooperatives to keep these grapes separate from the rest of the harvest. One of the cooperatives that has been able to do so is now selling an old vine Chenin Blanc under its brand at ZAR 200 (€10) a bottle at their cellar, instead of the usual ZAR 70 (€3.5) (SAW65). The cooperative manager stated that 'with old vines, you buy legacy . . . we are now making the best Chenin in the country, and this brings status to the winemaker and the area where the vineyards are. Farmers are now proud; they make more of an effort' (SAW65). Also, because of the old vine project and sales, the cooperative was able to expand the tasting area: 'we are full every weekend and old vine is also opening markets for our non-old vine premium wines' (SAW65).

However, not all old vines make good wine. As a representative of the project behind the heritage vine certification system told me, 'some are good vines that have been looked after, others can be regenerated for good production, but the unhealthy ones should be let go' (SAW29). The total area of old vines in South Africa is large enough to provide volume and visibility, but also small enough as a proportion of the total to sustain a premium and provide a unique selling point. These wines are perceived to be of higher quality and have built a good image, not only in South Africa but also internationally (SAW23, SAW38).

Image 8 A Certified Heritage Vineyard (bushvine), South Africa. Source: Author.

As indicated above, almost half of certified old vines are still grown as bush vines, a heritage and aesthetic valorization element that is leveraged by some producers. The director of sales of a cooperative that includes some certified producers told me that

> bush vine is one of the most underrated vineyard planting methods currently ... If you trellis your vineyard, it produces more because this way you increase the surface area of the vine. But if you don't have irrigation, a bush vine regulates itself, it will only carry as many branches as it can to preserve itself ... The best way to protect the grape bunches from the sun is under natural canopy and that's what the bush vine does, it goes up and then sprawls and the grapes are always underneath leaves ... It's a beautiful way for nature to grow.
>
> SAW17 (see Image 8)

The project personnel argues that there are clear economic and environmental sustainability elements in saving old vines, and in tending existing vines to grow old (adopting practices that can lengthen the lifespan of the vine) (SAW35). They consume less water and show more resistance to high temperatures (SAW38). If one selects the correct site, stock and clone combination, then vines can actually live for over eighty years (SAW29). Since it is very expensive to replant a vineyard, farmers can save quite a lot of money by replanting less (SAW29, SAW35). Also, South African Chenin Blanc has been building an international reputation for high quality and uniqueness in style, which can be combined with heritage vine certification to offer a unique proposition. However, there is a massive economy invested in vine replanting, so part of the industry is not happy with this idea (SAW35). All in all, this is one of the rare valorization initiatives where grape producers have been able to draw clear financial benefits, at least so far.

4.5 PLACE AND 'FINE WINES'

Distinction vis-à-vis the 'democratization of taste'

Wine for a long time was considered a simple commodity, blended from various vineyards, and stored and sold in large wooden barrels (and amphoras in ancient times, see Work 2018) under broad regional or varietal designations. Spoilage and oxidation were common and thus the freshest wines were more valued. In the seventeenth century, however, a series of innovations led to differentiation, including the establishment of discrete vineyards, the sale of wines under the name of an estate and by vintage, the adoption of techniques to increase the quality of wine, and the use of glass bottles and cork closures (Howland 2013). 'These developments enabled wine to be transported, cellared, and to evolve additional taste characteristics in the bottle. Consequently, wine transformed into a hyper-differentiated commodity valued for its distinctive varietal, vineyard and vintage characteristics; conspicuously consumed as a mark of distinction in public theatres of consumption' (Howland 2013, 328–39). In France, this process took a clear class dimension during the emergence of gastronomy in the nineteenth century – and led to the distinction between 'table wines', consumed by the working class as a form of conviviality and indulgence, and 'place wines' sought by the bourgeoisie under an ethics of sobriety and aspirations of *savoir boire*.[41]

While the valuation of intrinsic quality elements plays an important role in wine, it occurs within specific political economies. We should recall that wine appreciation as a sign of distinction developed first through interactions between powerful producers and traders in Bordeaux and their aristocratic British (and later French) clientele in the eighteenth century, with the French petty bourgeoisie starting to imitate aristocratic etiquette and taste in the nineteenth century (Garcia-Parpet 2011). Increasing interest in wine appreciation was also built on the novel publication of books on wine tasting and quality, and on wine keeping and serving (Howland 2013). Later, and especially from the 1970s onwards, a progressive process of democratization of taste took place – especially with the introduction of varietal labelling in New World production countries, which significantly simplified the need for consumers to know the specificities of different wine regions and localities. A more approachable industry of taste also emerged, which includes tasting events, wine appreciation courses, and specialized publications that help consumers learn not only how to perceive certain physical properties of a wine but also how to judge them (Smith 2007). Information is now more easily accessible to all consumers, from the back label on the bottle to online sources. Reviews and ratings in specialist and lifestyle media, and quality rankings and medals/awards affixed on the bottle (or displayed on retail shelves) are also part of this movement. A new and potentially radical set of changes in the wine appreciation world could come with new AI applications, which can synthetize human reviews of wines with large-scale data input from chemical analysis.[42]

These trends are compounded by larger discourses on the 'democratization of luxury'. For example, many Prosecco producers in interviews made statements such as: 'The democratic price of Prosecco makes a luxury experience more affordable for everyday use than Champagne' (P4). 'Prosecco is a democratic luxury that helps to live better – it is easy to drink, less complex than Champagne . . . and can be consumed in many different occasions and situations' (P5). Overall, these processes of 'democratization . . . ensure the wine industry a thoroughly open market, while simultaneously retaining the mechanisms and hierarchies of elite distinction based on connoisseurship' (Howland 2013, 326).

Social media is also partly upending the industry of taste making. One prominent wine journalist in South Africa told me that

> traditional wine critics tend to be older people and reach only a tiny fraction of a broader audience on social media . . . Lots of people who do not know much about wine now write comments on social media. Some influencers are photogenic and pretty and have a huge following in wine . . . They may know nothing about wine, but they are very trendy and make a huge difference.
>
> SAW23

The wine course industry in South Africa is reaching out to new audiences and consumers (and especially Black professionals in Johannesburg). One of the main wine distributors in the country has recently acquired the Cape Wine Academy (SAW14). Wine operators elsewhere are also explicitly talking about wine valorization through social media.[43]

The market for fine wines

At the same time as some degree of democratization of taste is taking place, we can also observe an expansion of the market and financial value of rare wines, collection pieces and investment wines, especially in highly income-unequal countries (Donzé and Katsumata 2022). Fine wines are the pinnacle of 'place wine' and can increase their value over time, but they can also lose it when flavour and bouquet dissipate. The potential for wines to age well and increase their value in time depends on terroir, vinification methods and the vagaries of the weather. Vintages of the same wines are valued differently by experts according to the predominant weather and climate conditions in a specific locale during a specific grape-growing and -harvesting season. Variability in lower echelons of place wines can be regulated to some extent, as irrigation tends to homogenize a wine style vintage after vintage. But appellation rules for many high-end wines in Europe do not allow irrigation. They are in fact seeking to valorize vintage, thus uniqueness not only in relation to place but also to time. Just like art, such wines are then presented as unique and thus impossible to reproduce (Daynes 2013; Karpik 2010). The value of a vintage can also be related to its coincidence with important events – whether collective (e.g. the year of independence of a country) or individual (e.g. one's birth year) – or to previous ownership by famous people. For example, wines previously owned by former French president Jacques Chirac and British prime minister Winston Churchill are particularly valuable (Garcia-Parpet 2011).

Transactions of fine wines are usually conducted through brokers, intermediary agencies and online platforms. Suppliers may be professionals who are specialists in these wines or individuals who may need to sell to solve liquidity problems (Garcia-Parpet 2011). The very top fine wines are often sold at auctions. While wine connoisseurs may buy wine for ageing and future consumption, others see wine mainly as a financial investment. Rare wines, and especially the top Bordeaux growths can fetch extraordinary prices. For example, a bottle of 1945 Romanée-Conti was sold for $558,000 at Sotheby's in New York in 2018, a world record at that time (Le Fur and Outreville 2019, 196). Auctions for fine wines have been a key instrument of valuation for a long time and are now increasingly carried out online. There are also mutual funds that specialize in wine, which are managed like hedge funds (Sanning, Shaffer and Sharratt 2008).

As a financial asset, wine has some characteristics that are similar to those of other tangible assets, such as collectable art: it does not pay dividends; it incurs costs for storage; items can break or lose value if stored improperly; and it takes time to liquidate a collection (Garcia-Parpet 2011). But there is also considerable uncertainty about the quality of fine wine prior to purchase. Buyers rely heavily on information provided on the label, by wine experts, and through the reputation of the winemaker and/or the auction house. A wine journalist told me that 'fine wine is like fine paintings, you need expert advice, somebody who has the credentials' (SAW23). Still, making sure that a very old vintage or rare wine is authentically coming from a specific place remains a challenge. Scandals such as that chronicled in the 2016 documentary *Sour Grapes* (directed by Jerry Rothwell and Reuben Atlas) have also raised doubts and uncertainty in the fine wine market. It recounts how, in 2003, a wine collector named Rudy Kurniawan started selling large quantities of wine from his cellar at auction – raising questions among some wine producers and private collectors. In April of 2008, a Burgundy winemaker asked for the removal of a wine lot at a live auction that was being sold by Mr Kurnavian. This winemaker claimed that he had not released such wine for the vintage on sale. Following a four-year investigation, Mr Kurnavian was eventually sentenced to ten years in prison and ordered to pay a large fine, in what amounted to the largest case of fine wine fraud in history (Fougere, Kaplan and Collins 2020).

Conspicuous production

The valuation of fine wine is also linked to its mode of acquisition, purpose (delayed consumption, resale, financial investment) and social characteristics of the seller (Garcia-Parpet 2011). In a way, we can observe both 'conspicuous consumption' (Veblen 2012 [1899]) of fine wines by the elites (and aspiring elites) and 'conspicuous production' by wineries owned by celebrities, the wealthy and corporations (Overton and Banks 2015; Overton and Murray 2016). This is particularly evident in South Africa, where profitability in wine, and especially in grape production (see Chapter 3 for details), is very tight or non-existent. Similar instances can be found in Prosecco and Valpolicella as well but are less prominent.

An increasing number of wine estates in South Africa are owned by independently wealthy South Africans (also by members of the 'Black elite', see Chapter 6), foreign magnates and corporations. For them, winemaking is a hobby (SAW4), a status symbol, a sign of distinction and a way of hosting the domestic and cosmopolitan upper class in beautiful surroundings. The winemaker of a large estate told me that 'our board members really like to come here for their meetings' (SAW56). These are 'prestige projects of very wealthy individuals. They are pet projects of the rich ... who do not need to be making money from wine' (SAW6). The manager of another estate stated that they 'have been successful in building a luxury brand because the owner has been subsidizing the wine business from making money in the property business' (SAW81).

Conspicuous production in South Africa is often tied to conservation efforts (more on this in Chapter 5). In the words of the winemaker of a large estate, 'rehabilitation is a major drive for our approach to sustainability. We spent 20 million Rand so far just to clear alien vegetation. We are also working on anti-erosion measures and have spent 25 million on it. In some sections of our conservation land, we have found species that were thought to have been extinct' (SAW56). This has implications for the feasibility of sustainability efforts more generally. The manager of another wine estate told me that

> it's impossible for an estate to make money from wine. So, moving to a green economy is only possible if you are a billionaire and you have money available – that way you can afford it ... Billionaires can spend their money on many things, making their businesses 'green and Black' [referring to environmental certifications and Black Economic Empowerment measures, see Chapters 5 and 6], but the regular guys can't afford a lot of these things.
>
> SAW4

And while we can observe a big environmental drive by large wine buyers to use lighter bottles for everyday wine, 'heavy bottles and their premium appearance are important for the top end, light bottles won't do', as stated by the representative of another wine estate (SAW8). One particularly sharp observer and journalist summarizes it well: 'It takes bravery to stand for your principles, but it is much easier if you are wealthy and privileged' (SAW23). In sum, valuation in fine wines is also linked to the identities of who is selling and who is buying.

4.6 TASTING WINE IN PLACE: WINE TOURISM

Wine tourism refers to travel to wine regions and/or specific wineries for the purpose of tasting wines in the context of specific landscapes. At the minimum, it includes a visit to individual or collective wine shops and tasting rooms but can also involve visits to cellars, wine tours, walks through – and picnics in – vineyards, meals or events at co-located restaurants, wine tasting workshops and/or attending winemaking events. Visits often end with the purchase of wine to take away (Picard, Moreira and Loloum 2018). Wine tastings are usually offered in packages (typically three to five wines); they are sometimes run by trained personnel and may include pairings with finger food. Some wineries offer participatory events, such as grape picking, old-style stomping grapes at harvest time, or filling bottles with customized blends and labels.

Wine tourism can be seen as a cultural process, one that is located between place and space, between image and representation (Demossier 2020, 36, citing Hirsch and O'Hanlon, 1995), and between experience and memory. 'Pre-existing cultural and social values are promotionally attached to [wine which is] then "sold back" to consumers with the promise that lifestyle consumption . . . will ensure their personal experience of the same-self values, ideals and practices' (Fournier 2019, 164). But wine tourism is also a way of experiencing terroir (and nature, see Chapter 5) in situ through heavy mediation and editing.

> If the trade of wine defines the circulation of a perceived magical essence extracted from a given terroir . . . tourism can be seen as an inverse circulation in which wine consumers become tourists and travel to wine terroirs. In the first case, terroir is circulated toward consumers; in the second, wine-consumers-as-tourists are circulated toward terroir. Both forms of circulation seem complementary instances of the same social phenomenon, both grounded in . . . cosmological metanarrative opposing a magical place of distance to a quotidian place of ordinary life.
>
> Picard, Moreira and Loloum 2018, 533

While chateaux in Bordeaux have been entertaining the French elite for centuries, wineries in general started to open their doors to a wider audience only in the 1960s. In many countries and regions, they actually started to do so only well into the 1990s or later. Producers entering the wine tourism circuit have to rethink the way they present themselves to the public (personally and through their employees, infrastructure and landscape), including how they communicate their values and identities. With the development of hospitality infrastructure, architecture has also become an important way through which to express styles, identities and terroir: 'oak barrels, Italianate towers, haciendas, warehouses, cellars, stainless steel tanks and wind turbines have become the backdrop for storytelling' (Danielmeier 2014, 213) (see Image 9). Wineries seek to appeal to customers through 'the prominent display of beauty, cleanliness, and tradition in the organization of the landscape; in the use of distinctive and onerous processes of cultivation and maturing (e.g., the handpicking of grapes, the use of new oak barrels); and in an emphasis on science and technique, sometimes embodied in the hiring of celebrated winemakers and consultants' (Fourcade 2012, 536). In short, appreciation of landscapes allows the explicit linking of wine to a specific place (Tomasi, Gaiotti and Jones 2013).

Many tasting rooms also offer a glimpse, typically through a glass wall, of 'adjacent cellars with aging barrels, carefully curated with pleasing arrangements, light effects, and even the decorative use of dust' (Picard, Moreira and Loloum 2018, 534). In more sophisticated and well-organized wine tourism regions (for example, Napa in California, Stellenbosch in South Africa), tourists can walk into a winery any day of the week, especially during the high tourist season. Other wineries and regions have much more restricted offerings, with many wineries closed to the public or only offering visits upon previous booking and/or on specific days (this is often the case in Valpolicella). Wine tourism experiences in the Old World, including in Italy, have been historically centred on a whole region or village (Moran 1993). They are also organized along festivals and wine routes, which are demarcated itineraries linking member wineries through a wine region or geographical indication that is valorized by highlighting a set of distinctive landscape and cultural attributes (Hall et al. 2002). In the New World, including in South Africa, wine tourism offerings are usually focused on activities in specific wineries (Mitchell, Charters and Albrecht 2012), but more collective efforts have also emerged –

Image 9 Tasting room with winemaking facility in the background, South Africa. Source: Author.

including those organized along wine routes (Bruwer 2003; Ferreira and Hunter 2017). Again, distinctions between Old and New Worlds are becoming more blurred, with wine routes becoming key in promoting regional branding everywhere.

Destination marketing in wine is based on the distinctiveness of place and territorial identity, in other words, a form of tourism terroir (Albrecht 2014). It is increasingly linked to regional festivals that not only feature wine but also offer a wide variety of local crafts and foods. These are common means of bringing 'the various professional actors, buyers, and wine consumers together in a festive environment. The aims are multiple, including direct sale, branding and customer relationship marketing, social festivity, and the reinforcement of a sentiment of regional wine and gastro terroir among producers and clients' (Picard, Moreira and Loloum 2018, 536). With increasing competition among many brands and geographical appellations, wine destinations try to differentiate from competitors by leveraging territorial heritage and tradition (Gačnik 2014). Thus, in wine tourism, 'value directly depends on a socially mediated, carefully curated image of a given place that allows certain wine regions to stand out . . . [so that consumers can] define social belonging, demonstrate aspirational social standing, and display cultural capital' (Senese, Hull and McNicol 2019, 139–40).

Tasting experiences and wine-centred hospitality are an increasingly important part of selling wine and ensuring overall profitability for wineries. These encounters at their best encourage direct contact with small-scale producers and conviviality. 'Learning the grammar of the site and the language of its products can thus become integral to the experience of drinking and to the social forms and shared sociability underpinning it' (Demossier 2020, 149). But wine tourism can also involve large, corporate wineries that offer generic, branded experiences embedded in architectural features having little to do with 'the local'. Vineyards around a tasting room or cellar may be an integral part of the production infrastructure of a winery, providing a glimpse into actual viticultural practices – but they can also be visual tokens of productive realities where most grapes are bought from contractors. 'Wineries that once used to be cultural expressions of connections between land, produce and people, have separated into machines for production and into performative places that offer hospitality functions . . . with winemakers often display[ing] an historical and romanticized picture of winemaking' (Danielmeier 2014, 214; see also Overton and Murray 2013).

Wine tourism can be seen as a pilgrimage, an escape from everyday urbanized existence. Travellers seek to materially connect with idealized places and escape 'the mundane present in which wealthy, urban Westerners live . . . Wine tourism away from home, but also wine consumption back at home, hence seem specific ceremonial instances that enable the material transfer of magical qualities between a terroir and the body of a consumer' (Picard, Moreira and Loloum 2018, 537). When combined with wine route itineraries, this picture is spiced with a dash of adventure, discovery and exploration – as tourists move from one winery to the next in a literal and metaphorical journey.

> Wine tourists anywhere in the world literally move from one locale to another in search of knowledge, sensory stimulation, and pure pleasure. Yet, many also see

themselves as being on a metaphorical journey toward wine connoisseurship or other knowledge, which will involve more than just tastings. Landscape, nature, and architecture thus take on a different significance as a backdrop to consumers' and guides' inner growth.

Joy et al. 2018, 168

Wine tourism is often wrapped up in romantic, nostalgic discourses and rural idyllic material setups, with almost ornamental vineyards surrounding a winery (Howland 2019b, 243) and with wine guides that often stage authenticity and try to 'find a performing equilibrium between their own interests, the clients, the local people, and their employers' (Joy et al. 2018, 167). In South Africa, some wineries offer tastings that pair specific wines with the olfactory experience of different *fynbos*, shrub vegetation that is typical of the Cape Floral Kingdom, which includes around 6,000 endemic species. Stellenbosch and surrounding areas (including the top destination Franschhoek) are tourism-driven areas, with wine tourism one of their many possible offerings. The representative of a winery told me that they 'want to make it possible for people to have a more personal and memorable experience . . . It's all about aesthetics . . . When somebody visits us, they feel history and tradition. We can provide a direct visual connection between the vineyard and the actual wine; it is a far better experience than digital traceability' (SAW66). Another wine producer stated that 'wine tourism has a halo effect for wine brands' (SAW84). A third argued that 'restaurants may not be profit centres, but they are important to attract customers for the wine . . . We sell them stories. They are an important part of the experience' (SAW71). A label designer told me that 'wine tourism offerings should be pleasant and uncontroversial . . . People are overloaded, when they visit a winery, they want to take a break. They want to forget and tune out' (SAW74).

In both South Africa and Italy, some companies that prize wine tourism to a large extent externalize grape growing to contract farmers but will always keep a 'vineyard for show' (SAW49, V11) around the winery to show tourists, or as a landscape where they offer tastings and picnics. In Italy, this is often combined with dominant imagery depicting 'the natural world as splendid, often sublime and the culture that tends it, hard-working and even heroic' (Senese, Hull and McNicol 2019, 127). This is particularly the case in hilly areas of Valdobbiadene in the Prosecco DOCG, where vineyards are perched on very steep hills and are tended exclusively by hand (see depiction in Image 10). Heroic viticulture has a formal definition as that either located on land with a slope greater than 30 per cent; located at an average altitude greater than 500 metres; distributed on terraces; or grown on small islands.[44] Heroic vineyards are formally recognized in Italian wine legislation[45] and receive special support. A heroic narrative is also used in an Italian-Greek project seeking to valorize 'Volcanic Agriculture of Europe', which featured prominently at the ProWein fair in 2023.[46] The project 'aims to promote, emphasize and make consumers know about the extraordinary characteristics of a form of agriculture and dairy production that differ from the rest thanks to the volcanic origin of the soil'.[47]

Beauty, together with terroir, can be used to raise nostalgia for natural lifestyles and hard work, thus valorizing them by embedding place-based production into

Image 10 Depiction of 'heroic viticulture', Italy. Source: Photo of an image by Beatrice Pilotto in the magazine *Visit Conegliano Valdobbiadene*, issue 02/2020, 8–9, published by the Consorzio di tutela del vino Conegliano Valdobbiadene Prosecco and the Strada del Prosecco e vini dei colli Conegliano Valdobbiadene.

modern economies (Senese, Hull and McNicol 2019). But agro-chemical spraying also affects contiguous communities, leading to protests and pushbacks (see the example of Prosecco in Chapter 5). And while the imagery and discourses of heroic viticulture are often built around the (usually male) figure of the hard-working small farmer and his family, even the smallest operation needs to hire labour at least for harvesting – often also for other operations. What is *not* on show in most wine tourism experiences are labourers toiling in the vineyard, especially when they are immigrants or members of a disadvantaged or minority ethnic group (see Chapter 6). When tourists are around, vineyards seem to magically take care of themselves. Wine experiences are thus built upon selective associations and disassociations with place (Ibert et al. 2019; Lang 2024; Overton and Murray 2013; Rainer 2021; Thomsen and Hess 2022).

4.7 WORLDS OF VALUATION AND VALUE STRUGGLES RELATED TO PLACE

Placeless wines

In this chapter, I focused on the role of place as a site of value struggle in wine – distinguishing between placeless wines and wines that are in one way or another linked to a place (including fine wines and wine tourism). In placeless, wine valuation is based on retailers' demands related to three elements: intrinsic quality and packaging; codified solutions to food safety and basic aspects of sustainability; and impeccable logistics. These are typical features of an *industrial* world of valuation (see Table 10) – entailing the enrollment of technical expertise and skills at the levels of logistics and clean winemaking (as opposed to unique or fancy). Retailers communicate very specific demands on intrinsic quality and packaging to their suppliers: what to bottle (colour, maybe a varietal or blend, body, level of acidity, residual sugar, no taints), what kind of label and cork to use, the weight and shape of the bottle and the recycling possibilities. Specifications on material quality at this level can be measured or described easily for purchasing purposes. These factors are then translated into 'clean winemaking techniques' and further upstream into systematic viticultural practices. Once this basic step is cleared, then price (the main instrument of a *market* world) operates as a valuation device. Therefore, a compromise of *market* and *industrial* worlds provides the reference framework for processes of valuation and struggles around most internationally traded wine. This entails a blending of common principles articulated around efficiency and competition, and valuation processes merging objective technical measurement of material properties and price.

Place wines

Value struggles for place wines instead coalesce around terroir in relation to ideas and operationalizations of tradition, authenticity and heritage. Terroir is leveraged to transmit a sense of (often romanticized) connection to the location of production, with trust embedded in a particular region, a processing system that is typical of an area, and/or the skills of people who produce the grapes and the wine. To a large extent, terroir and geographical origin relate to a *domestic* world of valuation – where intimate knowledge of the land, and long-term and repetitive fine-tuning of practices and varieties, embed the natural features of land and climate into the wine. Valuation processes linked to terroir are built upon the idea that good wine can come only from specific locations and only after centuries of experimentation and close knowledge of the land. When terroir is institutionalized in larger indications of geographical origin, it still refers to a domestic world but in less immediate ways – as it can relate to fairly large and internally diverse regions.

But where geographical indications are collectively owned by consortia of producers, an important element of the valuation of place also relates to a *civic* world, which is based on collective solidarity and representation. Geographical appellations tend to provide a rent to all producers within the demarcated area. At the same time, there are vast differences in the wine-producing world on what an indication of geographical origin actually means and how it is operationalized. Collective identities and bottom-up control are more in evidence in smaller geographical denominations, where regulation tends to be stricter and more detailed than in larger ones. But even in larger appellations, smaller operators can still exert some level of indirect control

Table 10 Worlds of valuation and value struggles in wine (place)

	Worlds of valuation (general)					
	Market	Industrial	Domestic	Civic	Inspired	Opinion
Common principle	Competition	Efficiency	Traditional benevolence	Collective solidarity	Spiritual or creative enhancement	Fame
Qualified objects and processes	Product units	Plans, systems, controls, forecasts	Specific assets	Negotiation, consultation, distributional arrangements	Innovation, creation	Public relations, brand names, social media recognition
Questions underpinning valuation processes	Is it economic?	Is it technically efficient, scalable, functional?	Does it follow tradition? Can it be trusted?	Is it collectively safe, healthy, socially and environmentally sound?	Is it new or unique? Is it a breakthrough?	Is it accepted by the public/ consumers?
Valuation focus	Price	Scalability, and proper functionality	Trust, history, repetition	Social, labour, environmental, collective impacts	Creativity, novelty, personality	Renown, visibility

	Worlds of valuation in wine (place)					
Valuation focus	Price	Availability at technical specification and scale	Tradition, authenticity, heritage	Collectively owned or controlled	Unique, inspiring	Famous, recognized
Value struggles						
Geographical appellation			x	x		(x)
No appellation			x		(x)	(x)
'Fine wines'			x			x
Wine tourism	(x)		x		(x)	(x)
(Placeless wines)*	x	x				

Legend: x = currently dominant world(s) (darker shading); (x) = antagonistic world(s) underpinning value struggles (lighter shading).
* The valuation of placeless wines by definition does not relate to place; they are included in the table for comparative purposes.
Source: Own elaboration.

through their cooperatives and/or membership in consortia, and benefit from rents linked to producing wine with a geographical denomination. Geographical indications that are not built around an appellation system can also provide a rent to producers as long as they are able to maintain a good reputation. However, these geographical indications tend to lack the collective and institutional element that provides (especially smaller) producers with some control from below, thus the civic world element in valuation tends to be weaker. The valuation of place in these situations often departs from an exclusive set of domestic considerations to also include an *inspiration* world – with producers focusing on uniqueness and aesthetic or emotional attachments to the place where the wine comes from.

Wine valuation in place wines of all kinds is also increasingly shaped by the endorsement by renowned wine writers, judges, publications or through social media – a set of features of a world of *opinion*. Here, valuation rests on the aesthetic approach of endorsers towards wine (including his/her preferences for one place or style over another), and their perceived independence from industry interests. The main factors here are ratings by top wine writers (e.g. Jancis Robinson, Robert Parker, Tim Atkins) and by influential publications (e.g. *Wine Spectator*, *Decanter*). Which experts, and in what markets, come to be recognized as being of worthy opinion is the topic of entire books (McCoy 2006; Osborne 2004). Place, location and/or terroir are thus mediated by wine experts – given that even the most knowledgeable consumers need to be guided through the great diversity of wines available in the market. At the same time, expertise is being reframed with the rise of influencers and peer advice via social media. Yet, opinion makers will not have an impact on wine styles unless producers make wines that appeal to their palate. Therefore, the rise, consolidation and fizzling out of a particular wine style and/or aesthetics will depend on actors that can translate it into actual practices in the vineyard and the winery – for example, the so-called flying winemakers who deliver portable solutions to winemakers and viticulturists around the world and do the hidden work of shaping an opinion world of valuation into real-world practices (Colman 2008; Lagendijk 2004).

Fine wines

When it comes to fine wines, it makes sense to start the interpretation of valuation from insights on the enrichment economy (Boltanski and Esquerre 2020) and the economy and society of singularities (Karpik 2010; Reckwitz 2020). As indicated in Chapter 2, Boltanski and Esquerre (2020) see the enrichment economy as an economy focused on enhancing the value of things through narratives that form differences and identities. These are things that already exist and that are usually intended for the wealthy. Wines in the enrichment economy are meant to be kept for delayed consumption or even just to be stored to accrue value. When wine is purchased to fill a collection (e.g. acquiring a range of vintages of a particular wine), demand does not decrease as one purchases more. It tends to increase as the collection grows, contrary to what one would expect from marginal utility theory.

Terroir from the perspective of the enrichment economy is akin to producing local cultural singularities that allow monopoly rents (Boltanski and Esquerre 2020). At the same time, we can observe an increasing incorporation of fine wine producers into larger luxury groups (e.g. Moet Hennessy and Louis Vuitton have merged to form LVMH; several top Bordeaux chateaux have been acquired by luxury conglomerates) (Boltanski and Esquerre 2020, 21). International investment groups have also taken over many prestigious properties, in France and elsewhere, primarily as a financial investment (Garcia-Parpet 2009).

Karpik (2010)'s delineation of different regimes of coordination in the markets for singularities is also particularly relevant for the valuation of fine wines (see details in Chapter 2). These regimes account for different ways of qualifying a product and the judgement devices that are attached to each qualification. He characterizes the market for fine wines as an 'authenticity regime' that relies especially upon two judgement devices: appellations, which in the case of wine are geographical appellations but also the names of top chateaux or brands; and *cicerones*, which build on the infrastructure of wine criticism, including the development of language and expressions, protocols of judgement for comparative tasting and sensorial techniques (Karpik 2010).

Especially before the 1970s, fine wines were understood as incomparable, defined by a plurality of taste judgements, and supposed to be kept. Since then, wine valuation devices have multiplied and reached a broader public, with critics occupying a more central function (Karpik 2010, 138). The increasing number and granularity of different terroirs, combined with different vintages, yields many singularities. Therefore, wine guides, expert opinion and now social media provide key instruments in sifting through these. Yet, they do so from the vantage point of specific aesthetics. In Italy, for example, two points of reference for the valuation of wine are the Luigi Veronelli guide (slightly more traditionalist) and the wine magazine *Gambero Rosso* (slightly more modernist) (Negro and Hannan 2022). Globally, the scores provided by the Wine Advocate (originally established by Robert Parker), the specialist magazine Wine Spectator, and critics like Jancis Robinson and Tim Atkin are important points of reference. Wine guides do not usually take into consideration price, therefore the focus of the fine wine market is not price competition (Karpik 2010).

A quantitative application of Karpik's theory to the market for wine singularities shows that purchases are indeed strongly correlated to a variety of valuation devices, which 'reduce the opacity of the market by giving reasons for product choice' (Schenk 2021, 179). But the effect of different devices varies substantially: wine critics and guides play a major role in explaining purchases, while personal networks and confluences seem to be playing only subordinate roles. Geographical appellations do not actually seem to shape purchasing decisions for the most expensive wines, and rankings are mostly relevant for lower-priced wines and for the very top end of the price distribution (Schenk 2021). These results also suggest that valuation devices do not simply provide information to fill a gap – they offer 'knowledge on the symbolic content of singular products and the composition of relevant evaluation criteria' (Schenk 2021, 196). To translate these insights into the language of worlds of valuation, fine wines relate to a world of *opinion*, but also to the valuation of place authenticity that is characteristic of a *domestic* world.

Wine tourism

Wine tourism can be thought of as terroir experienced in person – steeped in a *domestic* world of valuation related to inhabiting tradition and authenticity, experiencing 'local nature', and authentically living a (reinvented and idealized) place. However, these valuations are increasingly entwined with representations of beauty, aesthetics, architecture and landscaping, and are linked to relaxing and even spiritual experiences of connection to place and terroir – markers of an *inspiration* world. Wine tourism can offer a lived experience of unique sites, interaction with 'mad winemakers' and the storytelling behind any of these. Valuation processes can be linked to experiencing the places presumably inhabited by those making or marketing the wine – with expertise based not necessarily on technical competence but on the host's capability to enact an 'artistic moment'. Wine tourism experiences of this kind are partly linked to performance and partly embedded in design (a unique label, a funky name for the wine or a special bottle shape). Technical skills in winemaking and viticulture can also be part of an inspiration world, provided that they are used in unique or alchemical ways and relate to the creativity and personality of the host.

Some elements of an *opinion* world of valuation are also at play in wine tourism. Given the large number of properties that are available for tourist experiences, key reference points for valuation processes are provided by celebrity and social media endorsement, scores and reviews in tourist guides and websites such as Tripadvisor, and by celebrities themselves owing wineries. At the same time, we can also trace the progressive emergence of packaged wine tourism solutions, where nostalgia for natural lifestyles is even more sanitized and sold through more generic, branded and homogenized place-based offerings based on price competition – thus drawing a *market* world of valuation.

4.8 CONCLUSION

The analysis of place in shaping wine value struggles provided in this chapter has important implications for the way we understand power dynamics in the overlaps of value chains and chains of values. For placeless wines, calculations showing the distribution of value added along the chain, and among different operators and social groups in each value chain node, can be an appropriate way to understand bargaining power (see Chapter 3 for a South African example). However, in place wines and wine tourism, other key forms of power are also at play. Value struggles occur around whether one can taste place in a wine, and conversely how wine can be valued differently by experiencing it in specific places. These are key features of constitutive power. These considerations coalesce around discussions on tradition, authenticity and heritage in constantly redefining terroir and geographical origin. In fine wines, they are framed through the registers of exclusivity and uniqueness, with important place dimensions as well.

In general, place is a site of value struggle that allows (smaller) wine producers (individually, but especially collectively) to leverage worlds of valuation that can weaken or at least challenge the market/industrial compromise that is at the basis 'placeless wines'. At the same time, we can also detect a watering down of these effects when place is sold as a brand, and when the peculiarities of different places get lost through the tendential homogenization entailed in the spatial expansion of geographical appellations. The specific implications of these reflections for power dynamics will be further examined in Chapter 7 – in conjunction with the findings arising from the two other sites of value struggle (nature and people) examined in the next two chapters.

Chapter 5

NATURE

5.1 INTRODUCTION

Compared to other agro-food products, wine has been a relatively late mover in handling sustainability issues, with some initiatives starting in the late 1990s and the bulk of attention towards environmental sustainability standards and certifications emerging in the past ten to fifteen years. Organic certification was an early mover in addressing environmental concerns in wine, as in many other agro-food industries. Although organic wine is still a minor proportion of total production globally, it has been growing rapidly. Biodynamic wine, whether certified or not, is also spreading worldwide, but remains a small niche. In addition to organic and biodynamic certification, integrated production of wine systems (based on 'best practices' in viticulture and winemaking) are spreading in all regions, as is the production of 'natural wines'. In France and Italy, small vineyards in traditional wine-producing regions are also laying claims of 'reasonable' viticultural practices (*viticulture raisonée*) based on the characterization that traditional local techniques are similar to those used in organic production.

Although there have been several environmental sustainability initiatives in various wine-producing countries (Ponte 2019), they are still mainly local or regional. A concerted effort to set up a global sustainability initiative (the Sustainable Wine Roundtable) was initiated only very recently. In this context, New World producing countries have been at the forefront of broad initiatives that encompass various aspects of environmental (and social) sustainability in wine (Borsellino et al. 2016). Programmes of this kind are present in Australia, the state of California, Chile, New Zealand (Flint, Golicic and Signori 2016; Sautier et al. 2018), Italy and South Africa (see below). For example, Sustainable Winegrowing New Zealand, an industry group that introduced its formal environmental management system as early as 1997, now certifies both grape growers and wine producers on the basis of a scorecard and a benchmarking system.[1] In 2014, it claimed to cover 90 per cent of vineyard areas, of which 7 per cent also held organic certification (Gilinsky et al. 2015). Similarly, the California Sustainable Winegrowing Program promotes 'green' and 'sustainable' practices and has developed a certification program that 'provides verification by a third-party auditor that a winery or vineyard implements sustainable practices and continuous improvement'.[2] By 2017, around one-quarter of vineyard area and two-thirds of wine production in California had gained various forms of sustainability certification or verification.[3]

Environmental sustainability is one of the main sites of value struggles in the South African and Italian wine industries. The South African wine industry has been a pioneer on sustainability management (SAW37), with internationally recognized standards such as the voluntary Integrated Production of Wine (IPW) protocol dating back to 1998. Sustainability in South Africa has become increasingly important in policy, strategic and marketing discourse, especially in the past decade (SAW2). It is becoming a minimum requirement demanded by domestic and international wine merchants and retailers (SAW6, SAW19). Italy has also embraced sustainability in wine through several initiatives. Although demand for sustainability from domestic retailers is not as pressing in Italy as it is in South Africa, interest is growing from international buyers. These observations do not mean that environmental sustainability is necessarily improving. As a Valpolicella wine producer told me in an interview:

> People want to know what they drink, they are not just posing because it's cool. But this also means that it is difficult to distinguish between those who say something about their environmental stewardship and then do not do it; those who are not saying anything, but they are doing it; and those who say it and do it as they say ... I am actually one of those who do not say it. I avoid telling stories because then the larger producers copy them and they can do things at a larger scale, whether the stories and practices are theirs or not.
>
> V16

In this chapter, I focus on value struggles related to nature, the environment and climate change. Value struggles that have strong place elements (including references to tradition, authenticity, and heritage) were covered in Chapter 4. Those that are mainly revolving around labour and social conditions of production will be examined in Chapter 6. In the rest of this chapter, I examine four layers of value struggle related to nature. The first is around the regulation and governance of environmental sustainability through standards, codes of conduct and certifications. The second concerns viticulture as part of a broader ecology (as in organic and biodynamic viticulture and winemaking), traditional vine training systems, biodiversity conservation and the beauty of nature. The third layer coalesces around discussions on what is 'natural wine'. The fourth is about climate change and the role of innovation and technology in shaping adaptation and mitigation measures. This is followed by an analysis of the visibility of sustainability concerns at wine trade fairs as a way of gauging their valuation within professional circles. Finally, I will interpret these empirical findings through the lenses of different worlds of valuation.

5.2 REGULATION AND GOVERNANCE OF ENVIRONMENTAL SUSTAINABILITY

Differently from many other agro-food products, there is currently no *global* certification system on sustainability for wine. However, there are some international reference guidelines provided by the International Organization of Vine and Wine (OIV) and the International Federation of Wines and Spirits (FIVS). OIV is a technical intergovernmental body with forty-nine member states that provides information to develop regulations, avoid barriers to trade and promote sustainability in the wine sector. Following the introduction of sustainability guidelines back in 2004, it developed a 'Guide for the implementation of principles of sustainable vitiviniculture' in 2016, providing a benchmark document that contains five principles and a series of actions that wine operators are encouraged to take, two of which focus on environmental issues:[4] (1) the implementation of a sustainable approach that integrates environmental, social and economic aspects (overview and analysis of existing regulations; and integration of sustainable production approaches within the governance structure of an organization); and (2) sustainable vitiviniculture that respects the environment (selection of the vineyard and winery site; soil management; preserving biodiversity and the landscape; input and output management; limiting noise and air pollution; and adaptation to climate change and mitigation of climate change).

FIVS is an international organization that advises the wine, spirit and beer sectors on public policy issues. It is more oriented towards the distribution end of the value chain than OIV and has developed its own 'Global Wine Producers Environmental Sustainability Principles' and a 'Greenhouse Gas Accounting Protocol'[5] for its members, which include producers but are mostly distributors, importers, exporters and trade associations. The FIVS principles are organized under three rubrics: prosperity, people and planet. Their planet rubric includes guidelines for vineyard and winery operators on how to 'implement environmentally sustainable activities based on the unique characteristics of their geographical regions and associated environmental risks'. These activities, cover (but are not limited to): water and energy efficiency, soil health, waste management, air quality, climate resilience, pest management and biodiversity/ecosystems. The FIVS guidelines also indicate the possible contributions to wine tourism, employment and the legal protection of viticultural landscapes and terroirs.[6]

A comparative study of sustainability initiatives in six countries (Flores 2018) shows that most include certifications or labels that are voluntary and employ qualitative methods to check whether producers meet the standards set in guidelines, but without mandating the improvement of performance. Other reviews of sustainability initiatives find that they are no longer a source of differentiation (Golicic 2022; Rosin et al. 2017; Rosin, Campbell and Reid 2017), although they differ widely in their processes, certification costs and levels of transparency – thus making it difficult for the consumer to know the difference between them. A general lack of cooperation among them is also observed (Moscovici and Reed 2018). Specific programs for carbon footprint are also starting to be considered in the wine industry. For example, the state of Oregon has set up a 'Carbon Neutral Challenge' and New Zealand has developed a 'carboNZero' label.

A comprehensive picture of wine sustainability certifications worldwide is provided by a benchmarking exercise carried out by the Sustainable Wine Roundtable (SWR; more on this organization below), which covers thirty existing national and regional wine standards (as of the end of 2022).[7] SWR found several areas of commonality across these standards, including on environmental issues:

> Most standards cover issues of good farm environmental practices, for example water use, energy consumption, use of chemical inputs and pest control . . . A small number of standards go further on the environmental journey and include requirements around issues such as carbon sequestration and regenerative agriculture . . . Only a small number of standards . . . include factors such as winery design, packaging choices, use of renewable energy, modern slavery and living wage.[8]

Other broad sustainability initiatives that are not wine-specific but are relevant to the sector include: the Sustainable Supply Chain Initiative, developed by the Consumer Goods Forum (a trade body with 400 retailer members);[9] the Amfori Business Social Compliance Initiative code of conduct, developed in collaboration with the 2,400 Amfori members (Amfori is a global business association of mostly retailers, importers, and brand owners);[10] the International Sustainability Standards Board, which is developing a global baseline for sustainability information for financial investors and global capital markets;[11] and the International Standards Organization 26000 standard on social responsibility.[12]

Driving change: Alcohol monopolies, finance and wine experts

Many of the current demands for sustainability in wine have been driven by the alcohol monopolies of the Nordic countries (Sweden, Finland, Norway, Iceland and the Faroe Islands) and some Canadian states (Quebec, Ontario). These demands are now spreading to private retailers in the UK and other countries in Europe, but less so in southern Europe and the US (SAW1). Some domestic retailers in South Africa are also starting to place similar demands on their suppliers (SAW34). Table 11 summarizes the current portfolio of retailers' sustainability requirements that have been commonly reported during fieldwork in South Africa and Italy. They include several certifications that will be examined later in this chapter (organic, biodynamic) and in Chapter 6 (Fairtrade, WIETA, Equalitas), but also new demands for alternative packaging solutions (lighter bottles, alternative containers, bulk shipping). Providing carbon footprint information has become the most recent addition to the panoply of demands

Table 11 Main environmental demands by international retailers on wine suppliers[13]

Retailers demands	Main demanders
Organic and biodynamic certification	Germany, UK, alcohol monopolies
Lighter glass bottles	Mainly alcohol monopolies
Recyclable or greener forms of packaging	Mainly alcohol monopolies
Alternative containers (BiB, PET bottles, cans)	Alcohol monopolies (US/UK for cans)
Bulk exports (from South Africa)	Germany, Denmark, UK
Carbon footprint	Just started, mainly EU markets

Source: Elaboration by the author based on Das Nair, Chisoro and Ponte (2023).

placed by wine buyers and retailers in the EU on their suppliers, also because the EU is expected to implement Carbon Border Adjustment Measures (CBAMs) in the near future. South Africa has delayed the implementation of its own carbon tax law to 2026 (the original deadline was 2023). In response to these anticipated changes, some international retailers are demanding that their suppliers develop five-year carbon plans (SAW12, 49).

Systembolaget, for example, has been seeking to increase the proportion of 'sustainable wine' it buys for over a decade. Systembolaget is a state-controlled company that has the exclusive rights to sell alcohol in Sweden – through a retail network of around 450 stores and almost 500 agents serving smaller communities. It carries about 21,000 items in its range, 3,000 of which in what they call the 'Set Range' (representing 95 per cent of sales). These are purchased through tenders where products are blindly evaluated by a panel of three tasters. It also carries out about 2,900 temporary launches a year for seasonal and exclusive items. Systembolaget purchases wine from around 900 suppliers around the world.[14]

Systembolaget's code of conduct for sustainable purchasing is considered a point of reference for many other sustainability initiatives, both collective/associational and individual/corporate. In March 2022, it launched its 'Sustainable Choice' range to guide its customers to find the most sustainable options in relation to the environment, climate and working conditions (this is in addition to its organic range, which accounts for around 14 per cent of total sales by volume). To carry the Sustainable Choice label, a product has to have Systembolaget-approved environmental certification, it must be sold in packaging with a lower climate footprint than ordinary glass bottles and must pass Systembolaget's analysis of working conditions. However, since its launch, sales of beverages with the Sustainable Choice label have amounted to only around 9 per cent of total sales.[15]

Systembolaget has started working with branch organizations to create tools for carbon calculation and reporting, and to share experiences and solutions for Scope 3 emissions (those generated outside of a firm's boundaries and along the value chain) related to packaging and transport. It now includes specific demands on containers in its tenders, such as lighter glass bottles for lower carbon footprint, PET bottles, Bag-in-Box, Tetrapack, and on recyclable or 'greener' forms of packaging for closures, boxes, and labels (WG1, SAW1, SAW17, SAW26, SAW31, SAW33). A Systembolaget representative told me that

> for every tender, we have requirements related to certification and packaging (for example, a lightweight bottle under 420 g). These specifications are different for different tenders and types of wine... We also introduced tenders for wine in PET bottles. We want to expand deliveries in Bag-in-Box: it is very efficient when it comes to climate change impacts. Size and stacking are good, and they are less tricky than pouches. The carton outside is made of recycled fibres... But the perception of consumers is still a challenge. Glass is a great material and wine can stay in it for many years.
>
> WG1

There is also innovation taking place around screw caps (driven by the UK), pouches for wine (although these have limited consumer uptake), and canned wine (driven by the US market) (SAW6).

In 2022, Systembolaget also revised its carbon emissions targets to seek to halve them through the entire value chain by 2030 and reduce them in their direct operations by 90 per cent by 2025 (from a 2019 baseline). Only about half of total emissions are linked to viticulture and winemaking, while the rest is related mainly to transport and packaging. The difference of GHG emissions per litre of wine between heavier and lighter bottles is substantial, as is the difference between glass bottles and bag-in-box solutions.[16] Eventually, Systembolaget expects to develop different solutions for transport and logistics and then choose the ones that are more climate friendly (WG1).

In addition to retailers, another emerging driver of sustainability in wine is the financial sector. According to a representative of FederDoc (the Italian federation of geographical appellation consortia), the role of finance is becoming very important when companies approach banks and other financial institutions. The president of one of the wine sustainability certifications told me that 'when the Norwegian sovereign fund and BlackRock say that you get cheaper financing if you are sustainable, the others listen' (IG3). A media representative told me that 'the Fondazione Gambero Rosso is working with banks such as Intesa San Paolo to develop a point system linked to sustainability for obtaining credit. The financial system is important, it can really push producers in the right direction' (IG17).

Wine guides and prominent wine experts (tasters, journalists, judges) and social media influencers are also waking up to the sound of environmental sustainability. Jancis Robinson has been a major factor in the push to decrease the weight of glass bottles for everyday wine (see below). Robert Parker's *Wine Advocate*, one of the global institutions of wine now part of the Michelin group, in 2021 started assigning the green emblem award to wineries (IG13). Its aim is to 'recognize and celebrate the most extraordinary cases of sustainable efforts in the wine industry. It is a symbol of honour and distinction granted to wine producers that have demonstrated outstanding achievements in sustainability and environmental stewardship.'[17] Fifty wineries worldwide have now received this award (including eight in Italy and three in South Africa). In Italy, every year, Gambero Rosso[18] awards a 'three glasses' distinction to top-quality wines (in 2024, 498 wines achieved this feat).[19] Recently, it has also started to award a 'three green glass' distinction to wines which distinguish themselves in the area of sustainability (in 2024, 174 won this award).[20] These awards are assigned through the deliberation of a committee of experts (IG13). South Africa's premier wine guide, *Platter*, does not seem to have an equivalent 'green' award or evaluation criteria linked to sustainability, even though the country is at the forefront of sustainability efforts.[21]

Broad sustainability certifications and initiatives in South Africa and Italy

South Africa has a rich portfolio of broad sustainability initiatives, including the IPW scheme; the World Wildlife Fund (WWF) Conservation Champions programme; and Carbon Heroes, which I cover in this chapter. I examine the Wine and Agricultural Ethical Trading Association (WIETA) certification and various Black Economic Empowerment (BEE)/transformation initiatives in Chapter 6.

The IPW system is focused mostly on plant protection, food safety and, to a lesser extent, on environmental and climate change issues. IPW is a voluntary sustainability scheme managed by the public sector and applies to farms and cellars (SAW 1, SAW31). As of 2022, 95 per cent of all vineyards, 94 per cent of wineries and 95 per cent of wine sold were certified with this standard (SAW1, SAW2, SAW25). South Africa was the first country in the world to develop a sustainability certification system for wine: the scheme was established back in 1998, the first harvest was certified in 2000, and the seal was first affixed to wine bottles in 2010 (SAW25, SAW1).

IPW includes environmental sustainability criteria for viticulture and winemaking – covering production, processing and packaging. The sustainability seal is affixed together with the Wine of Origin seal that covers traceability and integrity issues. Producers that do not obtain or use the IPW seal can still have their wine certified under the Wine of Origin system (SAW25).[22] Cellars, farms and bottling companies carry out annual self-assessments, while external audits take place every three years. For cooperatives, a random selection of farmers is audited (SAW2). Farms and wineries need a 63–65 per cent or above score to pass. IPW certification is particularly important for qualifying for some of the tenders by monopoly buyers in the Nordic countries (SAW26).

While in its early years IPW was focused mostly on plant protection and food safety, environmental sustainability and climate change issues are now being gradually embedded in its standard. Although it does not yet incorporate specific goals for reducing carbon footprints, the IPW protocol allows extra points to be scored for using a specific carbon calculator (see below). 'Demand for carbon footprint information is growing, so we need to step up or we will be left behind. We are getting more and more inquiries from our members on carbon and water neutrality' (SAW25). IPW has also started bringing in elements of conservation (influenced by the WWF Conservation Champion programme, see below) and includes water conservation issues both at the farm and cellar levels (SAW25). Auditors are allowed to provide recommendations on how to improve the situation at the farm and winery levels and these notes are included in the auditing reports. However, IPW does not have the resources to hire consultants to help farms and wineries improve. This gap in funding points to missed opportunities for setting up an expert group to provide advice to farms and wineries on how to improve their compliance with IPW.

One of the outstanding critical issues with IPW is that it allows the use of glyphosate (a much-criticized herbicide) for weed control. This herbicide is still legally registered in South Africa, but at the time of fieldwork, there was a sense that its days were numbered. The EU, however, after banning two fungicides commonly used in viticulture, has recently approved the use of glyphosate until 2033.[23] A representative of a government regulatory agency stated that 'farmers are using glyphosate because it is a cost-effective way of managing weeds in the vineyards, when used according to guidelines and in a safe way . . . but this is a risky approach as you are limiting your market possibilities' (SAW25). Given the implications for market access in the mid-term, a common view in South Africa is that these issues require research and development to prevent loss of market access.

Like in South Africa, the broad wine sustainability certifications operating in Italy are the result of national and local initiatives (Corbo, Lamastra and Capri 2014). Equalitas will be examined in parallel to South Africa's WIETA in Chapter 7. The World Biodiversity Association (BWA) scheme will be covered below in the section on conservation. Here, I briefly cover two national schemes: 'Sistema Qualità Nazionale Produzione Integrata' or SQNPI, and 'V.I.V.A. Sustainability and Culture'.

SQNPI certification was developed by the Italian Ministry of Agricultural, Food and Forest Policy starting in 2016. It organized various regulations that were scattered around different regions and harmonized them in view of providing a set of guidelines for integrated production (including that for wine grapes). The SQNPI standard includes a set of 'good agricultural practices' and integrated pest management. It is certified by accredited third-party auditors. What makes SQNPI unique is that in other countries these standards are offered as general guidelines, within which producers must work out the details, often by calling in consultants to help them. This ends up being a complex and expensive process. SQNPI instead provides specific strategies and practices for each crop, and a set of precise indicators and solutions to pest and disease control. The system is tuned to different agro-ecological situations – for example, the amount of agro-chemicals needed in viticulture in a hot, dry climate such as Sicilia is much lower than in the north, where it is colder and rainfall is higher. According to one of its representatives, SQNPI cuts the cost of certification and allows smaller producers to access it (IG1). SQNPI certifies the grape must and the bottled wine, which can carry the bee logo. To some extent, SQNPI can be equated to South Africa's IPW in that they are both focused on integrated production and have been developed by public sector institutions.

In parallel to SQNPI, the Italian Ministry of Ecological Transition has also developed a sustainability certification specifically targeted at wine production – called 'V.I.V.A. *Sustainability and Culture*'. It includes technical specifications for calculating sustainability performance in vineyards and wine production in relation to four aspects: air, water, territory and vineyard (IG16). However, this certification has not taken off – as of 2021, only seventy-nine firms had been certified.

Towards a global wine sustainability certification?

The recently established SWR is seeking to develop a global reference standard for the wine industry – if not a certification system per se. The initiators of SWR in the late 2010s identified a sustainability gap in the wine industry and sought to create a hub for information and opportunities to organize events and conferences, and to provide information and a discussion forum (WG2). In 2020, they held their first conference online and a key issue that arose from it was a lack of alignment and global definition of sustainability in wine. A representative of SWR told me that 'there are over forty standards at the regional and local levels, with some commonalities, but they lack coordination . . . There is also an inconsistent approach to packaging' (WG2). He also stated that SWR first aimed at benchmarking existing standards against a global reference, then will work with

> standards owners to address gaps where they exist . . . and with retailers to create a shared position on sustainability issues. The goal is to develop individual standards which address specific needs of different geographies, but which can be cross-compared by retailers and wine consumers. The outcome would be a one-stop shop to support producers deliver progress on sustainability in wine and retailers on the evaluation of sustainability in wine.[24]

For the time being, SWR is framed as a global platform and discussion forum for producers and existing certification schemes aiming to develop collaborative action and tools on labour standards, packaging, agro-chemical use, and low-carbon logistics[25] – with the possibility of developing a global sustainability reference standard for the wine industry.[26] SWR counts fifty founding members in its roster – including one from South Africa (Wines of South Africa, WOSA) and one from Italy (Equalitas). On packaging, SWR is proposing the increased use of alternative formats. In late 2023, it announced a 'Glass Weight Accord' among nine of its retailer members,[27] which seeks to reduce the average weight of the wine bottles from the current average of 550 g to 420 g by 2026 – a reduction of around 24 per cent. On viticulture, SWR seeks to create a decision-making protocol with regional variations to guide, inter alia, input choices and usage, spraying frequency and other key viticultural functions. On human rights, it wants to develop tools, guidance and capacity building for compliance.[28] At the time of writing, SWR has over seventy members, including nine retailers.[29]

A representative of one of the Nordic monopolies told me in an interview that there are major differences in climate between different regions, so it is good that we have different sustainability programs with different ideas, values and priorities. Very impressive work has been done in this field, but these programs are often owned by branch organizations which have unique institutional and historical profiles, so it has been difficult to expand them. Consumers and retailers do not want too much diversity ... The best thing is to have a unique wine but a sustainability standard that is internationally accepted.

WG1

This statement may suggest that, despite the variety of local and regional certification schemes, a global reference standard may be in the making – although it is not yet clear whether it will turn into a certification system with a label to be placed on the wine bottle.

SWR is currently focusing on harmonization and mutual recognition. One of their representatives told me that 'SWR is likely to build on what is there already, it cannot be a totally new standard. It will not be too detailed and will seek mutual recognition of different standards' (WG1). In 2023, SWR initiated a Global Reference Framework for Sustainability in Wine. This framework contains six main elements: governance; environmental performance in the vineyard; environmental performance in the winery; human and social issues; packaging; and logistics and distribution. This framework is not meant to be a certification system – at least for now. It is a statement based on best practice, a global reference point which does not provide localized and detailed guidance. SWR states that 'the concept of terroir is crucial in how we regard wines themselves. It is important that a similar recognition is made that the detail of sustainability will also differ between locations'.[30]

5.3 ECOLOGY, BIODIVERSITY CONSERVATION AND BEAUTY

A second layer of value struggle related to nature concerns contrasting ideas and practices of ecology around organic and biodynamic viticulture and winemaking, the use of traditional vine training systems, biodiversity conservation and the beauty of landscapes. I will examine these in turn and then conclude with a deeper examination of the environmental value struggles that are taking place in Prosecco and Valpolicella.

Organic wine

Organic wines are still a minor proportion of total production globally, but they have been growing rapidly (Gilinsky et al. 2015: 42). From 2005 to 2019, the area of certified organic vineyard globally increased by an annual average of 13 per cent (conventional vineyard area decreased by an average of 0.4 per cent during that time).³¹ As of 2019, Spain, Italy and France accounted for 75 per cent of the world's certified organic vineyard surface. Italy has the highest proportion of organic vineyards (15 per cent of the total planted area), followed by France (14 per cent) and Austria (14 per cent). Organic standards are slightly different in different countries, but according to OIV,³² organic vitiviniculture is a production system that excludes the use of genetically modified organisms (and inputs derived from genetically modified organisms) and that seeks to:

- maintain ecosystems and the fertility of soils in the long term;
- increase biodiversity and the protection of natural resources;
- promote the use of ecological processes and cycles;
- minimize or eliminate external interventions and viticultural practices that require the use of chemical synthesis products; and
- use organic products and processes in transformation and production, trying to avoid all techniques that have a considerable negative impact on the environment.

Until 2012, the EU only allowed the labelling of 'wine made from organic grapes'. Since then, regulations have been put in place in all countries for cellar management and winemaking and therefore it can now be sold as 'organic wine'. This required a compromise on the levels of sulphur that can be used in winemaking, depending on the levels of residual sugar in different wines.³³

Organic wine represents a small proportion of South African production, but demand for it is increasing (SAW1, SAW2; SAW13, SAW14; SAW30; SAW50). South Africa has actually recorded the second-highest growth rate of organic vineyard expansion in the world in the 2005–2019 period, with a 30 per cent yearly average (but starting from a low base).³⁴ One of the main problems with certification from the point of view of South African producers is that it requires auditors to be sent from the EU (SAW1, SAW2, SAW82). The owner of a private winery told me that

> it is understandable that the EU needs to avoid greenwashing and make sure that certification is provided with integrity. But the cost is too high, plus you need different audits for North America and for the EU. The system is fundamentally unfair. If you export wine from the EU, their audits are recognized as equivalent for the US market, but we cannot use our EU certification to export to the US. It is absurd.
>
> SAW50

A representative of the main South African wine industry association told me that 'organic certification is important in Nordic markets, but it is also risky to invest in a certification if you are not sure you will win the tender anyway' (SAW1). Many South African wine producers argue that it does not pay to export organic wine. One of them, for example, stated that 'the Swedish monopoly offers too low of a price because they think there is a subsidy for organics like in EU producing countries, but this is not the case in South Africa' (SAW 17). Therefore, some argue that

> there is a disconnect between the costs of production and the price they want to pay for organic wine. Costs are higher for organics: yields are lower, you use more labour and more fuel because you need to go through the vineyard more often ... You should charge a higher price to consumers ... But in the wine market, consumers do not see the difference, they think that all wine is 'natural' to begin with.
>
> SAW 17; similar views were also expressed in SAW 3, SAW 5 and SAW 82

As an organic wine producer put it: 'organic farming is a lot more complicated and there is much bigger management input. This is because the expertise on the production side of organics is underdeveloped. Hence, it's very difficult to find answers to problems – one can't approach universities, can't find the suppliers that are selling chemicals to help them, can't speak to a neighbouring farmer' (SAW 82). A wine wholesaler also made the point that 'you have 30 per cent more tractor driving if you farm organically and you need to spray more times ... Unless you use an electric tractor and you are careful with compaction, this is a problem' (SAW 63).

A representative of one of the main South African wholesalers stated in an interview that:

> Three of our farmers got certified, but... they had challenges with the certification process (had to buy organic seedlings, etcetera). It took extra work; the paperwork was very demanding ... and then they did not get a premium. That, combined with lower yields meant that they went under. Organic is not profitable, unless you are in Elgin [a 'cool climate' area on the Southern Coast] ... Ploughing for weed control is more expensive. The carbon footprint is also higher, with more sprays and more tractor trips, and then you have higher levels of copper in the soil. It is better to build organic matter in the soil through regenerative agriculture and plant cover crops as much as possible in the winter, then work them into the soil in the spring ... Organic grape-growing for wine is not sustainable, farmers are going under.
>
> SAW 62

Another wholesaler, however, painted a different picture:

> There is good demand for organic wine in bulk, but growers do not think they can farm this way. There is a lack of knowledge. Retailers are willing to pay a premium and those who do not pay a premium for organics tend to buy lower-quality wine. Buyers understand the need to be paid more for organics. We sold two containers in bulk last year and got a 40 per cent premium for the same quality ... But you need to make buyers understand that they cannot have organic wine at the same price as conventional. It is wine buyers who make

decisions, not consumers. We need to stop fantasizing about consumers and need to work on retail buyers.

SAW73

In Prosecco and Valpolicella, organic wine has been only tepidly pushed by the consortia and there is still relatively limited uptake – only 3.3 per cent of the planted area in Prosecco DOCG and 10 per cent in Valpolicella are organic, even including areas under conversion.[35] This was much lower than the national average in 2022,[36] but higher than in South Africa (where it is less than 1 per cent).[37] Several producers in the hilly areas of Prosecco argue that it is very difficult to make organic Prosecco, and nearly impossible to make it biodynamic due to high rainfall and thus the need to spray fungicides (P1). In Valpolicella, several of the large wine producers argued that they need to have organic wine to be able to win tenders with the Nordic monopoly buyers.

One producer claimed that:

It is technically feasible to make organic wine in Valpolicella, although it needs more manual labour and more hours of machine operation, because one needs to go more often to the vineyard. In the first years of conversion, we observed a lowering of yields (-15 per cent) which affected the balance sheet of the farms – also because grape farmers had to buy more machinery for mechanical weeding, etcetera. This is also why organic wine should cost more . . . Yet, it is difficult to sell organic wine, as supermarket chains demand the same price as for non-organic wine and the pressure to cut corners is definitively there to meet these demands.

V4

One of the major producers of organic wine in the Prosecco area argued that Italian consumers and retailers lack a deep culture of organic agriculture – they focus mostly on margins and price not on quality. As a result, this organic producer sells almost all his production abroad, especially in Germany, Austria and Switzerland. In recent years, this producer also started to apply vegan certification because it is in demand.

Consumers, even if they are not vegan, think that the wine is healthier . . . It is a joke, but one that pays. Nobody uses animal products these days in the winemaking process. Most wines are vegan by default.

P11

A producer in Valpolicella confirmed that 'the consumer understands the value of organic, but the supermarket buyer wants it at the same price. It is absurd! . . . We even sell some of our organic wine without the label. It is better than selling it at the same price as conventional wine' (V12). Another stated that 'sometimes it does not make sense from a financial point of view, but we do it anyway to make buyers happy' (V8).

But critique of organics is not only related to financial returns. Some farmers are moving beyond organics and towards regenerative viticulture and biodynamic wines. An iconic biodynamic producer in Valpolicella told me that

> some of the products that are used in organic viticulture are very problematic, copper for example. You have a biological system but at the same time you are polluting the soil with a heavy metal. ... If you really need to use copper, it makes more sense to have a higher dosage and spray fewer times – also with lower dosages we are facilitating the emergence of resistance ... The welfare of the plant itself is not at the centre of attention in mainstream organic approaches. Vines need to have the possibility of self-defending from diseases and pest attacks. It's ok to use fewer agro-chemicals but the vine needs to be healthy. It is useless to avoid spraying synthetic inputs if you then need to pass through with the tractor many more times to spray organic inputs. It becomes more expensive and if you can't make a profit then just as well if you do not farm to begin with. Agriculture is about bringing home a product after all. Choices related to agro-chemicals are important but there are a lot of other factors at play, they cannot be the only things that one focuses on in organic agriculture.
>
> V3

Biodynamic wines and regenerative viticulture

Biodynamic wine production, whether certified or not, is also spreading worldwide, but remains a small niche and is regarded as somewhat esoteric (Flint, Golicic and Signori 2016). Biodynamic viticulture is built on the foundations of a philosophy developed by Rudolf Steiner, who applied rational thought to spiritual experience. Farms are considered themselves as organisms with their own individual nature, which are also connected to other forces in the universe (Negro and Hannan 2022; Joly 2012). Steiner outlined the features and practice of biodynamic agriculture in a series of eight lectures to farmers in 1924 in what is now Poland (Dhalla 2019).

Instead of approaching viticulture as a monoculture, biodynamic methods seek to achieve 'the greatest possible diversity of plants and insects to create a balanced and stable environment for the vines'.[38] Biodynamic viticulture makes use of eight specific biodynamic substances and soil supplements, follows a calendar of operations guided by astrological configurations and cosmic rhythms, and highlights the articulation of biological and spiritual processes. Biodynamic viticulture pays particular attention to regenerating soil health and seeks for 'the humus layer of the soil [to grow] continuously so that [the] vineyard can withstand both droughts and heavy rainfall, allowing a variety of micro-organisms to settle in it'.[39] In a way, biodynamic viticulture also claims to truly express place, as it embeds biological and cultural/spiritual processes into a very specific locality.[40]

Demeter International, a Germany-based federation of certification bodies in forty-five countries, owns the trademark for 'biodynamic' and certifies farms worldwide (Negro and Hannan 2022).[41] As of March 2023, there were over 1,400 Demeter-certified vineyards worldwide – accounting for 25,000 hectares. This is a very small proportion of global vineyard area but has grown rapidly in recent years, more than doubling from around 12,000 hectares in 2018.[42] Castellini, Mauracher, and Troiano (2017) report that the largest number of biodynamic vineyards is in France (around 300) and Italy (over 70), with four countries accounting for more than 1,000 certified hectares each (Italy, Spain, the USA and Chile). Biodynamic wines remain a very small proportion of production in both South Africa and Italy, but some producers in both places have achieved cult status. Many do not seek certification and instead communicate their specific philosophy of production directly to buyers and consumers. Biodynamic viticulture is part of an increasing interest in regenerative agriculture more generally – in view of preserving healthy soils (Gonzalez-Maldonado et al. 2024).

The South African biodynamic wine producers I interviewed argue that regenerative viticulture can be an important venue not only for value addition but also for long-term sustainability. This must start from the perspective of preserving soil health as key for plant resilience, especially in view of climate change. One argued that 'an increase by 5 per cent of the humus content in the topsoil will increase the resilience of the plants by 300 per cent, so in the long term it pays off' (SAW13). Another stated:

> The key to regenerative farming is that, in the short term, we are farming with grapes; but in the long term we are farming with soil ... We need a new look at biodiversity: 30 per cent of all species are already extinct; it is an exponential trend. Currently, there are 200,000 plant species alone that are threatened by vineyard expansion ... Microbial terroir is not just about the physical part (chemistry of the soil) but also about the biological content of the soil, and this adds an additional variable to terroir; you need to link it all up ... This is where land caring and land sparing can meet and help viticultural production on multiple levels: to improve quality but also to reduce risk, to increase sustainability and self-sufficiency. You need to take care of biodiversity and apply regenerative agriculture principles. It is not one or the other. It is not enough to protect wilderness; you need to integrate nature holistically in the farm ... But agro-chemical companies have no interest in this, and their prices are increasing very fast. Small farmers struggle to stay in the game, and they are bought up by larger companies, which then reproduce industrial agriculture – it's a vicious circle. And because you destroy biodiversity, you will need larger and larger farms to keep up.
>
> SAW50

A third South African biodynamic producer confirmed the view that

> the biggest sustainability opportunity is regenerative viticulture, which leads to healthier soils and therefore healthier plants. The reason we do not have healthy soils is because we add nitrogen in them. If you use nitrogen as fertilizer, you get

a higher yield in the short term, but you tie up these elements in the soil and it becomes unbalanced. Plants become weak and more susceptible. Then, you need to use more agro-chemicals to kill weeds. And these chemicals damage the soil even more. Regenerative agriculture can right these wrongs in three–four years, a blink of an eye.

SAW63

A similar set of views emerged from interviews with biodynamic producers in Valpolicella, Italy. As the following quotes show, environmental concerns are also related to the abandonment of traditional practices that were deemed to be more sustainable. Land preparation is a first concern for these producers: 'To produce top wines, you need a terrain that has not been touched by bulldozers, because these so-called land improvements destroy the soil, and you then force the vine to grow roots that are not fitting their original purpose in that particular place. The "progress" that we witnessed in the 1970s was not progress at all' (V3). A second concern is about irrigation: 'We do not use irrigation in the vineyard because this way the roots go deeper and the taste improves' (V3).

A distinct but related valuation struggle concerns the kinds of training systems used in viticulture, and the different degrees of mechanization processes they allow. In Valpolicella, much of this debate is around the traditional *pergola veronese* system of training vines and the more 'modern' Guyot, which is much in vogue as it allows the mechanization of many operations, including harvesting (see Image 11). One of the producers who support the more traditional pergola system argued that:

> viticulture that does not take into consideration the match between a training system and the soil cannot produce high quality. Mechanized harvesting cannot impart selection and ruins the product already at the farm. The grape skin is no longer healthy and whole. It is a brutal form of harvesting as you break the skin and extract substances that are not desired in the wine, which you then must intervene to take away during winemaking.

V3

He also stated that

> one must understand what is best for the welfare of the vine. With Guyot, you place the vine under the sun the whole day. The pergola is horizontal, the light filters through differently, with inclined rays in the morning and evening, while the grapes are protected during the hottest hours of the day. Humidity, speed of maturation and health of the vineyard are all impacted. Also, you do not need to cut the grass under the pergola, while with Guyot you need to do so because it increases the degree of humidity, which is bad for Guyot-trained vines as they are closer to the ground. Guyot also allows a more intensive form of planting, with distances of 2–2.6 metres between vines, while a pergola usually needs a spacing of 3.6–5.5 metres. This leads to more compacted soils, rows that are closer to each other and thus more interventions, which in turn means more

Image 11 Pergola veronese semplice (left) and Guyot (right) vineyard training systems, Italy. Source: Author.

tractor passages, each time placing more weight on the soil and compacting it further. Compact terrain lacks enough oxygen and has lower water retention properties. It has less capacity for ionic exchange. As a result, the vine has higher needs from a point of view of nutrition and water. Forcing the vines this way means that they are more prone to be affected by disease, they live shorter lives and lose the typicality of flavour that comes from a long-term match with the soil. Then, you need to set up irrigation systems or even deliver nutrition with drip irrigation and fertilization. It becomes almost like a hydroponic system!

V3

Another producer stated:

Our vineyards are planted with the *pergola veronese* system, which allows you to make fewer treatments and thus you save in costs. The pergola protects the grape bunches during the hot hours of the day, which is important because Corvina is a delicate grape ... The Guyot system has become popular because it allows you to harvest mechanically once you have harvested selected grapes for Amarone production [by regulation, Amarone can only be harvested by hand]. With the pergola system, all harvesting is manual.

V1

These training systems also have implications for the size of production units.

With the pergola system, you must do everything by hand – and an individual family can only handle seven or eight hectares on its own with the help of their relatives. The implementation of the Guyot training system and the emergence of work cooperatives has helped farms to grow. Smaller farmers are selling their land or rent it out.

V5

Biodiversity conservation and beauty

An important set of concerns among organic, biodynamic and conservation-oriented farmers (and those who are moving in these directions) concerns three interlinked components of biodiversity. The first is about viticulture as monocropping: a Valpolicella wine producer told me that 'old-style viticulture was not a monoculture system. There were rows of grape vines, but they were far from each other because we needed to pass through with the oxen plough. In between vines, you planted maize, vegetables, whatever' (V3). Another said that: 'the problem is that farmers have now become entrepreneurs, they have resorted to monoculture which is both an environmental and a nutritional disaster. But the wine industry is full of *prenditori* [an Italian euphemism for 'those who take'], not of *imprenditori* [entrepreneurs]' (V16).

A second element of biodiversity in viticulture has to do with the diversity of grape varieties: A wine producer argued that

> grape vines have the great property that they self-select. In the past, farmers kept their own plantlets to be grafted in the new plantings and this facilitated a lot of natural hybrids. The grape vine is very good at making genetic variants. It is very important therefore to avoid homogenization, and this is why I think it's important to rediscover the genetic diversity of vines in the fields, to preserve the variants that have developed in time. For example, I found a grape vine in a hilly area that had been abandoned for a long time and now I am doing a DNA analysis to find out what species it is.

V3

This is part of a broader movement for the rediscovery and valorization of species. A group of Italian enologists is very active in seeking to rediscover vine cultivars that had been lost or abandoned and discover new ones in nature that had never been vinified before. In addition to collecting grape varieties and analysing their DNA, they are carrying out micro-production with these varieties.[43]

A third aspect is about the natural biodiversity of the ecosystem within which the vineyard is integrated:

> This is preserved not only by avoiding herbicides, but also leaving the grass to grow high and not cutting it when it is still full of wildflowers. It is important to maintain an equilibrium between species where there is no predominance by one kind over the others. Grasses tend to self-regulate and maintain a natural equilibrium. I sowed a mix of grasses in the fall in between the vineyard rows for

four–five years, then they regenerated by themselves. Increasing biodiversity means maintaining an equilibrium, for example, between clover that fixes nitrogen and other plants with bigger roots that keep the soil aired. There are also mechanical solutions that do not create problems, for example a roller that bends but does not cut grass. If one does not cut grass, or does it after the flowering period, useful insects remain in the vineyard and do not migrate. Since we started this approach, we have not had any problems with aphids and mites ... There is scientific evidence that tall grass slows down infections. Although vines are self-pollinating, it is good for the environment that there are other pollinators. With our methods, soil is rich with micro-organisms and is soft, not compacted.

V3

Another producer stated: 'The response of the vineyards to these practices is amazing – you see new grasses, useful insects coming back. You see a completely new ecosystem emerging' (V5).

In South Africa, the valuation of nature as ecology in wine is often articulated through a combination of conservation and beauty. The motto of South Africa Wine, the apex organization that sets strategic objectives for the industry, clearly tells us to 'discover diversity in a glass'. Although SA Wine is a new organization (established in 2023), the diversity approach is not. A previous version was developed by WOSA in the early 2000s, at that time with the motto 'variety is in our nature'. The original idea at that time was that the rich biodiversity that the Western Cape can boast translates into a great variety of wines, and conversely, that appropriate stewardship of the winelands helps preserve this biodiversity. What WOSA wanted to portray was a South Africa as a 'dynamic country of enormous diversity ... [with a winemaking tradition blending] the restrained elegance of the Old World with the accessible fruit-driven styles of the New World ... [yielding] wines which eloquently express the unique *terroir*, extraordinary biodiversity and fascinating people of the Cape'.[44] In the early days, this translated into a specific initiative, the Biodiversity and Wine Initiative (BWI), in collaboration with WWF with co-funding from the World Bank.

Its aims were to achieve:

- no further loss of habitat in critical sites;
- a positive contribution to biodiversity conservation through setting aside natural habitat in contractually protected areas;
- changes in farming practices to enhance the suitability of vineyards as habitat for biodiversity, and a reduction in farming practices that have negative impacts on biodiversity, both in the vineyards and in the surrounding natural habitat;
- benefits to the wine industry by using the biodiversity of the Cape Floral Kingdom (CFK), and the industry's proactive stance of implementing biodiversity guidelines, as a unique selling point to differentiate South African wine.

According to WWF and WOSA,

> the Cape Floral Kingdom (CFK) is the smallest and richest plant kingdom on earth ... internationally recognized as a global biodiversity hotspot and listed as South Africa's newest World Heritage Site ... As 80 per cent of the CFK is in private hands, conserving the CFK requires getting biodiversity conservation into the hearts and minds of the landowners. The most effective way of doing this is through the industries that represent them. The Biodiversity & Wine Initiative is the first project in this new conservation strategy, working directly with the South African wine industry.[45]

About 90 per cent of wine production in South Africa is said to occur within the CFK. According to WWF and WOSA, the growth of the wine industry can endanger some areas of vulnerable natural habitat (like *renosterveld* and lowland *fynbos*) – although the area under viticulture in South Africa is actually decreasing. Still, BWI was promoted as presenting 'a great opportunity to both the wine and conservation sectors. The wine industry benefits from using the biodiversity of the CFK as a competitive marketing advantage, and from contributing to sustainable natural resource management ... The conservation sector benefits from pioneering biodiversity best practices in the wine industry and conserving the CFKs most threatened habitats'.[46]

BWI awarded the status of 'Biodiversity Champions' to producers that scored 85 per cent of the total points in a self-assessment of biodiversity and complied with additional demands, including setting aside 10 per cent of their land for conservation in perpetuity. Vergelegen, the farm established in 1700 by the then governor of the Cape, Willem Adriaan van der Stel, and currently owned by mining conglomerate Anglo-American, became the first champion in March 2005. Requirements for regular membership of BWI were less stringent: to comply with the biodiversity guidelines 'where appropriate, to the best of the company's ability'; to supply BWI with a copy of an aerial photo map of the property; to 'responsibly conserve' the demarcated biodiversity area to obtain the IPW certificate (see Chapter 3); to supply the property's 'biodiversity story' for marketing purposes; and to set aside two hectares for conservation purposes. The last requirement, which could be difficult to achieve for smaller properties, was later allowed to be met by rehabilitating a portion of own land or in a neighbouring farm, and by donating to a conservation fund project.

The experience of BWI lasted a decade and was celebrated in a beautiful coffee-table book entitled *The Wine Kingdom: Celebrating Conservation in the Cape Winelands*, published by WWF South Africa in 2015. The beauty of the CFK and the properties of featured Biodiversity Champions are front and centre in this publication – wrapped in discourses of renewal, wilderness, wonder and harmony with nature. Of the eleven chapters that constitute the book, only one is on 'human nature' (entitled 'the spirit of community'), framed through the idea of 'united in our diversity' and featuring stories of employment creation, training workers for conservation, facilitating small business development, providing educational infrastructure and opportunities, and featuring a land reform programme through an empowerment initiative.

BWI had a clear focus on the beauty of the CFK and the conservation of its biodiversity. This aesthetic approach is still present in its successor, the WWF 'Conservation Champions' (CC) programme, which was established in 2015/16 (SAW1, SAW7). The image symbolizing this initiative features a sugarbird perched on a *Protea repens* (also known as Common Sugarbush). The basic principle of the new programme is still to recognize the best performers in the field of conservation but in a broader perspective covering three overall conservation criteria: energy, water and nature (SAW7). In the CC programme, a producer can qualify by meeting only one of these criteria, although most producers comply with two or three – and all seem to be meeting the water criteria. The programme is also considering extending its coverage to carbon footprint (SAW33). A total of fifty-five farms for a total of 25,000 ha were 'Conservation Champions' (SAW1, SAW2, SAW7) in 2022. A representative of the main wine industry association told me that

> 50 per cent are family owned by generations and have made sustainability their philosophy; 25 per cent are big brands, and their main interest is marketing – it is not a certification as yet but they want to be able to use the attractive stickers featuring a protea and a sugarbird on the wine bottle; the last 25 per cent are companies that do not need it but still value the initiative and the advice they get from it.
>
> SAW2

WWF personnel carry out annual assessments in all farms and check for possible changes in their environmental plans, consult the IPW audit report and advise them on possible ameliorations. They also provide technical advice to champions. The main funder of this initiative is an individual philanthropist, who has indicated that the programme will soon need to be completely self-funded. No membership fee is being charged for the time being, but this may change in view of reaching financial self-sufficiency (SAW7).[47] In terms of markets, WWF is trying to get more shelf space with domestic retailers for wines carrying the CC label, but this is proving to be difficult. In export markets, this certification still has limited traction, although some retailers seem to have started showing interest (SAW7).

While the CC programme is more than just nature conservation, it is still aesthetically anchored to the beauty of the CFK – in a way, it is indirectly helping to aestheticize issues that are less easy to beautify, such as energy and water conservation. This broadening aesthetic is not confined to the CC programme. It is also taking place at the industry strategy level. While the original motto promoted by WOSA in the late 2000s and 2010s was focused on nature, the current motto of SA Wine takes a 'diversity' angle. From a nature focus, the industry is now signalling a broader casting that also includes cultural diversity, thus wrapping post-apartheid relations of power and domination under a diversity cloak – harking to Archbishop Desmond Tutu's portrayal of South Africa as a 'rainbow nation' (more on this in Chapter 6) (Howson, Murray and Overton 2020). In a way, this is an attempt to turn a troubled history into a competitive advantage (Howson et al. 2023, 153).

But linking nature and beauty is not simply an institutional task in South Africa. It is at the centre of marketing and storytelling among many individual wine producers. This is epitomized by a statement made by the manager of a CC winery: 'good wine is made from vineyards in beautiful surroundings' (SAW66). Another champion has set aside 1,000 ha of land for a conservation park under the stewardship of CapeNature[48] in perpetuity. 'Our central aim . . . is to keep this land from being developed . . . We are not doing conservation to attract more customers; it is just part of our value system' (SAW75). This is not uncommon, as other champions have set aside up to 4,000 ha for conservation and are often part of regional conservancies (SAW76, SAW52). Many wine producers who set aside land for conservation focus particularly on alien vegetation clearing and replanting indigenous varieties. This is usually also good for water management. But given the long history of land appropriation during colonial times and exclusion of the Black majority from land ownership during apartheid, combined with the current pressure under which landowners are in view of BEE initiatives (see Chapter 6), one must wonder whether conservation efforts based on setting land aside for perpetuity are more than just about biodiversity.

The valuation of wine around stories of conservation and beauty, both in relation to wine and to wine tourism facilities, also makes sense financially. The head of sales of a winery told me: 'You can be biodiverse as much as you want, but if you go bankrupt it goes down the drain' (SAW71). The representative of another cellar stated: 'We have planted 100,000 indigenous trees on our farm, which are attracting bird populations; in turn, these attract tourism; this is good for the

Image 12 'Clean' vineyards (left) and more biodiverse vineyards (right), South Africa. Source: Author.

company; it also provides employment at our wildlife sanctuary' (SAW9). Another winery uses the proceeds of conservation activities for a rhino protection project with two NGOs – something that is very popular among tourists coming to the winery and restaurant as 'rhino conservation is an emotional discussion' (SAW28). But other interviewees argued that South African producers need to be better at communicating biodiversity and conservation by bringing the beauty of nature more forcefully into the tasting room to build memories and facilitate storytelling.

Finally, beauty in South Africa does not only refer to conservation areas, but also to the changing perceptions of what a 'beautiful vineyard' is (see Image 12): The representative of one of the largest wine producers in South Africa told me:

> We want to move away from 'dead vineyards' to a more biodiverse situation with better soils ... I think that if you look at a vineyard, the classic view in South Africa is that it has to be with pristinely clean rows and a trimmed canopy. It is quite impressive, but if you really look at what happens it's actually quite dead in the middle of the row underneath the vines. You get the growth, and you get the fertilizer, and you get the water, but it is obviously an aberration and you've got so much carbon that is released into the air because people are saying it should be pristine, so they are constantly keeping it clean ... But what we have seen in many places in the world is that cover crops are a big benefit and you shouldn't cut the cover crops off or till them into the soil ... So now we are rolling flat all these cover crops ... and they can actually inhibit weed growth ... The soil still gets the benefit of having more moisture ... So, there's a lot of benefits to having what we viewed in the past as a 'dirty vineyard' ... And the financial benefits of using less fertilizer and less water are immediate. You can have natural beauty instead of a clinical situation.
>
> SAW20

In Italy, the wine industry has its own biodiversity initiative, the World Biodiversity Association's (BWA), which assigns a 'Biodiversity friend' certification. Despite 'world' featuring in its name, this is a local initiative developed by a group of ecologists in Verona that helps assess the impact of production processes on the biodiversity of production areas (in wine but also other agri-food products) (IG10). BWA is based on a decalogue of agricultural sustainability covering aspects from soil fertility to water conservation and energy conservation. Its operational focus is on three direct indicators of biodiversity for water, soil and air quality; thus, certification is based on outcomes and is agnostic on what processes are followed to reach them. Like in South Africa, the biodiversity logo that can be affixed on the bottle is somewhat known in domestic markets, but not so far in international markets.

Although there is less strategic attention paid in the Italian wine industry to the link between biodiversity conservation and beauty, it is present among a sub-set of producers – especially among biodynamic farmers. One of them, told me:

> I want to eliminate the use of plastic to tie the vines – there are now threads you can use that are biodegradable in six months. In some vineyards, I use willow branches to tie the vines. In a vineyard I just replanted I am using wooden and bamboo poles instead of iron and plastic poles. It is quite beautiful to set up a vineyard like that. I will be leveraging this aesthetics for wine tourism purposes. I am also trying to maintain drywalls, which happen to be very good natural environments for useful insects and are very beautiful.
>
> V5

Another producer said:

> I started being interested in biodynamics because of an interest in soil fertility, in what nutrients I provide to the earth. I get to know what I give to the soil – these days farmers have no idea what they put into the earth. But it's also an aesthetic choice, I make biodynamic wine with a consciousness of the beauty attached to it.
>
> V16

Environmental value struggles in Prosecco and Valpolicella

The increases in area and production volumes that the Prosecco and Valpolicella areas went through in the past few decades indicate that there is an important dynamic of land and frontier expansion at play (Moore 2015). Vineyard expansion has enabled producers to meet increasing demand for Prosecco and Valpolicella wines, but it has also had implications on soil erosion and other environmental and health issues. These dynamics are key in understanding the processes of appropriation of nature that underpin capital accumulation. Soil erosion is a particularly contentious issue in Valdobbiadene and Valpolicella Classico areas, both located mostly on hills.

In Prosecco, there seems to be a large gap between the picture provided by the consortia and what transpires in some of the media and in independent scientific publications when it comes to soil erosion and other environmental impacts of viticultural expansion. A Prosecco DOCG consortium representative, for example, stated:

> The area under viticulture in the hilly zone of the DOCG increased dramatically in the 1990s and 2000s, but growth has now stopped. In the plains of Conegliano and Vittorio Veneto, there has also been expansion. In these areas, many viticulturists left farming in the 1970s to work in the rapidly expanding industry, and the remaining farmers moved on to other crops. However, they have now reverted to vineyards because it is much more profitable. But these are not new expansion areas; it is agricultural land that has reverted to viticulture. These days there is also more attention paid to how land is prepared. In the past, hills were simply flattened, and the topsoil was damaged as a result. There is more awareness now.
>
> P4

A wine producer located on the Valdobbiadene hills also argued that their vineyards are small and are often located on steep hills and that there has been little or no deforestation or planting of new vineyards. The owner of a Prosecco producing company stated that 'even in the plains, vineyards did not take the place of forest. They were planted where in the past there was maize cultivation. You can make €21,000 in net profit per hectare with Prosecco, much less if you plant maize' (P1). Another producer stated that 'it is actually good for nature that we have vineyards in Valdobbiadene, otherwise you would have brambles and impenetrable forest. Where there are vineyards there is no soil erosion because the structural work done to establish the vineyard helps water drainage and consolidates the ground' (P2).

However, several local media articles report stories on new deforested areas that are leading to landslides.[49] For example, a landslide that occurred in 2014 in Refrontolo led to a heated debate. On the one hand, a media report claimed that it was related to the lack of upkeep of the forested area, rather than the construction of new vineyards.[50] On the other hand, an academic study claimed that it was related to the deforestation of five hectares of vineyard, with the draining systems along its sides accelerating the speed of runoff water (Basso and Vettoretto 2020, 8). The expansion of planted area is reported in some cases to be causing major changes in the gradient of slopes to make room for mechanical harvesting and thus is facilitating soil erosion and landslides (De Nardi 2016; Visentin and Vallerani 2018).

A number of other academic studies have shown that land use in the Conegliano and Valdobbiadene DOCG area has changed quite dramatically – with vineyard expansion replacing traditional cropland, grassland and woodland (Basso 2019). Pappalardo et al. (2019) modelled the potential soil erosion in the Prosecco DOCG area in view of the large increase of converted area to vineyard production and estimated a much higher potential erosion impact than in other viticulture areas in Italy. Yet, theirs is not a study of actual erosion based on local monitoring, as the DOCG consortium has vociferously argued.[51] Others have characterized some of these changes as 'viticulture sprawl' – the colonization of natural, semi-natural and agricultural land and woodlands that is changing the landscape and creating 'a globalized wine territory' (Basso and Vettoretto 2020, 5). Something similar is also occurring in Valpolicella.[52] These instances suggest a process of extraction of surplus from nature for capital accumulation (Havice and Campling 2017) – a frontier expansion that may be reaching its limits (Moore 2015).

Some of these issues became a topic of great debate in Italy, starting in November 2016, when the popular investigative journalism programme *Report*, produced by the public broadcaster RAI3, dedicated one of its episodes to Prosecco.[53] In addition to a critical take on the expansion of the Prosecco denomination (see Chapter 4), the one-hour documentary brought attention to the negative health impacts of agro-chemical spraying in Valdobbiadene, where almost every little piece of land is planted with glera vineyards, including in locations very close to homes and schools. The DOCG consortium recommends twelve agro-chemical applications during the growing season, but these can go up to twenty if it rains more often than usual. The documentary footage shows indiscriminate spraying with powerful pressure sprayers very close to homes and streets, even if hand sprayers should be used at distances under ten metres from them. Local inhabitants complain of having to close their windows very often and of not being able to let their children play outdoors for days following a spraying.

The documentary includes claims by local individuals that incidences of asthma and cancer are increasing in the communities of Valdobbiadene and shows the rise of local committees to fight against what they see as an indiscriminate application of agro-chemicals.[54] A follow-up episode aired in 2017[55] returned to the Conegliano Valdobbiadene area to check if the situation had changed. The footage of this second documentary includes an interview with the president of the Prosecco DOC consortium – where he indicates that new rules have banned the use of glyphosate given that spraying is creating social conflict in the area. But members of the local committees are still unsatisfied with the progress made.[56] This saga suggests pressure from below from local committees is also important in value struggles, not only from international buyers of Prosecco (Basso and Vettoretto 2020; Ponte 2021; Ponte et al. 2023; Visentin and Vallerani 2018).

Both Prosecco consortia have also started a series of environmental initiatives to counter the particularly bad press they have been facing. One of these is the development of a collective concept of sustainability to produce Conegliano Valdobbiadene Prosecco Superiore DOCG. This is elaborated in a flagship publication by the DOCG consortium,[57] which highlights five broad dimensions of sustainability: (1) reduction and substitution of agro-chemical application; (2) water management; (3) soil management and biodiversity; (4) CO_2 emissions and energy use; and (5) reuse of by-products and ecological packaging. Absent from these considerations are the issues of land use change and the impact of vineyard expansion on soil erosion and the landscape. In other words, environmental management is approached in relation to existing viticultural areas, but not to their expansion. As for agro-chemical use, two main approaches are indicated in their manifesto. One is a (tepid) push for conversion to organic and biodynamic grape production – including a special effort to reduce copper use, which is allowed in organic agriculture but is increasingly being questioned because of its residual presence in the soil. A second approach, much more in focus in the manifesto, is captured under the broad umbrella of 'innovative solutions'. The DOCG Prosecco consortium has also started working towards obtaining SQNPI certification for 50 per cent of its farmers by the end of 2022 and 100 per cent by 2029.[58] When achieved, winemaking establishments and bottling enterprises will be able to use the SQNPI bee-inspired logo on their products. This process is being supported by a network of 'smart agriculture' solutions coordinated by the consortium, including nineteen meteorological stations, remote sensing and continuous pest monitoring.[59]

When it comes to the larger Prosecco DOC consortium, a report on their sustainability activities for 2019 includes a number of important environmental sustainability elements and activities.[60] Notably, the DOC consortium has allocated the latest increase in viticulture area (by 1,200 ha in 2017/18) according to a points system that assigned: 230 ha to organic farms; 148 ha to farms that follow sustainable practices; and 1,113 ha that meet their own 'mosaico verde' standard (meaning at least 5 per cent of viticulture area planted includes hedges and forest). A Prosecco DOC consortium representative argued that

> sustainability demands are not the result of buyers asking for it, but of local community protests. Producers and cooperatives first did not want to have anything to do with it, but now have understood that something must be done.
>
> P21

Valpolicella has avoided negative publicity related to environmental and health issues, and indeed a representative of one of the main cooperatives argued that 'sustainability is important to keep good relations with local populations'. (V8) Another Valpolicella interviewee stated that they have had

> similar problems as in Valdobbiadene, with local populations complaining about the spraying of agro-chemicals, but without the media attention so far. Local committees protested with their municipal administrations first. The municipalities wanted to contain the possible reputational damage and worked to promulgate local regulations to limit the use of agro-chemicals, but not all municipalities have done so.
>
> V9

Part of this lack of open confrontation is that, in Valpolicella, the consortium developed its own certification system for the sustainable production of wine grapes (RRR – Reduce, Retrench, Respect), which was based almost exclusively on integrated crop management practices. RRR was developed in response to the perceived limitations of SQNPI:

> We developed RRR because we perceived the national-level protocol as insufficient for us – these standards were too rigid and did not reflect local realities. For example, they did not include the safeguarding of local populations and the impacts of agro-chemical application on those who live in the area . . . The idea was to eventually expand it to other DOC areas and merge it with SQNPI, but this did not happen. SQNPI has high technical value, but it has not been sold well to the wine industry. But RRR is now used only in Valpolicella. It is difficult to have it recognized by the monopoly buyers in Scandinavia.
>
> V9

One of the main incentives for RRR certification was provided in the regulations to produce Amarone. Only a certain percentage of total grape production is allowed to be vinified for the highly priced Amarone, the rest goes to produce other, cheaper Valpolicella wines. But if grape producers meet the RRR standard, they are allowed an extra 5 per cent of grapes to be used for Amarone production (V8). As of 2021, 1,210 ha had been RRR-certified in Valpolicella (or 15 per cent of the total area).

However, at the 2022 Vinitaly expo, a representative of the consortium announced that they were moving away from RRR certification protocols and instead focusing on SQNPI certification (awarded automatically to holders of RRR).[61] The consortium realized that a scheme that was only applied in one geographical appellation would not be easily accepted by large supermarket chains, and thus decided to throw its weight behind a much larger Italian scheme, SQNPI.

Environmental contestation and adjustments in Prosecco and Valpolicella areas of production have not emerged in an institutional vacuum, as they are the result of large increases in viticulture (see Chapter 3), which are supported directly and indirectly through several instruments that are seen as helping industry players rather than other stakeholders. These include: the regional allocations of the EU Agricultural Fund for Rural Developments; the regional territorial plan (Piano dell'Assetto del Terrritorio, 2004)[62] and its modifications (the so-called Piano Casa, 2009)[63] that allow new or expansion of buildings in agricultural areas (these are not available in more urban areas); and a 2006 decree stipulating that conversion from non-cultivated areas into intensive cultivation does not require an environmental impact assessment if under ten hectares (Basso and Vettoretto 2020: 8).

These instruments have facilitated an increase in the value of viticultural land, while demand is falling for houses that are contiguous to vineyards due to agro-chemical spraying – leading to new forms of social stratification and some degree of depopulation on the hills. Conflicts are also accentuated by the fact that farmers since 2017 have been exempted from paying a fixed income tax from agricultural land that other land uses incur (Basso and Vettoretto 2020, 14). A recent reform that would have reintroduced this tax spurred protests and direct action by farmers. In February 2024, the national government changed course on its reintroduction.

5.4 'NATURAL' WINES

From a wine landscape perspective, there is very little that is 'natural' in a conventional vineyard – it is a monoculture that suppresses biodiversity and approaches pests and diseases with aggressive agro-chemical management. Viticulture is organized around neatly trained and pruned vines, carefully arranged in linear rows and often supported and shaped by metal or cement poles, metal wires and plastic thread. Harvesting is increasingly done mechanically. Precision viticulture entails the use of sophisticated sensors, irrigation and fertilization systems, and sometimes drones. Winemaking usually requires intervention at every step of the way, from fermentation to bottling. Vineyards and cellars are thus heavily shaped by human hands and technology. So, how can a wine be natural and what does it mean to valorize wine through nature – or, in other words, what does it mean to naturalize wine?

Naturalizing wine is a process of construction of authenticity which is distinct from that operating under a narrower notion of terroir (see Chapter 4), but the two also overlap. It is based on portraying wine as a simple and pure product, where the job of viticulturists and winemakers is to intervene as little as possible – to let nature express itself as much as possible into the wine (Chazal 2024; Inglis 2019; Kaplonski 2019; Smith Maguire 2019). The natural wine movement is in a way a rejection of post-war productivism and interventionism, a countermovement to the industrialization and homogeneization of viticulture and winemaking, and a call for less interventionist approach – where winemakers become stewards over the natural world, rather than the shapers of it (Chazal 2024). But for some, it is also 'an ill-defined and rag-tag movement . . . [that] defines itself just as much by what it stands against, as what it stands for' (Black 2013, 280).

Born in France and heavily influenced by the writings and scientific experiments of Jules Chauvet (Cohen 2013), natural winemaking has spread across Europe and beyond in the past few decades. Because it lacks a legal definition or a certification process, what constitutes natural is negotiated among different actors. It may variously entail organic, biodynamic or 'more natural' viticulture (whether certified or not) and the use of yeasts that are naturally present on grapes to ferment the must (instead of synthetic yeasts). It can also be linked to the rejection or minimization of specific practices: adding sugar before fermentation to heighten alcohol levels (where allowed); fining and filtering techniques; using sulphur to combat unwanted micro-organisms; and/or ageing wine in new wood barrels which impart specific characteristics to a wine (Smith Maguire 2019). Sometimes, these approaches are combined with the use of rediscovered indigenous, and/or less-known, grape varieties. Altogether, this amounts to a reimagination of what constitutes authentic wine, both at the level of discourse and of practice, guided by a set of principles but also constituting a moving target (Cohen 2013; Inglis 2019). Smith Maguire (2019, 179) argues that natural wine is part of an 'omnivorous taste regime that prizes provenance and authenticity'. It is legitimized through transparency (geographical origin but also biographic specificity), heritage (linking to tradition and nostalgia), and genuineness (lack of artifice and disavowing commercial prioritization).

Natural winemaking also entails value struggles around what quality means from an olfactory and visual perspective. Because natural wine is made with little or no sulphur, unwanted yeasts may develop in the wine – giving off funky odours arising from Brettanomyces, for example. While fans defend these characteristics as indicators of nature expressing itself in the glass, these odours and volatile acidity, when predominant, actually tend to obscure the more subtle expressions of nature (Black 2013). Natural wines also tend to be cloudy, thus providing a different aesthetic reference from conventional wines, which are usually clear. Some natural white wines are left to macerate for longer periods of time and are then aged in amphoras, imparting an orange colour and exhibiting higher levels of oxidation. As discussed in Chapter 4, ageing wine in amphoras has experienced a revival in the past decade or so, along with a general movement away from full-body, high alcohol wines and towards more elegant wines that spend less time in new oak barrels. Amphoras, and especially the high-tech versions that are currently circulating in the top-end of the market (and not only in the realm of natural wines), have a much softer impact on the wine. Redefining these organoleptic features and the practices that shape them as attractive is thus a key (re)valuation process for both producers and consumers.

Natural wine shops have become an urban feature in cities such as Montreal, Tokyo and Copenhagen, favouring a specific aesthetics of roughness, messiness and artisanship – and attracting moneyed hipsters who can spend at least €15 for a glass of wine. In these spaces, there is also a conscious breaking away from the conventional language of wine appreciation, for example arguing for the sterility of filtration or using terms such as 'funky' in an appreciative way. In this context, natural wine is seen as honest, made in the vineyard and not manipulated in the cellar. On the one hand, natural wine shops are seen as crafty and entrepreneurial spaces, productive of immaterial and affective labour, and part of the creative industry. On the other hand, they are also often built upon precariousness and immigrant labour.[64]

In Italy, some producers of natural wine have attained cult status in some markets, such as the USA (Black 2013). Natural wine is increasingly visible at trade fairs, such as Vinitaly, but the domestic market is still quite limited. Associations of militant natural wine producers are emerging, such as 'Vini Veri'[65] and 'Triple A' (Artigiani, Artisti, Agricoltori; Italian for 'Artisans, Artists, Farmers').[66] In South Africa, natural wines are a minuscule niche and are not very well known internationally. However, the natural wine movement has sparked a repositioning of previously unremarkable wines, especially in what Chazal (2024) call previously 'empty spaces' of quality – for example in Swartland. Many mainstream wine producers, however, remain sceptical of natural wines. A representative of one of the larger wine producers stated the following during an interview:

> There are natural wines in South Africa, but you will not find them in retail because they are expensive and in my opinion a lot of them are faulty wines that are actually not good. Most of them are just funky ... For example, orange wine is quite oxidated, with long skin contact in maceration. A lot of times this means that it extracts a lot of bad phenolics like cabbage. Still, I think natural wine makers push people to think differently about wine, to go beyond only making cookie-cutter wines ... The natural wine movement creates journalist and media interest ... I think South Africa is making some movements in this area production ... For now, we tell stories about our carbon cutting exercises, we talk about our social and ethical sustainability. We do not have natural wines to offer ... This can be a problem. Thirty-somethings do not want to drink what their fathers and mothers drank, and people in their twenties say they want everything natural.
>
> SAW17

5.5 WINE AND CLIMATE CHANGE

Climate change and related carbon calculation issues are becoming a new frontier of valuation (SAW17, SAW12, IG3, IG7) and will shape value struggles in the years to come. Questions about the carbon footprint of viticulture, winemaking, packaging and logistics have started to be raised by retailers in the past few years, first simply as requests for more information, and more recently by developing requirements to report on carbon emissions along the value chain – in view of future reductions. Systembolaget, for example, is developing a special tender for carbon neutral wine. From a regulatory perspective, the EU is expected to place carbon emission requirements also on imports from outside its block, which may entail decreasing the use of fertilizer, increasing the use of greener sources of electricity and fuel, and lowering the quantity of agro-chemical applications or changing their sources. The EU is also considering applying a border carbon adjustment tax and is pushing forward on environmental labelling. As a result, larger wineries and wholesalers are starting to use carbon calculators. Yet, South African and Italian wine producers still have limited awareness of the importance of carbon footprint.

Drastic changes in weather will also affect grape farming, hence farmers need to adapt (Vink et al. 2012). In South Africa, larger operators are starting to set up solar panels, battery storage and water recycling systems. They are also constructing excess and underground drainage water systems which go into dams and are conducting soil carbon analysis to improve soil health (SAW4, SAW9, SAW17, SAW22). In Italy, carbon calculators are starting to be implemented by larger and more structured wine producers, also as part of a more general embrace of 'Viticulture 4.0' approaches and related subsidies and incentives (see below). However, Italy lacks a collective recognition of these efforts, while South African is already developing a programme and certification system – to which I now turn.

The Confronting Climate Change programme in South Africa

South Africa's Confronting Climate Change (CCC) programme is run by a consulting outfit called Blue North Sustainability, which helps value chain actors to carry out carbon footprint calculations. Originally funded by the UK bilateral aid agency, it was later taken over by the South Africa Department of Agriculture and eventually by the fruit and wine industry bodies – which now own the actual tool. In 2019, it was commercialized and is now run based on a user pays model. The tool is used to generate calculations of carbon emissions along the chain in view of comparing them with benchmarks by region and commodity. It is accompanied by online training tools and local support (SAW12).[67]

A CCC officer told me that this tool is used to help value chain actors to monitor carbon footprints all the way to the harbour overseas: 'Farmers can input data and generate calculations of carbon emissions along the chain, then compare them with benchmarks by region and commodity. At the farm level, carbon calculation is not too complex. Farmers have data on the main headlines, that is fertilizer, electricity, fuel, and agro-chemicals' (SAW12). CCC is also pushing farmers to break down the different uses of fuel so they can better minimize its use. This is to identify hotspots and find solutions. At the cellar level, different business models make it more complex to calculate carbon emissions. The idea behind CCC is that the whole industry should conduct these calculations. But data do not mean anything unless companies adopt a strategy for reducing carbon emissions. Such a strategy requires 3–4 years of data on average to be able to get a proper assessment, because carbon emissions are also related to varying weather conditions (SAW 12).

The Carbon Heroes feature of the CCC programme is used to recognize the journey that the more advanced firms have made in this field. It allocates a label for a period of one or three years depending on the score.[68] The Carbon Heroes label can be used on websites and for marketing and communication purposes but cannot be affixed on the bottle yet. As of 2022, 39% of all cellars had completed the carbon footprint exercise, and 17% of all producers had done so. They get one bonus point in the IPW score. The administratively intensive and costly nature of compliance suggests a need for supporting (smaller) farmers and producers.

Other initiatives in carbon abatement are taking place at the individual company level. One of the major producer-wholesalers in South Africa has started a project on carbon neutral wine, which is part of their social responsibility portfolio. In one of their operations, they are moving towards carbon neutral operations, also by using offsets. So far, they can only say that they are 'carbon responsible' because there is not yet a carbon neutral certification system for food and beverages that is verified by an auditor. Many others are claiming to produce 'carbon neutral' wine already, but there is no clear traceability for these claims yet (SAW 62). One of the major wine exporters in South Africa expressed a sense of frustration with these demands, which is also shared by many others:

> What is the point? Why have a plan if there is no pathway to compliance? The retailers ... will not be able to verify the situation. All our suppliers now have to provide a carbon plan, but it is a box-ticking exercise. Supermarkets are arrogant, they can ask for anything they like. And we need to adapt or die.
>
> SAW 62

New packaging forms and the weight of bottles

South Africa has seen some recent innovations on wine packaging. Bag-in-box (BiB) packaging was launched to deal with surplus wine during the lockdown period of the Covid-19 pandemic and proved to be very popular in the domestic market, together with 1.5 litre wine bottles, wine coolers and low alcohol wines (SAW 5, SAW 13, SAW 34). Canned wine is also emerging. The single serving can appeal to the conscious drinker. It is also suited to outdoors lifestyles. The recyclability of the can makes it appear more environmentally friendly as well. However, so far it has not taken off as much in South Africa as in other countries like the US and the UK (SAW 77). In Italy, BiB consumption is quite limited and is mainly used for exports, especially to the Nordic countries, where there is demand for BiB wine of good quality.

But the most visible discussion related to packaging relates to the weight of bottles (in addition to bulk exports, see Chapter 3). As seen above, SWR has started a glass weight initiative, prompted by demands from the Nordic monopolies to lower the average bottle weight for everyday wine to a maximum of 420 grams, and by the activism of guru wine taster Jancis Robinson. South Africa, however, has serious problems with the supply of glass bottles, of any weight. After the second producer of glass bottles, Nampak Glass, was sold in 2019, the supply of glass bottles in South Africa has been essentially controlled by a quasi-monopolist, Consol Glass. Several concerns were raised by interviewees around the lack of availability of glass bottles and their increasing cost, as all wine producers are directly or indirectly reliant on Consol Glass (SAW1, SAW2, SAW22). As the sales director of a wine estate noted, 'the whole industry is reliant on a monopoly glass supplier – Consol. This is a big, big problem as there is not enough glass' (SAW31; similar views were also expressed in SAW5 and SAW53). Another wine producer highlighted that there was a shortage of see-through bottles in 2022 and because of that, 'you get what you get when it comes to glass' (SAW57).

This glass shortage became even worse during the Covid-19 pandemic as furnaces were shut down and Consol's expansion plans had to be halted due to low demand because of an alcohol sales ban (SAW2, SAW5). Even though the ban was subsequently lifted, and the expansions are continuing, some industry players claim that it will take some time before the supply constraint is eased (SAW19 and 49). This has resulted in upward price pressures for glass. One producer estimated that Consol's prices increased by 14 per cent during the Covid-19 period (SAW5). A lack of adequate supply locally means that glass bottles had to be imported, with possibly negative carbon footprint implications (SAW 17 and SAW 20). However, it is not necessarily the case that imported bottles have a higher carbon footprint. It depends on the energy used to make them (coal in South Africa and China, a renewable energy mix in Germany and other EU countries). Local production, on the other hand, creates local jobs – a key political aspect in South Africa.

Technology and innovation

Spurred by incentives at the national and regional levels, in both Prosecco and Valpolicella many of the larger wine companies are attempting to improve their environmental footprint and impacts on climate change – mainly through technology adoption and innovation linked to the language of Industry 4.0 adapted to viticulture, or Viticulture 4.0. This broad spectrum includes the adoption of mechanical defoliage solutions, precision spraying machines to avoid dispersion of agro-chemicals in the air and what is presented as precision viticulture (digital management of viticulture, geo-differentiated maps, drone-based data collection). Precision viticulture is recommended especially in those morphological contexts, such as the Prosecco and Valpolicella hills, with steep inclines and difficult access to the vineyards – an instance of technology marrying what is popularly referred to as heroic viticulture (see Chapter 4).[69] A similar, techno-focused approach is applied in relation to water management and soil management solutions. In the fields of greenhouse gas emission reduction and energy management solutions, as well as the reuse of by-products and ecological packaging, some companies are making progress. They are moving towards lower-emissions vehicles, LED-based illumination systems, solar panels, geo-thermal energy, cold accumulation systems, ecological materials for packaging, the use of pomace for distillation and pruning biomass for compost, energy and biochar production processes.

In Valpolicella, a large wine producer reported a similar set of approaches:

> We protect the environment with specific agronomic techniques, such as mechanical weed control and the use of pheromones ... We also have a circular economy approach beyond the vineyards. For example, we use thermoregulators for winemaking... One of the main current challenges is related to packaging, especially light glass, recycling and other materials – such as paper instead of aluminium capsules... The monopoly buyers in Scandinavia are pushing hard on materials and packaging. This trend is there, and we cannot ignore it, although demands are very different in other export markets. We follow a logic of continuous improvement.
>
> V2

Another area of innovation is related to the development of varieties that are resistant to certain pests and diseases, and (to a lesser extent) more tolerant of drought. These varieties are not new, as research on resistance had already started in the nineteenth century in relation to phylloxera, but the first hybrids (crosses between *vitis vinifera* and other kinds) exhibited poor organoleptic characteristics at that time. Renewed interest in these hybrids took place in the 1970s and 1980s in Germany, where researchers developed some resistant varieties to fungi. They were able to successfully address these issues and did not encounter strong opposition from producers. In more traditional wine-producing countries there is a stronger focus on preserving wine as the exclusive product of *vitis vinifera* as a way of protecting their terroir and geographical indications (IG12). But given the impact of climate change and increased agro-chemical inputs costs, interest in these hybrid varieties is returning also in countries such as France and Italy. In these hybrids, the genome of *vitis vinifera* provides the organoleptic qualities that are expected in wine, while the other species can provide resistance against powdery mildew and downy mildew.

Efforts on alleviating heat and/or water stress is focused on improving rootstocks on which *vitis vinifera* is grafted, but this strand of research is very recent and will not be commercially available for a while (IG5). An alternative is to adopt species of *vitis vinifera* that do well in hot and dry climates, such as some Greek varieties. But because much of the value of a wine is linked to its grape variety (e.g. Cabernet Sauvignon, Chardonnay), this is a commercially tricky path (IG15). In addition to rootstocks, researchers are also working on better ways of managing the canopy – by adopting specific strategies during green pruning that can help maintain the quality of the grape during hot summers. However, as a researcher involved in these efforts told me, farmers are still too preoccupied with pests and diseases, not enough with environmental stress such as temperature and water ... Also, agro-chemical use and abuse is a major problem: research shows that cover crops can provide important results in relation to water retention. Intensive viticulture is abhorring. There is great variation in relation to water stress among different clones of the same vine species. One could act differently for different clones and optimize the interventions according to different areas. However, industry is not interested in this kind of approach because it entails lower agro-chemical use.

IG15

A second researcher told me that

modern science allows you, in hybrids of fourth and fifth generations, to insert genetic traits from other species that allow an increase in resistance without changing the genome of *vitis vinifera* in sensorial terms ... But then you must convince consumers as well: if you cannot sell these wines, there is no point in improving their resistance, so the commercial part is very important.

IG12

For a third researcher, 'wine producers are interested in resistant varieties because they can decrease agro-chemical application by 70 per cent and so they can save a lot of money, but the EU and the input lobby are pushing a lot for using agro-chemicals instead. The wine industry is responsible for 50 per cent of all agro-chemicals used in agriculture in Europe' (IG5).

The market is currently on the fence. Those who are against hybrids argue that they are contrary to the culture and tradition of winemaking (IG12). There is also the problem of what to call them: they could have a fantasy name or a name that is somewhat similar to the parent variety (such as Cabernet Eidos and Sauvignon Kretos). DOC consorzia in Italy are unlikely to allow any name that is related to their successful wines (such as derivations from Nebbiolo or Prosecco). The hybrid varieties that have been registered so far in Italy can now be vinified (if allowed by regional authorities), but the resulting wine cannot be sold under a DOC denomination, only as IGT.[70] Supporters of these hybrids include some of the most influential wine experts, including the president of a winemaker association, who told me:

The fight against hybrids is a mistake ... Yes, the organoleptic profile of these resistant varieties can be improved, but their rejection is not an option. If you use these clones, you are not 'de-naturing' the wine or the environment. In the vineyard, you can do a lot with mechanical solutions and resistant clones, you do not have to resort to agro-chemicals all the time.

IG4

Several producers I interviewed in Valpolicella have started to plant new vineyards with resistant varieties. One reported that 'you only need two treatments instead of a dozen, it is much better. With organic, every time it rains you need to go out and spray copper ... The extra cost of planting resistant varieties is absorbed in only three years. But we need these varieties to be included in the DOC regulations to really take off' (V19). Another producer reported having made wine from a resistant variety for three years now: 'the organoleptic profile is different but not worse ... And you save money on gasoline and pollute less. They could be very useful when planted in more sensitive areas where spraying is a problem, such as close to homes, schools and cycling paths' (V12).

Wines made from these hybrids are growing in visibility and market acceptance in Germany, where they were first developed. At the ProWein 2023 wine fair, several thematic tasting panels were organized for PIWI wines (fungus resistant varieties in German). At the seminars organized around these events, producers claimed that they make 80 per cent fewer agro-chemical applications, and that around 3 per cent of all viticulture area is currently planted with PIWIs in Germany. Contemporary varieties have more genetic material from *vitis vinifera* than the earlier versions from the 1970s, thus their organoleptic profile has improved. PIWI awards have also been assigned for many years by the association PIWI International[71] Some varieties have been designed to delay their ripening period, allowing longer and slower ripening that improves their quality. This is one of the problems of regular varieties, which are now ripening faster and earlier and yield grapes with high sugars but poor aroma. With climate change, farmers of regular varieties are unable to solve this problem unless they move up in altitude with their new plantings. But these areas may not be available or can entail new deforestation. PIWI producers argue that young consumers are very interested in minimizing the environmental and climate impacts of wine production, and that PIWI wines can be a market to fulfil these demands.[72]

These sets of observations suggest that there are important technological innovation dynamics at play in response to climate change, especially among large operators. The big difference between Italy and South Africa is not the quality of research (which is quite advanced in both countries),[73] but that in Italy various layers of government provide important incentives for the purchase of Viticulture 4.0 technology. In South Africa, this support is lacking. As a result, the incorporation of these technologies in viticulture and winemaking is not widespread, also because of the crisis of profitability in viticulture. At the same time, some of the larger players in South Africa are taking a strategic approach to climate change from a risk management perspective. One of the large producer-wholesalers, for example, has carried out a climate change study to assess the probability of quality non-compliance by its suppliers – in view of securing their portfolio of grape and wine supplies at the specified volumes, styles and quality. This company is also putting together related product innovation and mitigation activities and monitoring meteorological data for all wine-producing districts in South Africa. Its team of viticulturists has estimated the likely impact of climate change on quality, yield and style. For example, higher temperatures affect the sugar level in Sauvignon Blanc grapes, changing both yields and styles. This means that the company may have to start sourcing from a cooler area. It is also carrying out adaptation measures, using modelling tools to adjust actual practices in the vineyard – such as pruning techniques, adoption of cover crops to manage moisture retention, irrigation, rootstock treatments – and is considering switching to cultivars that are resistant to specific diseases and/or drought.

> If we do nothing, we estimate that we could lose 25–30 per cent of the yield. We work with our suppliers to develop joint planning, forecasting and information exchange. But the rest of the industry is not quite there yet. We do it because it is part of our due diligence practice, it's a standard operating procedure. There is a big vacuum in the South African industry, which is only now starting to consider these issues.
>
> SAW49

5.6 THE LIMITED VALORIZATION OF SUSTAINABILITY AT WINE TRADE FAIRS

Trade fairs offer an opportunity for wine producers and marketers to valorize their approaches to wine styles, aesthetics, branding and environmental sustainability through direct communication to a specialist audience. From a research perspective, it is therefore an ideal space to discern what kind of approach wine companies take in communicating different kinds of values to their commercial buyers (these trade fairs are not open to the public, so this is not consumer marketing). I attended four wine fairs for this purpose: CapeWine 2022 in Cape Town, South Africa (in collaboration with Reena Das Nair and Shingie Chisoro); Vinitaly on two occasions (2022 and 2024) in Verona, Italy (see Image 13) and ProWein 2023 in Dusseldorf, Germany (widely considered *the* global wine trade fair). At each site, among other fieldwork activities, I/we carried out a one-by-one inspection of all relevant exhibitor stands that had been set up by individual or groups of wine producers and marketers. I took note of whether there was any visual communication embedded in the features of the stand and/or on the bottles – and what kind of representation was used (a logo, pictures, overall design, videos). I approached sustainability communication in broad terms, including environmental, social and transformation issues (thus these observations are also relevant to the findings included in Chapter 6). However, I took a narrow focus in relation to delivery: I only analysed the stand design and/or the bottle label as an immediate communication device, rather than the brochures that may or may not have been visible or available.

The overall theme of the CapeWine 2022 fair in South Africa was 'Sustainability 360 – Better wine for a better future', which indicated the strategic intent on the part of industry bodies to highlight South Africa as a supplier of sustainable wine to trade journalists, to the political system, and especially to wine buyers (both domestic and international). Given this overall framing, it is relatively unsurprising that the sustainability thematic focus was embedded in the general marketing material and that the visual presentation of the trade fair was organized explicitly around social, environmental and transformation issues in the South African wine industry. The collective visual design of the exhibition space also included

Image 13 Main design of the Veneto pavilion at Vinitaly 2024. Source: Author.

many banners highlighting the many sustainability initiatives that are active in this sector.

As stated by the CEO of WOSA, Siobhan Thompson, during the opening seminar, the wine 'industry is facing a lot of uncertainties caused by drought and climate change and this is what this conference is all about – developing a framework of sustainability. The theme for this year's fair is Sustainability 360 and it comprises all three pillars – planet, people and prosperity'.[74] CapeWine 2022 included a rich programme of seminars and thematic tastings around sustainability – including sessions on transformation, organic and biodynamic wines, regenerative viticulture, biodiversity conservation, fair trade, old vines and canned wine.

Out of around 450 exhibitors at CapeWine 2022, 61 (or 13.5 per cent of the total) visually communicated one or another aspect of sustainability in their exhibition stands. While this proportion is significant, it is far from indicating a mainstreaming of sustainability communication. However, this does not mean that the other exhibitors do not practice sustainability one way or another, only that they chose not to communicate it at the fair. Of the 61 that communicated sustainability, 41 did so through only one signifier (a logo, a picture, some writing on the stand itself), 17 with two signifiers, and only three with three or more – for a total of 98 sustainability signifiers. Only two exhibitors designed the whole stand to primarily communicate sustainability. Some of the others did so primarily through selected images or storytelling on posters/writings/back-label of wine bottles (a total of 19). The large majority, however, communicated sustainability only through the logos of existing initiatives without additional information or storytelling (40). In terms of thematic areas, most stands focused narrowly on single issues related to conservation (21) and old vine certification (17), others focused on transformation/social issues (7) or organic and other environmental issues (6); the rest took a broad/comprehensive approach to sustainability (10). In general, these can be interpreted as relatively light forms of engagement in sustainability communication, when done at all.

Sustainability as a theme did not feature as prominently at Vinitaly 2022. Very few seminars were offered on this topic. In terms of incidence of sustainability communication by individual producers with exhibition stands at the fair, the picture emerging is actually similar to the one at CapeWine 2022. I used the same system of observation and recording of sustainability communication at both fairs. At Vinitaly, I applied it to all Prosecco and Valpolicella exhibition stands in the Veneto pavilions (thus I did not examine those located in the dedicated organic pavilion). Only 16 per cent of all stands in the Veneto pavilions had any signalling of sustainability (30 out of 184). When there was signalling at all, reference to one or another certification or logo was the preferred method (22 instances). Only three stands featured more than one logo. Organic certification was the most featured logo (13 instances), followed by BWA (on biodiversity, six), Equalitas (broader sustainability approach including social issues, four), SQNPI (focus on integrated production, three), and V.I.V.A. (broader sustainability, one). Only eight stands had any story communicated on sustainability, and only two of these were designed mainly around sustainability issues. The thematic focus was almost exclusively on

Image 14 The 'organic world' space at ProWein. Source: Author.

environmental issues (except for the four instances where Equalitas or V.I.V.A. logos were displayed). Italian wine marketers obviously do not think they face social and labour challenges or, if they do, they would rather not talk about it (see Chapter 6).

A similar picture emerged at Vinitaly 2024, where 26 stands had signalling of sustainability out of 179 (less than 15 per cent). But this time, almost all of them only communicated sustainability through one or another logo, and only four had any other text or image that drew attention to sustainability issues. Even the few that had adopted a sustainability thematic framing in 2022 subsequently toned down this kind of visual messaging in 2024. The stands of consortia that claim to take sustainability seriously (including the two Prosecco consortia and the Valpolicella consortium) had no explicit visual or textual reference to sustainability in their dedicated spaces at the fair. Veneto region's motto ('Veneto, natural intelligence', see Image 13) featured prominently, but natural intelligence here was meant as a pun vis-à-vis artificial intelligence. It was not a concern with nature. Finally, at Vinitaly 2024, there was only one seminar focused on sustainability issues, and even then, it was on the impact of climate change on the organoleptic characteristics of wine.

While the proportion of exhibitors engaging in sustainability communication in their domestic fairs was similar in the two countries, it is clear that South Africa has a longer history of engagement in sustainability standards and certification in wine, and a much more diversified set of sustainability stories to tell. Also, while in the South African wine fair, organic and other sustainability-featured wines were an integral part of the regular pavilions, in Italy, organic and biodynamic wines were featured mostly in a specialized space on their own, signalling that concerns with sustainability may not be well integrated with the everyday operations of most mainstream wine operators.

Finally, in 2023, I applied the same methodology at ProWein, which is generally considered the most important global wine trade fair. Overall, the little that was flagged on sustainability (organics, biodynamics, natural wines) was placed in a special 'organic and biodynamic' area that covered half of one of the thirteen halls used for the expo (see Image 14). The ProWein program of seminars and thematic tastings featured very little sustainability content, although the term itself was included in some titles, without relevant content to follow. The only exceptions were a few special tasting events of resistant grape varieties, a seminar on sustainability in Prosecco and a seminar run by the Sustainable Wine Roundtable.

South Africa's exhibition space at ProWein was placed in the same pavilion with other New World producers. The common aesthetic, branding and messaging organized by WOSA did contain some sustainability content (depictions of the SA sustainability and integrity seal, pictures of happy farmworkers), but much of the focus was on beauty (pictures of proteas, tourist attractions, Cape Dutch architecture) and on attractive images of viticulture and winemaking (pristine vineyard landscapes, bunches of grapes, interiors of wine cellars and piles of oak barrels; see some examples in Image 15). Beyond the collective branding exercise, the proportion of individual South African exhibitors which signalled one or another form of sustainability (14 out of about 100 exhibitors) was fairly similar to that observed at CapeWine 2022. Only two had the whole stand designed to attract

Image 15 South Africa's collective designs at ProWein. Source: Author.

attention to sustainability. Strangely, very little effort was dedicated to presenting the unique offering that South Africa can provide, Heritage Vine certification.

Italy had a series of distinct regional themes and designs instead of a unitary message at ProWein. The Valpolicella consortium's campaign (at ProWein and more generally) was framed around love (*amore*), given its proximity to Verona of Romeo and Juliet. The DOCG Prosecco consortium featured its UNESCO heritage recognition, while the Prosecco DOC consortium focused on 'Italian genius' and related 'art of living'. All in all, a clear conclusion is that sustainability communication for South Africa played a lesser role at ProWein than at CapeWine, while for Italy (Prosecco and Valpolicella) it had a low profile both at ProWein and Vinitaly. This is odd, given the amount of attention that sustainability is receiving from regulators, the media and consumers. Overall, the observations provided in this section suggest that concerns with environmental sustainability (and thus the value of nature) are not paramount in mainstream professional circles where wine sellers and buyers meet, such as wine trade fairs.

5.7 WORLDS OF VALUATION AND VALUE STRUGGLES RELATED TO NATURE

In the following discussion, I return to the analytical framework of worlds of valuation to make theoretical sense of the empirical observations provided in this

Table 12 Worlds of valuation and value struggles in wine (nature)

	Worlds of valuation (general)					
	Market	Industrial	Domestic	Civic	Inspired	Opinion
Common principle	Competition	Efficiency	Traditional benevolence	Collective solidarity	Spiritual or creative enhancement	Fame
Units of valuation	Product units	Plans, systems, controls, forecasts	Specific assets	Negotiation, consultation, distributional arrangements	Innovation, creation	Public relations, brand names, social media recognition
Questions underpinning valuation processes	Is it economic?	Is it technically efficient, scalable, functional?	Does it follow tradition? Can it be trusted?	Is it collectively safe, healthy, socially and environmentally sound?	Is it new or unique? Is it a breakthrough?	Is it accepted by the public/consumers?
Valuation focus	Price	Scalability, and proper functionality	Trust, history, repetition	Social, labour, environmental, collective impacts	Creativity, novelty, personality	Renown, visibility

	Worlds of valuation in wine (nature)					
Valuation focus	Good/service, form of capital	Managed, functional	Proximate, conserved	Available to all, provider of collective services	Aesthetic, emotional	Mobilized by celebrities and experts, through SoMe
Value struggles						
Regulation & governance	x	x	(x)	(x)		
Ecology, conservation, beauty	(x)	(x)	x	x	x	
'Natural wines'	(x)	(x)			x	
Climate change	x	x				x

Legend: x = currently dominant world(s) (darker shading); (x) = antagonistic world(s) underpinning value struggles (lighter shading)
Source: Own elaboration.

chapter (see summary in Table 12). One of the most relevant debates in the sociology of value and valuation is whether there is an underlying and coherent logic that makes up a specific 'green' world of valuation (Blok 2013; Centemeri 2023; Lafaye and Thévenot 2017; Latour 1998). Blok (2013) argues that green arguments seem to need constant reassertion in view of conflicting interpretations of the value of nature. Likewise, Chiapello (2013, 74) contends that 'ecological criticism is highly adaptable to all regimes' and has no preference for any particular political model, thus making it unsuitable as a world on its own. Drawing on pioneering work by Godard (1990), Plumecocq (2023) argues that valuations of nature can be usefully analysed through the existing six worlds delineated by Boltanski and Thévenot (2006), rather than constituting their own green world. I concur with these arguments and therefore in Table 12, I draw from Plumecocq's work to identify different worlds of valuation related to nature (summarized in the line 'valuation focus') and how they can explain various value struggles in wine.

In a *market* world of valuation, nature is treated like a commodity (even when fictional), such as in 'ecosystem services' or 'environmental good' (Plumecocq 2023). Nature is the object of a market transaction, and its valuation can be attached to the willingness to pay for accessing a site or a landscape, or safeguarding wildlife or biodiversity. Nature can also be seen as a form of capital valued through its price (e.g. raw materials). In an *industrial* world, the valuation of nature is carried out by assessing the most efficient way of using it functionally (e.g. minimizing the cost of water for irrigation, rather than valuing it for its beauty when accumulating in a lake). Environmental concerns in the industrial world are managed through procedures, codes of conduct, standards and/or certifications. In a *domestic* world, the valuation of nature is related to proximity and conservation, often wrapped around discourses of heritage and historical landscape preservation. In a *civic* world, nature is valued in relation to whether it is free and available to everyone, whether it serves the common good and/or whether it provides collective (non-marketized) services – such as parks or freely accessible landscapes, or biodiversity conservation that benefits broad ecosystems. In an *inspired* world, the valuation of nature relates to the emotional responses it generates from aesthetics and spirituality (e.g. the beauty of a landscape, the quality of life facilitated by regenerative agriculture), sometimes in relation to an emblematic plant or animal. Finally, in a world of *opinion*, the valuation of nature is mobilized through public opinion (Plumecocq 2023; see also Plumecocq et al. 2018), including in social media and through support by celebrities (e.g. Brad Pitt), well-known organizations (e.g., Greenpeace) and/or famous experts (e.g. Jane Goodhall).

In the empirical analysis of wine value struggles related to nature carried out in this chapter, four sometimes overlapping layers have emerged: first, struggles around environmental concerns that are regulated and governed through standards, codes of conduct and certifications; second, in relation to ecology, beauty and the imperatives of biodiversity conservation; third, around debates on the meaning of natural wines; and fourth, concerning climate change adaptation and mitigation – including the role of innovation and technology in facilitating these processes.

Regulation and governance

Regulation and governance of nature through broad sustainability certifications in wine can be seen as instruments of an *industrial* world of valuation, even though they do not yet coalesce into a globally recognized set of principles and standards. Because certifications are increasingly required by retailers as a condition for market entry in specific wine segments, they also draw partially from a *market* world, as they provide a competitive advantage (mostly market entry, but occasionally also a price premium). A key value struggle in this realm concerns the future survival of more local control on how to manage nature through regional and national governance systems (such as SQNPI and V.I.V.A. in Italy; and IPW in South Africa) – given the decoupling from place-based specificities that the emergence of a global standard such as SWR would entail. In other words, these concerns relate to a possible weakening of a *domestic* world of valuation and the strengthening of a *market/industrial* compromise, as broad certifications are becoming minimum requirements and the Nordic alcohol monopolies (and other retailers copying them) develop matrices of mutual recognition and equivalence among existing certification systems. A similar dynamic is taking place also through the increasing environmental demands that are being embedded in regulation (e.g. in Italy through the potential EU ban on some agro-chemicals, but also in South Africa through the expansion of IPW into environmental issues beyond integrated management). The key actors involved in these struggles are, on the one hand, the Nordic monopolies (and increasingly other retailers) and the financial sector, which are seeking common/global systems and indicators to manage environmental sustainability equally across jurisdictions. On the other hand, we find national or regional sustainability certification systems that are seeking to keep a more local and diversified character to environmental management.

Another dimension of value struggle related to regulation and governance sees many grape and wine producers resisting the increasing pressures to certify, whether the certifications are global or local. Many grape and wine producers express frustration at being asked to deliver 'greener' grapes and wine without gaining clear financial benefits beyond maintaining market access. This resistance is taking place with substantial political and institutional support in Italy, while in South Africa it takes a more diffuse dynamic. The main moral claim leveraged in this struggle is one of survival of farming as a profitable economic activity (in both countries) – and harks to *domestic* and *civic* worlds of valuation based on the preservation of a traditional economic activity and the collective benefits it provides to rural areas that otherwise would be abandoned (especially in Italy). A third dimension is more specific to Italy and sees local communities protesting what they perceive as the excessive and indiscriminate spraying of agro-chemicals close to residential areas, and the deforestation of tracts of land for viticulture expansion. This kind of resistance is based on *civic* valuations as they highlight the impact of nefarious practices on the collective health of a community or landscape.

Ecology, biodiversity conservation and beauty

A second layer of value struggle related to nature revolves around ecology, biodiversity conservation and beauty. Biodynamic viticulture/winemaking and biodiversity conservation are built upon a compromise of *inspired* and *civic* worlds of valuation, with an element of *domestic* valuation embedded in the idea 'proximate nature'. *Inspired* valuation surfaces through the spiritual dimensions of Steiner's approach to regenerative agriculture, and discourses of beauty related to practices and perceived norms of how a vineyard should look. *Civic* valuation appears through the stewardship of nature and its biodiversity – not only for the health of soils and the vineyard per se, but for the balance of overall ecologies. Civic valuations are also leveraged in organic viticulture, but these are becoming marginalized by a *market/industrial* compromise based on certification and fulfilling market demand. This is happening to a lesser extent also in certified biodynamic wines.

The main value struggles related to biodynamic and organic viticulture and winemaking are happening around claims of wholeness and ecological balance by biodynamic operators vis-à-vis the power of science at the service of efficiency and competitiveness. This is reflected in accusations of esoterism levelled by mainstream winemakers and their associations against biodynamic farmers. These debates also spill over into characterizations of the appropriate scale of production in both vineyard and cellar, different kinds of vineyard training systems (e.g. between *pergola veronese* and Guyot in Valpolicella), and the use of machinery and irrigation in the vineyard – with substantial support in favour of intensive systems from mainstream institutions and the agro-chemical industry.

While the conservation of biodiversity and landscapes is an important component of organic and especially biodynamic wines, it is also part of valorization processes in conventional wines through certification systems such as the WWF Conservation Champions programme in South Africa and the World Biodiversity Association certification system in Italy. Marketization and selling stories wrapped around nature conservation are also very common in South Africa, where 'diversity' (of nature and people) is the main motto of the apex wine institution, and where wealthy or corporate owners of wine estates can afford to set aside large tracts of land for conservation in view of preserving *fynbos* and the rich diversity of the CFK. In Italy, biodiversity concerns tend to revolve around the defence of commercial autochthonous varieties (such as Corvina in Valpolicella) and less around the biodiversity of larger ecosystems, although some interest is also detectable in rediscovering old and commercially abandoned varieties. Conservation issues are also embedded in initiatives for the preservation of cultural landscapes, as seen in the case of the UNESCO heritage recognition of the Prosecco Hills of Conegliano and Valdobbiadene (see Chapter 4).

Natural wine

A third layer of value struggle operates around ideas and practices of natural wine, a construction of authenticity that is distinct from that leveraged under the narrower notion of terroir (see Chapter 4) – although the two also overlap. Natural wine is valorized for being a simple and 'pure' product, where the job of viticulturists and winemakers is to intervene as little as possible and let nature express itself in the wine. Natural winemakers and marketers do not want to conform to mainstream valuation discourses and often seek to rely on the inspirational personality of celebrity natural winemakers – thus leveraging a compromise between *inspiration* and *opinion* worlds. The beauty of nature here is intended as a general aesthetic, not necessarily a proximate one based on a *domestic* world of valuation.

One of the contradictions of natural wines is that even if they are promoted as hyper-local, they may be sold in global markets and shipped to distant destinations, often through a kind of anti-brand branding (Chazal 2024). Some critics also contend that natural wines actually betray place. They claim that without human intervention these wines may all actually taste the same because they exhibit the same typical faults – an unintended homogenization outcome (Inglis 2019, 40). We can interpret these aspects as a creeping of *market/industrial* dynamics into the proud *inspiration/opinion* compromise that underpins valuation in natural wines. Finally, we should note that natural wine usually results in more work, rather than less – given the heightened level of attention needed to avoid negative outcomes both in the vineyards and the cellar (Cohen 2013). In their focus on minimizing technology and connecting with the winemaker, natural wine discourses can obscure the role of migrant workers, who are overshadowed by narratives of the small family farm and the dedicated artisan making wine. We can then observe a double movement – the valorization of the work nature does in shaping the wine, and the concurrent devalorization of the hidden human work entailed in making wine more 'natural' (more on this in Chapter 6).

Climate change

A fourth and final layer of value struggle is related to climate change. Current approaches to climate change in wine are primarily focused on adaptation strategies, and much less so on mitigation – except for diatribes on the importance of lighter-weight bottles and emerging concerns with minimizing carbon emissions. An *industrial* logic of valuation is dominant in this field, with a substantial component of technical innovation (often embedded in so-called Viticulture 4.0 discourses). This is confirmed by the current focus on measuring and decreasing carbon emissions, and on adopting resistant varieties. Some of these measures are being included in carbon (and broader sustainability) certification initiatives, thus leaning partially on a *market* world as well. But climate change poses fundamental challenges to viticulture and winemaking that would require more collective responses, which could be based on a *civic* world of valuation but are currently lacking. Rising temperatures are reshaping what grape varieties should be planted where, and with what canopy management systems. Weather conditions are becoming more erratic and water for irrigation scarcer.

For vineyards that are already planted, harvests are happening earlier, grapes are ripening faster and lack acidity. Quicker ripening also raises labour challenges where grapes are harvested by hand (see Chapter 6). New areas that used to be unsuitable for grape growing are now being exploited (parts of Denmark and Holland, for example), with large Champagne houses investing in new sparkling wine production on the southern coast of England, which has similar soil characteristics to Champagne. Yet, these responses are happening as if climate change did not challenge the actual survival of wine in many current production locations.

5.8 CONCLUSION

The typical global capitalist pressure to maintain or increase efficiency and competitiveness, and the underlying compromise of market/industrial worlds of valuation that underpin it, is becoming more dominant in value struggles around nature. This compromise is prevailing in relation to value struggles around the regulation and governance of environmental concerns, where they are displacing the role of domestic and civic worlds of valuation. An industrial logic is also prevailing in response to climate change. Domestic/civic compromises are still playing a major role in value struggles around ecology, biodiversity conservation and beauty, and inspired/opinion compromises in natural wines. However, these two realms refer to niche phenomena, and market/industrial valuation logics are creeping into them as well. The result of these struggles will determine to what extent environmental concerns will be used for the further homogenization of wine offerings (and the strengthening of a market/industrial compromise) or as an extra source of diversification alongside or in combination with terroir (safeguarding the domestic and civic elements of valuation). The relative invisibility of environmental concerns in wine trade fairs suggests that the market/industrial compromise is having the upper hand. The relegation of biodynamic, organic and natural wines to their own 'special pavilions' at these fairs suggests that they are still seen as a somewhat separate phenomenon from mainstream winemaking – despite increasing market demand and the threat of climate change.

In combination with the findings on value struggles related to place presented in Chapter 4, these observations entail that nature is becoming an important site of value struggle. The role that terroir has historically played in attempting to retain diversification, segmentation and uniqueness for decades is to an extent being replaced by, or integrated with, valuation concerns related to the environment, biodiversity, climate change and naturalness. On the one hand, environmental stewardship could bring mainstream wines closer to the philosophy of terroir. On the other hand, it could indicate a process of naturalization of wine more generally, and thus a further delinking of production from place (Teil et al. 2011). The human element of intimate knowledge and artisanship that is embedded in terroir is lost when general environmental concerns become predominant – and especially when they are codified in global standards, codes of conduct and certification systems. Larger and more generic geographical denominations have watered down the uniqueness of site and very specific terroirs. Likewise, the certification and mainstreaming of environmental sustainability is providing new venues for re-homogenization processes.

Chapter 6

PEOPLE (CLASS, RACE AND GENDER)

6.1 INTRODUCTION

In the previous two chapters, I have shown that place and nature are two key sites of value struggle in wine. Place and environmental protection and conservation can be used, at least nominally, against the tendential globalization and homogenization of wine and in favour of better economic and environmental conditions of production. This is better achieved when place is valorized through regulatory and institutional interventions that are at least partly driven and controlled by (small-scale) producers. But environmental sustainability initiatives, especially when driven by large wine merchants and retailers, create important operational and financial burdens on smaller wine producers and especially on grape farmers. These burdens can be best overcome when a price premium is paid for wine that has been produced in environmentally conscious ways. However, these premia in practice are rarely paid. In this chapter, I examine the composite value struggles that operate around the qualification of people, both as labourers (thus in terms of social and work conditions of production) and as owners of material and intellectual property. In other words, this chapter is about unpacking class, race and gender intersectionality to properly understand struggles around the valuation of people (Heinich 2022).[1]

That the labour and social conditions of farmworkers in agriculture are problematic is an established fact, not only in South Africa but also in other countries in both the Global North and the Global South. Wine is no exception to this. Accordingly, a large critical literature has highlighted how surplus value is extracted from farm labour by capital – many of these contributions engaging with Marx's labour theories of value and derivative reflections. In parallel to this, a rich debate has also emerged on racial capitalism and post-coloniality (see Chapter 2). In wine, these aspects have been examined mainly in relation to racialized labour in South Africa. Labour in the wine industry is clearly gendered and racialized elsewhere as well – although outside South Africa race is usually subsumed under discussions on immigrant labour, seasonal labour and indentured/modern slavery labour. As seen in previous chapters, racialized labour fetishism is clearly at play in wine tourism, where the valorization of place and of nature are built on hiding people of colour from view – even though they do much of the manual labour in vineyards and cellars.

In the first part of this chapter, I highlight some of the value struggles operating around social and labour conditions in viticulture and winemaking.[2] Given the focus on farmworkers and lower-skill cellar workers, this is an implicit discussion of class – intertwined with race and gender. I place this analysis in the context of the legacy of labour exploitation under apartheid in South Africa, but also argue that in different guises these issues are relevant in other wine-producing countries as well. I show how these concerns are typically managed through various certifications that include social and ethical components, thus continuing the analysis of environmental aspects of sustainability certifications started in Chapter 5. In the second part of this chapter, I examine changes (or lack thereof) in racialized and gendered patterns of ownership and control in South African wine, where the state is pushing the industry to (racially) transform under the rubric of so-called 'Black Economic Empowerment' (BEE). This is also a reflection on class through the analysis of which social groups are benefitting from these initiatives – a new 'empowered' capitalist class vis-à-vis small entrepreneurs and farmworkers. At the end of the chapter, I interpret the empirical findings through the worlds of valuation framework in view of combining the insights of value struggles around people with those related to place and nature in the final chapter of the book.

6.2 RACIALIZED AND GENDERED LABOUR EXPLOITATION IN WINE

Labour relations in South Africa and Italy[3]

Labour relations on wine farms in South Africa cannot be understood without acknowledging their historical roots in slavery, paternalism and neo-paternalism (Du Toit 2002; Ewert and Du Toit 2005; Ewert and Hamman 1999) and gender discrimination (Barrientos 2019; Bell 2022; Greenberg 2013). Labour arrangements on wine farms after the end of slavery in the 1830s and up to the 1980s have been described in the literature as 'authentic, undiluted paternalism' (Ewert and Hamman 1999, 208) – a mixture of punishment and rewards, with workers receiving social dividends (housing, water, electricity) in exchange for low wages, no unionization, the part-payment of wages in alcohol (the infamous *tot* system) and generally appalling working conditions (McEwan and Bek 2009b, 2006; Nugent 2024a; Williams 2016), especially for women (Bek, McEwan and Bek 2007; Bell 2022). In the 1980s, initiatives for the 'social upliftment' of farmworkers aimed at reducing the social costs of this system and at improving productivity and the poor image of the industry – but failed in ending sanctions. Rather than transforming labour relations, they created a kind of 'neo-paternalism' – a combination of modern and paternalist farm management (Ewert and Du Toit 2005; Kruger, Du Toit and Ponte 2006).

These racialized and gendered power relations of subjection and dependency existed not only on farms – white power was also embodied in local government and agricultural institutions through (mostly male) membership and control of cellars, producer cooperatives, and financial institutions (Du Toit 1993). One important legacy from this past was the development of a complex regulatory system managed by KWV, which included planting quotas, buying surplus wine, establishing minimum prices, and other instruments that protected farmers from price pressures and the vagaries of the market (Howson, Murray and Overton 2020; Nugent 2024a). A second legacy was the perpetuation of a paternalistic, misogynist and racialized labour regime that saw Black workers as minors, subject to the sovereign authority and protection of white masters, and which denied them the protection of any but the most basic rights (Du Toit, Kruger and Ponte 2008). This entailed that farmworkers were cast not as the victims of white power but rather of alcohol abuse itself – and of pregnant women's drinking habits, which led to high incidences of foetal alcohol syndrome. Discourses of improvement were therefore linked (and to a large extent still are) to development projects rather than to addressing the structural power of white male domination (Du Toit, Kruger and Ponte 2008).[4]

The political transition of the 1990s brought the new democratically elected African National Congress government into power. Labour and employment legislation was lifted up to a minimum ILO level and beyond, and a burst of union activity started to take place in agriculture. At the same time, farm owners started to casualize and externalize labour recruitment in order to mitigate the consequences of increased labour costs and the costs of complying with new labour legislation (Ewert and Hamman 1999; Kruger, Du Toit and Ponte 2006). They cut down their permanent workforce, adopted technologies and mechanization that minimized the need for manual labour, and started restricting job security through hiring younger workers (Ewert and Du Toit 2005; Ewert and Hamman 1999). This movement towards the minimization of a permanent labour force and the casualization of (especially female) unskilled and low-skilled labour is not confined to the wine industry. It is part of a wider process in South Africa that is taking place in other labour-intensive sectors as well. These casual workers are excluded from the basic entitlements that permanent workers have now gained and face higher livelihood vulnerability and insecurity (Alford 2020; Alford, Visser and Barrientos 2021; Barrientos 2019; Kritzinger, Barrientos and Rossouw 2004).

In short, plenty of research has confirmed that labour conditions for farmworkers remain very problematic in post-apartheid South Africa (Bek, McEwan and Bek 2007; Devereux 2020; Ewert and Du Toit 2005; McEwan and Bek 2006, 2009b; Nelson, Martin and Ewert 2005).[5] This literature has also shown that female workers are concentrated in lower-paid, more fragmented and insecure employment – and that they are still subjected to gender-based intimidation, multiple forms of violence, and discrimination (Bell 2022; Devereux 2020; Eriksson 2018; Greenberg 2013). This situation is continuing even following a number of initiatives targeted at improving it, including a spate of adversarial actions from farmworker unions and women-oriented NGOs, such as Women on Farms (Alford 2020; Alford, Visser and Barrientos 2021; Barrientos 2013; Eriksson 2018; Howson et al. 2023). The weakening of labour power emerging from casualization has been compounded by a wave of mechanization in grape farming and agriculture more generally. As the winemaker of an estate put it: 'While a decade ago it was still cheaper to use manual labour than machines, now the reverse is true' (SAW56). Farm labour struggles play out not only through discussions on sustainability standards and codes of conduct (see below) but also through local protests, strikes and activism, via international media and NGO exposure.[6] Occasionally, farmworkers' storytelling (placed on websites or the label on wine bottles) is also used to stake claims of ethicality (Smith Maguire 2019).

Many of the wine producers I interviewed in South Africa are clearly frustrated by more adversarial actions, and especially by what they perceive as the incessant negative media exposure of their industry internationally. They recognize the underlying problems but frame this level of attention as unfair vis-à-vis the problematic labour conditions of (often illegal) immigrants in Italy, Spain and California. The media and NGOs, however, have shown increasing interest in the labour conditions of grape farms in Italy as well. Most recently, an Oxfam report[7] for the Swedish monopoly buyer Systembolaget chronicled human rights violations in selected wine farms in four regions of Italy. It reports instances of health and safety risks, excessive working hours, instances of forced labour, restrictions of freedom of association, and poor, unsafe and unsanitary housing – together with low wages, lack of access to remedy, gender discrimination and discrimination against migrant workers. The report places these findings in the context of widespread labour rights challenges in Italian agriculture more generally. 'About 1,500 agricultural workers died in Italy between 2013 and 2019 because of exploitative working conditions. While the labour force is a mixture of Italian citizens and migrants, the number of migrants working in agriculture has increased by 90 per cent in the past decade'.[8] Although the Oxfam report did not examine producers in the Veneto region, it highlights that some of these issues are found not only in southern Italy (Sicilia, Puglia) but also in Toscana and Piemonte, regions that have received less scrutiny on labour conditions in farms. According to Oxfam, low wages, excessive overtime and lack of adequate access to remedy are spread across all four regions. And 'cases of labour exploitation have also been detected in the north, where grapes are harvested mainly by migrant workers ... under conditions that have been described as close to slavery'.[9]

There is also a clear gender dimension to labour exploitation in Italian vineyards. For example, the death of a 49-year-old female grape picker in 2015 led to media attention and a police investigation. The investigation unveiled what

> authorities, labour experts and union organizers described as an elaborate system of modern-day slavery – involving more than 40,000 Italian women, as well as migrant and seasonal labourers ... [Women are] favoured because of their smaller, nimble hands ... Farm owners regularly paid middlemen to [transport them to the farms]. Sometimes, the middlemen pocket two-thirds of the women's pay and deduct transportation costs. Five-hour trips are not counted on the clock.[10]

Waves of illegal immigration have also been related to the increasing employment of undocumented workers in vineyards in southern Italy (Valente and Seifert 2018).

As the representative of a wine sustainability initiative told me in an interview:

> There is a wall of silence in the wine sector in Italy, a lot of decorative façade. It is a cunning world, where everything is beautiful and everyone is good. But because there is pressure for better transparency, things are now changing, especially in relation to social issues and employment conditions ... We still have serious problems with labour exploitation, not only in the south but also in regions where we produce our most famous wines. We need more self-criticism. Instead of reacting to scandals, we should deal with labour issues proactively to create opportunities for improvement, growth and development.
>
> IG13

A Prosecco wine producer highlighted the labour recruitment challenges they face:

> All farms use immigrant labour, it is an important resource. During Covid, many seasonal labourers could not come to Italy, and this created huge problems ... We use labour cooperatives, which provide up to 200–300 workers at a time. They are all trained by these cooperatives ... Recently, relatives of farmers have been allowed again by labour regulation to work in the vineyards like in the past, but under some conditions.
>
> P2

Another said that

> it is very difficult to find labourers and to give them proper contracts ... In small farms, many manual labour operations are made by farmers and their families. Up to five hectares, we can make do with family labour, even for pruning and harvesting. It is the larger farms that hire contract labourers ... Some of the bigger producers in the flatlands have invested in mechanical harvesting to manage this problem – one machine does the job of 100 harvesters.
>
> P5

The apparent problem in finding workers is compounded by climate change: 'The harvesting season has been shortening because of the heat. It now lasts fifteen days, in the past it was up to thirty days. So, you need to do the same job in fewer days, meaning you need more workers for shorter periods' (P1). In other words, climate change is also making labour management even more complex and susceptible to exploitation.

A representative of a labour union of farmworkers in the Veneto region stated in an interview:

> The current approach in Prosecco is towards industrial agriculture – maximization of production, high intensity of agro-chemical application ... Value creation is not transferred to the broader community or workers. Wineries make a lot of money, workers do not. Many workers come to the union to report

that many hours are paid outside their salary slip, and not everyone receives a slip. When immigrant workers use a tractor, they are often paid as unskilled labourers. It is very difficult to punish labour exploitation as in the whole province ... there are only two labour inspectors for all economic sectors. A firm has one probability over 35,000 to be visited. Many immigrants have residence permits that have expired and are in a weak legal position. They usually come to the area with a debt of €5,000 or more that they owe to labour intermediaries. Local labour facilitators manage arrivals and recruitment – when illegal immigrants arrive, they are sometimes recruited directly in refugee centres in the south and sent up north.

P6

A labour union representative also stated that

immigrant workers without a contract get paid as low as €3 per hour for unskilled manual labour – while with a contract they may get €5-7. Italians usually ask for €10 an hour. Those who have regular contracts see that the hours they work are many more than the ones declared in their salary slips. Therefore, even if the contract says that they are paid €10/hour, when counting the effective number of hours they get paid a lot less per hour. Also, seasonal contracts do not stipulate that labourers work every day – for example, a contract can cover a period of four months, but includes only a minimum of forty working days ... There are also reports that rent for housing is deducted from salary slips at a high cost. Sometimes, workers receive a salary slip and bank transfer only to be asked to return part of the salary to the farmer in cash.

P6

These quotes suggest that the exploitation of racialized and gendered labour is not the exclusive purview of the wine industry in South Africa, it also happens in Italy – where racially motivated attacks and sexual violence are not unusual in agriculture.

In the rest of this section, I examine three wine certification systems (one global, one specific to South Africa, and one specific to Italy) that have substantial components dealing with labour and social conditions of production – in view of ascertaining to what extent they are addressing the exploitation challenges discussed so far.

Certification systems on social and labour conditions

Fairtrade wine

Fairtrade wine was first certified in 2003 (Herman 2019; Staricco and Ponte 2015). According to Fairtrade International, it was developed to address increasing concerns around the labour conditions of workers on large wine estates, as well as the difficulty faced by smallholder wine growers in developing countries to earn a decent living ... Vineyards that are Fairtrade certified receive at least the Fairtrade Minimum Price ... [which amount depends] on the cost of living and business in each origin area and on its cultivation method. The Fairtrade Premium – extra funds paid on top of the sales price – enables small-scale farmers and vineyard workers to invest in social, economic and environmental improvements.[11]

Only wines from Argentina, Chile, Lebanon and South Africa are currently allowed to receive Fairtrade certification,[12] with South Africa accounting for around two-thirds of total Fairtrade wine sales globally (Back et al. 2019; Bell 2022; Herman 2012, 2018, 2019; Howson, Murray and Overton 2020; Moseley and McCusker 2008; Overton, Murray and Howson 2019).[13]

As indicated in Chapter 5, formally meeting environmental and social sustainability standards has become essential in some wine markets, especially in view of winning a tender to supply the Nordic and Canadian alcohol monopoly systems (SAW1). Some of these tenders specifically require Fairtrade certification. South Africa's Fairtrade wine sales have been increasing significantly in recent times (SAW1, SAW33, SAW81, SAW83). In export markets, retailers want Fairtrade because it is a globally recognized certification, while WIETA is a local initiative (see below). Some South African producers are doubly certified (SAW1).

There are 7,000 ha of certified Fairtrade vineyards in South Africa (8 per cent of the total area planted), for an equivalent harvest of around 90,000 tons of grapes. These are farmed by about thirty certified wine grape growers, a mix of cooperative members and other standalone growers and estates (SAW33). From 2015 to 2020, sales of Fairtrade wine from South Africa increased by 180 per cent in value, with the largest destinations being the UK, Germany and the Nordic countries. According to a representative of Fairtrade Africa, the main drivers for this growth are the Nordic monopolies, which have a strong emphasis on Fairtrade products, and the Co-op retailer in the UK, which is converting to 100 per cent Fairtrade supplies. There are signs of an increasing focus on going towards higher quality Fairtrade wines, but also a recognition among suppliers that 'big retail will always try to bring prices down' (SAW33).

Fairtrade wine is purchased with a price premium, amounting to 0.6 ZAR (0.03 USD) per Kg of grapes delivered and 0.68-0.7 ZAR (around 0.04 USD) per bottle. In 2021, Fairtrade paid a total of €1.5 m in premia in South Africa (SAW33). Fairtrade premium committees at the farm level are nominally in charge of deciding how to use this premium. They are made up of elected representatives of farmworkers and require fair representation of women. Popular uses of the premium include building nurseries for children of farmworkers, educational support and scholarships, health and nutrition projects, and pension schemes (SAW33). However, there are also concerns that decisions on how to spend the premiums are not always driven by workers but indirectly by farm owners (SAW44). A recent change of the rules allows these committees to retain part of the premium to be distributed in cash to farmworkers (SAW78, SAW80).

A representative of a wine industry body in South Africa, however, argues that some farm owners are not happy with what they get from Fairtrade in terms of financial benefits: 'It is all well to have projects with farmworkers and the community, but Fairtrade has to pay for the farmer as well. Producers are paying the fees, but the price of Fairtrade wine at the retail level is too low' (SAW1).

Farm certification (which is carried out by FLOCert through local auditors) requires that farms comply with social and (some) environmental standards. Social standards include meeting good labour practices, work conditions and freedom of association, while environmental standards require that farmers improve soil and water quality, manage pests, avoid using harmful chemicals, manage waste, reduce greenhouse gas emissions and protect biodiversity. Certain listed chemicals are banned. Water, waste and pest management are required and enforced. Fairtrade Africa[14] supports farmer compliance and/or facilitates external support.

Fairtrade seeks to address farmworker housing quality and evictions; labour issues, including overtime; industrial relations (between farmworkers and manager, especially in relation to issues of intimidation); and what happens to the right of living on the farm when a farmworker retires (contingency help, transition help). In 2016, the Fairtrade Foundation published a Fairtrade Gender Strategy, following critiques showing that women involved in Fairtrade farmed products were receiving fewer benefits due to gender inequality (Smith 2015). This gender strategy includes three goals: (1) to improve the active and equal participation of women in Fairtrade-certified smallholder and hired labour organizations; (2) to facilitate equitable access to Fairtrade benefits; and (3) to challenge systemic issues that impact the realization of greater gender equality along the value chain.[15]

Herman (2018) has examined several Fairtrade initiatives in South Africa – including Fairhills, Bosman Family Vineyards and Tukulu/Earthbound. At the time of her fieldwork (2008-2014) Fairhills was structured around a long-term supply relationship with Origin Wine (a wine distributor) and the Co-op group in the UK, with the Du Toitskloof cooperative cellar as the main supplier. Fairtrade accreditation, reached in 2005, was followed by several social development projects financed from the Fairtrade premium and an additional premium provided by the Co-op. Herman shows that these projects brought significant changes in the communities involved, including upgrades to the local primary school, the establishment of sports clubs, a health centre, a mobile medical unit and support for children's school fees.

My own interviews with Fairhills indicate that Origin Wine has stopped its supply agreement with Du Toitskloof, and taken the Fairhills brand with it, creating some confusion among farmworkers. This is also a clear instance of intangible value (the brand name) being controlled from above by merchants, and not below by farmers or farmworkers. The Fairhills association also had to change name to Dutoitskloof Fairtrade Initiative.[16] The winery is still exporting Fairtrade wine to some major UK supermarkets but under a different brand (SAW78). The premium is still used to continue funding key projects (a mobile library, a clinic, a nursery) and educational activities to help youth find different ways of remaining engaged in the community, but not necessarily as farmworkers (as nurses, extension officers, teachers). These projects receive additional funding from other international retailers and monopoly buyers. The association is heavily involved in helping retailers add value to these wines by telling stories about its activities, with one retailer recently featuring these stories on the neck tag of the bottle (SAW78). Similar projects and initiatives are also being carried out at other Fairtrade farms, even though they do not receive explicit additional support from distributors and retailers. Some of these projects have important gender dimensions, including campaigns against gender violence (SAW54, SAW56, SAW60, SAW80).

Herman (2018) argues that the material and relational improvements that Fairtrade has facilitated in the relevant communities are important, but also points out that they have not been accompanied by unequivocal empowerment. The farm owner always has the power to decide whether to maintain certification or delist. This is also why Herman (2018) argues for Fairtrade to engage more strongly in the broader project of transformation and BEE (more on this in the second part of this chapter), as farmworkers, even in an environment of improved working and living conditions, are still part of a system of unequal power relations structured along race and gender lines. When certification started in South Africa in 2003, Fairtrade started a unique reflection on what fairness would mean in the context of a history of racial exploitation. All certified producers had to comply with requirements related to worker ownership, management control, employment equity and skills development – with no exception based on annual turnover. While a few farmers carried out BEE transactions to become Fairtrade certified, some farm owners within Fairhills raised concerns over their global competitiveness, given the demanding requirements that BEE processes would have entailed. However, by 2010, Fairtrade Label South Africa had dropped the BEE requirement – partly as the result of competitiveness fears and partly because of a perceived lack of alignment between the requirements of BEE transactions and Fairtrade principles. One of South Africa's BEE brands (Tukulu) moved to a less 'ethnic' brand (Earthbound) to forefront its double organic-Fairtrade status (the only one in South Africa at that time) rather than highlighting its BEE ownership. This highlights how BEE credentials are seen as less important in international markets than in the domestic political economy (Herman 2018).

International market conditions limit the space for manoeuvre for Fairtrade in the South African wine industry in other ways as well. For example, the chief operating officer of a private cellar told us that

> Fairtrade should be banned because it has such a bad image – not because of bad quality, but because hardly any money makes it back to the farmer or the winery. How can it be sold for seven pounds a bottle in the UK? This means a free-on-board price of one and a half pounds a bottle. It is not possible to make money this way, considering the import duty, excise, and supermarket chain markup . . . Fairtrade is taking from farmers, not giving.
>
> SAW76

At the same time, a Fairtrade representative pointed out that 'Fairtrade can be a vehicle for other benefits, both philanthropic and commercial. The downward price pressure on South African wine applies to all wines, not only Fairtrade' (SAW33). As a representative of a Fairtrade-certified winery told us,

> we get additional funding from the Co-op and the Finnish monopoly on top of the Fairtrade premium. This way, we have been able to expand the primary school. Another retailer provided funds for the medical centre. These contributions are bigger than the Fairtrade premium fund. Fairtrade also brings in other clients because we can tell stories about our community projects.
>
> SAW78

In some ways, these stories (which almost always have a race and gender angle) are as important in wine valuation as Fairtrade certification itself.

Two other significant international initiatives compete in the Fairtrade space in agriculture and wine. One is 'Fair for Life', which is controlled by one of the main organic certification companies and is not considered as strict or empowering as Fairtrade. It was 'created in 2006 by the Swiss Bio-Foundation in cooperation with the IMO Group, then taken over by the Ecocert Group in 2014 to meet a specific demand from organic farming stakeholders'.[17] One of the main organic wine cellars in South Africa has recently moved from Fairtrade to Fair for Life certification. Another initiative, mainly focused on viticulture, is 'Fair'N Green', originally founded in 2013 in Germany and now expanding into other European countries.[18]

The Wine and Agricultural Ethical Trading Association (WIETA)

WIETA is a multi-stakeholder initiative focused on wine in South Africa that grew out of a UK government Ethical Trade Initiative pilot project. It has been active in South Africa since the early 2000s (Bek, McEwan, and Bek 2007; Du Toit 2002; Herman 2018; Howson, Murray and Overton 2020; McEwan and Bek 2009b). According to its website, WIETA represents 'the interests of trade unions, civil society groupings, wine brands and their producers . . . [It promotes] fair working conditions within the wine industry and [provides] a platform for dialogue around ethical trade'.[19] WIETA has developed and manages an ethical code of conduct that includes provisions against discrimination (the only passage that includes explicit references to race and gender issues).[20] WIETA carries social audits to ascertain legal compliance with South Africa's labour and occupational health and safety legislation. It also requires beyond-compliance demands to make sure that 'management systems reflect sustainable ethical principles, policies and practices . . . [and] that farmworker housing not only meets prescribed safety, health and sanitation standards but also promotes the right to dignity, family life and broader community development'.[21] The WIETA protocol also demands that employment contracts are properly explained to farmworkers, given that many of them cannot read. Despite these efforts, there are still many outstanding challenges related to poor working conditions on farms and cellars in South Africa, including deteriorating wage conditions and farmworker evictions, especially for women

(SAW2, SAW44). Farmworker communities often lack access to programs and services such as public transport, health services and education in remote farms. This has led to the development of community projects such as the Pebbles project and the Anna Foundation to address these issues (SAW15, SAW40). These problems are compounded by the government's poor law enforcement in the industry (SAW11, SAW44).

Although adherence to the WIETA code is voluntary, 77 per cent of the total vineyard area in South Africa is certified (SAW1, SAW2). A WIETA representative stated that 'in the past, it was not recognized by buyers and especially retailers, but now in the UK and elsewhere in Europe it is accepted' (SAW10). In Sweden, Systembolaget has special tenders for WIETA wines from South Africa (SAW2). At the time of fieldwork, 1,400 grape growers were either certified or are carrying ongoing certification efforts (SAW10). Depending on the risk matrix, grape growers obtain different grades: an A grade allows them to maintain certification for three years until the next audit; a B grade ensures certification for two years; a C grade only for one year; and D grade indicates that they did not pass and need to address specific outstanding issues before reauditing (SAW2). Producers have one year to address corrective actions and WIETA helps them with training and capacity building, or by advising them on how to get funding for such purposes. WIETA does not help operators with the actual implementation of corrective actions as it would constitute a conflict of interest (SAW2, SAW10). Since 2019, accredited third-party auditors have been in charge of certification. While WIETA is helping producers to valorize South African wine in export markets, uneasiness about the requirements demanded by retailers is pervasive. A representative of one of the main wine cooperatives told me: 'Squeezed margins affect grape growers. At our cooperative, we have gone down from thirty-seven to twenty-three producers as margins are very low' (SAW79). Several other interviewees stated that social issues are placing increasing pressure on the financial viability of their companies. They recognize that sustainability certifications have become a necessity for market access, but also argue that they do not provide a producer competitive advantage (SAW19, SAW41, SAW49).

Equalitas

Equalitas is a sustainability certification system that is taking hold in Italy. Established in 2015, Equalitas seeks to cover three main dimensions of sustainability: its '3E' logo stands for Environmental, Ethical and Economic. Both Equalitas and WIETA are recognized by alcohol monopolies in the Nordic countries as all-round approaches to sustainability and are accepted for qualification to selected tenders. Differently from WIETA, however, Equalitas is driven by producers – it is controlled by the DOC/DOCG consortia through their federation (FederDoc) (IG3). Its standard includes: integrated production management, which is focused on minimizing the application of agro-chemicals and on rationalizing fertilizer use; good communication with stakeholders and communities; good practices within firms and with their suppliers; and measures against labour exploitation on farms.²² On good economic practices it includes a list of practices for employees, such as worker development plans for wages; financial incentives in view of environmental and social goals; and regular meetings with the owners.²³ On good economic practices for suppliers, it requires criteria for equal pricing for purchased products and the setting of 'tolerable payment terms'.²⁴ Equalitas has been supportive of the government's work on a national standard for sustainability in the wine industry (SQNPI, see Chapter 5). One of Equalitas's representatives sees SQNPI as 'providing a low bar standard upon which Equalitas can provide higher standards' (IG3).

Equalitas offers three possible foci of certification: the winery, the wine and the geographical denomination (once 60 per cent of the total area under production is certified) (IG3, IG11). As we have seen in Chapter 5, the Prosecco Conegliano Valdobbiadene DOCG consortium and the Valpolicella consortium decided to prioritize SQNPI certification, which is more focused on integrated production and selected environmental issues and less on social and labour issues. However, individual producers are still seeking Equalitas certification. As of March 2024, there were more than 3,000 Equalitas-certified wineries and more than 6,000 labelled wines in Italy.²⁵ Many certified wineries are in the Prosecco DOC area, where the consortium is seeking the certification of the whole geographical denomination. But there are also twenty-nine individual wineries certified in the Verona province (most of which have production facilities in Valpolicella).²⁶ Finally, there are currently two certified geographical denominations (Rosso di Montepulciano and Vino Nobile di Montepulciano). A representative of the Prosecco DOC consortium stated in an interview that

> sustainability has to become a prerequisite of the productive system, but producers need time to come along. The ban on glyphosate we introduced in the Prosecco DOC area, for example, was carried out too quickly, and many producers remain unhappy with it. Also, the Ministry has not included it in their regulations yet, because it claims it does not relate to quality, so the ban is for the time being only applied in the Prosecco area. We do not believe that organic certification is a strategic priority, we would rather go beyond that to integrate economic, social and environmental sustainability ... For this reason, we are working with Equalitas to seek a sustainability certification for the whole DOC area ... This allows us to claim that we operate ethically but in the context of the right competitiveness framework.
>
> P5

The representative of an Equalitas-certified winery I interviewed in Valpolicella stated that

> it is a good system for continuous improvement ... In relation to social issues, we have noticed that employees are now happier, work better, they fully engage, and as a result, they are more productive. They are more involved in decisions, they provide their opinions and recommendations, and they have become part

of the family ... On farming practices and environmental issues, we did not have to change much because we are organic already, but Equalitas asks us to decrease water consumption and energy use, which is good. It pushes us to set objectives and monitor progress, provides new stimuli ... We have a new photovoltaic system now, and want to expand it ... On carbon footprint, Equalitas asks us to calculate it, but there is no requirement in terms of decreasing it ... We have now started to put the 3E label on our bottles. It is appreciated by buyers but was not demanded by them. It helps to get extra points for the tenders by Nordic monopolies.

V22

The representative of another winery in Valpolicella told me that they decided to seek Equalitas certification because they 'saw a lot of producers abusing the concept of sustainability, so decided to provide a serious message to the consumer' (V23). However, they also raised some critical issues:

There are parts of the standard that are difficult to manage. For example, we need to manage relations with neighbours – including advance warnings before we spray agro-chemicals – and we need to set up continuative and professional dialogue. Also, it is not always easy to evaluate grape suppliers. You should in theory visit them and assess how they manage their operations, especially in relation to social issues (for example, seasonal labour during harvest), but it is difficult to handle short-term labour directly, so many suppliers use labour cooperatives. They may try to use the best ones, but sometimes it is hard to know.

V23

In sum, the analysis of the wine sustainability certifications that include social and labour issues suggests that, as well intentioned as they may be, they are not equipped to deal with the structural imbalances that underpin labour exploitation. I will expand on these reflections in the last section of this chapter, together with those emerging from the analysis of racialized and gendered issues in ownership patters to which I now turn.

6.3 OWNERSHIP AND CONTROL: 'BLACK ECONOMIC EMPOWERMENT' IN SOUTH AFRICA[27]

Wine value struggles around people are playing out not only in relation to the exploitation of labour. They are also linked to the nationality, race and gender of the owners of material and intellectual property. I focus on South Africa in the rest of this section because, for historical reasons, these issues are at the centre of current debates on the legitimate characteristics of the individuals who produce, brand and/or market wine.[28] The nationality of owners of vineyards and wineries is a particularly delicate issue in South Africa, which until recently had escaped the international takeovers of wineries that have characterized the wine industry in the past decades (Anderson and Pinilla 2018). Many interviewees in South Africa perceive foreign investment with a mixture of resignation (because of low profitability and the incremental need for additional capital for investment and marketing) but also worry. The representative of one of the largest wineries with a substantial BEE component stated: 'Our farm has been with the family since 1810. Currently, it is the eighth generation of owners who runs it. Some of the workers are part of the fifth generation on the farm. It is an advantage to have such history, we are not some rich guys coming in and then moving on after a bit' (SAW54). The representative of another winery also questioned the motives of foreign investors: 'They are getting hold of cheap land and labour. They are scooping up lots of properties of all sizes. The question is whether they will help South Africa. What is their commitment to the country?' (SAW64). In the rest of this section, I focus on the race and gender dimensions of ownership, which is the fulcrum of major discussions and initiatives under the banner of BEE in South Africa.

Brief history and current status

In the now thirty-year pursuit of transformation objectives, the South African wine industry has put in place numerous initiatives and structures to support the entry and participation of 'historically disadvantaged people' (HDPs).[29] In the early 1990s, the promise of democratic transformation posed a powerful challenge to KWV, which had hitherto regulated and largely controlled the South African wine industry (see Chapter 3). To protect its assets, KWV needed to mitigate the risks of government intervention and radical transformation of the industry. They did so by converting into a private entity in 1997, at the condition of funding an industry trust that would provide services to the industry and support its (racial) transformation in terms of ownership and control (Du Toit, Kruger and Ponte 2008; Kruger, Du Toit and Ponte 2006; Nugent 2024a; Williams 2005).

In February 1999, the South African Wine Industry Trust (SAWIT) was established to be the custodian of KWV funds. The functions of the trust were separated into two not-for-profit companies: Busco (Wine Industry Business Support Company) and Devco (Wine Industry Development Company). The objective of Busco was to finance services in research, development and competitiveness in the industry, some of which had previously been provided by KWV. For this purpose, it established Winetech for technology transfer; the South African Wine Industry Information System (SAWIS) for collecting and managing statistical data; and Wines of South Africa (WOSA) for generic promotion of South African wine. The objective of Devco was to develop and support new entrants into the industry and to improve the conditions of farmworkers and their communities. In reality, Devco provided little support to new entrants in comparison with that available to established industry through Busco (Du Toit, Kruger and Ponte 2008; Kruger, Du Toit and Ponte 2006; Nugent 2024a; Williams 2005).

In 1999, Winetech developed its Vision 2020 document, which laid down a process of research and consultation for building an innovation – and market-driven industry that would be globally competitive and highly profitable. In effect, it announced the end of the high-yield and low-quality productivist system. Vision 2020 was couched in technical and market language and avoided any real engagement with the burning racial questions facing the industry. It did not include any discussion of changes in ownership or redistribution, nor any reference to BEE (Du Toit, Kruger and Ponte 2008; Kruger, Du Toit and Ponte 2006). In 2002, the two main producer-wholesalers in the industry at that time (KWV and Distell) formed the South African Wine and Brandy Company (SAWB) to be the 'inclusive and representative' body of the wine industry. But its four chambers, representing producers, cellars, trade and labour, only the latter represented Black interests, as 99 per cent of ownership and control over the assets of the wine industry was in white hands at that time (Kruger, Du Toit and Ponte 2006; Nugent 2024a; Williams 2005).

The SAWB was tasked with finding a path to transformation in the industry, but by 2003 had not developed any initiatives in this direction. The enactment of the Broad-Based BEE Act of 2003 altered this situation by setting a new national objective and a framework within which it could be achieved. It also provided a new language of 'empowerment' that could be used by a representative stakeholder institution to formulate the transformation agenda in the wine industry. SAWB's Wine Industry Plan, presented in October 2003 at the Black Economic Empowerment Consultative Conference, aimed at creating a 'harmonious, prosperous non-racial agricultural sector'. In 2003, the first BEE corporate deal took place when Anglo American Farms (Amfarms) sold the Boschendal wine farm to a consortium of investors that included an empowerment group. This was followed by a BEE deal for KWV in 2004 (for a detailed review of this deal, see Williams 2005), Distell in 2005, and a number of others in the mid-2000s (Du Toit, Kruger and Ponte 2008).

At the same time, SAWIT started working towards the creation of a 'BEE charter' for the industry, and a number of BEE wine labels such as Thandi and Lindiwe emerged (Herman 2019). In 2007, a Wine Industry Transformation Charter was announced, which adapted the generic BEE scorecard to the specific characteristics of the wine industry. In practice, it exempted 80 per cent of wine producers due to their small turnover (Herman 2018, 36). By 2010, only thirty-five empowerment projects and thirty Black-owned brands had been established (Herman 2018). The wine charter was not implemented and an industry vacuum remained until 2012, when the more general AgriBEE Charter became the code of reference for the whole sector (Sato 2013). In addition to ownership (25 points), the AgriBEE scorecard includes four other elements: management control (19 points); skills development (20 points); enterprise and supplier development (40 points); and socio-economic development (15 points).[30]

In the past decade, transformation of the wine industry has become a key government agenda and is now finally seen (at least rhetorically) as an imperative (SAW3) – with the inclusion of Black SMEs and Black women entrepreneurs as special foci.[31] Several mechanisms have been attempted under this agenda: (1) various forms of land ownership redistribution; (2) full or partial control of wineries and/or wine brands, and related support for business operations;

(3) opening up management control to HDPs (this is happening mostly in larger companies); (4) initiatives related to skills development and preferential supplier agreements – including the outsourcing of services (often low skilled, such as cleaning and security) to Black-owned business providers, sometimes run by former employees; and (5) socio-economic development projects, which remains the most popular way of scoring BEE points for companies – and is also the most paternalist of these instruments.

In the next two sub-sections, I focus on the first two mechanisms. While in the early days share equity schemes were the most popular instruments in attempting to tackle land ownership, joint ventures are now in ascendancy. In general, non-land-based models of transformation are now the most common. WOSA currently lists forty-eight empowerment projects of various kinds.[32]

Land ownership initiatives

Ownership and management of grape farms and wine cellars have been historically dominated by white men, and entry and expansion of Black entrepreneurs, and of Black women in particular, has been limited (SAW3). As of the mid-2020s, there is still a general understanding in the industry that, when it comes to land ownership, 'transformation has a long way to go. The industry wants to double the land owned by previously disadvantaged people from 2.5 per cent of the vineyards to 5 per cent by 2025' (SAW1). This is still far from the government's transformation targets of transferring 20 per cent of land and water rights into the hands of HDPs by 2025 (SAW3, SAW18).

Land ownership transformation initiatives have taken various forms. One has been a model where HDP individuals or groups take over full ownership of a farm and/or cellar. There are two main variants of this model: a) the willing buyer/willing seller variant, where government buys land from a willing seller, then leases it to beneficiaries; this is problematic as the beneficiaries cannot use vineyards for collateral to get funding from banks; this was a big part of the original idea of land redistribution in the country but is now mostly stagnant (SAW3); and b) the land restitution variant, where a community files a claim to reclaim ancestral land and the government then buys the land and gives it back to the community; there have been very few successful transactions of this kind in the wine sector, the largest of which involved fifteen farms for a total of 160 ha of land (SAW3).

Other business models that involve Black land ownership include contract farming with a winery; joint ventures between farmworkers and an existing farmer; share equity distributed to farmworkers; and Black-controlled cooperative entities (Herman 2018, 37). In farmworker ownership schemes, vineyard owners usually transfer part of their farmland to workers as part of BEE transformation projects. Farmworkers then sell grapes to the winery at harvest – with income from sales going into a trust (SAW83). In other variations, farmworkers are involved in both grape growing and wine production, with the winery owner providing technical expertise and assistance in developing a farmworkers' wine brand (SAW81). These projects often include community initiatives in primary and secondary education, healthcare, sports, housing, social clubs and transport-related projects and sometimes combine worker ownership of parts of the land with Fairtrade certification (SAW2, SAW3, SAW54) or with guaranteed offtake by a supermarket chain (SAW34, SAW53).

Very few of these projects have been successful so far (SAW3, SAW17, SAW19, SAW22) and tend to include those with solid corporate backers, such as Earthbound, which was established in 2004 as a spinoff of South Africa's largest producer-wholesaler (Distell). In this case, shareholding includes Distell (49 per cent), a group of Black businessmen (36 per cent) and a community trust of farmworkers (15 per cent), with the transformation project focusing on skills development and training. Yet, Herman (2018) reports that the trust has played a very limited role in shaping strategic choices and that farmworkers have been receiving limited dividends. An even more problematic example is the Solms-Delta transformation project, which was established in 2001 by neuroscientist Mark Solms and British philanthropist Richard Astor, the two original owners who then transferred over a third of the company to farmworkers. After years of losses and operational challenges, and a government-backed injection of funding in 2016, it went into liquidation and a rescue process in 2018. It remained mostly idle until 2023, when an African American investor purchased it. He is now the sole owner of the company.[33] In another case (Reyneke), farmworkers indicated a preference for home ownership rather than farm shares (SAW13, SAW50).

In general, only a very few HDPs have managed to enter the wine industry through land ownership (SAW17; SAW19; SAW22). This model requires substantial capital investment in land, infrastructure and facilities, and access to water rights. Land is particularly expensive in areas such as Stellenbosch and Franschhoek (SAW3). Land-based entry also requires expertise at multiple levels of the value chain and is further challenging given the lead times to get products to market. One needs to plant a vineyard for three years, and then it takes time to produce a wine like the sparkling Methode Cap Classique (SAW3). It is only after several years, and assuming the product sells well, that any return on investment is realized. Long lead times have severe implications for cash flow, as running costs continue to accumulate before sales are made. Overall, the land ownership projects that seem to have been more successful include those that have involved wealthy Black investors (Herman 2018).

Brand ownership and business support initiatives

Most Black entrepreneurs who were successful in entering the wine industry have done so through a 'virtual winery' model focused on branding. There are two variants of this model: (1) HDPs manage grape purchasing and make and sell their own wine, often in rented facilities; and (2) they buy wine from different cellars (in bulk or already bottled) and sell it under their own brand (SAW3, SAW11, SAW68). In both cases, HDPs enter through a commercial (or sometimes co-ownership) partnership with established wine producers who have vineyards and/or wine production and bottling facilities. Currently, less than 3 per cent of total industry sales are accounted for by HDP-owned brands, while other estimates indicate this figure as being less than 1.5 per cent of sales (SAW18, SAW3).

These models allow Black entrepreneurs to scale up by leveraging their partners' economies of scale in production, packaging material, branding, marketing, logistics and access to markets (SAW11) – without the need for substantial capital to set up their own production facilities. In addition, in some instances, partners extend credit on payment of the wine – providing Black entrepreneurs with the flexibility to pay after sales have been made (SAW55, SAW68). Partners can also support other practical aspects of production, business skills and market access given their experience and history in the wine industry (SAW3, SAW55, SAW68). The new entrant in these partnerships is typically responsible for creating and growing the brand, often for niche product spaces and/or linked to unique stories and messaging (Das Nair, Chisoro and Ponte 2023).

Given the substantial political and water-rights problems around land ownership in South Africa, the virtual model reduces barriers to entry. But new entrants still require space where they can host customers for tastings and food pairings. This is important for building a brand and for exposure. Showcasing a small vineyard as part of the tasting experience is also visually valuable, given the growing importance of wine tourism. A brand also needs a facility to produce small batches of boutique-style wine (SAW55). To address these challenges, SAWITU set up 'The Wine Arc' facility in Stellenbosch to provide a brand home for Black wine producers who may not have physical or land-based facilities. The Wine Arc is a one-stop place for Black-owned brands (and a research farm). It provides cost-sharing support in terms of market access (through a physical location to meet clients and undertake tastings), e-commerce facilities, access to labs, cellars, rootstock, testing and research and innovation facilities (SAW55, SAW18). SAWITU conducts company evaluations and assesses each brand in relation to commercial positioning/success, brand strategy and technical viability, design, packaging, story and benchmark testing for quality. SAWITU also helps them assess whether a product story is creating market interest (SAW18) (Das Nair and Chisoro 2023; Das Nair, Chisoro and Ponte 2023).

While BEE brands have achieved relative success selling into international markets, they face key challenges selling in local markets (SAW53, SAW55, SAW68). BEE wine producers argue that 'Black-named brands', and especially those owned by women, have not yet achieved broad acceptance in the domestic wine market because of the continuing legacies of patriarchy, racism and misogyny (SAW55, SAW18, SAW68). New entrants are often treated with scepticism and thus it is not sufficient for them to simply market a brand as Black-owned or just compete on the strength of their story (SAW3, SAW81). These challenges have led to some HDP producers retaining or using more traditional 'white-named brands' because they tend to sell better in South Africa (SAW3). In general, it is difficult for Black producers to get Black wine consumers interested in their stories, as they favour established, more traditional and well-known brands (SAW18, SAW68,

SAW3). As stated by the wine buyer of a South African retailer, 'you have Black brands that interest white customers, and white brands that interest Black customers; we are missing Black brands for Black customers' (SAW34).

On-trade sales through restaurants are dominated by two distributors in South Africa, which control the list of wines that they present to restaurants for possible purchase. From the restaurant side, owners or managers also control the brands that go into their wine lists. These factors together mean that Black new entrants without established brands struggle to be placed in restaurant wine lists (SAW68, SAW81). The owners of some of the few Black brands that have managed to supply restaurants say that large and possibly excessive markups are charged by restaurants on their wine sales, and this further discourages consumers from experimenting with new wines (SAW45).

Off-trade sales in South Africa are dominated by supermarket chains (SAW81). Black-owned brands struggle to supply them (SAW6). First, given the intense competition for shelf space in supermarket chains, less well-known and established Black wine brands that do not yet have a track record of strong sales find it difficult to secure a listing (SAW68, SAW81). When a brand gets listed with a supermarket but does not sell, the supermarket can delist the product, and this is costly for a producer (SAW3, SAW81). However, domestic retailers as part of their BEE commitments are starting to procure wine from Black-owned producers, often for their own private or house brands (Das Nair and Chisoro 2023). This ensures guaranteed offtake and support in terms of packaging and branding for smaller Black suppliers (SAW4).

SAWITU currently supports sixty-seven members – ranging from HDPs owning land, farming grapes, and producing and bottling wine, to HDPs ordering a particular style of wine from a wine cellar and then bottling with their own brand (SAW1). Central to SAWITU's transformation objectives is also a specific focus on increasing representation of Black women-owned wine businesses. Of the sixty-seven Black-owned wine brands supported by SAWITU, 75 per cent are women-owned (SAW18). Furthermore, of the twenty or so Black brands supported under the Wine Arc facilities, the majority are women-led or women-owned. The entry and participation of Black women-owned businesses is particularly important given the continuing gender disparities in the wine industry (SAW44, SAW47). Women-owned businesses comprise some of the Black entrepreneurs that have achieved relative success through producing high-quality wines (some of which are award-winning) with strong brands. These Black women entrepreneurs are directly involved in the production of their own wines through virtual wineries, rented cellar facilities or privately owned cellar facilities (Das Nair and Chisoro 2023). Their experiences make for great stories to market, but they are still very few. Their entry experiences have been challenging, also given that many do not come from a background or long family history of wine production. In addition to the continuing racial stigma in a still very white industry, the significance of generational knowledge in the wine business is particularly striking (Das Nair, Chisoro and Ponte 2023). This goes together with the need to build networks and brands over time and for close collaboration with suppliers and distributors.

Without this history, owners of Black brands typically enter through pursuing a passion they develop for winemaking after exposure to the industry, including by working in wineries or vineyards, in retail or in wine tourism (Das Nair, Chisoro and Ponte 2023).

Overall, new entrants in the wine industry are seen by established actors as in need of mentorship, coaching, enterprise supplier development and access to markets (SAW18). The owner of a wine wholesale operation argued that HDPs need 'positive mythology, education, uplifting and social fabric repair . . . instead of BEE to make money for yourself' (SAW63). These are discourses that often hark back to the paternalism discussed earlier in this chapter in relation to farm labour. These views are also often accompanied by the framing of racial and gender inequalities as simply a question of capital, highlighting the large gaps in funding to make the necessary investments to support the aggressive entry and ownership by Black entrepreneurs (Das Nair, Chisoro and Ponte 2023). But it will take far more than just capital to facilitate transformation. At least the emergence of brand-focused transformation initiatives is a sign of recognition in the wine industry that saddling HDPs with high-risk and low-margin ventures, such as grape farming, is not particularly empowering – and that ownership of intangible assets can be a more fruitful venue.

6.4 WORLDS OF VALUATION AND VALUE STRUGGLES RELATED TO PEOPLE (CLASS, RACE AND GENDER)

In the previous two sections, I have provided empirical evidence of how people's qualifications can be enrolled in various processes of valuation. I focused on two aspects – people as labourers, and people as owners of means of production and intellectual property – and highlighted some of the class, race and gender dimensions of concomitant value struggles. In this section, I interpret these findings through the lenses of different worlds of valuation. In relation to people as labourers (see Table 13), we can identify an important presence of a market world of valuation. An industrial world is also at play, valuing labour in relation to the skill sets held by different categories of workers. As seen in previous chapters, these two worlds are often conjoined with the workings of contemporary capitalism. When value struggles coalesce around social and labour conditions of production, this *market/industrial* compromise is strengthened through the codification and standardization efforts that lay behind social sustainability certifications. Initiatives such as Fairtrade, WIETA and Equalitas can valorize wines to be exported to specific markets in Europe, especially the UK and Nordic countries, but they are unable to challenge the structural inequalities that push margins down, especially at the farm level – where the most problematic work conditions persist. This provides extra strength to a market/industrial valuation compromise in view of keeping labour costs down and further casualizing work – in a context of certification systems that have limited or no explicit concern with the gendered and racialized aspects of exploitation.

Certification initiatives attempt to address some of the actual social and labour conditions on wine farms, but they do so in ways that generally promote negotiation and compromise – and thus inherently weaken the more collective and adversarial approaches to labour struggle, such as strikes or media and NGO pressure. This means that, in value struggles over people as labour, a market/industrial compromise is not only dominant but also consolidated through *domestic* valuations of labour as tamed and subjugated. This is the case not only for the race and gender legacies of apartheid in South Africa but also for the historical subjugation of gendered and racialized family and immigrant labour in Italian agriculture. These mutually supporting valuations provide the main base through which surplus labour is extracted. But an antagonistic *civic* world can also be detected, which values dignified labour and collective action. For example, Fairtrade wine certification can transfer some of the value extracted from racialized and gendered labour back to the collective Fairtrade committee, where farmworkers can to some extent redirect it to community projects that they are able to at least partially shape. Equalitas can be seen as a sustainability system that is indirectly driven by farmers, and thus has collective valuation elements as well, given that it is controlled by the FederDoc, the Italian federation of DOC/DOCG consortia.

In relation to the valuation of people as owners of the means of production and intellectual property, the dominant *market/industrial* compromise operates through the prioritization of concerns with financial viability and the minimum scale of production that allows economies of scale to ensure competitiveness (this is a key discussion in both South Africa and Italy; see Chapter 3). But challenges to this compromise are arising through civic, domestic and inspiration worlds of valuation. *Civic* elements are emerging in view of reshaping the ownership structures of the industry in South Africa – to increase Black and female participation and control under the banner of BEE. These transformation initiatives, as limited as they have been, seek to collectively redress racial- and gender-based historical inequalities. *Domestic* valuation repertoires can also be detected. In South Africa, they are linked to: 1) Black producers resorting to the use of more traditional 'white brand names' because they tend to sell better; 2) the continuing presence of paternalist discourses on empowerment, with new Black entrants seen as needing mentorship, coaching and development; and 3) a more general backlash against selling properties to foreign capital. Finally, an *inspiration* world of valuation is becoming more visible, embedded in discourses of promoting entrepreneurship and innovation among Black, and especially Black women, winemakers in South Africa. However, this is accompanied by a focus on brand ownership rather than on controlling the means of production.

6.5 CONCLUSION

In this chapter, I have unpacked some of the struggles that play out around the valuation of people through their class, race and gender intersectionality. I covered the social and work conditions of production of people as labourers as well as the

Table 13 Worlds of valuation and value struggles in wine (people)

	Market	Industrial	Domestic	Civic	Inspired	Opinion
			Worlds of valuation (general)			
Common principle	Competition	Efficiency	Traditional benevolence	Collective solidarity	Spiritual or creative enhancement	Fame
Units of valuation	Product units	Plans, systems, controls, forecasts	Specific assets	Negotiation, consultation, distributional arrangements	Innovation, creation	Public relations, brand names, social media recognition
Questions underpinning valuation processes	Is it economic?	Is it technically efficient, scalable, functional?	Does it follow tradition? Can it be trusted?	Is it collectively safe, healthy, socially and environmentally sound?	Is it new or unique? Is it a breakthrough?	Is it accepted by the public/consumers?
Valuation focus	Price	Scalability, and proper functionality	Trust, history, repetition	Social, labour, environmental, collective impacts	Creativity, novelty, personality	Renown, visibility
			Worlds of valuation in wine (people)			
Valuation focus in relation to (racialized and gendered) labour	Wage	Skilled	Subjugated	Dignified	Innovative	Popular among peers
Value struggles	x	x	x	(x)		
Valuation focus in relation to (racialized and gendered) ownership	Financially sustainable	Operator on a large(r) scale	National, local	Disadvantaged group	Entrepreneur	Famous
Value struggles	x	x	(x)	(x)	(x)	

Legend: x = currently dominant world(s) (darker shading); (x) = antagonistic world(s) underpinning value struggles (lighter shading)
Source: Own elaboration.

qualifications of people as owners of tangible and intangible assets. The devaluation of labour is taking place through a double movement: the further casualization of work and the substitution of manual operations with machinery and digital technologies. At the same time, grape farmers are under financial pressure and are asked to deliver social (and environmental, see Chapter 5) sustainability solutions, while their margins are being squeezed from actors downstream of the value chain. In other words, the value farmers are extracting from racialized and gendered labour is itself extracted upstream – especially from retailers, and eventually by consumers.

Finally, I have also shown how efforts to facilitate a racial (and to some extent gender) transformation of ownership and control in South African wine have had very limited success – often benefiting a new and politically connected Black elite or being restricted to a small number of emerging Black women entrepreneurs through brand ownership. Transformation through land and winery ownership has been difficult for many legacy, family-owned operations as they want to maintain ownership and management control. Therefore, most wine companies (and especially the smaller ones) prefer to go the easier routes of transformation – facilitating skills development, outsourcing services to Black-owned providers, and setting up community projects for socio-economic upliftment.

Chapter 7

LOOKING AT CAPITALISM THROUGH THE WINE GLASS

7.1 INTRODUCTION

Value chains are an important cog of contemporary capitalism and understanding power dynamics in and around them is essential in view of unveiling how value is created, appropriated and distributed among different actors and what valuation practices underpin these processes. Much research has documented the unequal distribution of value added along chains, showing that (especially smaller) operators based in the Global South retain very small proportions of the value they help create (see Chapter 2). Research focused on *bargaining* power (dyadic, direct) in value chains has helped us explain how value added is skewed along the value chain because of the disparity that often characterizes the links between (many small) suppliers and (a few large) buyers. We also know that the benefits of value chain participation, when present, are unequally distributed among actors of different sizes and social characteristics (e.g. along class, race and gender lines).

Work examining *institutional* power (collective, direct) has provided key insights into the regulatory frameworks, standards and certifications that shape entry barriers and the conditions of participation in value chains among different social groups (see Chapter 2). But so far, we have known much less about why we observe these results beyond the unequal endowment of resources among different actors and social groups, and the limited power or willingness of the state in addressing these imbalances. In this book, I sought to provide a more nuanced understanding of how *constitutive* power (collective, indirect) shapes key 'value struggles' and with what consequences. Future efforts should be undertaken to better understand *demonstrative* power (dyadic, indirect) as well. While some of the normative values that underpin it may be similar to those shaping constitutive power, the distinctive transmission mechanisms of demonstrative power (mimicking, isomorphism) warrant dedicated attention.

In the rest of this chapter, I build on the analysis of three sites of value struggle (place, nature and people) carried out in the previous chapters to delineate how different configurations of 'worlds of valuation' can shape *constitutive* power in wine. I do this in view of explaining how power operates in value chains as imbricated in chains of values – and with what consequences for different groups of actors. I conclude with a reflection on what wine tells us about contemporary capitalism. Those who have not read the previous three chapters in detail will be able to get in the next section a summary picture of how a plurality of worlds of valuation are enrolled at different sites of value struggle in wine and how they are linked to power dynamics and inequality. Those who have read through the three previous chapters may want to read only the last part of the next section, which contains a synthesis of the findings.

7.2 VALUE STRUGGLES, CONSTITUTIVE POWER AND INEQUALITY IN WINE

Place

In Chapter 4 I have shown that a major value struggle is taking place between 'placeless wines' and 'place wines'. In placeless wines, retailers lean on a compromise of industrial and market worlds of valuation – thus between common principles articulated around efficiency and competition and through processes combining objective technical measurement of material properties and price (see Table 14 for a summary). This compromise applies to most wine that is traded internationally. The dominance of this widely accepted valuation of placeless wines means that as long as it remains uncontested, value distribution along the chain will continue to be skewed against upstream operators (wine producers, but especially grape farmers and farm labourers) and in favour of downstream operators (and especially retailers).

Another way this kind of value struggle is manifested is through discussions on how to increase the unit price of the wine that is sold/exported – this is a key issue in both Italy and South Africa. In Italy, this effort is focused on strengthening sales of appellation wines. In South Africa, premiumization efforts are taking place chiefly through attempts to ramp up price premia for higher-end brands, wines and properties, rather than through the valorization of geographical indications or terroir. Yet, the proportion of South African wine exported in bulk is increasing, and premiumization efforts are mostly carried out at the individual property level – lacking the regulatory framework and collective organization that could underpin place wines.

For 'place wines', value struggles coalesce around worlds of valuation drawing from (changing) ideas of tradition, authenticity and heritage. This is where constitutive power has the potential to benefit producers. Valuation based on terroir and geographical origin mainly relates to a domestic world – drawing from claims that intimate knowledge of the land and historical fine-tuning of practices can impart the taste of place into a wine. But when terroir is institutionalized in larger indications of geographical origin, domestic valuations operate in less immediate ways. In this case, origin relates to internally diverse regions to the point that place can be perceived as a (generic) brand. Where geographical indications are collectively owned by consortia controlled by producers, a civic

Table 14 Worlds of valuation and value struggles in wine*

	Worlds of valuation					
	Market	**Industrial**	**Domestic**	**Civic**	**Inspired**	**Opinion**
	Price	Availability at technical specification and scale	Tradition, authenticity, heritage	Collectively owned or controlled	Unique, inspiring	Famous, recognized
Place						
Geographical appellation			x			(x)
No appellation system	x				(x)	(x)
'Fine wines'			x		x	x
Wine tourism	(x)		x		(x)	(x)
(Placeless wines)*	x	x				
Nature	Good/service, form of capital	Managed, functional	Proximate, conserved	Available to all, provider of collective services	Aesthetic, emotional	Mobilized by celebrities, experts, through SoMe
Regulation & governance	x	x	(x)	(x)		
Ecology, conservation, beauty	(x)	(x)	x	x	x	
'Natural wines'	(x)	(x)			x	x
Climate change	x	x				x
People						
As (racialized and gendered) labour	Wage	Skilled	Subjugated	Dignified	Innovative	Popular among peers
	x	x	x	(x)		
As (racialized and gendered) owners	Financially sustainable	Operator on a large(r) scale	National, local	Disadvantaged group	Entrepreneur	Famous
	x	x	(x)	(x)	(x)	

Legend: x = currently dominant world(s) (darker shading); (x) = antagonistic world(s) underpinning value struggles (lighter shading)
* The valuation of placeless wines by definition does not include place; they are included in the table for comparative purposes.
Source: Own elaboration based on findings presented in Tables 10, 12 and 13.

world of justification is also at play. Here, valuation is based on collective solidarity and representation – facilitating the provision of place-based rents to *all* producers within a demarcated area. Collective identities and bottom-up control tend to be more evident in smaller geographical denominations than in larger ones.

But terroir, and the domestic world of valuation that relates to it, is not necessarily an instrument of redistributive change. In a way, terroir can be seen as both de-fetishizing the role, identities and attachments of some (local) people in the making of a wine, while also fetishizing the role of others, such as non-local actors and workers (Ulin 2013). In other words, terroir both 'challenges the idea of mass-produced commodities and non-distinction and ... [at the same time] accentuates privilege and the marginalization and concealment that account for the historical and social production of privilege' (Ulin 2013, 70). Indeed, 'the weight of history ends up serving as the gatekeeper for truly tasting terroir, requiring a commitment to the power of tradition, heritage, and experience' (Trubek 2008, 248). The taste of place is 'the product of a global hierarchy of value that gives preferences to certain forms of sensory experiences and knowledge over others' (Demossier 2020, 85). This means that terroir can help producers to retain more of the value they create but can also be the source of exclusion and inequality.

Terroir is after all another form of morality (Howland 2019a) – emerging from 'political domination, historical classism, and the marketing strategies of profit-maximizing entrepreneurs' (Swinburn 2019, 221). It is an entanglement of symbolic projections and specific economic interests (Fourcade 2012) that can reproduce a strongly hierarchical structure (Carter 2018; Moran 1993), although the progressive multiplication of appellations has meant a tendency towards more inclusiveness. Terroir can thus create (new) winners and losers, and lead to place actually losing its character through excessive commercialization and upscaling (Demossier 2020, 4). Furthermore, most forms of terroir rarely include an articulation of the role of seasonal, often immigrant, labour that may be utilized even in smaller viticulture and winemaking realities.

More generic geographical indications (those that are *not* based on terroir) can also provide a rent to producers. However, they lack the collective elements that facilitate some control from below by producers. Their civic valuation elements tend to be weaker. More generally, the valuation of place wines where there are no geographical appellations tends to be based on inspiration – as producers focus on individualistic aspects related to uniqueness and the emotional attachments to the place where the wine comes from. Place wines (whether coming from appellations or not) are also increasingly valued through the endorsement by renowned wine writers, judges or publications – thus leaning on a world of opinion. These types of valuations are actually dominant in fine wines.

Finally, valuation processes in wine tourism are often steeped in a domestic world that is linked to experiencing tradition and authentically living a (possibly reinvented and idealized) place. These valuations are also often entwined with representations of beauty and aesthetics through architecture and landscaping and are linked to relaxing and spiritual experiences of connection to place – characteristics of a world of inspiration. Some opinion valuations are at play as well, as celebrity and social media endorsements, scores and reviews in tourist guides and websites provide key guidance to consumers. At the same time, we can also trace the emergence of packaged solutions to wine tourism, where nostalgia for natural lifestyles is extremely sanitized and sold through generic, branded and homogenized offerings, thus drawing on elements of the market world. Finally, wine tourism can be seen as a form of escapist entertainment built upon the illegibility and hiding of labour (and its possible exploitation), the highly polluting agro-chemical management of the vineyard and the heavy-handed shaping of landscapes – including possible deforestation when opening up new plots.

Wine tourism allows the inhabiting of safe spaces of small luxury that are separate from the rest of humanity and nature (Latour 2018). It allows a glimpse of what it could mean to inhabit tradition and authenticity and often builds an idealization of place as an idyllic perfection of nature as wild and completely tamed at the same time. Wine tourism offers a combination of offshored, cleansed experiences of belonging and detachment – a form of escapism from the daily grind and stress of urbanity. It is a clear example of the literal consumption of space (Goodman and Goodman 2016), place (Urry 2002) and nature (Moore 2015; Tsing 2015) – and revolves around value struggles along the lines of industry operators against other residents, capital against labour and small-scale conviviality against branded corporatism.

Overall, constitutive power in place wines and wine tourism is still articulated in significant ways through a domestic world of valuation, with civic, inspiration and opinion worlds also playing varying roles – depending on whether we examine place with or without geographical appellations systems, fine fines or wine tourism. These combinations contrast with the industrial/market valuation compromise that is dominant in placeless wines.

Nature

The empirical analysis of nature as a site of wine value struggle carried out in Chapter 5 highlighted four layers where different worlds of valuation overlap and clash: 1) value struggles occurring around the regulation and certification of environmental concerns; 2) value struggles related to ecology, biodiversity conservation and beauty; 3) value struggles around the meaning of 'natural wines'; and 4) value struggles concerning climate change adaptation and mitigation. Understanding the complexity of valuation processes behind these struggles is key to further unpacking the various layers and dynamics of constitutive power (see Table 14).

First, broad sustainability certifications in wine can be seen as instruments of an industrial world of valuation, even though they are not yet assembled into a global certification. Most of the existing certification systems are based on specific local conditions thus embedding some elements of a domestic world. But because these certifications are now required by retailers (especially in Nordic countries where alcohol monopolies operate), they also draw from a market world. A domestic world is also being leveraged through the dominance of locally adapted certification systems (instead of a fully fledged global one), the valorization of autochthonous varieties that are considered to be more suited to local environments, and through claims that farmers should not be asked to deliver environmental management without gaining financial benefits – otherwise the survival of a traditional economic activity would be at stake. Thus, constitutive power in this realm is based on an industrial/market compromise but faces important antagonistic pulls from the domestic world of valuation.

One of the contradictions of certifications on environmental sustainability is that they deal with the management of viticultural land as it had no alternative uses. But where land and frontier expansion are occurring (such as in Prosecco and Valpolicella), viticulture sprawl is leading to the colonization of natural, semi-natural and agricultural land and woodlands. It is changing landscapes and creating 'a globalized wine territory' (Basso and Vettoretto 2020, 5). As the value of viticultural land increases, demand falls for houses that are contiguous to vineyards due to agro-chemical spraying – leading to new forms of social stratification and a degree of depopulation in some areas. These are instances of frontier expansion and the extraction of surplus from nature for capital accumulation (Havice and Campling 2017; Moore 2015), leading to possible environmental devastation (Tsing 2015). They are also new forms of social stratification.

A second way of understanding constitutive power in relation to nature is to examine worlds of valuation around ideas of ecology, biodiversity conservation and beauty. One of the main value struggles in this realm relates to biodynamic and organic wines and operates around an inspiration world of valuation based on spirituality, wholeness and ecological balance (especially by biodynamic wine farmers). There are also important tensions between civic valuations based on the common good of ecology on the one hand, and industrial claims based on the power of science at the service of efficiency and competitiveness on the other hand. These debates also spill over into claims regarding the appropriate scale of production, different kinds of vineyard training systems, and the use of machinery and irrigation. Conservation of biodiversity and landscapes can also be based on an industrial world of valuation when embedded in certifications, and via the marketization and selling of stories wrapped around nature conservation. Sometimes, these are embedded in initiatives for the preservation of cultural landscapes, for example through UNESCO recognition in Italy. In South Africa, nature conservation efforts include the setting aside of land for perpetuity – ostensibly leaning on a civic world of valuation by aiming to preserve biodiversity for collective benefit. But given the long history of land appropriation during colonial times – and the exclusion of the Black majority from land ownership during apartheid – these conservation efforts also tend to solidify existing inequalities.

Third, value struggles around natural wines revolve around attempts to portray wine as a simple and pure product, where the job of viticulturists and winemakers is to intervene as little as possible to let nature express itself in the wine. But critics contend that natural wines actually betray place – without human intervention, they all may taste the same because they exhibit the same typical faults. This is an unintended creeping of market/industrial dynamics into the proud inspiration/opinion compromise that underpins the valuation of natural wines. Fourth, actions related to climate change in wine are primarily focused on adaptation, much less on mitigation – with the exception of current discussions on whether and how to reduce the weight of bottles, and of some concerns with reducing carbon emissions more generally. Therefore, an industrial world of valuation is dominant here, with a substantial focus on technical innovation, techniques and metrics for measuring carbon emissions, and the adoption of disease-resistant varieties. Some of these measures are being included in certification initiatives that include carbon components, thus leading to a market/industrial compromise.

In sum, constitutive power in value struggles around nature is built around a currently dominant market/industrial valuation compromise. It is prevailing in value struggles around the regulation and governance of environmental concerns, where it threatens to displace the role of domestic and civic worlds of valuation – thus further solidifying the current power imbalances between upstream and downstream value chain actors. It is also prevailing in valuations related to the impact of wine-related operations on climate change. This overall configuration of constitutive power is being challenged by domestic/civic compromises around ecology, biodiversity conservation and beauty, and by inspired/opinion compromises in relation to natural wines. However, these two latter realms refer to niche wine segments, and market/industrial logics are also creeping into them as well.

People (class, race and gender)

A market world of valuation that considers labour as a factor of production (which value is expressed in a wage) is dominant in value struggles related to people as labour – together with industrial approaches that value the skill sets that different categories of workers have (see Table 14). This combination allows producers to keep labour weak – a class-based extraction of value facilitated by keeping the labour force unorganized, tamed and portrayed as generic in its race and gender characteristics. But rising concerns about the social and labour conditions of production have forced wine industries to develop codified and standardized interventions embedded in sustainability certifications – a sign of the changing features of constitutive power.

Certification initiatives require negotiation and compromise – and thus inherently weaken more adversarial approaches, such as union strikes and/or media or NGO pressure. This means that the dominant world of valuation based on a market/industrial compromise is being consolidated also through domestic principles that value labour as tamed and subjugated. These mutually supporting worlds of valuation provide the main basis from which surplus labour is extracted – even in situations where civic principles (such as in Fairtrade wines) can return a small part of this value back to workers (partly directly, partly through community projects). At the same time, at least in South Africa, efforts are taking place to explicitly highlight the racial and gender aspects of labour exploitation in view of addressing past and current injustices – with limited success. Overall, value in wine is being extracted from (racialized and gendered) labour through a double movement of further casualization of work and the substitution of manual operations with machinery and digital technologies. At the same time, grape farmers are under financial pressure and are asked to deliver standardized social sustainability solutions while their margins are being squeezed from other actors downstream in the value chain. In other words, the value grape farmers are extracting from racialized and gendered labour is itself accumulated upstream – especially by retailers.

Finally, people as owners of tangible and intangible assets in wine are subject to a dominant market/industrial compromise as well – manifested through discussions about the financial viability and the minimum scale of production that allows enough economies of scale to ensure competitiveness. But this dominant compromise is being challenged by civic, domestic and inspiration worlds of valuation, especially in South Africa. Some of these have emancipatory potential: for example, civic valuations are emerging in view of reshaping the ownership structures of the industry to increase Black and female participation and control under the banner of Black Economic Empowerment; and inspiration approaches are playing out through the valuing of entrepreneurship and innovation, especially among Black female winemakers. But these worlds of valuation can also consolidate existing inequalities – for example, discourses on empowerment are often couched in paternalist terms, a domestic valuation narrative. Also, they have not yet travelled beyond South Africa, with the partial exception of the Nordic alcohol monopolies.

Worlds of valuation and inequality

In the rest of this section, I build on the analysis of how worlds of valuation operate in various sites of value struggle in wine to delineate how constitutive power operates in wine value chains more generally – together with some observations on what consequences these dynamics have on inequality. Place has been an important site of value struggle in wine, with producers (individually, but especially collectively) being able to shape constitutive power partly to their advantage through worlds of valuation that can weaken or at least challenge the dominant market/industrial compromise. Rising concerns with environmental and (racialized and gendered) labour conditions of wine production raised the hope that similar antagonistic shifts could strengthen the constitutive power exercised by labour, disadvantaged groups and small producers to retain more of the value they create. However, the typical global capitalist pressure to maintain or increase efficiency and competitiveness, and the underlying market/industrial valuation compromise that underpins it, are becoming even more dominant. The 2008 EU wine reform entailed a shift from a regulatory system based on supply to one based on demand, further weakening the position of farmers and farmworkers (Itçaina, Roger and Smith 2016). That this is happening in one of the most fragmented and diversified industries in the agro-food sector does not bode well for the potential of constitutive power to address past and current inequalities.

Nature has started to become an important site of value struggle only recently in wine. At the same time, the role that place (and terroir in particular) has historically played in shaping constitutive power – to retain diversification, segmentation and uniqueness – is to an extent being replaced by, or integrated with, valuation concerns related to the environment, biodiversity conservation, climate change and 'naturalness'. On the one hand, environmental stewardship could bring mainstream wines closer to the philosophy of terroir. On the other hand, it could indicate a process of naturalization of wine more generally, and thus a further delinking of production from place (Teil et al. 2011). The human element of intimate knowledge and artisanship that is embedded in terroir is lost when general environmental concerns become predominant – and especially when they are codified in standards and certification systems. Larger and more generic geographical denominations are watering down the uniqueness of site and more specific terroirs. This, together with the mainstreaming of environmental, labour and social sustainability concerns through certification, is providing new venues for re-homogenization processes and thus strengthening the position of large buyers and retailers. The total lack of visibility of labour concerns and the relative invisibility of environmental concerns in wine trade fairs (see Chapter 5) suggest that a market/industrial valuation compromise is still having the upper hand for now. The relegation of biodynamic, organic and natural wines in their own special pavilions at trade fairs also indicates that they are still seen as a somewhat separate phenomenon from mainstream winemaking – despite increasing demand.

In a way, terroir is also being remade by nature through the impact of capitalism on climate change. Climate change is upending centuries of accumulated knowledge that is the backbone of arguments for terroir – thus actually weakening the existing, even if constantly changing, place-based domestic valuations that underpin constitutive power. Ecological change is taking place much faster than the relatively slow adaptations of yesteryears, to the point that 'particular associations between wine and place will be difficult or impossible to maintain' (Inglis 2019, 38). As capitalism affects climate change, it weakens both the ecology and the taste of place, ultimately reinforcing the domination of placeless wines and the depletion of nature – at least until wine can be made somewhere and somehow (probably with machinery rather than manual labour).

That 2023 saw a historic low in global wine production, with volumes declining by 10 per cent in the EU, should ring a bell in the ears of the wine industry. In Europe, harvest volumes were affected by excessive rainfall in some places, leading to mildew and floods, and severe drought or wildfires in others (especially in southern Europe). Italy saw a 23 per cent drop in production due to heavy rainfall, floods and hail. In 2024,

> late spring frosts ... caused damage across many of Europe's largest wine-producing regions ... Just as winemakers in Chablis, France, were recovering

from the late April frosts, they got hit by a supercell thunderstorm with hail in early May. The storm affected roughly half of the appellation, resulting in crop losses and floods in wineries . . . Adverse weather events are nothing new, but the frequency and volatility of chaotic weather patterns are on the incline'.[1]

Warmer temperatures at the time of harvest also entail shorter harvesting seasons and the need for more workers for shorter periods of time, or a further switch to mechanization. Either way, these are negative outcomes for labour.

Overall, a compromise of market and industrial worlds of valuation is dominant in shaping constitutive power in wine. Important resistance elements are still occurring through domestic valuations, with civic, opinion and inspiration worlds also playing a role. At the same time, opinion and inspiration worlds of valuation tend to facilitate the individualization of sites of struggle, thus indirectly further weakening civic valuations that are based on solidarity and collective action by producers and workers. These individualization processes in the longer term open the door for a further strengthening of the market/industrial compromise and solidify the dominant position of larger wine buyers.

How these struggles develop in the near future will determine to what extent labour concerns, together with social and environmental issues and the valorization of place, will be used for further homogenization of wine offerings or as an extra source of diversification alongside or in combination with terroir. For the time being, inequality continues to characterize the wine world, but through far more sophisticated and multifaceted processes than just the extraction of surplus value from labour.

7.3 LEARNING FROM WINE TO UNDERSTAND CONTEMPORARY CAPITALISM

Understanding contemporary capitalism requires an explicit engagement with processes of value creation, appropriation and redistribution, and how they feed different forms of power – in view of building a more just, cooperative and sustainable economic system. In the past half century, advances in information and communication technology have facilitated the global outsourcing and offshoring of production activities – as a more flexible and spatially dispersed mode of manufacturing progressively emerged and consolidated (Whittaker et al. 2020). In the last part of the twentieth century and up to the onset of the financial and economic crisis of 2008, this led to the progressive reorganization of economic activity away from markets or vertical integration within multinational corporations and towards the formation of global value chains and production networks – where conception, production, and distribution of a good or service are distributed among many firms in different places around the world. These network forms of organization are not coordinated spontaneously through market exchange but are governed centrally by a group of lead firms (Gereffi, Korzeniewicz and Korzeniewicz 1994; Ponte, Gereffi and Raj-Reichert 2019). These firms, but also other actor groups, govern value chains through different forms of power (Dallas, Ponte and Sturgeon 2019), including constitutive power that is built on changing and overlapping normative foundations (the worlds of valuation examined in this book).

These trends have been accompanied by the progressive financialization of the global economy, with the 'ratio of financial assets to aggregate gross domestic product—rising from 120% in 1980 to 600% in 2020' (Bair et al. 2023, 2). Lead firms in value chains sought to outsource and offshore their operations not only to take advantage of new technology, lower labour costs in the Global South, and trade liberalization – but also in view of minimizing productive capital investment and inventory, and as a way of focusing on value capture to deliver greater shareholder value (Froud et al. 2000). This also meant a move away from long-term investment in productive assets and more attention paid to managing finance per se, as opposed to leveraging it for productive investment (Milberg and Winkler 2013). In more recent years, and particularly in the past decade, geopolitical factors and more active industrial policies have returned to the fray. There has been a partial return to more direct control of strategic inputs and materials by lead firms in value chains and an increase in the provision of public incentives for the creation of national or regional champions in key strategic industries.

Lazonick and Shin (2019) term contemporary capitalism's growing imbalance between value creation and value extraction in corporate activities as 'predatory value extraction'. They argue that this process is built largely on extracting value from labour, which wages have not kept up with productivity gains. Value extraction is manifested through the transformation of a retain-and-reinvest corporate regime, accompanied by long-term employment practices, into a downsize-and-redistribute system based on short-term employment relations. In the latter system, corporations seek to downsize their labour force and redistribute value to shareholders through cash dividends and stock buybacks (which tend to boost stock market valuations) instead of reinvesting in productive assets. In the US, this system is led by corporate executives under pressure from activist shareholders and corporate raiders, and is enabled by regulators (Lazonick and Shin 2019). In this book, I showed that predatory accumulation is related to extracting value not only from people's labour but also from their identities as owners of tangible and intangible assets, and from place and nature.

Corporations are also increasingly seeking to optimize tax liabilities and wealth distributions – not only by dispersing production activities around the globe but also by disaggregating themselves legally and financially to locate value, profit and (preferably intangible) assets in jurisdictions offering them lower taxes or secrecy (Bair et al. 2023; Seabrooke and Wigan 2022).

> The use of more sophisticated financial vehicles by both individuals and corporations has accelerated, including the ever-increasing use of offshore jurisdictions, which allow multinational corporations to avoid taxes ...That capital increasingly took financial and intangible forms expanded these opportunities. While it is logistically difficult and costly to relocate a factory, the

location of financial and intangible assets is easily achieved via amendments to contracts, changes in financial accounts, or the execution of a financial trade.

Bair et al. 2023, 2–3

Another way these trends have been characterized in extant discussions in international political economy is that contemporary capitalism has come to reward rent seekers over value creators. As discussed in Chapter 2, rent arises from 'overcharging above the "competitive" price and undercutting competition by exploiting particular advantages (including labour)' (Mazzucato 2018, 4) and/or from blocking potential competitors from entering an industry to retain a monopoly. Rent extraction is also one of the factors behind the rise of the so-called 1 per cent of the population – the very wealthy. Their wealth is increasingly deriving from income generated mainly by creating entry barriers to competitors and from the deregulation of finance, which is now disproportionately large in comparison to the rest of the economy (Stiglitz 2015). Wealth inequality is increasing dramatically, especially, but not only, in the US. For individuals, 'during the 1980–2020 period, wealth as a whole has been growing almost twice as fast as income. The result is that relative to what is produced and earned in a given year, the wealth of the rich has skyrocketed' (Saez and Zucman 2020, 11; see also Zucman 2019).

In terms of global income inequality, the middle classes in emerging economies (especially in Asia) and the global plutocracy (the top 1 per cent) have benefited in relative terms – with stagnant or small gains for the very poor in developing countries and the lower-middle classes in rich countries (Milanovic 2016). In absolute terms, however, a large share of the gains have actually accrued to the very rich. These dynamics were strengthened by the effects of the financial and economic crisis of 2008 and the following years. When it comes to within-country income inequality, Milanovic (2016) shows that, after having decreased for much of the twentieth century, it took an upswing in rich countries since the 1980s – contrary to the expectations embedded in the so-called Kuznets curve, according to which, as countries industrialize, inequality first increases and then decreases as average incomes rise. Given that between-country inequality has been narrowing (see also Baldwin 2016), Milanovic (2016) argues that it becomes even more important to tackle within-country inequality.

The rate of return to capital in the global economy has been higher than that of economic growth for decades now. Wealth inherited through generations is not being taxed sufficiently – further feeding a vicious circle of inequality (Piketty 2014, 2020). But, as Piketty (2020) eloquently argues, there is nothing natural about income and wealth inequalities (the two are related but have different dynamics; see Pfeffer and Waitkus 2021). Societies across centuries have justified inequality (or tried to dismantle it) through ideological and political work. Each of these ideologies has been based on a specific theory of borders (internationalist vs nativist) and a theory of property (egalitarian vs unequal) (Piketty 2020). Inequality therefore is not attributable to some innate economic or technological factors – it is built on ideological, normative and political work.

In this book, I have shown that, while concerns with rent-seeking are important, inequality also arises in competitive markets where value is created by some actors and appropriated or redistributed by others. I have indicated that dominant actors in wine value chains (and especially large merchants and retailers) benefit disproportionately from specific configurations of valuation, in particular a compromise of market and industrial norms. What wine has taught us is that material processes are still important in value chains, despite the immaterial basis of much wealth in contemporary capitalism. At the same time, intangible assets can be both a vector of accumulation and of collective action by weaker players, such as producers and labour, albeit with limited results so far. Wine also provides relevant examples of how wealth accumulated in other sectors of the economy can be invested in conspicuous production projects by large corporations and the very wealthy. Freed from the need to turn a profit in these wine vanity projects, these investments also distort the picture of competitiveness in the rest of the sector. Finally, we have learned that much capital accumulation arises not only from the exploitation of labour but also from place, nature and the identity of the owners of material and intangible assets (Hardt and Negri 2017; Moore 2015). This is why facilitating competition to address rent-seeking and reforming taxation systems on income and wealth, important as they may be, are not enough to address current inequalities and injustices.

Looking at capitalism through the wine glass has shown how inequality is continuously justified through normative work about the value of place, nature and people. Contemporary societies since the 1980s have been justifying increasing inequality by reifying property, valuing enterprise and idealizing meritocracy. The losers in these processes have been seen as lacking in merit, virtue and diligence (Piketty 2020). Therefore, the inequalities we observe in contemporary capitalism are far from natural occurrences. If that is the case, then the way we organize our economy should not be set in stone either. Supply chain shocks during the Covid-19 pandemic and the war in Ukraine have taught us that 'established mantras, such as just-in-time stock management, outsourcing and the minimization of inventory to improve returns over investment ratios are being reconsidered, at least as long as supply strictures persist... Reinvestment in tangible assets rather than distribution of dividends is no longer taboo' (Bair et al. 2023, 11). Geopolitics is becoming more important in shaping the geography of investment,[2] together with new technologies that have allowed some degree of reshoring, nearshoring or friend-shoring of functions that were previously carried out in locations with lower ratios of labour-to-competence cost (Coe and Yeung 2015). To the extent that reshoring occurs, it may also lead to 'greater state insistence that the wealth arising from those chains accumulates to their jurisdictions rather than "offshore"' (Bair et al. 2023, 11). Furthermore, civil society organizations have been pressuring corporations to be accountable for labour and environmental conditions of production that eventually shape inequality; intergovernmental organizations are trying to push for more stringent tax transparency requirements; activists are developing sophisticated strategies for tracing value chains and targeting lead firms; and the new EU Corporate Sustainability Due Diligence Directive is now requiring corporations to set up due diligence procedures along their value chains. These processes can open up new venues of action by environmental and labour groups.

But these opportunities for antagonism can also be thwarted, watered down or mummified by established interest groups – and their consultants and lawyers (Mazzucato and Collington 2023). In this book, I have chronicled how different and potentially more emancipatory worlds of valuation are counteracted by normative pushbacks or new valuation discourses and practices that ultimately reinforce inequality, labour exploitation and environmental destruction (see also Buller 2022; Ponte, Noe and Brockington 2022). Wine is one of the most diversified and fragmented industries in the agro-food sector. If there were hope for better ways of organizing economic activity, wine is surely where one should start looking. While change may be taking place in some corners of the wine industry, the majority of wine sold globally is supplied by industrial operations and/or through the exploitation of (racialized and gendered) labour. The valorization of place and the possibility of thoughtfully managing the environment are being homogenized and codified in standards and certifications that facilitate further capital accumulation by wine merchants and retailers. This further squeezes the margins of smaller wine producers and especially grape growers – with cascading effects on the labour conditions of farmworkers.

The analysis of constitutive power provided in this book shows that the appropriation of value arising from changing interpretations of how to handle place, nature and and people also hides the drivers of inequality and its manifestations. The inroads of market-industrial valuation compromises entail that 'rather than appraise our economy from the perspective of supporting life – recognizing the ways in which our economic institutions and systems currently drive social and ecological crises – instead we [still] appraise life, and any action taken to protect it, in economic terms' (Buller 2022, 9–10). These valuations operate a diffusion of responsibility by design and serve the interests of the private sector, rather than meeting key social and environmental objectives (Gabor 2021). Therefore, an examination of valuation processes remains central for unveiling forms of power, such as constitutive power, that despite being subtle, are no less impactful on inequality.

Overall, these reflections suggest that the exercise of power in contemporary capitalism draws from valuation devices that, while appearing to address labour exploitation and environmental destruction, actually manage to defuse the possibility of radical change. Capital is able to extract value from place, nature and people through the material political economies of access to, and exploitation of, natural and human resources. That capital accumulation is also based to a large extent on intangible assets is well known, but this book shows that it operates not only through the monopolization of intellectual property rights but also by leveraging ideals, identities and experiences related to tradition, authenticity and heritage. In this context, valuation 'increasingly involves activating subjectivities in a network, capturing, siphoning off, and appropriating what they make in common . . . [This way, identities have come to serve] as a privileged means to property and also a form of property itself, which promises to maintain or restore the hierarchies of the social order' (Hardt and Negri 2017, 28, 53).

In conclusion, current modes of value extraction still include conquest, dispossession and exploitation, but also operate through monopolizing intellectual property, leveraging winner-takes-all network effects and privately appropriating the common – place, nature and (badly paid or unpaid) social work and knowledge. Therefore, accumulation is based not only on superior bargaining power and regulatory and institutional setups that benefit capital against labour and nature but also on manoeuvrings around conflicting valuation narratives and practices – in other words, on constitutive power. A continued involvement in researching valuation processes in the global economy, and in value chains in particular, is therefore essential. Ultimately, global and local inequalities and the protection of the natural environment will be addressed only when we combine the politics of access to resources, production and processing with the normative work that shapes power relations between capital, labour and nature.

APPENDIX TABLES

Appendix Table 1 List of interviews (South Africa)

Interview #	Date	Function(s)	Type of actor
SAW1	02/11/21	Communications Director	Industry Association
SAW2	15/03/22	Communications Director	Industry Association
SAW3	17/03/22	Director of Enterprise Development	Industry Association
SAW4	22/03/22	CEO	Private Winery
SAW5	22/03/22	Export Manager	Wine Cooperative
SAW6	23/03/22	Manager	Wholesaler
SAW7	23/03/22	Director	NGO
SAW8	24/03/22	Sales and Marketing Director	Wine Estate
SAW9	24/03/22	Director	Private Winery
SAW10	24/03/22	CEO	NGO
SAW11	25/03/22	Chairperson	Industry Association
SAW12	25/03/22	Director	Consulting Company
SAW13	28/03/22	Owner	Private Winery
SAW14	28/03/22	Principal	Training Institution
SAW15	29/03/22	CEO	NGO
SAW16	29/03/22	Operations and Export Managers	Distributor
SAW17	28/10/22	Head of Sales	Producing Wholesaler
SAW18	29/03/22	Operations Manager	Industry Association
SAW19	30/03/22	Head of Corporate Strategy	Producing Wholesaler
SAW20	30/03/22	Head of Sales	Producing Wholesaler
SAW21	30/03/22	Executive Manager	Research Institution
SAW22	31/03/22	COO and Owner	Wholesaler
SAW23	31/03/22	Wine Master, Writer	Wine Journalist and Taster
SAW24	31/03/22	Lecturer	Wine Educator and Taster
SAW25	31/03/22	Section director	Government agency
SAW26	01/04/22	Financial Manager	Wine Cooperative
SAW27	01/04/22	Owner	Investor
SAW28	04/04/22	Managing Director, Cellar Master	Private Winery
SAW29	04/04/22	Director	NGO
SAW30	04/04/22	Freelancer	Wine Journalist
SAW31	05/04/22	Sales Director	Wine Estate
SAW32	05/04/22	Destination Director, Researcher, Head of Research Unit	Government Agency
SAW33	05/04/22	Commercial Manager, Senior Programme Officer	Sustainability Certification
SAW34	06/04/22	Wine Buyer	Retailer
SAW35	06/04/22	Associate Professor	Research Institution
SAW36	06/04/22	Professor	Research Institution
SAW37	12/04/22	Director	Importer of SA Wine
SAW38	22/04/22	Director	NGO
SAW39	05/10/22	Project Manager	NGO
SAW40	05/10/22	Education Officer	NGO

(Continued)

SAW41	07/10/22	Systems Manager	Wine Cooperative
SAW42	07/10/22	Sales and Marketing Director	Wine Estate
SAW43	07/10/22	Owner	Private Winery
SAW44	05/10/22	Director	NGO
SAW45	06/10/22	Owner and Winemaker	BEE Winery
SAW46	06/10/22	Owner	BEE Winery
SAW47	06/10/22	CEO and Project Manager	BEE Winery
SAW48	07/10/22	Sales Manager	BEE Winery
SAW49	11/10/22	Head of Corporate Strategy	Producing Wholesaler
SAW50	12/10/22	Owner	Private Winery
SAW51	07/10/22	Director	Private Winery
SAW52	13/10/22	Winemaker and Assistant Winemaker	Wine Estate
SAW53	13/10/22	Managing Director, Tasting Room Manager, BEE Shareholder	Wine Cooperative
SAW54	13/10/22	Communications Director	Private Winery
SAW55	12/10/22	Brand Owner	BEE Winery
SAW56	14/10/22	Winemaker	Wine Estate
SAW57	14/10/22	Export Manager	Private Winery
SAW58	14/10/22	Specialist Pruner	Service Provider
SAW59	19/10/22	Owner	Marketer
SAW60	21/10/22	Compliance Officer	Private Winery
SAW61	24/10/22	Owner and Director	Wine Estate
SAW62	24/10/22	Production Director and Group Winemaker	Producing Wholesaler
SAW63	24/10/22	Owner and Director	Wholesaler
SAW64	25/10/22	COO and Chief Winemaker	Private Winery
SAW65	26/10/22	Managing Director	Wine Cooperative
SAW66	26/10/22	CEO, Marketing Manager, Winemaker	Private Winery
SAW67	21/10/22	Owner	Wine Estate
SAW68	24/10/22	Brand Owner, Sales and Marketing Dir.	BEE Winery
SAW69	27/10/22	International Sales and Marketing Manager	Wine Cooperative
SAW70	27/10/22	Head of Marketing and Sales	Wine Estate
SAW71	27/10/22	Head of Sales and Cellar Master	Private Winery
SAW72	31/10/22	Production Manager	Wholesaler
SAW73	31/10/22	Owner and CEO	Wholesaler
SAW74	31/10/22	Owner	Label Designer
SAW75	01/11/22	Cellar Master	Private Winery
SAW76	02/11/22	Chief Operating Officer	Private Winery
SAW77	02/11/22	Owner	Wholesaler
SAW78	03/11/22	Project Manager and Fairtrade Officer	NGO
SAW79	03/11/22	Systems Manager	Wine Cooperative
SAW80	03/11/22	Owner	Private Winery
SAW81	12/11/22	General Manager, Marketing and Information Officer	Wine Estate
SAW82	16/11/22	Owner	Wine Estate
SAW83	12/11/22	Marketing Manager	Wine Estate
SAW84	18/10/22	Owners, HR Director, Viticulturist, Cellar Master	Private Winery

Appendix Table 2 List of interviews (Italy and Europe)

Interview #	Date	Function(s)	Type of actor
P1	20/10/20	General Manager, Owner	Private Winery
P2	20/10/20	Marketing Manager	Private Winery
P3	20/10/20	General Manager, Owner	Private Winery
P4	20/10/20	Professor	Research Institution
P5	20/10/20	President, Communications Officer	Geographical Appellation Consortium
P6	20/10/20	Communications Officer	Geographical Appellation Consortium
P7	26/10/20	President	Geographical Appellation Consortium
P8	26/10/20	Director	Geographical Appellation Consortium
P9	26/10/20	Communications Officer	Geographical Appellation Consortium
P10	16/11/20	Secretary General	Farmworker Labour Union
P11	16/11/20	Former Inspector	Farmworker Labour Union
P12	16/11/20	Secretary of Confederation	Farmworker Labour Union
P13	22/01/21	Director	Wine Cooperative
P14	22/01/21	Director of Production	Wine Cooperative
P15	22/01/21	Marketing and Export Manager	Wine Cooperative
P16	23/01/21	Owner	Private Winery
P17	23/01/21	Marketing Manager	Private Winery
P18	29/01/21	Owner	Private Winery
P19	29/01/21	Owner	Private Winery
P20	29/01/21	Marketing Manager	Private Winery
P21	12/02/21	President	Geographical Appellation Consortium
P22	19/02/21	Owner	Private Winery
V1	15/04/21	Owner	Private Winery
V2	29/04/21	General Manager	Private Winery
V3	04/05/21	Owner	Private Winery
V4	04/05/21	Director Of Wine Production	Private Winery
V5	06/05/21	Owner	Private Winery
V6	06/05/21	Owner	Private Winery
V7	06/05/21	Communications and Marketing Director	Private Winery
V8	06/05/21	Enologist, Quality Manager	Wine Cooperative
V9	06/05/21	Technical Department	Geographical Appellation Consortium
V10	06/05/21	Technical Department	Geographical Appellation Consortium
V11	07/05/21	General Manager, Owner	Private Winery
V12	07/05/21	Owner	Private Winery
V13	31/05/21	Communications and Marketing Director	Private Winery
V14	07/07/21	Owner	Private Winery
V15	08/07/21	Marketing Manager	Private Winery
V16	08/07/21	Owner	Private Winery
V17	08/07/21	President	Wine Route Association
V18	08/07/21	Owner	Private Winery
V19	09/07/21	Owner	Private Winery
V20	09/07/21	Owner	Grape Supplier
V21	29/06/22	Enologist	Private Winery
V22	29/06/22	Owner	Private Winery
V23	07/07/22	Owner, Marketing Manager	Private Winery
IG1	22/01/21	Director	Sustainability Certification
IG2	09/07/21	Owner	Winemaking Input Supplier
IG3	17/06/22	President	Sustainability Certification

(Continued)

IG4	27/06/22	President	Winemaker Association
IG5	28/06/22	Consultant and Researcher	Research Institution
IG6	29/06/22	Professor	Research Institution
IG7	30/06/22	Product Certification Officer	Sustainability Auditing Firm
IG8	30/06/22	Product Certification Officer	Sustainability Auditing Firm
IG9	30/06/22	Director, Consultancy and Training	Wine Industry Association
IG10	30/06/22	General Manager	Sustainability Certification
IG11	01/07/22	Technical Support Officer	Sustainability Certification
IG12	01/07/22	Researcher	Research Institution
IG13	01/07/22	Chairperson of the Board of Directors	Sustainability Certification
IG14	07/07/22	President	Sustainability Certification
IG15	07/07/22	Researcher	Research Institution
IG16	07/07/22	Professor	Sustainability Certification
IG17	11/07/22	Executive Vice President	Media Company
WG1	21/06/22	Sustainability Manager	Monopoly Importer
WG2	27/06/22	Outreach and Development Manager	Sustainability Certification
WG3	27/06/22	Consultant	Sustainability Certification
WG4	01/07/22	Climate Change Director	Sustainability Association
WG5	27/03/23	Head of Logistics and Sustainability	Wine Importer (Germany)
WG6	29/03/23	Director of Off-Trade Sales	Wine Importer (UK)

Legend: P = Prosecco; V = Valpolicella; IG = Italy General; WG = World General.

NOTES

Chapter 1

1 Source: Interview SAW63.
2 Source: Interview V16.
3 Source: Interview SAW79.
4 Bacchus is the Roman name of the mythological Greek god Dionysus, son of Zeus.
5 I owe this formulation to Lisa Ann Richey, who has published widely on the paradoxes of ethical solidarity and the selling of 'values' (Richey 2024; Richey and Ponte 2011).
6 Some of these interviews were carried out in collaboration with Reena das Nair and Shingie Chisoro, University of Johannesburg, as part of my activities as a Distinguished Visiting Professor there in 2019–2024.
7 For definitions of wine value chain actors, see Chapter 3.
8 Some of these interviews were carried out in collaboration with Valentina de Marchi, Eleonora di Maria and Marco Bettiol of the University of Padova.

Chapter 2

1 Parts of this section draw, in edited form, from Dallas, Ponte and Sturgeon (2019) and Ponte (2019).
2 Value chain research that has applied a governmentality approach to power and governance include Gibbon and Ponte (2008) and Raj-Reichert (2013); neo-Gramscian approaches include Levy (2008), Palpacuer and Roussey (2023), and Palpacuer (2008).
3 There is of course a much larger literature on legitimacy in the social sciences (e.g. Foret 2008; Johnson, Dowd and Ridgeway 2006), including in business studies (e.g. Haack, Schilke and Zucker 2021; Suchman 1995). In this book, I chose to focus on normative issues from the standpoint of valuation and thus I do not discuss legitimacy in depth.
4 Kaplinsky (2005) distinguishes between: monopoly rents, such as tariffs or geographical indications, which protect markets and restrict price competition; Schumpeterian rents, such as state subsidies or intellectual property rights, which protect profits arising from innovation or invention; redistributive rents, which arise from policies that target specific social and political necessities; and learning rents, which are embedded in initiatives that seek to enhance skills or organizational capabilities.
5 For a dissenting view, see Stark (2009) for whom the multiplicity of evaluative principles is actually creating uncertainty.
6 Karpik (2010) delineates different regimes of coordination that characterize 'markets for singularities' – accounting for different ways of qualifying a product and different judgement devices that are attached to each qualification. Karpik lists five possible types of judgement devices: cicerones (judgement provided by critics and in

guidebooks); rankings (ordering singular products along an ordinal scale); appellations (names defining singular products); confluences (spatial arrangements of products in retail and/or sales techniques); and personal networks (acquiring knowledge by word of mouth). He also identifies a series of regimes of coordination that are linked to these devices, depending on: whether knowledge is personal or impersonal; whether knowledge is substantial (related to the specific content of the good or service, such as reviews and guides) or pertains to formal devices (as in rankings); and whether it serves small or large markets.
7 Boltanski and Esquerre (2020) distinguish different forms of valuation by identifying two relevant axes: the form of presentation (in the analytic language related to the distinct properties of the thing; or in the form of a narrative featuring or evoking events or persons); and the commercial potential (the expectation that things may lose or acquire value in time). These combinations yield four forms of valuation: standard (analytic presentation, negative commercial potential; e.g. industrial products); trend (narrative presentation, negative potential; e.g. fashion items); asset (analytic presentation, positive potential; e.g. works of art); and collection (narrative presentation, positive potential; e.g. collectibles).
8 Other research has shown how specific quality conventions are behind collective approaches seeking to promote specific localities (Cidell and Alberts 2006; Guthey 2008; Lindkvist and Sanchez 2008; Sánchez-Hernández, Aparicio-Amador and Alonso-Santos 2010) and/or have identified which innovation systems and regulation enable firms to move between different conventions (Barbera and Audifredi 2012; Lindkvist and Sanchez 2008; Stræte 2004). Finally, others (Prosperi, Vergamini and Bartolini 2020; Quiñones-Ruiz 2020; Raynolds 2012; Raynolds, Murray and Heller 2007) have leveraged convention theory to explain how quality contestations arise and are resolved along the value chains for fair trade and organic products; how collective enrolment in particular conventions facilitates forms of control at a distance; and how these may lead to the mainstreaming of these certifications (Raynolds 2009; Renard 2005). Raynolds (2009) in particular highlights that it is not ethics per se that challenges power structures in value chain governance, but rather how ethics content is embedded in different conventions.
9 Other common worlds have been proposed in the literature, including the 'network world' (Boltanski and Chiapello 2005), the 'green world' (Blok 2013; Latour 1998; Thévenot, Moody and Lafaye 2000) and the 'information world' (Thévenot 2007). I will not engage with these worlds as they do not appear to hold explanatory power in wine (but see a full discussion on why I do not apply the 'green world' in Chapter 5).

Chapter 3

1 See, inter alia, the *International Journal of Wine Marketing*, the *International Journal of Wine Business Research* and the *Journal of Wine Economics*.
2 See also OIV, State of the World Vine and Wine Sector in 2022, April 2023. https://www.oiv.int/sites/default/files/documents/2023_SWVWS_report_EN.pdf.
3 See:
https://www.oiv.int/public/medias/5958/oiv-state-of-the-vitiviniculture-world-market-april-2018.pdf;
https://www.oiv.int/public/medias/7298/oiv-state-of-the-vitivinicultural-sector-in-2019.pdf;

https://www.oiv.int/public/medias/7909/oiv-state-of-the-world-vitivinicultural-sector-in-2020.pdf;
https://www.oiv.int/sites/default/files/documents/eng-state-of-the-world-vine-and-wine-sector-april-2022-v6_0.pdf;
https://www.oiv.int/sites/default/files/documents/OIV_State_of_the_world_Vine_and_Wine_sector_in_2022_2.pdf;
https://www.oiv.int/sites/default/files/2024-04/OIV_STATE_OF_THE_WORLD_VINE_AND_WINE_SECTOR_IN_2023.pdf.

4 Source: Calculated from 'OIV - State of the world vine and wine sector 2023'. Available at: https://www.oiv.int/sites/default/files/2024-04/OIV_STATE_OF_THE_WORLD_VINE_AND_WINE_SECTOR_IN_2023.pdf.
5 Ibid.
6 Ibid.
7 Source: Various presentations at the ProWein 2023 and Vinitaly 2024 wine fairs.
8 However, various forms of diversification of wine go back to ancient Egypt, Greece and Rome, while the concept of *clos* was developed by Cistercian monks in the twelfth century (Howland, 2019a; Unwin, 1991).
9 This system subsequently found its equivalent adaptations in various European countries (including in Italy from the 1960s onwards) and eventually at the EU level.
10 Source: https://www.wipo.int/wipolex/en/treaties/details/231.
11 Source: https://www.wipo.int/treaties/en/registration/lisbon/.
12 Parts of this section draw in edited form from two working papers (Das Nair and Chisoro 2023; Das Nair, Chisoro, and Ponte 2023).
13 See in particular the documentary 'Bitter Grapes' by Tom Heinemann: http://www.bittergrapes.net.
14 Source: SAWIS Statistical Booklets, 2006 and 2021.
15 Source: Interviews SAW66, SAW75, SAW41, SAW79.
16 Source: SAWIS Statistical Booklet, 2021.
17 Sources for the following bullet points (unless otherwise mentioned): SAWIS Statistical Booklet, 2021 and https://www.wosa.co.za/The-Industry/Overview/.
18 Source: SAWIS Statistical Booklets, 2006 and 2021.
19 Source: SAW6.
20 Source: SAWIS Statistical Booklets, 2006 and 2021.
21 Source: https://www.gov.za/sites/default/files/gcis_document/202106/44701gen353.pdf.
22 Of relevance are also government organizations in wine tourism, such as the Cape Town and Western Cape Tourism Trade and Investment Agency (Wesgro), which aims to position the Western Cape as a leading cultural and adventure capital in wine. The wine industry is also supported by various educational organizations such as Stellenbosch University, which offers several pre- and post-graduate courses in viticulture, oenology and wine biotechnology, in addition to laboratories for testing and chemical analysis. The Cape Wine Academy offers courses for wine professionals and enthusiasts at various levels. Programmes such as the Pinotage Youth Development Academy provide skills development opportunities and certifications for youths from historically disadvantaged backgrounds (source: https://www.pyda.co.za/know-us).
23 Source: https://www.news24.com/fin24/companies/new-central-body-for-sa-wine-industry-announced-20230119.
24 Source: https://www.wosa.co.za/The-Industry/Overview/.

25 Sources: https://www.sawis.co.za/info/download/Vineyards_2015_1.pdf and SAWIS Statistical Booklets, 2007 and 2022.
26 A similar set of observations is also provided in Nugent (2024a).
27 Production costs include day-to-day cash expenditure as well as provisions for renewal. Production costs, however, exclude entrepreneurial remuneration, interest obligations and tax. Cash expenditure includes direct costs, labour costs, general expenses and non-capital related expenses on mechanization and fixed improvements (Source: Vinpro Production Plan Survey, 2022, obtained from Vinpro).
28 See also: Nedbank Vinpro Day presentation, slide 10, available at https://vinpro.co.za/wp-content/uploads/2023/01/2.-Nedbank-Vinpro-Info-Day-2023-Winning-in-Wine-by-Rico-Basson.pdf.
29 Source: Nedbank Vinpro Day presentation, slide 10.
30 Source: https://vinpro.co.za/liquor-sales-open-but-wine-industry-hit-with-other-setbacks/#:~:text=Sales%20cut%20off,20%20weeks%20since%20March%202020.
31 A partial exception to this picture is the Swartland Independent Producers (SIP) initiative within the Wine of Origin Swartland area, where prescriptive elements in viticulture and winemaking guide members' practices (Nugent 2024a, 293–6).
32 Source: https://www.wosa.co.za/wosadocs/72020/Wine%20Map%202020-07%20-%20150dpi.jpg.
33 Source: https://www.wosa.co.za/Wine-Country/Wine-Tourism/Wine-Routes/.
34 Source: I and M Futureneer Advisors, SAWIS and South Africa Wine, 'The economic value of the South African wine tourism industry in 2022', available at https://www.sawis.co.za/info/download/Economic_Value_of_Wine_Tourism_in_SA_2022_FINAL_2024.pdf.
35 Source: http://dati.istat.it/.
36 Ibid.
37 Ibid.
38 Source: https://www.inumeridelvino.it/solo-numeri/solonumeri-italia/esportazioni-di-vino-italia-valore-e-volume.
39 Source: https://www.areastudimediobanca.com/it/product/sintesi-il-settore-vinicolo-italia-ed-2023?check_logged_in=1.
40 Source: ISMEA, 'Il settore vitivinicolo alla sfida della PAC post-2020: complementarietà degli interventi tra i e ii pilastro e prospettive'. Available at: https://www.ismea.it/flex/cm/pages/ServeBLOB.php/L/IT/IDPagina/10565.
41 Since 2018, wine consortia have been allowed by Italian regulation to seek alignment between demand and supply. This market management system works as follows: a) when supply exceeds demand, stocks of base wine that are within the annual limit are set aside for a possible sparkling process and bottling later in the season, or eventually to be sold as base wine; and b) when demand exceeds supply, a maximum 20 per cent of total production of base wine over the annual production limit can be sold as DOC/DOCG following a regional decree (P4). The management of volumes and certification of DOC and DOCG bottles is carried out by Valoritalia, a private company appointed by the Ministry of Agriculture to certify grape variety, vintage and geographical origin.
42 Source: Elaboration of data provided by the Prosecco DOC and Conegliano and Valdobbiadene Prosecco DOCG consortia. Data for 2023: https://www.winemeridian.com/mercati/prosecco-doc-bilancio-2023-contrazione-prevedibile-pronte-iniziative-mirate/; https://news.unioneitalianavini.it/i-numeri-2023-del-prosecco-doc-e-docg-sul-cv-4-2024/#:~:text=el%202023%20la%20produzione%20della,638%2C6%20milioni%20di%20bottiglie.
43 Source: https://www.tb.camcom.gov.it/uploads/SST/pdf/Economia_Territorio/2022_Il_Prosecco_e%20_le_sue_tre_denominazioni_DOC_e_DOCG.pdf.

44 Source: Elaboration from data provided by Consorzio Prosecco DOC.
45 Source: OIV, The Global Sparkling Wine Market, April 2020. Available at: https://www.oiv.int/public/medias/7291/oiv-sparkling-focus-2020.pdf.
46 Source: Consorzio per la Tutela Vini Valpolicella, Valpolicella Annual Report 2023. https://www.consorziovalpolicella.it/wp-content/uploads/2023/06/dossier-valpolicella-annual-report-2023-interattivo.pdf.

Chapter 4

1 For a poignant discussion on 'placeless' food more generally, see inter alia Morgan, Marsden and Murdoch (2006).
2 Unit export prices as presented by Ettore Nicoletto of Nomisma at the seminar 'The values of wine: The socioeconomic impact of the Italian supply chain tested by markets and new consumption trends', Vinitaly 2024, organized by Federvini. Heated discussions on limiting grape yields and increasing quality also featured at the seminar 'Il vino e' . . . Made in Italy', also at Vinitaly 2024, organized by the Ministry of Agriculture, Food Sovereignty and Forests.
3 For a more optimistic take on the potential role of terroir and geographical origin in valorizing South African wine, see Nugent (2024a).
4 Consorzio Tutela del Vino Conegliano Valdobbiadene Prosecco (2020) 'I terroirs del Conegliano Valdobbiadene Prosecco: Studio sull'origine della qualità nelle colline del patrimonio UNESCO', Pieve di Soligo (TV), p. 15 (translation by the author). *Rive* are steep and difficult to reach plots.
5 Source: https://winenews.it/en/the-pdo-economy-of-italian-wine-is-worth-11-3-billion-euros-with-still-many-challenges-to-overcome_516814/ and https://www.politicheagricole.it/flex/cm/pages/ServeBLOB.php/L/IT/IDPagina/4923.
6 RAI 3 Report, 'Piccoli chimici', documentary first aired on 17 December 2023. Available at: https://www.raiplay.it/video/2023/12/Piccoli-chimici---Report-17122023-21df958a-e253-4c34-9382-9bd248d4bdfc.html.
7 The lack of requirement for nutritional and ingredient information on wine bottles was a unique situation in the food industry in the EU until recently (while a list of allergens had already been required). This situation has now changed with new EU regulation (1308/2013 as amended by 2021/2017) that came into force on 8 December 2023. Bottled wine is now required to indicate nutritional values and a list of all the ingredients that have been used to make the wine. Only the energy values need to be placed on the label, while the complete nutritional information and list of ingredients can be made available through a QR code. One possible interpretation for this flexibility is that there is not enough space on the label for all the information required. Another is that some of the ingredients, if listed on the label, would scare off consumers. Therefore, the industry preferred to have the possibility of placing an extra burden on the consumer to find such information by scanning a QR code. See https://eur-lex.europa.eu/legal-content/EN/TXT/?uri=celex%3A32013R1308 and https://eur-lex.europa.eu/legal-content/EN/TXT/HTML/?uri=CELEX:3202 1R2117.
8 RAI 3 Report, 'Piccoli chimici', documentary first aired on 17 December 2023. Available at: https://www.raiplay.it/video/2023/12/Piccoli-chimici---Report-17122023-21df958a-e253-4c34-9382-9bd248d4bdfc.html.
9 Source: https://www.sawis.co.za/cert/productionareas.php.

10 Hart Feuer and Daniel Monterescu, 'Recalibrating terroir for Asia: Heritage sake and wine in Japan', presented at the international workshop 'Wine, Space, Place: Global geographies of wine cultivation, production and consumption', Catholic University of Eichstätt-Ingolstadt, 22–23 February 2024.
11 For an engaging discussion of authenticity, including in relation to food consumption and tourism, see Lipovetsky (2021).
12 Source: Vasco Boatto, Eugenio Pomarici and Luigino Barisan, 'Conegliano Valdobbiadene Prosecco DOCG — Oltre il 2019', available at: https://www.prosecco.it/wp-content/uploads/2019/12/Rapporto-Economico-2019.pdf.
13 Ibid.
14 Source: https://www.thedrinksbusiness.com/2011/08/top-10-wine-scandals/7/.
15 Sparkling wines in Italy were traditionally drunk at Christmas and Easter, but they are now purchased more evenly throughout the year, with a peak in November in preparation for the holiday season (P4).
16 Source: Consorzio Tutela del Vino Conegliano Valdobbiadene Prosecco (2020) 'I terroirs del Conegliano Valdobbiadene Prosecco: Studio sull'origine della qualità nelle colline del patrimonio UNESCO', Pieve di Soligo (TV), 26.
17 Producers wanted to avoid what had just happened to 'Tocai' wine in Friuli (now called 'Friulano') after the name was assigned for exclusive use to Hungarian Tokai (P4).
18 Source: https://www.theguardian.com/world/2006/sep/24/italy.foodanddrink.
19 This observation was made by local interviewees featured in *Report*, a popular Italian programme of investigative journalism. See https://www.raiplay.it/video/2016/11/La-frazione-di-Prosecco-e7aa7183-4c34-4f3b-9e0d-b84e4e409d7f.html.
20 RAI 3 Report, 'La frazione di Prosecco, Part 1', 14 November 2016. Available at: https://www.rai.it/programmi/report/inchieste/La-frazione-di-prosecco-82f70b9c-ce75-461d-b98d-cb5b8894fd58.html.
21 RAI 3 Report 'La frazione di Prosecco, Part 2', 20 November 2017. Available at: https://www.youtube.com/watch?v=WWAc4UIB8CQ.
22 Source: https://www.trevisotoday.it/attualita/prosek-zaia-progetto-aggregazione-roma-14-giugno-2022.html.
23 Source: https://winenews.it/en/reform-of-the-eu-gi-system-green-light-unanimously-in-the-agriculture-commission_495349/.
24 Other cases against individual producers using similar names in Germany (such as Prisecco, Perisecco or PrimaSecco) were brought to the EUIPO office, which ruled in favour of the Italian plaintiffs. See RAI 3 Report, 'Il Prosecco e i suoi fratelli', 10 July 2023. https://www.raiplay.it/video/2023/07/Il-Prosecco-e-i-suoi-fratelli---Report---10072023-31fe20f4-2985-4b31-ae4c-cd3b2c98ec86.html. The Prosecco DOC consortium also won a case at the Appeals Court in Singapore against 'Australian Prosecco' exports to Singapore. However, Australia will continue to produce and sell 'Prosecco' wine domestically following the breakdown of trade agreement negotiations with the EU. See https://www.meiningers-international.com/wine/news/italy-wins-against-australia-prosecco-dispute.
25 Daniel Monterescu, 'The uses and abuses of terroir: Wine across imperial borders and colonial frontiers', presented at the international workshop 'Wine, Space, Place: Global geographies of wine cultivation, production and consumption', Catholic University of Eichstätt-Ingolstadt, 22–23 February 2024.
26 Labelling requirements for South African wine, art. 12. https://www.sawis.co.za/winelaw/download/LABELLING_REQUIREMENTS_FOR_SOUTH_AFRICAN_WINE_2019.pdf.
27 Ibid., art. 13.

28 Negro and Hannan (2022) also compare the evolution of Barolo styles with that of Brunello di Montalcino, a wine produced in Toscana. Like Barolo and Amarone della Valpolicella, Brunello di Montalcino is considered one of the most iconic wines of Italy. While small family production is the norm in Barolo, in Montalcino large firms from outside the region, and family farms that do not have local origins, are much more important. Contrary to Barolo, in Montalcino there was very little commercial wine production before the establishment of the DOC in 1966 (and later the DOCG). Because of the voting system applied in the *consorzio* (with voting rights proportional to the volume of production), larger producers exercise predominant control over decisions in Montalcino (thus diminishing the degree of collective action). Because larger producers wish to make a wine that can be commercialized faster from the time of vinification, various alterations to the rules are now allowing them to use smaller oak barrels and to release the wine after only one year in the bottle, down from three and a half years in the 1980s.

29 Source: https://www.consorziovalpolicella.it/wp-content/uploads/2024/02/DisciplinareAmarone-della-Valpolicella.pdf.

30 The Cape Floral Kingdom was added to the UNESCO World Heritage list in 2004, but it is not related to the vineyards that are planted within or contiguous to the protected area. Yet, it spurred an effort to present viticulture as 'environmentally defensible', including the development of the 'Integrity and Sustainability' seal and the Biodiversity and Wine Initiative (Nugent 2024a, 256–7) (see also Chapter 5).

31 The valorization of heritage can also take less formalized incarnations through individual wineries' storytelling about place, architecture, type of fermentation/ageing vessel and landscape beauty. In South Africa, this is often linked to the beauty of Old Dutch architecture, even though it brings with it a heritage of colonialism, slavery and apartheid. In Italy, in addition to Tuscan-style landscaping and architecture, the use of amphoras has also been linked to heritage, given that the Romans used them to transport all sorts of grains and liquids, including wine. Amphoras can also help express terroir better because they do not impart forced flavours into the wine and they are attractive and aesthetically pleasing to visitors (SAW71).

32 Source: https://whc.unesco.org/en/list/.

33 Source. Consorzio Conegliano Valdobbiadene DOCG (2019). Conegliano Valdobbiadene Dossier: L' amore per la terra parla con i fatti. Pieve di Soligo, Italy, p. 9. Translation by the author.

34 Ibid., 9–10, 15.

35 Ibid., 11.

36 Ibid., 12-13.

37 Source: https://www.consorziovalpolicella.it.

38 Source: https://famigliestoriche.it.

39 In 2017, a court in Venice had decreed that the term 'Amarone' could not be used by the *Famiglie dell'Amarone d'Arte* association, and that it had to change its name to *Famiglie storiche*. In 2019, the court of appeals confirmed this outcome. However, the European Union Intellectual Property Office ruled against the consortium, as it did not consider the name of the association misleading for the consumer. Eventually, in 2023, the two parts came to an amicable agreement and there is now talk of (some of the families) rejoining the consortium. See: https://www.consorziovalpolicella.it/vino-fine-contenzioso-consorzio-valpolicella-famiglie-storiche/; https://nordesteconomia.gelocal.it/imprese/2021/05/20/news/amarone-fine-della-guerra-del-nome-le-famiglie-storiche-rinunciano-1.40295221; https://famigliestoriche.it.

40 See also https://oldvineproject.co.za.
41 Olivia Lindsay, 'Winemakers in Languedoc-Roussilion: Resilience, "good taste" and "bad" reputations', presented at the international workshop 'Wine, Space, Place: Global geographies of wine cultivation, production and consumption', Catholic University of Eichstätt-Ingolstadt, 22–23 February 2024.
42 Regina Lee (Master of Wine), 'How AI will change the ways we work in the wine business', presentation at the Wine2Wine Business Forum, Verona, 13–14 November 2023.
43 Laura Catena, 'Enotourism: A social media journey to #1', presentation at the Wine2Wine Business Forum, Verona, 13–14 November 2023.
44 Source: https://www.cervim.org.
45 Article 7 of 'Testo unico della vite e del vino Legge 238 del 12/12/2016' https://www.politicheagricole.it/flex/cm/pages/ServeBLOB.php/L/IT/IDPagina/12012.
46 The 'Volcanic Agriculture of Europe' project focuses on selected wines and cheeses: Soave DOC, Soave Superiore DOCG, and Lessini Durello DOC in Verona, Italy (all whites, some in areas overlapping with Valpolicella reds); Santorini DOP, and Monte Veronese Formaggio DOP.
47 Source: https://volcanicagricultureofeurope.com.

Chapter 5

1 Source: https://www.nzwine.com/en/sustainability/swnz/?submit=.
2 Source: https://www.sustainablewinegrowing.org.
3 Source: https://www.forbes.com/sites/thomaspellechia/2017/02/01/the-u-s-wine-industry-focuses-on-a-sustainable-future/#73c10c6d51e2.
4 For more details, see https://www.oiv.int/standards/oiv-guide-for-the-implementation-of-principles-of-sustainable-vitiviniculture-#_Toc146287452.
5 Source: https://www.fivs.org/environmental-sustainability/.
6 Source: https://globalsustainablewine.wordpress.com/principles/#definition-of-sustainable-winegrowing-and-winemaking.
7 A complete list of the thirty standards covered in the SWR benchmarking exercise is not available. A partial list includes: Bodegas de Argentina (Argentina), California Sustainable Wine (USA), Equalitas (Italy), Fair'N Green (Germany), Fairtade (International), Fish Friendly Farming (USA), Low Impact Viticulture and Enology (LIVE) (USA), Lodi Rules (USA), Long Island Sustainable Winegrowing (USA), Napa Green (USA), Salmon Safe (USA), SIP Certified (USA), Sustainable Wine Ontario (Canada), Sustainable Winegrowing Australia (Australia), Sustainable Winegrowing New Zealand (New Zealand), Sustainable Wine Great Britain (United Kingdom), Terra Vitis (France), Vinos de Chile (Chile), Wine & Agricultural Ethical Trade Association (WIETA) (South Africa) and Wines of Alentejo (Portugal). Source: 'SWR Global Reference Standard Benchmarking sustainability standards in wine: Meeting on progress to date', presented at a SWR webinar on 11 October 2022.
8 Peter Stanbury, 'Benchmarking Sustainability Standards in Wine: The SWR Global reference Framework for Sustainability in Wine', Sustainable Wine Roundtable, November 2023, 13.
9 Source: https://www.ssciglobal.org.
10 Source: https://www.amfori.org/en/solutions/social/about-bsci.

11 Source: https://www.ifrs.org/groups/international-sustainability-standards-board/#:~:text=The%20ISSB%20has%20set%20out,to%20global%20capital%20markets%3B%20and.
12 Source: https://www.iso.org/iso-26000-social-responsibility.html.
13 Wine buyers in the UK, Germany, Holland and the Nordic countries are increasingly requiring Fairtrade certification (for supplies from South Africa). Nordic alcohol monopolies are also setting up special tenders which require WIETA or Equalitas certification (see Chapter 6).
14 Systembolaget, 'Different for a reason: Responsibility report 2022'. https://www.omsystembolaget.se/globalassets/pdf/ansvarsredovisning/systembolagets-ansvarsredovisningen_20230504_eng_final_interaktiv.pdf.
15 Ibid.
16 Ibid., pp. 32–3.
17 https://www.robertparker.com/free-publications/green-emblem.
18 *Gambero Rosso* is a company that has been publishing magazines, guides, wine, cookery and travel books since 1986. In time, it has expanded into cooking schools, professional training, and the production of television and online content. It is considered the most important companies of this kind in the gastronomy and wine sector in Italy. See https://www.gamberorosso.it.
19 Source: https://www.gamberorosso.it/notizie/notizie-vino/guida-vini-ditalia-2024-sono-498-i-vini-premiati-con-i-tre-bicchieri-e-12-i-premi-speciali/.
20 Source: https://www.tastinglife.it/2024/03/06/tre-bicchieri-verdi-2024-gambero-rosso-premia-leccellenza-sostenibile/.
21 Source: https://www.wineonaplatter.com.
22 See also https://www.ipw.co.za.
23 Source: https://food.ec.europa.eu/plants/pesticides/approval-active-substances-safeners-and-synergists/renewal-approval/glyphosate_en#:~:text=Glyphosate%20is%20currently%20approved%20as,to%20certain%20conditions%20and%20restrictions.
24 SWR presentation at the ProWein trade fair, Dusseldorf, 21 March 2023.
25 Source: https://swroundtable.org.
26 SWR presentation at the ProWein trade fair, Dusseldorf, 21 March 2023.
27 The retailers included in the accord at the time of writing were: Laithwaites, Lidl GB, Naked Wines UK, Naked Wines USA, Sweden's Systembolaget AB, The Wine Society, Virgin Wines, Waitrose and Whole Foods Market.
28 SWR presentation at the ProWein trade fair, Dusseldorf, 21 March 2023.
29 Source: https://swroundtable.org/wp-content/uploads/2022/11/SWR-Master-Document-2022_23-.xlsx-Membership-Management.pdf.
30 Peter Stanbury, 'Benchmarking Sustainability Standards in Wine: The SWR Global reference Framework for Sustainability in Wine', Sustainable Wine Roundtable, November 2023, 23.
31 Source: OIV (2021), 'Focus OIV the world organic vineyard', 11. Available at: https://www.oiv.int/public/medias/8514/en-focus-the-world-organic-vineyard.pdf.
32 Resolution OIV-ECO 460–2012. Available at: https://www.oiv.int/public/medias/1903/oiv-eco-460-2012-en.pdf.
33 IFOAM EU group (2013) 'EU rules for organic wine production: Background, evaluation and further sector development'. Available at: https://www.organicseurope.bio/content/uploads/2021/02/ifoameu_regulation_eu_rules_for_organic_wine_production_2013_compressed.pdf?dd.

34 Source: OIV (2021), 'Focus OIV the world organic vineyard', 12–13.
35 Sources: Consorzio Prosecco DOCG, 'I futuri del vino italiano — Qualità, sostenibilità e territorio. Il presente e le sfide del Conegiano Valdobbiadene Prosecco Superiore DOCG, 2020, 40; and Consorzio per la Tutela dei Vini Valpolicella, Valpolicella Annual Report 2021, 42.
36 Source: Panel discussion on 'CAP. . .SUS: The common agricultural policy towards sustainability', organized by Legambiente at Vinitaly 2022.
37 Source: https://www.sawis.co.za/info/download/BI_Daagliks_30092021.pdf.
38 Source: https://demeter.net/demeter-products/wine/.
39 Ibid.
40 Source: various presentations at the '2024: Cento anni dalle conferenze di Koberwitz: quali verità per l'agricoltura biodinamica?', organized by Demeter at Vinitaly 2024.
41 Another certification body is Biodyvin, which is focused only on biodynamic wines. Only 202 growers are certified with Biodyvin, mostly in France. http://www.biodyvin.com/en/home.html.
42 Source: https://demeter.net/wp-content/uploads/2023/06/2023_Demeter-wineries-worldwide.pdf.
43 Source: Panel discussion 'Future viticulture between sustainability and climate change' at Vinitaly 2022. See also: Aldo Lorenzoni, Luigino Bertolazzi, Giuseppe Carcerieri De Prati, GRASPO (2022), 'La biodiversità viticola: Vitigni dal passato per i vini del futuro', Associazione G.R.A.S.P.O. and https://swite.com/graspo.
44 WOSA (Wines of South Africa) (2005) 'The wines of South Africa: Variety is in our nature' (brochure). Stellenbosch: WOSA, 5.
45 Source: *Wineland* magazine, January 2005 issue.
46 Source: *Wineland* magazine, January 2005 issue.
47 See also https://www.wwf.org.za.
48 CapeNature is a government agency that manages and maintains nature reserves in the Western Cape Province of South Africa. https://www.capenature.co.za/about-us.
49 Source: https://www.trevisotoday.it/politica/miane-frana-premaor-11-ottobre-2019.html and *La Tribuna di Treviso*, 14/3/2020.
50 Source: https://www.qdpnews.it/index.php/refrontolo/3216-tragedia-al-molinetto-le-cause-lucchetta-ecco-gli-elementi-dei-tecnici-nessuna-frana-o-diga.
51 See also https://www.trevisotoday.it/attualita/erosione-prosecco-replica-consorzio-valdobbiadene-5-giugno-2019.html.
52 Source: Consorzio per la Tutela dei Vini Valpolicella (CTV), Valpolicella Annual Report 2021. Available at: https://www.federvini.it/images/Dossier_Valpolicella_Annual_Report_2021.pdf.
53 RAI 3 Report, 'La frazione di Prosecco, Part 1', 14 November 2016. Available at: https://www.rai.it/programmi/report/inchieste/La-frazione-di-prosecco-82f70b9c-ce75-461d-b98d-cb5b8894fd58.html.
54 A representative of the confederation of cooperatives operating in the wine sector in Veneto argues in the documentary that the incidence of cancer in the area is no different than for the rest of the region – he argues that, as a matter of fact, it is slightly under the average.
55 RAI 3 Report 'La frazione di Prosecco, Part 2', 20 November 2017. Available at: https://www.youtube.com/watch?v=WWAc4UIB8CQ.
56 The 2020 Viticulture Protocol indicates that the consortium, under pressure from local committees, has adopted some practices that go beyond EU and Italian regulatory standards – including a ban on the use of glyphosates and the obligation of putting up

signs 48 hours in advance of the application of agro-chemicals in vineyards. See https://www.prosecco.it/it/protocollo-viticolo-2020/.
57 Fondazione Symbola and Consorzio di Tutela Conegliano Valdobbiadene DOCG (2020), 'I futuri del vino italiano — Qualità, sostenibilità e territorio. Il presente e le sfide del Conegiano Valdobbiadene Prosecco Superiore DOCG', Pieve di Soligo (TV).
58 Sources: P5; Consorzio Prosecco DOCG, Bolle d'annata 2019. Rapporto tecnico — Distretto del Conegliano Valdobbiadene DOCG. Pieve di Soligo, p. 35.
59 Consorzio di Tutela Conegliano Valdobbiadene DOCG, 'Bolle d'annata 2019. Rapporto tecnico — Distretto del Conegliano Valdobbiadene DOCG', Pieve di Soligo (TV), 36-7.
60 Consorzio di Tutela Prosecco DOC, 'Relazione inerente alle attività di sostenibilità — Annualità 2019', Treviso.
61 Source: Panel discussion 'Future viticulture between sustainability and climate change' at Vinitaly 2022.
62 Source: https://www.regione.veneto.it/web/ambiente-e-territorio/pat.
63 Source: https://www.regione.veneto.it/web/ambiente-e-territorio/piano-casa-veneto.
64 Marlene Spanger and Magnus Andersen, 'Spaces of natural wine in Copenhagen: Labour, migration and a just green transition,' presented at the international workshop 'Wine, Space, Place: Global geographies of wine cultivation, production and consumption', Catholic University of Eichstätt-Ingolstadt, 22–23 February 2024.
65 Source: https://www.viniveri.net.
66 Source: https://www.triplea.it/it/.
67 See also https://www.climatefruitandwine.co.za.
68 See also https://carbonheroes.co.za.
69 Source: Vasco Boatto, Eugenio Pomarici and Luigino Barisan, 'Conegliano Valdobbiadene Prosecco DOCG — Oltre il 2019', available at: https://www.prosecco.it/wp-content/uploads/2019/12/Rapporto-Economico-2019.pdf.
70 Attilio Scienza, 'What does natural mean in wine? How to engage wine lovers with science', presentation at the Wine2Wine Business Forum, Verona, 13–14 November 2023.
71 See https://piwi-international.org/en/.
72 Sources: interviews WG8, WG9 and various presentations at the seminar 'Sustainable Red PIWIs' at ProWein, 21 March 2023.
73 For example, in South Africa, Winetech is financing pre-breeding research to develop breeding of resistant varieties. In particular, they are looking at genetic markers showing resistance to two fungal diseases. Drought resistance research however is not as high in their priorities (SAW21). On innovation in the South African and Italian wine industries more generally, see Cusmano et al. (2010) and Giuliani et al. (2011).
74 Source: author's audio recording of the opening seminar at CapeWine 2022.

Chapter 6

1 There are other qualifications of people (skills, knowledge) that could be relevant for a discussion of value and valuation in wine, which I do not cover in detail in this book – for example, the skills, knowledge and role of wine experts, influencers and writers/journalists, who are key in modulating wine valuation processes, are only discussed briefly in Chapter 4. I do not explicitly examine workers in the wine value chain

beyond manual labour at the level of farm and cellar, such as managers, marketers and those employed in retail, restaurants and bars in consumption markets – although I briefly discuss labour employed in wine tourism. In this book, due to limited space, I focus on the valuation of people as labour employed in grape and wine production, and as holders of material and intellectual property.

2 I recognize that labour exploitation takes place at the trade and retail levels as well, but I do not have the space or the empirical evidence to examine this aspect in detail in this book.

3 Parts of this section draw in revised form from Kruger, Du Toit and Ponte (2006) and Du Toit, Kruger and Ponte (2008).

4 This 'project approach' to addressing the social outcomes of racialized and gendered labour relations continues, with a spate of contemporary initiatives that seek to address alcoholism, domestic violence, and lack of education attainment among farmworker communities (SAW15, SAW40, SAW43). These are laudable and needed initiatives but tend to address the manifestations of racism rather than its causes.

5 See also Finnwatch (2023). 'Human rights in South African wineries: The responsibility of Alko's supply chains'. Available at: https://finnwatch.org/fi/julkaisut/ihmisoikeudet-etelae-afrikan-viinitiloilla.

6 See, for example, the documentary 'Bitter Grapes' by Tom Heinemann: http://www.bittergrapes.net and a recent report from Finnwatch on Human rights in South African wineries. https://finnwatch.org/fi/julkaisut/ihmisoikeudet-etelae-afrikan-viinitiloilla.

7 See details in the Oxfam's report on working conditions on wine farms in Italy: Oxfam (2022) 'The workers behind Sweden's Italian wine: An illustrative Human Rights Impact Assessment of Systembolaget's Italian wine supply chains' https://oxfam.se/wp-content/uploads/2022/11/Oxfam.The-Workers-Behind-Swedens-Italian-Wine.2021.pdf.

8 Source: Oxfam 'The workers behind Sweden's Italian wine', 10.

9 Source: Oxfam 'The workers behind Sweden's Italian wine'.

10 Gaia Pianigiani, 'Grapes, death and injustice in Italian vineyards', *The Independent*, April 16, 2017. https://www.independent.co.uk/news/long_reads/grapes-death-and-injustice-in-italian-vineyards-a7682921.html. On illegal labour brokers in the agricultural sector, see also Fondazione Rizzotto 'VI Rapporto agromafie e caporalato', 23/10/2023; https://www.fondazionerizzotto.it/vi-rapporto-agromafie-e-caporalato/.

11 Source: https://www.fairtrade.net/product/wine.

12 Source: https://www.fairtrade.org.uk/farmers-and-workers/wine-farmers-and-workers/.

13 Source: https://www.fairtrade.org.uk/farmers-and-workers/wine-farmers-and-workers/.

14 Source: https://fairtradeafrica.net/.

15 Source: https://files.fairtrade.net/publications/2016FairtradeGenderStrategyEN.pdf.

16 Source: https://www.dtkfairtrade.org.

17 Source: https://www.fairforlife.org/pmws/indexDOM.php?client_id=fairforlife&page_id=home.

18 Source: https://www.fairandgreen.com/en/.

19 Source: https://wieta.org.za/who-are-we/.

20 Source: http://www.wieta.org.za/wp-content/uploads/2019/03/WIETA-Code-Version-3-2016.pdf.

21 Source: https://wieta.org.za/who-are-we/.

22 Source: https://www.equalitas.it/en/.

23 On 'environmental sustainability', the Equalitas standard includes indicators on biodiversity (drawn from BWA certification, see Chapter 5), carbon footprint and water footprint. It also covers good agricultural practices (soil management, fertility management, irrigation, plant management, pest management, harvest management, biodiversity management, prohibition of applying chemical herbicides in between rows, and exclusion of dangerous pesticides) and good winery and bottling practices (related to harvesting, winemaking and bottling, cleaning and sanitation of premises and equipment, and packaging). See https://www.equalitas.it/en/.
24 Source: https://www.equalitas.it/en/sustainability/.
25 Source: https://www.equalitas.it/en/labels/.
26 Source: https://www.equalitas.it/en/sustainable-wineries/.
27 Parts of this section draw in revised form from Du Toit, Kruger and Ponte (2008), Ponte et al. (2023), and Das Nair et al. (2023).
28 In Italy, wine valuation linked to the identity of the owners of material and intangible assets does not appear prominently in public debates, the trade literature and my interview material. A partial exception is a reference to the difficulties that 'small family wine farms' are facing in maintaining a niche profile vis-à-vis large wine corporations. This discourse extends to agriculture more generally and is linked to EU and Italian regulatory efforts to promote the multifunctionality of agriculture, attract or retain younger generations in this sector, and address the depopulation of rural areas – especially in hilly and mountain areas. A distinctive domestic valuation strategy based on small-scale family wine farms, however, is difficult to push forward, as many of the largest wine producers in the country are also 'family-owned' (see Chapter 3). There are also associations and marketing initiatives showcasing wines produced by women winemakers in Italy, such as the 'Associazione nazionale le donne del vino' (V13, V18, https://ledonnedelvino.com). These are important political movements in a male-dominated sector in a chauvinist society but have not yet coherently articulated a civic valuation discourse based on gender. A much more prominent discussion related to ownership is that of cooperative forms of organization (in both Italy and South Africa), where they are among the largest players. Cooperatives originally focused on producing bulk wine for wholesalers, but are now increasingly also branding and marketing their own wine. However, this is not a wine valuation approach framed around class, race or gender – it is about a particular form of organization. I refer readers interested in debates around the changing role of cooperatives, their successes, struggles and innovation paths, and to what extent they are becoming just another form of corporate player, to the rich available literature on this topic (on Italian wine cooperatives see, inter alia, Begalli, Capitello and Codurri 2014; Borsellino et al. 2020; Carter 2012; Nazzaro et al. 2022; Rizzo 2009; see also Chapters 3 and 6 on South Africa).
29 The term historically disadvantaged person (HDP) refers to any person, category of persons or community disadvantaged by unfair discrimination before the Constitution of the Republic of South Africa, 1993 (Act No. 200 of 1993) came into operation. Some South African legislation specifically refers to the empowerment of 'Black people', defined as 'a generic term that means Africans, Coloureds and Indians' (Broad-Based Black Economic Empowerment Act. Act No. 53 of 2003, 2). In this book, I use the terms 'Black people' and 'HDPs' interchangeably.
30 These scores relate to the scorecard for larger enterprises; for smaller enterprises (with an annual revenue of less than ZAR 10 million), the score on skills development has more weight, while the scores for management control and for enterprise and supplier development have less weight. http://webapps.daff.gov.za/AgriBEE/scorecard.do.

31 For a broader discussion of transformation in South Africa beyond wine, see inter alia Alessandri, Black and Jackson (2011); Andreasson (2010); Iheduru (2004); and Ponte, Roberts and Van Sittert (2007).
32 Source: https://www.wosa.co.za/Sustainability/Socially-Sustainable/BEE/Empowerment-Projects/.
33 Sources:
https://www.dailymaverick.co.za/article/2018-08-14-the-solms-delta-way-or-how-not-to-do-land-reform/.
https://www.dailymaverick.co.za/article/2018-09-11-the-solms-delta-saga-the-perspective-of-mark-solms-and-richard-astor/.
https://www.businesslive.co.za/fm/life/travel/2024-01-11-cheers-to-second-chances-as-solms-delta-gains-new-investor/.
https://weeklysamirror.news/re-imagined-solms-delta-opens-new-chapter/.

Chapter 7

1 Hanna Halmari, 'The SW Summary: On the impact of climate change, how bats benefit the vineyard, the need for greater transparency in Champagne, and more', Sustainable Wine Newsletter, 30 May 2024. https://sustainablewine.co.uk/the-sw-summary-the-impact-climate-change-benefits-of-bats/.
2 Shawn Donnan and Enda Curran, 'The global economy enters an era of upheaval', Bloomberg 18 September 2023 https://www.bloomberg.com/graphics/2023-geopolitical-investments-economic-shift/.

REFERENCES

Albrecht, Julia. 2014. 'Online terroir: Wine and regional identity in online destination marketing'. In *Wine and identity*, edited by Matt Harvey, Leanne White and Warwick Frost, 230–42. Routledge.

Alessandri, Todd M, Sylvia Sloan Black and William E Jackson. 2011. 'Black economic empowerment transactions in South Africa: Understanding when corporate social responsibility may create or destroy value'. *Long Range Planning* 44 (4): 229–49.

Alford, Matthew. 2020. 'Antagonistic governance in South African fruit global production networks: a neo-Gramscian perspective'. *Global Networks* 20 (1): 42–64.

Alford, Matthew, Margareet Visser and Stephanie Barrientos. 2021. 'Southern actors and the governance of labour standards in global production networks: The case of South African fruit and wine'. *Environment and Planning A: Economy and Space* 53 (8): 1915–34.

Allaire, Gilles and Robert Boyer, eds. 1995. *La grande transformation de l'agriculture: Lectures conventionnalistes et régulationnistes*. Inra-Quae.

Allaire, Gilles and Benoît Daviron, eds. 2018. *Ecology, capitalism and the new agricultural economy: The second great transformation*. Routledge.

Anderson, Kym. 2004. *The world's wine markets: Globalization at work*. Edward Elgar Publishing.

Anderson, Kym and Signe Nelgen. 2011. *Global wine markets: A statistical compendium, 1961–2009*. University of Adelaide Press.

Anderson, Kym and Vicente Pinilla. 2018. 'Introduction'. In *Wine globalization: A new comparative history*, edited by Kym Anderson and Vicente Pinilla, 3–23. Cambridge University Press.

Anderson, Kym, Signe Nelgen and Vicente Pinilla. 2017. *Global wine markets, 1860 to 2016: A statistical compendium*. University of Adelaide Press.

Andreasson, Stefan. 2010. *Africa's development impasse: Rethinking the political economy of transformation*. Bloomsbury Publishing.

Appadurai, Arjun. 1988. *The social life of things: Commodities in cultural perspective*. Cambridge University Press.

Archer, Matthew. 2024. *Unsustainable: Measurement, reporting, and the limits of corporate sustainability*. New York University Press.

Aspers, Patrik and Jens Beckert. 2011. 'Value in markets'. In *The worth of goods: Valuation and pricing in the economy*, edited by Jens Beckert and Patrik Aspers, 3–38. Oxford University Press.

Back, Robin M, Xinyang Liu, Britta Niklas, Karl Storchmann and Nick Vink. 2019. 'Margins of Fair Trade wine along the supply chain: Evidence from South African wine in the US market'. *Journal of Wine Economics* 14 (3): 274–97.

Baglioni, Elena and Liam Campling. 2017. 'Natural resource industries as global value chains: Frontiers, fetishism, labour and the state'. *Environment and Planning A: Economy and Space* 49 (11): 2437–56.

Baglioni, Elena, Liam Campling and Gerard Hanlon. 2020. 'Global value chains as entrepreneurial capture: Insights from management theory'. *Review of International Political Economy* 27 (4): 903–25.

Bair, Jennifer and Matthew C Mahutga. 2023. 'Power, governance and distributional skew in global value chains: Exchange theoretic and exogenous factors'. *Global Networks* 23 (4): 814-31.
Bair, Jennifer and Florence Palpacuer. 2012. 'From varieties of capitalism to varieties of activism: The antisweatshop movement in comparative perspective'. *Social Problems* 59 (4): 522-43.
Bair, Jennifer and Florence Palpacuer. 2015. 'CSR beyond the corporation: Contested governance in global value chains'. *Global Networks* 15 (s1): S1-S19.
Bair, Jennifer, Christian Berndt, Marc Boeckler and Marion Werner. 2013. 'Dis/articulating producers, markets and regions: New directions in critical studies of commodity chains'. *Environment and Planning A: Economy and Space* 45 (11): 2544-52.
Bair, Jennifer, Stefano Ponte, Leonard Seabrooke and Duncan Wigan. 2023. 'Entangled chains of global value and wealth'. *Review of International Political Economy* 30 (6): 2423-39.
Baldwin, Richard. 2016. *The great convergence*. Harvard University Press.
Banks, Glenn and John Overton. 2010. 'Old world, new world, third world? Reconceptualising the worlds of wine'. *Journal of Wine Research* 21 (1): 57-75.
Barbera, Filippo and Stefano Audifredi. 2012. 'In pursuit of quality. The institutional change of wine production market in Piedmont'. *Sociologia Ruralis* 52 (3): 311-31.
Barham, Elizabeth. 2003. 'Translating terroir: The global challenge of French AOC labeling'. *Journal of Rural Studies* 19 (1): 127-38.
Barrientos, Stephanie. 2013. 'Corporate purchasing practices in global production networks: A socially contested terrain'. *Geoforum* 44: 44-51.
Barrientos, Stephanie. 2019. *Gender and work in global value chains: Capturing the gains?* Cambridge University Press.
Bartley, Tim. 2007. 'Institutional emergence in an era of globalization: The rise of transnational private regulation of labor and environmental conditions'. *American Journal of Sociology* 113 (2): 297-351.
Basso, Matteo. 2019. 'Land-use changes triggered by the expansion of wine-growing areas: A study on the Municipalities in the Prosecco's production zone (Italy)'. *Land Use Policy* 83: 390-402.
Basso, Matteo and Luciano Vettoretto. 2020. 'Reversal sprawl. Land-use regulation, society and institutions in Proseccotown'. *Land Use Policy* 99: 105016.
Batifoulier, Philippe. 2001. *Théorie des conventions*. Economica Paris.
Beckert, Jens. 2011. 'The transcending power of goods: Imaginative value in the economy'. In *The worth of goods: Valuation and pricing in the economy*, edited by Jens Beckert and Patrik Aspers, 106-28. Oxford University Press.
Begalli, Diego, Roberta Capitello and Stefano Codurri. 2014. 'Cooperatives, wine clusters and territorial value: Evidence from an Italian case study'. *Journal of Wine Research* 25 (1): 45-61.
Bek, David, Cheryl McEwan and Karen Bek. 2007. 'Ethical trading and socioeconomic transformation: Critical reflections on the South African wine industry'. *Environment and Planning A: Economy and Space* 39 (2): 301-19.
Bell, Joshua. 2022. 'Social upgrading or dependency? Investigating the implications of the inclusion of commercial wine farms within South African Fairtrade certification'. PhD thesis, Political and International Studies, Rhodes University.
Bell, Martin and Elisa Giuliani. 2007. 'Catching up in the global wine industry: Innovation systems, cluster knowledge networks and firm-level capabilities in Italy and Chile'. *International Journal of Technology and Globalisation* 3 (2-3): 197-223.

Benjamin, Walter. 1935. *The work of art in the age of mechanical reproduction*. Penguin.
Bhambra, Gurminder K. 2014. 'Postcolonial and decolonial dialogues'. *Postcolonial Studies* 17 (2): 115-21.
Black, Rachel E. 2013. 'Vino naturale: Tensions between nature and technology in the glass'. In *Wine and culture: Vineyard to glass*, edited by Rachel E Black and Robert C Ulin, 279-94. Bloomsbury Academic.
Black, Rachel E and Robert C Ulin. 2013. *Wine and culture: Vineyard to glass*. Bloomsbury Publishing.
Blok, Anders. 2013. 'Pragmatic sociology as political ecology: On the many worths of nature(s)'. *European Journal of Social Theory* 16 (4): 492-510.
Bloomfield, Michael John. 2014. 'Shame campaigns and environmental justice: Corporate shaming as activist strategy'. *Environmental Politics* 23 (2): 263-81.
Bloomfield, Michael John. 2017. *Dirty gold: How activism transformed the jewelry industry*. MIT Press.
Boltanski, Luc and Eve Chiapello. 2005. *The new spirit of capitalism*. Verso.
Boltanski, Luc and Arnaud Esquerre. 2020. *Enrichment: A critique of commodities*. John Wiley & Sons.
Boltanski, Luc and Laurent Thévenot. 2006. *On justification: Economies of worth*. Princeton University Press.
Bonanno, Alessandro, Kae Sekine and Hart N Feuer. 2020. *Geographical indication and global agri-food: Development and democratization*. Taylor & Francis.
Borsellino, Valeria, Giuseppina Migliore, Marcello D'Acquisto, Caterina Patrizia Di Franco, Antonio Asciuto and Emanuele Schimmenti. 2016. '"Green" wine through a responsible and efficient production: A case study of a sustainable Sicilian wine producer'. *Agriculture and Agricultural Science Procedia* 8: 186-92.
Borsellino, Valeria, Francesca Varia, Cinzia Zinnanti and Emanuele Schimmenti. 2020. 'The Sicilian cooperative system of wine production: The strategic choices and performance analyses of a case study'. *International Journal of Wine Business Research* 32 (3): 391-421.
Bourdieu, Pierre. 1979. *La distinction: Critique sociale du jugement*. Les éditions de minuit.
Brunori, Gianluca and Adanella Rossi. 2007. 'Differentiating countryside: Social representations and governance patterns in rural areas with high social density - The case of Chianti, Italy', *Journal of Rural Studies* 23 (2): 183-205.
Bruwer, Johan. 2003. 'South African wine routes: Some perspectives on the wine tourism industry's structural dimensions and wine tourism product'. *Tourism Management* 24 (4): 423-35.
Buller, Adrienne. 2022. *The value of a whale: On the illusions of green capitalism*. Manchester University Press.
Çalışkan, Koray and Michel Callon. 2009. 'Economization, part 1: Shifting attention from the economy towards processes of economization'. *Economy and Society* 38 (3): 369-98.
Callon, Michel, Cécile Méadel and Vololona Rabeharisoa. 2002. 'The economy of qualities'. *Economy and Society* 31 (2): 194-217.
Callon, Michel and Fabian Muniesa. 2005. 'Peripheral vision: Economic markets as calculative collective devices'. *Organization Studies* 26 (8): 1229-50.
Callon, Michel, Yuval Millo and Fabian Muniesa, eds. 2007. *Market devices*. Blackwell.
Carter, Elizabeth Ann. 2012. 'Cooperation, competition, and regulation: Constructing value in French and Italian wine markets'. University of California, Berkeley.
Carter, Elizabeth Ann. 2018. 'For what it's worth: The political construction of quality in French and Italian wine markets'. *Socio-Economic Review* 16 (3): 479-98.

Castellini, Alessandra, Christine Mauracher and Stefania Troiano. 2017. 'An overview of the biodynamic wine sector'. *International Journal of Wine Research* 9: 1–11.

Cattaneo, Olivier, Gary Gereffi and Cornelia Staritz. 2010. *Global value chains in a postcrisis world: A development perspective*. World Bank Publications.

Centemeri, Laura. 2023. 'Green justification and environmental movements'. In *Handbook of economics and sociology of conventions*, edited by Rainer Diaz-Bone and Guillemette de Larquier. Springer Nature. https://doi.org/10.1007/978-3-030-52130-1_37-2.

Charters, Steve. 2019. 'Terroir wines in Champagne: Between ideology and utopia'. In *Wine, terroir and utopia*, edited by Jacqueline Dutton and Peter J Howland, 111–25. Routledge.

Charters, Stephen, Nathalie Spielmann and Barry J Babin. 2017. 'The nature and value of terroir products'. *European Journal of Marketing* 51 (4): 748–71.

Chazal, Clémentine. 2024. 'From the Cape of Good Hope to the Pointes de Graves: A study of the natural wine and its political challenges - Environmental movements and the transformation of wine production'. PhD thesis, Science Po Bordeaux.

Checchinato, Francesca, Vladi Finotto, Christine Mauracher and Chiara Rinaldi. 2024. 'Spreading the gains from geographical indications: A longitudinal study on the extension of the Prosecco GI'. *Journal of Rural Studies* 109: 103336.

Chiapello, Eve. 2013. 'Capitalism and its criticisms'. In *New spirits of capitalisms? Crises, justifications, and dynamics*, edited by Paul Du Gay and Glenn Morgan, 60–81. Oxford University Press.

Cidell, Julie L and Heike C Alberts. 2006. 'Constructing quality: The multinational histories of chocolate'. *Geoforum* 37 (6): 999–1007.

Cisterna, Nicolas Sternsdorff. 2013. 'Space and terroir in the Chilean wine industry'. In *Wine and culture: Vineyard to glass*, edited by Rachel E Black and Robert C Ulin, 51–66. Bloomsbury Academic.

Coe, Neil M and Henry Wai-Chung Yeung. 2015. *Global production networks: Theorizing economic development in an interconnected world*. Oxford University Press.

Coelho, Alfredo Manuel and Jean-Louis Rastoin. 2006. 'Financial strategies of multinational firms in the world wine industry: An assessment'. *Agribusiness: An International Journal* 22 (3): 417–29.

Cohen, Paul. 2013. 'The artifice of natural wine: Jules Chauvet and the reinvention of vinification in postwar France'. In *Wine and culture: Vineyard to glass*, edited by Rachel E Black and Robert C Ulin, 261–78. Bloomsbury Academic.

Colman, Tyler. 2008. *Wine politics: How governments, environmentalists, mobsters, and critics influence the wines we drink*. University of California Press.

Colombini, Donatella Cinelli. 2015. 'Wine tourism in Italy'. *International Journal of Wine Research* 7: 29–35.

Coq-Huelva, Daniel, Javier Sanz-Cañada and Florencio Sánchez-Escobar. 2014. 'Conventions, commodity chains and local food systems: Olive oil production in "Sierra De Segura"(Spain)'. *Geoforum* 56: 6–16.

Corbo, Chiara, Lucrezia Lamastra and Ettore Capri. 2014. 'From environmental to sustainability programs: A review of sustainability initiatives in the Italian wine sector'. *Sustainability* 6 (4): 2133–59.

Corsi, Alessandro, Eugenio Pomarici and Roberta Sardone. 2018. 'Italy from 1939'. In *Wine globalization: A new comparative history*, edited by Kym Anderson and Vicente Pinilla, 153–77. Cambridge University Press.

Coveri, Andrea and Antonello Zanfei. 2022. 'Functional division of labour and value capture in global value chains: A new empirical assessment based on FDI data'. *Review of International Political Economy* 30 (5): 1984–2011.

Craven, Emily and Charles Mather. 2001. 'Geographical indications and the South Africa–European Union free trade agreement'. *Area* 33 (3): 312–20.
Cross, Robin, Andrew J Plantinga and Robert N Stavins. 2017. 'Terroir in the New World: Hedonic estimation of vineyard sale prices in California'. *Journal of Wine Economics* 12 (3): 282–301.
Cusmano, Lucia, Andrea Morrison and Roberta Rabellotti. 2010. 'Catching up trajectories in the wine sector: A comparative study of Chile, Italy, and South Africa'. *World Development* 38 (11): 1588–602.
Dallas, Mark P. 2014. 'Cloth without a weaver: Power, emergence and institutions across global value chains'. *Economy & Society* 43 (3): 315–45.
Dallas, Mark P and Jing-Ming Shiu. 2023. 'Power in consensus: Legitimacy, global value chains and inequality in telecommunications standard-setting'. *Global Networks* 23 (4): 792–813.
Dallas, Mark P, Stefano Ponte and Timothy Sturgeon. 2019. 'Power in global value chains'. *Review of International Political Economy* 26 (4): 666–94.
Danielmeier, Tobias. 2014. 'Winery architecture'. In *Wine and identity: Branding, heritage, terroir*, edited by Matt Harvey, Leanne White and Warwick Frost, 213–29. Routledge.
Das Nair, Reena. 2018. 'The internationalisation of supermarkets and the nature of competitive rivalry in retailing in Southern Africa'. *Development Southern Africa* 35 (3): 315–33.
Das Nair, Reena. 2019. 'The spread and internationalisation of South African retail chains and the implications of market power'. *International Review of Applied Economics* 33 (1): 30–50.
Das Nair, Reena and Shingie Chisoro. 2023. Participation of SMEs and women-owned businesses in the South African wine value chain. *CCRED Working Paper*, March, University of Johannesburg.
Das Nair, Reena, Shingie Chisoro and Stefano Ponte. 2023. Sustainability in the South African wine industry: Status, opportunities and challenges. *CBDS and CCRED Working Paper* 2023/3: Centre for Business and Development Studies, Copenhagen Business School.
Das Nair, Reena, Shingie Chisoro and Francis Ziba. 2018. 'The implications for suppliers of the spread of supermarkets in Southern Africa'. *Development Southern Africa* 35 (3): 334–50.
Daviron, Benoît and Stefano Ponte. 2005. *The coffee paradox: Global markets, commodity trade and the elusive promise of development*. Zed books.
Daynes, Sarah. 2013. 'The social life of terroir among Bordeaux winemakers'. In *Wine and culture: Vineyard to glass*, edited by Rachel E Black and Robert C Ulin, 15–32. Bloomsbury Academic.
De Nardi, C. 2016. 'Poisoned Prosecco Vineyards and the Downside of an Italian Icon thesis: Analyses of pesticides' impact on the environment and human health'. Masters, Università delle Scienze Gastronomiche.
Dean, Mitchell M. 2009. *Governmentality: Power and rule in modern society*. Sage.
Demossier, Marion. 2020. *Burgundy: The global story of terroir*. Berghahn Books.
Devereux, Stephen. 2020. 'Violations of farm workers' labour rights in post-apartheid South Africa'. *Development Southern Africa* 37 (3): 382–404.
Dewey, John. 1939. *Theory of valuation*. University of Chicago Press.
Dhalla, Rumina. 2019. 'Ideals for sustainability in the Australian wine industry: Authenticity and identity'. In *Wine, terroir and utopia*, edited by Jacqueline Dutton and Peter J Howland, 178–96. Routledge.

Diaz-Bone, Rainer. 2016. 'Convention theory, classification and quantification'. *Historical Social Research/Historische Sozialforschung* 41 (2): 48–71.
Diaz-Bone, Rainer and Guillemette de Larquier. 2022. 'Conventions: Meanings and applications of a core concept in economics and sociology of conventions'. In *Handbook of economics and sociology of conventions*, edited by Rainer Diaz-Bone and Guillemette de Larquier, 1–27. Springer.
Digeser, Peter. 1992. 'The fourth face of power'. *The Journal of Politics* 54 (4): 977–1007.
Donzé, Pierre-Yves and Sotaro Katsumata. 2022. 'High-end luxury wine demand and income inequality'. *International Journal of Wine Business Research* 34 (1): 112–132.
Du Toit, Andries. 1993. 'The micro-politics of paternalism: The discourses of management and resistance on South African fruit and wine farms'. *Journal of Southern African Studies* 19 (2): 314–36.
Du Toit, Andries. 2002. 'Globalizing ethics: Social technologies of private regulation and the South African wine industry'. *Journal of Agrarian Change* 2 (3): 356–80.
Du Toit, Andries, Sandra Kruger and Stefano Ponte. 2008. 'Deracializing exploitation? "Black Economic Empowerment" in the South African wine industry'. *Journal of Agrarian Change* 8 (1): 6–32.
Durand, Cédric and Wiliam Milberg. 2020. 'Intellectual monopoly in global value chains'. *Review of International Political Economy* 27 (2): 404–29.
Engelbrecht, Josias A., Frikkie Herbst and Johan Bruwer. 2014. 'Region-of-origin (ROO) certification as marketing strategy in the South African wine market'. *International Journal of Wine Business Research* 26 (2): 139–62.
Eriksson, Åsa. 2018. 'Resisting feminised precarity: Farm workers in post-strike Western Cape, South Africa'. PhD thesis, Department of Ethnology, History of Religions and Gender Studies, Stockholm University.
Esau, Darcen and Donna M Senese. 2022. 'The sensory experience of wine tourism: Creating memorable associations with a wine destination'. *Food Quality and Preference* 101: 104635.
Espeland, Wendy Nelson and Mitchell L Stevens. 1998. 'Commensuration as a social process'. *Annual Review of Sociology* 24 (1): 313–43.
Ewert, Joachim and Andries Du Toit. 2005. 'A deepening divide in the countryside: Restructuring and rural livelihoods in the South African wine industry'. *Journal of Southern African Studies* 31 (2): 315–32.
Ewert, Joachim and Johann Hamman. 1999. 'Why paternalism survives: Globalization, democratization and labour on South African wine farms'. *Sociologia Ruralis* 39 (2): 202–21.
Eymard-Duvernay, Francois. 1989. 'Conventions de qualité et formes de coordination'. *Revue Economique* 40 (2): 329–59.
Eymard-Duvernay, Francois, ed. 2006. *L'économie des conventions, methodes et resultats*. La Découverte.
Farmer, Erica A. 2013. '"Local, loyal and constant": The legal construction of wine in Bordeaux'. In *Wine and culture: Vineyard to glass*, edited by Rachel E Black and Robert C Ulin, 145–60. Bloomsbury Academic.
Ferreira, Sanette LA and Caitlin A Hunter. 2017. 'Wine tourism development in South Africa: A geographical analysis'. *Tourism Geographies* 19 (5): 676–98.
Festa, Giuseppe, SM Riad Shams, Gerardino Metallo and Maria Teresa Cuomo. 2020. 'Opportunities and challenges in the contribution of wine routes to wine tourism in Italy–A stakeholders' perspective of development'. *Tourism Management Perspectives* 33: 100585.

Feuer, Hart N. 2019. 'Geographical indications out of context and in vogue: The awkward embrace of European heritage agricultural protections in Asia'. In *Geographical indication and global agri-food*, edited by Alessandro Bonanno, Kae Sekine and Hart N. Feuer, 39–53. Routledge.

Flint, Daniel J, Susan L Golicic and Paola Signori. 2016. *Contemporary wine marketing and supply chain management: A global perspective*. Springer.

Flores, Shana Sabbado. 2018. 'What is sustainability in the wine world? A cross-country analysis of wine sustainability frameworks'. *Journal of Cleaner Production* 172: 2301–12.

Foret, François. 2008. *Légitimer l'Europe*. Presses de Sciences Po.

Fougere, Emily, Erin K Kaplan and Courtney A Collins. 2020. 'Pricing uncertainty in wine markets following the Rudy Kurniawan scandal'. *Journal of Wine Research* 31 (1): 1–5.

Fourcade, Marion. 2011. 'Cents and sensibility: Economic valuation and the nature of "nature"'. *American Journal of Sociology* 116 (6): 1721–77.

Fourcade, Marion. 2012. 'The vile and the noble: On the relation between natural and social classifications in the French wine world'. *The Sociological Quarterly* 53 (4): 524–45.

Fournier, Vincent. 2019. 'The commercial basis of terroir utopias in Calabria'. In *Wine, terroir and utopia*, edited by Jacqueline Dutton and Peter J Howland, 163–77. Routledge.

Froud, Julie, Colin Haslam, Sukhdev Johal and Karel Williams. 2000. 'Shareholder value and financialization: Consultancy promises, management moves'. *Economy & Society* 29 (1): 80–110.

Fuchs, Doris A. 2007. *Business power in global governance*. Lynne Rienner.

Gabor, Daniela. 2021. 'The Wall Street consensus'. *Development and Change* 52 (3): 429–59.

Gačnik, Aleš. 2014. 'Slovenian wine stories and wine identities'. In *Wine and identity: Branding, heritage, terroir*, edited by David Harvey, Leanne White and Warwick Frost, 57–70. Routledge.

Gade, Daniel W. 2004. 'Tradition, territory, and terroir in French viniculture: Cassis, France, and Appellation Contrôlée'. *Annals of the Association of American Geographers* 94 (4): 848–67.

Garcia-Parpet, Marie-France. 2009. *Le marché de l'excellence: Les grands crus à l'épreuve de la mondialisation*. Le Seuil.

Garcia-Parpet, Marie-France. 2011. 'Symbolic value and the establishment of prices: Globalization of the wine market'. In *The worth of goods: Valuation and pricing in the economy*, edited by Jens Beckert and Patrik Aspers, 131–54. Oxford University Press.

Gereffi, Gary. 1994. 'The organization of buyer-driven global commodity chains: How US retailers shape overseas production networks'. In *Commodity chains and global capitalism*, edited by Gary Gereffi, Miguel Korzeniewicz and Roberto P Korzeniewicz, 43–71. Praeger.

Gereffi, Gary. 1999. 'International trade and industrial upgrading in the apparel commodity chain'. *Journal of International Economics* 48 (1): 37–70.

Gereffi, Gary. 2014. 'Global value chains in a post-Washington consensus world'. *Review of International Political Economy* 21 (1): 9–37.

Gereffi, Gary, John Humphrey and Raphael Kaplinsky. 2001. 'Introduction: Globalisation, value chains and development'. *IDS Bulletin* 32 (3): 1–8.

Gereffi, Gary, John Humphrey and Timothy Sturgeon. 2005. 'The governance of global value chains'. *Review of International Political Economy* 12 (1): 78–104.

Gereffi, Gary, Miguel Korzeniewicz and Roberto P Korzeniewicz, eds. 1994. *Commodity chains and global capitalism*. Praeger.

Gibbon, Peter and Stefano Ponte. 2005. *Trading down: Africa, value chains, and the global economy*. Temple University Press.

Gibbon, Peter and Stefano Ponte. 2008. 'Global value chains: From governance to governmentality?' *Economy & Society* 37 (3): 365–92.

Gibbon, Peter and Lone Riisgaard. 2014. 'A new system of labour management in African large-scale agriculture?' *Journal of Agrarian Change* 14 (1): 94–128.

Gibbon, Peter, Jennifer Bair and Stefano Ponte. 2008. 'Governing global value chains: An introduction'. *Economy & Society* 37 (3): 315–38.

Gilinsky, Jr, Armand, Sandra K Newton, Thomas S Atkin, Cristina Santini, Alessio Cavicchi, Augusti Romeo Casas and Ruben Huertas. 2015. 'Perceived efficacy of sustainability strategies in the US, Italian, and Spanish wine industries: A comparative study'. *International Journal of Wine Business Research* 27 (3): 164–81.

Giuliani, Antonio Paco, Gianni Lorenzoni and Marco Visentin. 2015. 'New wines in new bottles: The "renaissance" of the Italian wine industry'. *Industry and Innovation* 22 (8): 729–52.

Giuliani, Elisa, Andrea Morrison and Roberta Rabellotti. 2011. *Innovation and technological catch-up: The changing geography of wine production*. Edward Elgar Publishing.

Giuliani, Elisa, Andrea Morrison, Carlo Pietrobelli and Roberta Rabellotti. 2010. 'Who are the researchers that are collaborating with industry? An analysis of the wine sectors in Chile, South Africa and Italy'. *Research Policy* 39 (6): 748–61.

Godard, Olivier. 1990. 'Environnement, modes de coordination et systèmes de légitimité: Analyse de la catégorie de patrimoine naturel'. *Revue économique* 41 (2): 215–41.

Golicic, Susan L. 2022. 'Changes in sustainability in the global wine industry'. *International Journal of Wine Business Research* 34 (3): 392–409.

Gonzalez-Maldonado, Noelymar, Mallika A Nocco, Kerri Steenwerth, Amanda Crump and Cristina Lazcano. 2024. 'Wine grape grower perceptions and attitudes about soil health'. *Journal of Rural Studies* 110: 103373.

Goodman, Michael K and David Goodman, eds. 2016. *Consuming space: Placing consumption in perspective*. Routledge.

Gradin, Sofa. 2016. 'Rethinking the notion of "value" in global value chains analysis: A decolonial political economy perspective'. *Competition & Change* 20 (5): 353–67.

Graeber, David. 2001. *Toward an anthropological theory of value: The false coin of our own dreams*. Springer.

Gramsci, Antonio. 1988. *Lettere dal carcere, volume secondo*. L'Unità.

Greenberg, Stephen. 2013. 'A gendered analysis of wine export value chains from South Africa to Sweden'. *Agrekon* 52 (3): 34–62.

Guthey, Greig Tor. 2008. 'Agro-industrial conventions: Some evidence from Northern California's wine industry'. *Geographical Journal* 174 (2): 138–48.

Guy, Kolleen M. 2003. *When Champagne became French: Wine and the making of a national identity*. John Hopkins University Press.

Gwynne, Robert N. 2008. 'UK retail concentration, Chilean wine producers and value chains'. *Geographical Journal* 174 (2): 97–108.

Haack, Patrick, Oliver Schilke and Lynne Zucker. 2021. 'Legitimacy revisited: Disentangling propriety, validity, and consensus'. *Journal of Management Studies* 58 (3): 749–81.

Hall, C. Michael, Liz Sharples, Brock Cambourne and Niki Macionis, eds. 2002. *Wine tourism around the world: Development, management, markets*. Routledge.

Hall, Stuart, David Morley, Catherine Hall and Bill Schwarz. 2019 [1980]. *Foundations of cultural studies*. Duke University Press.
Hamann, Ralph, James Smith, Pete Tashman and R Scott Marshall. 2017. 'Why do SMEs go green? An analysis of wine firms in South Africa'. *Business & Society* 56 (1): 23–56.
Hardt, Michael and Antonio Negri. 2017. *Assembly*. Oxford University Press.
Harvey, Matt, Warwick Frost and Leanne White. 2014. 'Exploring wine and identity'. In *Wine and identity: Branding, heritage, terroir*, edited by Matt Harvey, Leanne White and Warwick Frost, 1–13. Routledge.
Hastings, Thomas. 2019. 'Leveraging Nordic links: South African labour's role in regulating labour standards in wine global production networks'. *Journal of Economic Geography* 19 (4): 921–42.
Havice, Elizabeth and Liam Campling. 2013. 'Articulating upgrading: Island developing states and canned tuna production'. *Environment and Planning A: Economy and Space* 45 (11): 2610–27.
Havice, Elizabeth and Liam Campling. 2017. 'Where chain governance and environmental governance meet: Interfirm strategies in the canned tuna global value chain'. *Economic Geography* 93 (3): 292–13.
Havice, Elizabeth and John Pickles. 2019. 'On value in value chains'. In *Handbook on global value chains*, edited by Stefano Ponte, Gary Gereffi and Gale Raj-Reichert, 169–82. Edward Elgar Publishing.
Heilbroner, Robert L. 1983. 'The problem of value in the constitution of economic thought'. *Social Research* 50 (2): 253–77.
Heinich, Nathalie. 2017. *Des valeurs. Une approche sociologique*. Gallimard.
Heinich, Nathalie. 2020a. 'A pragmatic redefinition of value(s): Toward a general model of valuation'. *Theory, Culture & Society* 37 (5): 75–94.
Heinich, Nathalie. 2020b. 'Ten proposals on values'. *Cultural Sociology* 14 (3): 213–32.
Heinich, Nathalie. 2022. *La valeur des personnes: Preuves et ereuves de la grandeur*. Gallimard.
Herman, Agatha. 2012. 'Tactical ethics: How the discourses of Fairtrade and Black Economic Empowerment change and interact in wine networks from South Africa to the UK'. *Geoforum* 43 (6): 1121–30.
Herman, Agatha. 2018. *Practising empowerment in post-apartheid South Africa: Wine, ethics and development*. Routledge.
Herman, Agatha. 2019. 'Asymmetries and opportunities: Power and inequality in Fairtrade wine global production networks'. *Area* 51 (2): 332–9.
Hira, Anil. 2013. *What makes clusters competitive? Cases from the global wine industry*. McGill-Queen's Press.
Howland, Peter J. 2013. 'Distinction by proxy: The democratization of fine wine'. *Journal of Sociology* 49 (2–3): 325–40.
Howland, Peter J. 2019a. 'Enduring wine and the global middle-class'. In *The Globalization of Wine*, edited by David Inglis and Anna-Mari Almila, 151–70. Bloomsbury Academic.
Howland, Peter J. 2019b. 'Plain-sight utopia: Boutique winemakers, urbane vineyards and terroir-torial moorings'. In *Wine, terroir and utopia*, edited by Jacqueline Dutton and Peter J Howland, 235–52. Routledge.
Howland, Peter J and Jacqueline Dutton. 2020. 'Making new worlds: The utopian potentials of wine and terroir'. In *Wine, terroir and utopia*, edited by Jacqueline Dutton and Peter J Howland, 1–23. Routledge.
Howson, Kelle. 2022. 'Discursive power in ethical value networks: An analysis of the South African wine industry'. In *Ethical value networks in international trade*, edited by Warwick Murray, John Overton and Kelle Howson, 94–111. Edward Elgar Publishing.

Howson, Kelle, Warwick Murray and John Overton. 2020. 'Certified utopia: Ethical branding and the wine industry of South Africa'. In *Wine, terroir and utopia*, edited by Jacqueline Dutton and Peter J Howland 145–62. Routledge.

Howson, Kelle, Hannah Johnston, Matthew Cole, Fabian Ferrari, Funda Ustek-Spilda and Mark Graham. 2023. 'Unpaid labour and territorial extraction in digital value networks'. *Global Networks* 23 (4): 732–54.

Huber, Matt. 2018. 'Resource geographies I: Valuing nature (or not)'. *Progress in Human Geography* 42 (1): 148–59.

Humphrey, John and Hubert Schmitz. 2002. 'How does insertion in global value chains affect upgrading in industrial clusters?' *Regional Studies* 36 (9): 1017–27.

Ibert, Oliver, Martin Hess, Jana Kleibert, Felix Müller and Dominic Power. 2019. 'Geographies of dissociation: Value creation, "dark" places, and "missing" links'. *Dialogues in Human Geography* 9 (1): 43–63.

Iheduru, Okechukwu C. 2004. 'Black economic power and nation-building in post-apartheid South Africa'. *The Journal of Modern African Studies* 42 (1): 1–30.

Iliopoulos, Panagiotis and Dariusz Wójcik. 2024. 'The Big Four: Multiple functions and power in global value chains'. *Global Networks* e12507.

Inglis, David. 2019. 'Wine globalization: Longer-term dynamics and contemporary patterns'. In *The Globalization of Wine*, edited by David Inglis and Anna-Mari Almila, 21–46. Bloomsbury Academic.

Inglis, David and Anna-Mari Almila. 2019. 'Introduction: The travels and tendencies of wine'. In *The globalization of wine*, edited by David Inglis and Anna-Mari Almila, 1–20. Bloomsbury Academic.

Isla, Anne. 2017. 'Evolution des conventions de qualité et enjeux de la singularité sur le marché du vin'. *Food Systems/Systèmes Alimentaires* (2): 197–217.

Itçaina, Xabier, Antoine Roger and Andy Smith. 2016. *Varietals of capitalism: A political economy of the changing wine industry*. Cornell University Press.

Jevons, William Stanley. 1879. *The theory of political economy*. Macmillan.

Johnson, Cathryn, Timothy J Dowd and Cecilia L Ridgeway. 2006. 'Legitimacy as a social process'. *Annual Review of Sociology* 32 (1): 53–78.

Joly, Nicholas. 2012. *What is biodynamic wine? The quality, the taste, the terroir*. Clairview Books.

Joy, Annamma, Russell W Belk, Steve Charters, Jeff Jian Feng Wang and Camilo Peña. 2018. 'Performance theory and consumer engagement: Wine-tourism experiences in South Africa and India'. In *Consumer culture theory*, edited by Samantha N. N. Cross, Cecilia Ruvalcaba, Alladi Venkatesh and Russell W. Belk, 163–87. Emerald Publishing Limited.

Kanamaru, Tomoaki. 2020. 'Production management as an ordering of multiple qualities: Negotiating the quality of coffee in Timor-Leste'. *Journal of Cultural Economy* 13 (2): 139–152.

Kaplinsky, Raphael. 2005. *Globalization, poverty and inequality: Between a rock and a hard place*. John Wiley & Sons.

Kaplonski, Christopher. 2019. 'Utopia regained: Nature and the taste of terroir'. In *Wine, terroir and utopia*, edited by Jacqueline Dutton and Peter J Howland, 197–210. Routledge.

Karlsen, Asbjørn. 2018. 'Framing industrialization of the offshore wind value chain: A discourse approach to an event'. *Geoforum* 88: 148–156.

Karpik, Lucien. 2010. *Valuing the unique: The economics of singularities*. Princeton University Press.

Kay, Kelly and Miles Kenney-Lazar. 2017. 'Value in capitalist natures: An emerging framework'. *Dialogues in Human Geography* 7 (3): 295–309.

Kritzinger, Andrienetta, Stephanie Barrientos and Hester Rossouw. 2004. 'Global production and flexible employment in South African horticulture: Experiences of contract workers in fruit exports'. *Sociologia Ruralis* 44 (1): 17–39.

Krüger, Anne K and Martin Reinhart. 2017. 'Theories of valuation: Building blocks for conceptualizing valuation between practice and structure'. *Historical Social Research/ Historische Sozialforschung* 42 (1): 263–85.

Kruger, Sandra, Andries Du Toit and Stefano Ponte. 2006. 'De-racialising exploitation: "Black Economic Empowerment" in the South African wine sector'. *Danish Institute for International Studies Working Paper* 2006: 34.

Kumar, Randhir and Niels Beerepoot. 2019. 'Multipolar governance and social upgrading in the international services value chains: The case of support-service workers in Mumbai'. *Geoforum* 104: 147–57.

Lafaye, Claudette and Laurent Thévenot. 2017. 'An ecological justification? Conflicts in the development of nature'. In *Justification, evaluation and critique in the study of organizations: Contributions from French pragmatist sociology*, edited by Charlotte Cloutier, Jean-Pascal Gond and Bernard Leca, 273–300. Emerald Publishing.

Lagendijk, Arnoud. 2004. 'Global "lifeworlds" versus local "systemworlds": How flying winemkers produce global wines in interconnected locales'. *Tijdschrift voor economische en sociale geografie* 95 (5): 511–26.

Lang, Juliane. 2024. 'Pristineness, heritage, and the dissociative power of place imaginaries: Marketing "dark places" in global value chains'. *Environment and Planning A: Economy and Space*: 0308518X241284117.

Lang, Juliane, Stefano Ponte and Thando Vilakazi. 2022. 'Linking power and inequality in global value chains'. *Global Networks* 23 (4): 755–71.

Latour, Bruno. 1998. 'To modernise or ecologise? That is the question'. In *Remaking reality: Nature at the millennium*, edited by Bruce Braun and Noel Castree, 221–42. Routledge.

Latour, Bruno. 2018. *Down to earth: Politics in the new climatic regime*. John Wiley & Sons.

Lazonick, William and Jang-Sup Shin. 2019. *Predatory value extraction: How the looting of the business corporation became the US norm and how sustainable prosperity can be restored*. Oxford University Press.

Le Fur, Eric and Jean-François Outreville. 2019. 'Fine wine returns: A review of the literature'. *Journal of Asset Management* 20 (3): 196–214.

Levy, David L. 2008. 'Political contestation in global production networks'. *Academy of Management Review* 33 (4): 943–63.

Lindkvist, Knut B and José L Sanchez. 2008. 'Conventions and innovation: A comparison of two localized natural resource-based industries'. *Regional Studies* 42 (3): 343–54.

Lipovetsky, Gilles. 2021. *Le sacre de l'authenticité*. Gallimard.

Lubinga, Moses Herbert, Simphiwe Ngqangweni, Stephanie Van der Walt, Yolanda Potelwa, Bonani Nyhodo, Lucius Phaleng and Thandeka Ntshangase. 2021. 'Geographical indications in the wine industry: Does it matter for South Africa?' *International Journal of Wine Business Research* 33 (1): 47–59.

Mafata, M, J Brand, V Panzeri and A Buica. 2020. 'Investigating the concept of South African old vine Chenin blanc'. *South African Journal of Enology and Viticulture* 41 (2): 168–82.

Malorgio, Giulio, Eugenio Pomarici, Roberta Sardone, Alfonso Scardera and Domenico Tosco. 2011. 'La catena del valore nella filiera vitivinicola'. *Agriregionieuropa* 7 (27): 14–19.

Marshall, Alfred. 2013 [1890]. *Principles of economics* (unabridged eighth edition). Palgrave Macmillan.
Martineau, Harriet. 1832. *Illustrations of political economy, Vol. IV (French Wine and Politics)*. William Clowes.
Marx, Karl. 1992 [1894]. *Capital: Volume III*. Penguin.
Matthews, Mark A. 2016. *Terroir and other myths of winegrowing*. University of California Press.
Mazzucato, Mariana. 2018. *The value of everything: Making and taking in the global economy*. Hachette UK.
Mazzucato, Mariana and Rosie Collington. 2023. *The big con: How the consulting industry weakens our businesses, infantilizes our governments, and warps our economies*. Penguin.
McCoy, Elin. 2006. *The emperor of wine: The rise of Robert M. Parker, Jr. and the reign of American taste*. Ecco.
McEwan, Cheryl and David Bek. 2006. '(Re)politicizing empowerment: Lessons from the South African wine industry'. *Geoforum* 37 (6): 1021–34.
McEwan, Cheryl and David Bek. 2009a. 'Placing ethical trade in context: WIETA and the South African wine industry'. *Third World Quarterly* 30 (4): 723–42.
McEwan, Cheryl and David Bek. 2009b. 'The political economy of alternative trade: Social and environmental certification in the South African wine industry'. *Journal of Rural Studies* 25 (3): 255–66.
McKinlay, Arthur Patch. 1953. 'Bacchus as Inspirer of Literary Art'. *The Classical Journal* 49 (3): 101–36.
Meloni, Giulia and Johan Swinnen. 2013. 'The political economy of European wine regulations'. *Journal of Wine Economics* 8 (3): 244–84.
Mignolo, Walter D. 2021. *The politics of decolonial investigations*. Duke University Press.
Milanovic, Branko. 2016. *Global inequality*. Harvard University Press.
Milberg, William and Deborah Winkler. 2013. *Outsourcing economics: Global value chains in capitalist development*. Cambridge University Press.
Mirowski, Philip. 1990. 'Learning the meaning of a dollar: Conservation principles and the social theory of value in economic theory'. *Social Research* 57 (3): 689–717.
Mitchell, Richard, Steve Charters and Julia Nina Albrecht. 2012. 'Cultural systems and the wine tourism product'. *Annals of Tourism Research* 39 (1): 311–35.
Monterescu, Daniel. 2017. 'Border wines: Terroir across contested territory'. *Gastronomica* 17 (4): 127–40.
Moore, Jason W. 2015. *Capitalism in the web of life: Ecology and the accumulation of capital*. Verso Books.
Moran, Warren. 1993. 'The wine appellation as territory in France and California'. *Annals of the Association of American Geographers* 83 (4): 694–717.
Morgan, Kevin, Terry Marsden and Jonathan Murdoch. 2006. *Worlds of food: Place, power, and provenance in the food chain*. Oxford University Press.
Morrison, Andrea and Roberta Rabellotti. 2009. 'Knowledge and information networks in an Italian wine cluster'. *European Planning Studies* 17 (7): 983–1006.
Morrison, Andrea and Roberta Rabellotti. 2017. 'Gradual catch up and enduring leadership in the global wine industry'. *Research Policy* 46 (2): 417–30.
Moscovici, Daniel and Alastair Reed. 2018. 'Comparing wine sustainability certifications around the world: History, status and opportunity'. *Journal of Wine Research* 29 (1): 1–25.

Moseley, William G and Brent McCusker. 2008. 'Fighting fire with a broken teacup: A comparative analysis of South Africa's land-redistribution program'. *Geographical Review* 98 (3): 322–38.

Muniesa, Fabian, Yuval Millo and Michel Callon. 2007. 'An introduction to market devices'. *The Sociological Review* 55 (2_suppl): 1–12.

Murray, Warwick E, Kelle Howson, Simon Bidwell, John Overton, Johannes Rehner and Peter BF Williams. 2022. 'Ethical value networks'. In *Ethical value networks in international trade*, edited by Warwick E. Murray, John Overton and Kelle Howson, 52–74. Edward Elgar Publishing.

Nazzaro, Concetta, Marcello Stanco, Anna Uliano, Marco Lerro and Giuseppe Marotta. 2022. 'Collective smart innovations and corporate governance models in Italian wine cooperatives: The opportunities of the farm-to-fork strategy'. *International Food and Agribusiness Management Review* 25 (5): 723–36.

Negro, Giacomo and Michael T Hannan. 2022. *Wine markets: Genres and identities.* Columbia University Press.

Neilson, Jeff and Bill Pritchard. 2011. *Value chain struggles: Institutions and governance in the plantation districts of South India.* John Wiley & Sons.

Neilson, Jeffrey, Josephine Wright and Lya Aklimawati. 2018. 'Geographical indications and value capture in the Indonesia coffee sector'. *Journal of Rural Studies* 59: 35–48.

Neimark, Benjamin, Sango Mahanty and Wolfram Dressler. 2016. 'Mapping value in a 'green' commodity frontier: Revisiting commodity chain analysis'. *Development and Change* 47 (2): 240–65.

Nelson, Valerie, Adrienne Martin and Joachim Ewert. 2005. 'What difference can they make? Assessing the social impact of corporate codes of practice'. *Development in Practice* 15 (3–4): 539–45.

Nickow, Andre. 2015. 'Growing in value: NGOs, social movements and the cultivation of developmental value chains in Uttarakhand, India'. *Global Networks* 15 (s1): S45–S64.

Nugent, Paul. 2024a. *Race, taste and the grape: South African wine from a global perspective.* Cambridge University Press.

Nugent, Paul. 2024b. 'Sour grapes and sweet harmony: Historicizing collective action problems in the South African wine industry'. *Journal of Wine Economics* 18 (4): 332–40.

Osborne, Lawrence. 2004. *The accidental connoisseur: An irreverent journey through the wine world.* North Point Press.

Ouma, Stefan. 2015. *Assembling export markets: The making and unmaking of global food connections in West Africa.* John Wiley & Sons.

Outreville, J François and Michael Hanni. 2013. 'Multinational firms in the world wine industry: An investigation into the determinants of most-favoured locations'. *Journal of Wine Research* 24 (2): 128–37.

Overton, John and Glenn Banks. 2015. 'Conspicuous production: Wine, capital and status'. *Capital & Class* 39 (3): 473–91.

Overton, John and Jo Heitger. 2008. 'Maps, markets and Merlot: The making of an antipodean wine appellation'. *Journal of Rural Studies* 24 (4): 440–9.

Overton, John and Warwick E Murray. 2011. 'Playing the scales: Regional transformations and the differentiation of rural space in the Chilean wine industry'. *Journal of Rural Studies* 27 (1): 63–72.

Overton, John and Warwick E Murray. 2013. 'Class in a glass: Capital, neoliberalism and social space in the global wine industry'. *Antipode* 45 (3): 702–18.

Overton, John and Warwick E Murray. 2016. 'Investing in place: Articulations and congregations of capital in the wine industry'. *The Geographical Journal* 182 (1): 49–58.

Overton, John, Warwick E Murray and Kelle Howson. 2019. 'Doing good by drinking wine? Ethical value networks and upscaling of wine production in Australia, New Zealand and South Africa'. *European Planning Studies* 27 (12): 2431–49.

Palpacuer, Florence. 2008. 'Bringing the social context back in: Governance and wealth distribution in global commodity chains'. *Economy & Society* 37 (3): 393–419.

Palpacuer, Florence and Clara Roussey. 2023. 'Entangling global chains of wealth and value through CSR-ization: A critical Polanyian perspective on Weda Bay Nickel'. *Environment and Planning A: Economy and Space*. doi: https://doi.org/10.1177/0308518X231191946.

Pappalardo, Salvatore E, Lorenzo Gislimberti, Francesco Ferrarese, Massimo De Marchi and Paolo Mozzi. 2019. 'Estimation of potential soil erosion in the Prosecco DOCG area (NE Italy), toward a soil footprint of bottled sparkling wine production in different land-management scenarios'. *PLOS ONE* 14 (5):e0210922.

Parker, Thomas. 2015. *Tasting French terroir: The history of an idea*. University of California Press.

Peters, Gary L. 1997. *American winescapes: The cultural landscapes of America's wine*. Routledge.

Pfeffer, Fabian T and Nora Waitkus. 2021. 'The wealth inequality of nations'. *American Sociological Review* 86 (4): 567–602.

Picard, David, Catarina Nascimento Moreira and Tristan Loloum. 2018. 'Wine magic: Consumer culture, tourism, and terroir'. *Journal of Anthropological Research* 74 (4): 526–40.

Piketty, Thomas. 2014. *Capital in the 21st century*. Harvard University Press.

Piketty, Thomas. 2020. *Capital and ideology*. Harvard University Press.

Pitts, Frederick Harry. 2021. *Value*. John Wiley & Sons.

Plumecocq, Gael. 2023. 'Approaches to ecological problems in convention theory: How legitimate is environmentalism?' In *Handbook of economics and sociology of conventions*, edited by Rainer Diaz-Bone and G de Larquier. Springer Nature. https://doi.org/10.1007/978-3-030-52130-1_24-1.

Plumecocq, Gael, Thomas Debril, Michel Duru, Marie-Benoît Magrini, Jean Pierre Sarthou and Olivier Therond. 2018. 'The plurality of values in sustainable agriculture models'. *Ecology and Society* 23 (1): 21.

Pomarici, Eugenio and Roberta Sardone. 2020. 'EU wine policy in the framework of the CAP: Post-2020 challenges'. *Agricultural and Food Economics* 8 (1): 1–40.

Ponte, Stefano. 2014. 'The evolutionary dynamics of biofuel value chains: From unipolar and government-driven to multipolar governance'. *Environment and Planning A: Economy and Space* 46 (2): 353–72.

Ponte, Stefano. 2016. 'Convention theory in the Anglophone agro-food literature: Past, present and future'. *Journal of Rural Studies* 44: 12–23.

Ponte, S. 2019. *Business, power and sustainability in a world of global value chains*. London: Zed Books.

Ponte, Stefano. 2021. 'Bursting the bubble? The hidden costs and visible conflicts behind the Prosecco wine "miracle"'. *Journal of Rural Studies* 86: 542–53.

Ponte, Stefano and Joachim Ewert. 2007. South African wine: An industry in ferment. *Tralac Working Paper 8/2007*: Trade Law Centre for Southern Africa.

Ponte, Stefano and Joachim Ewert. 2009. 'Which way is "up" in upgrading? Trajectories of change in the value chain for South African wine'. *World Development* 37 (10): 1637–50.

Ponte, Stefano and Peter Gibbon. 2005. 'Quality standards, conventions and the governance of global value chains'. *Economy & Society* 34 (1): 1–31.

Ponte, Stefano and Timothy Sturgeon. 2014. 'Explaining governance in global value chains: A modular theory-building effort'. *Review of International Political Economy* 21 (1): 195–223.

Ponte, Stefano, Jennifer Bair and Mark Dallas. 2023. 'Power and inequality in global value chains: Advancing the research agenda'. *Global Networks* 23 (4): 679–86.

Ponte, Stefano, Gary Gereffi and Gale Raj-Reichert, eds. 2019. *Handbook on global value chains*. Edward Elgar Publishing.

Ponte, Stefano, Christine Noe and Dan Brockington, eds. 2022. *Contested sustainability: The political ecology of conservation and development in Tanzania*. Boydell and Brewer.

Ponte, Stefano, Simon Roberts and Lance Van Sittert. 2007. '"Black Economic Empowerment", business and the state in South Africa'. *Development & Change* 38 (5): 933–55.

Ponte, Stefano, Valentina De Marchi, Marco Bettiol and Eleonora Di Maria. 2023. 'The horizontal governance of environmental upgrading: Lessons from the Prosecco and Valpolicella wine value chains in Italy'. *Environment and Planning A: Economy and Space* 55 (8): 1884–1905.

Porter, Michael E. 1985. *Competitive advantage: Creating and sustaining superior performance*. Free Press.

Priilaid, David and Jonathan Steyn. 2020. 'Evaluating the worth of nascent old vine cues for South African wines'. *International Journal of Wine Business Research* 32 (2): 283–300.

Prosperi, Paolo, Daniele Vergamini and Fabio Bartolini. 2020. 'Exploring institutional arrangements for local fish product labelling in Tuscany (Italy): A convention theory perspective'. *Agricultural and Food Economics* 8 (1): 1–16.

Quentin, David and Liam Campling. 2018. 'Global inequality chains: Integrating mechanisms of value distribution into analyses of global production'. *Global Networks* 18 (1): 33–56.

Quesnay, François. 1894. *Tableau oeconomique*. Macmillan.

Quiñones-Ruiz, Xiomara F. 2020. 'The diverging understandings of quality by coffee chain actors: Insights from Colombian producers and Austrian Roasters'. *Sustainability* 12 (15): 6137.

Rainer, Gerhard. 2021. 'Geographies of qualification in the global fine wine market'. *Environment and Planning A: Economy and Space* 53 (1): 95–112.

Rainer, Gerhard, Christian Steiner and Robert Pütz. 2023. 'Market making and the contested performance of value in the global (bulk) wine industry'. *Economic Geography* 99 (4): 411–33.

Raj-Reichert, Gale. 2013. 'Safeguarding labour in distant factories: Health and safety governance in an electronics global production network'. *Geoforum* 44: 23–31.

Raynolds, Laura T. 2009. 'Mainstreaming fair trade coffee: From partnership to traceability'. *World Development* 37 (6): 1083–93.

Raynolds, Laura T. 2012. 'Fair Trade: Social regulation in global food markets'. *Journal of Rural studies* 28 (3): 276–87.

Raynolds, Laura T, Douglas Murray and Andrew Heller. 2007. 'Regulating sustainability in the coffee sector: A comparative analysis of third-party environmental and social certification initiatives'. *Agriculture & Human Values* 24: 147–63.

Reckwitz, Andreas. 2020. *The society of singularities*. Polity.

Renard, Marie-Christine. 2005. 'Quality certification, regulation and power in fair trade'. *Journal of Rural Studies* 21 (4): 419–31.

Ricardo, David. 1821. *On the principles of political economy*. J. Murray.

Richey, Lisa Ann. 2024. 'Why does capitalism feel so right? Ethical imaginaries of prison labour and sisterhood solidarity'. *Economy & Society* 53 (2): 250–74.
Richey, Lisa Ann and Stefano Ponte. 2011. *Brand aid: Shopping well to save the world*. University of Minnesota Press.
Rizzo, Luca Simone. 2009. 'Wine cooperatives in the East of the Province of Verona. Company consolidation and networking: An update'. Proceedings-AIEA2 VII Congresso Internazionale.
Robertson, Morgan. 2012. 'Measurement and alienation: Making a world of ecosystem services'. *Transactions of the Institute of British Geographers* 37 (3): 386–401.
Robinson, Cedric. 2000 [1983]. *Black Marxism: The making of the Black radical tradition*. University of North Carolina Press.
Rosin, Christopher, Hugh Campbell and John Reid. 2017. 'Metrology and sustainability: Using sustainability audits in New Zealand to elaborate the complex politics of measuring'. *Journal of Rural Studies* 52: 90–9.
Rosin, Christopher J, Katharine A Legun, Hugh Campbell and Marion Sautier. 2017. 'From compliance to co-production: Emergent forms of agency in sustainable wine production in New Zealand'. *Environment and Planning A: Economy and Space* 49 (12): 2780–99.
Saez, Emmanuel and Gabriel Zucman. 2020. 'The rise of income and wealth inequality in America: Evidence from distributional macroeconomic accounts'. *Journal of Economic Perspectives* 34 (4): 3–26.
Salais, Robert and Michael Storper. 1992. 'The four "worlds" of contemporary industry'. *Cambridge Journal of Economics* 16 (2): 169–93.
Sánchez-Hernández, José Luis. 2023. 'Wine and conventions: A fruitful coupage'. In *Handbook of economics and sociology of conventions*, edited by Rainer Diaz-Bone and G de Larquier. Springer. https://doi.org/10.1007/978-3-030-52130-1_68-1.
Sánchez-Hernández, José Luis, Javier Aparicio-Amador and José Luis Alonso-Santos. 2010. 'The shift between worlds of production as an innovative process in the wine industry in Castile and Leon (Spain)'. *Geoforum* 41 (3): 469–78.
Sanning, Lee W, Sherrill Shaffer and Jo Marie Sharratt. 2008. 'Bordeaux wine as a financial investment'. *Journal of Wine Economics* 3 (1): 51–71.
Sato, Chizuko. 2013. 'Black Economic Empowerment in the South African agricultural sector: A case study of the wine industry'. *IDE Discussion Paper* 384.
Sautier, Marion, Katharine A Legun, Christopher Rosin and Hugh Campbell. 2018. 'Sustainability: A tool for governing wine production in New Zealand?' *Journal of Cleaner Production* 179: 347–56.
Schenk, Patrick. 2021. 'Karpik in the bottle: Can judgment devices explain the demand for fine wine?' *KZfSS Kölner Zeitschrift für Soziologie und Sozialpsychologie* 73 (2): 177–200.
Schumpeter, Joseph A. 2013 [1950]. *Capitalism, socialism and democracy*. Routledge.
Schurman, Rachel and William Munro. 2009. 'Targeting capital: A cultural economy approach to understanding the efficacy of two anti-genetic engineering movements'. *American Journal of Sociology* 115 (1): 155–202.
Seabrooke, Leonard and Duncan Wigan, eds. 2022. *Global wealth chains: Asset strategies in the world economy*. Oxford University Press.
Selwyn, Benjamin. 2014. 'Commodity chains, creative destruction and global inequality: A class analysis'. *Journal of Economic Geography* 15 (2): 253–74.
Selwyn, Benjamin. 2019. 'Poverty chains and global capitalism'. *Competition & Change* 23 (1): 71–97.

Senese, Donna M, John S Hull and Barbara J McNicol. 2019. 'Ecotopian mobilities: Terroir-driven tourism and migration in British Columbia, Canada'. In *Wine, terroir and utopia*, edited by Jacqueline Dutton and Peter J Howland, 126–44. Routledge.

Sibanda, Omphemetse S Sr. 2016. 'The prospects, benefits and challenges of sui generis protection of geographical indications of South Africa'. *Foreign Trade Review* 51 (3): 213–24.

Simmel, Georg. 1978. *The philosophy of money*. Routledge.

Smith, Adam. 1977 [1776]. *An inquiry into the nature and causes of the wealth of nations*. University of Chicago Press.

Smith, Andy. 2016. *The politics of economic activity*. Oxford University Press.

Smith, Barry C. 2007. 'The objectivity of tastes and tasting'. In *Questions of taste: The philosophy of wine*, edited by Barry C Smith, 41–77. Oxford University Press.

Smith Maguire, Jennifer. 2019. 'Natural wine and the globalization of a taste for provenance'. In *The globalization of wine*, edited by David Inglis and Anna-Mari Almila, 171–89. Bloomsbury Academic.

Smith, Sally. 2015. 'Fair trade and women's empowerment'. In *Handbook of research on fair trade*, edited by Laura T Raynolds and Elizabeth A. Bennett, 405–21. Edward Elgar Publishing.

Staricco, Juan Ignacio. 2022. 'Power and its sources in the governance of global value chains: The Argentina–European Union biodiesel value chain'. *Global Networks* 23 (4): 715–31.

Staricco, Juan Ignacio and Stefano Ponte. 2015. 'Quality regimes in agro-food industries: A regulation theory reading of Fair Trade wine in Argentina'. *Journal of Rural Studies* 38: 65–76.

Stark, David. 2009. *The sense of dissonance: Accounts of worth in economic life*. Princeton University Press.

Stark, David. 2011. 'What's valuable?' In *The worth of goods: Valuation and pricing in the economy*, edited by Jens Beckert and Patrik Aspers, 319–38. Oxford University Press.

Starosta, Guido. 2010. 'Global commodity chains and the Marxian law of value'. *Antipode* 42 (2): 433–65.

Steyn, Jonathan Daniel. 2021. 'Authenticity framing and market creation for meta organisations: The case of the Swartland Independent Producers in the South African wine field'. PhD thesis, Department of Commerce, Graduate School of Business, Graduate School of Business, University of Cape Town.

Stiglitz, Joseph E. 2015. *The price of inequality: How today's divided society endangers our future*. W.W. Norton.

Storper, Michael and Robert Salais. 1997. *Worlds of production: The action frameworks of the economy*. Harvard University Press.

Stræte, Egil. 2004. 'Innovation and changing "worlds of production": Case-studies of Norwegian dairies'. *European Urban and Regional Studies* 11 (3): 227–41.

Suchman, Mark C. 1995. 'Managing legitimacy: Strategic and institutional approaches'. *Academy of Management Review* 20 (3): 571–610.

Swinburn, Robert. 2013. 'The things that count: Rethinking terroir in Australia'. In *Wine and culture: Vineyard to glass*, edited by Rachel E Black and Robert C Ulin, 33–50. Bloomsbury Academic.

Swinburn, Robert. 2019. 'Deep terroir as utopia: Explorations of place and country in southeastern Australia'. In *Wine, terroir and utopia*, edited by Jacqueline Dutton and Peter J Howland, 221–34. Routledge.

Teil, Geneviève. 2012. 'No such thing as terroir? Objectivities and the regimes of existence of objects'. *Science, Technology, & Human Values* 37 (5): 478–505.

Teil, Geneviève. 2014. 'Nature, the coauthor of its products? An analysis of the recent controversy over rejected AOC wines in France'. *The Journal of World Intellectual Property* 17 (3–4): 96–113.

Teil, Geneviève, Sandrine Barrey, Antoine Hennion and Pierre Floux. 2011. *Le vin et l'environnement: Faire compter la différence*. Presses des Mines.

Thévenot, Laurent. 1995. 'Des marchés aux normes'. In *La grande transformation de l'agriculture: Lectures conventionnalistes et regulationnistes*, edited by Gilles Allaire and Robert Boyer, 33–51. INRA-Economica.

Thévenot, Laurent. 2007. 'The plurality of cognitive formats and engagements: Moving between the familiar and the public'. *European Journal of Social Theory* 10 (3): 409–23.

Thévenot, Laurent, Michael Moody and Claudette Lafaye. 2000. 'Forms of valuing nature: Arguments and modes of justification in French and American environmental disputes'. In *Rethinking comparative cultural sociology: Repertoires of evaluation in France and the United States*, edited by Michele Lamont and Laurent Thévenot, 229–72. Cambridge University Press.

Thomsen, Lotte and Martin Hess. 2022. 'Dialectics of association and dissociation: Spaces of valuation, trade, and retail in the gemstone and jewelry sector'. *Economic Geography* 98 (1): 49–67.

Tomasi, Diego, Federica Gaiotti and Gregory V Jones. 2013. 'The role of landscape in the productive context and in the quality of Prosecco wine'. In *The power of the terroir: The case study of Prosecco wine*, edited by Diego Tomasi, Federica Gaiotti and Gregory V Jones, 235–48. Springer.

Torquati, Biancamaria, Giulia Giacchè and Sonia Venanzi. 2015. 'Economic analysis of the traditional cultural vineyard landscapes in Italy'. *Journal of Rural Studies* 39: 122–32.

Trubek, Amy B. 2008. *The taste of place: A cultural journey into terroir*. University of California Press.

Tsing, Anna Lowenhaupt. 2015. *The mushroom at the end of the world: On the possibility of life in capitalist ruins*. Princeton University Press.

Tups, Gideon and Peter Dannenberg. 2023. 'Supplying lead firms, intangible assets and power in global value chains: Explaining governance in the fertilizer chain'. *Global Networks* 23 (4): 772–91.

Ulin, Robert C. 2013. 'Terroir and locality: An anthropological perspective'. In *Wine and culture: Vineyard to glass*, edited by Rachel E Black and Robert C Ulin, 33–50. Bloomsbury Academic.

Unwin, Tim. 1991. *Wine and the vine: An historical geography of viticulture and the wine trade*. Routledge.

Urry, John. 2002. *Consuming places*. Routledge.

Valente, Marica and Stefan Seifert. 2018. An offer that you can't refuse? Agrimafias and migrant labor on vineyards in southern Italy. *DIW Berlin Discussion Paper* No. 1735.

Veblen, Thorstein. 2012 [1899]. *The theory of the leisure class: An economic study of institutions*. Renaissance classics.

Vilakazi, Thando and Teboho Bosiu. 2022. 'Black Economic Empowerment, barriers to entry, and economic transformation in South Africa'. In *Structural transformation in South Africa: The challenges of inclusive industrial development in a middle-income country*, edited by Antonio Andreoni, Pamela Mondliwa, Simon Roberts and Fiona Tregenna, 189–212. Oxford University Press.

Vink, Nick. 2018. 'South Africa'. In *Wine globalization: A new comparative history*, edited by Kym Anderson and Vicente Pinilla, 384–409. Cambridge University Press.

Vink, Nick, Gavin Williams and Johann Kirsten. 2004. 'South Africa'. In *The World's wine markets: Globalization at work*, edited by Kym Anderson, 227–51. Edward Elgar Publishing.

Vink, Nick, Alain Deloire, Valerie Bonnardot and Joachim Ewert. 2012. 'Climate change and the future of South Africa's wine industry'. *International Journal of Climate Change Strategies and Management* 4(4): 420-41.

Visentin, Francesco and Francesco Vallerani. 2018. 'A countryside to sip: Venice inland and the Prosecco's uneasy relationship with wine tourism and rural exploitation'. *Sustainability* 10 (7): 2195.

Walras, Léon. 2014 [1883]. *Elements of theoretical economics: Or, the theory of social wealth*. Cambridge University Press.

Whittaker, D Hugh, Timothy Sturgeon, Toshie Okita and Tianbiao Zhu. 2020. *Compressed development: Time and timing in economic and social development*. Oxford University Press.

Williams, Gavin. 2005. 'Black Economic Empowerment in the South African wine industry'. *Journal of Agrarian Change* 5 (4): 476–504.

Williams, Gavin. 2016. 'Slaves, workers, and wine: The "dop system" in the history of the Cape Wine industry, 1658-894'. *Journal of Southern African Studies* 42 (5): 893–909.

Work, Henry H. 2018. *The shape of wine: Its packaging evolution*. Routledge.

Zelizer, V. 1979. *Morals and markets: The development of life insurance in the United States*. Columbia University Press.

Zuboff, Shoshana. 2019. *The age of surveillance capitalism: The fight for a human future at the new frontier of power*. Profile books.

Zucman, Gabriel. 2019. 'Global wealth inequality'. *Annual Review of Economics* 11: 109–38.

INDEX

action, collective 196
activists (activism) 15, 166, 199
actors 45, 94, 110, 188
  chains of value 14–16, 20, 26, 32
adaptations 41, 193
additives 79
affordability 33
African National Congress 165
agencies 79, 101
Amarone della Valpolicella (Amarone) 68, 88–91, 95–6
  see also Prosecco and Valpolicella
Amfori Business Social Compliance Initiative 118
amphoras, ceramic 54, 80, 86–7, 143
apartheid 46–7, 48, 51, 136, 183, 192
appellations 43, 44, 62, 78–81, 108, 190
Appellations d'Origine Contrôlées (AOC) 43
appellation systems 79, 87
appraising 30
appropriation 24, 196, 200
architecture 103, 190
Aspers, Patrik 26
assessments 135
assets 39, 101, 197, 199, 200
attachments 27, 110
auctions 40, 101
Australia 35
authenticity 142, 188, 191
  place 77–91, 93, 95, 112–13
  value chains 33, 43, 66
awards 34, 76, 100, 121

Bair, Jennifer 18
Barbaresco wines 88
bargaining 14, 16, 18, 187
Barolo wines 87–8
beauty 132–8, 159, 191, 192
Becket, Jens 26
Benjamin, Walter 78

best practices 17, 29
Biodiversity and Wine Initiative (BWI) 133
biodiversity conservation 159, 191, 192, 195
biodiversity conservation and beauty 132–8
Biodiversity Wine Initiative (BWI) 134, 135
biodynamic wines 128–32
Black consumers 52
Black Economic Empowerment (BEE) 47, 136, 171, 175–82, 194
Black SMEs 177
Black workers 165
blended wines 40
Blok, Anders 157
Blue North Sustainability 145
Boltanski, Luc 27, 28–30, 110, 157
books 99
borders theory 198
bottles 102, 123, 146–7, 193
bottling 40, 75
branding 45, 151, 154
brands 170
  ownership and business support initiatives 179–82
  place 74, 91, 105, 113
  value chains 39, 54, 60
brokers 101
Burgundy 80–1
Busco 176
buyers 20, 47

cahier des charges 43
calculation 26
California Sustainable Winegrowing Program 115
Campling, Liam 22
Cantine Aperte 66
Cape Floral Kingdom(CFK) 134, 135
capital, corporate 39

capitalism 24, 187–8
    contemporary 3–5, 182
    learning form wine to understand 196–201
    racial 163
    value struggles, constitutive power and inequality in wine 188–96
Carbon Border Adjustment Measures (CBAMs) 119
carbon calculation 145
carbon emissions 75, 145–6, 193
carbon footprints 118–21, 145
Carpené & Malvolti 81
cases, empirical 8–10
cash flows 56, 75
Castellini, Alessandra 129
celebrities 39, 82, 112, 190
certification 141–2, 183
    capitalism 191–3, 195, 200
    place 115, 117
    social and labour conditions 168–75
Certified Heritage Vineyards 96–8, 99
chains of value 5–8, 13
    governance and power 14–19
    sociology of value and valuation 25–8
    value in 19–25
    worlds of valuation 28–32
Champagne 42–3
Chauvet, Jules 143
Chazal, Clémentine 144
chemical fertilizers 17
chemical spraying 107, 140, 148–9, 170, 191
Chiapello, Eve 157
Chile 35
civic world 30
classifications 42
    wine 46
class, social 69, 77, 182–3
climate 69
climate change 81, 167
    capitalism 191, 193, 195
    nature 144–51, 160–1
collaboration 181
collections 27, 39, 110
collective constitution 18
collective representation 108
collectives 14–15, 16, 196
Colombini, Donatella Cinelli 66

colonialism 136, 192
commodification 73
commodities 22, 25, 27
Common Agricultural Policy (CAP) 44, 65
communities 170
companies, multinational 39
competition 19, 22–3, 26, 105, 111, 195
competitions 34, 76
competitiveness 45, 183, 192, 194, 199
compromise 188, 192, 193, 194
Conegliano 66, 77, 92–5
    see also Prosecco and Valpolicella
conflicts 142
Confronting Climate Change (CCC) 145–6
connoisseurship 77, 101
conservation 61, 192
Conservation Champions' (CC) programme 135
Consol Glass 147
consolidation 61–2
consortia 43, 108, 110
Consorzio Tutela Vini delllla Valpolicella 95–6
conspicuous consumption 99, 101–2
constitutive power 16–17, 187–8, 191–3, 195–6, 200–1
consumers 19
    place 82, 87, 99, 110
    value chains 33, 45, 51, 54
    see also Black consumers
consumption 20, 34, 41
    conspicuous 101–2
consumption, global 39
conventions 29–30
cooperation 14
cooperatives 46, 64, 75, 97, 110
Corporate Sustainability Due Diligence Directive 199
corporations 14, 197
costs 55, 97
    labour 197
Covid pandemic 56, 146, 147, 199
critics 87, 111
Croatia 84
cultural landscapes 92, 95
cultural values 103
customers 103

Dallas, Mark P. 14, 15, 17–18
Dannenberg, Peter 17
data 21
data sources 8–10
decoding 34
decolonialism 24
deforestation 139, 150
dehumanization 74
Demeter International 128–9
Denominazione d'Origine Controllata (DOC) 65–6
Denominazione d'Origine Controllata e Garantita (DOCG) 65–6, 67, 84
demonstrative power 16, 187
Demossier, Marion 80
depopulation 192
designation areas 58
designations, geographical 65
destination marketing 105
devastation 192
Devco 176
Dewey, John 28
differentiation 73, 91, 99
digital monopolies 21
digital platforms 21
disciplinare 89, 91, 96
discrimination 165
disease control 47
disease resistance 148, 193
distribution 40
distribution of value 22
diversification 195, 196
diversity 85
documentaries 139–40
domestic world 30
due diligence 199–200
dyadic power 16
dyads 15

ecological systems 23
ecology 159, 191, 192
    nature 159
    see also nature
economy, global 197
efficiency 82, 194
elites 3, 28, 103
    Black 102, 185
    place 74, 83, 100
    value chains 34, 40–2

emissions 119–20
employment 75, 137, 197
empowerment 177
energy consumption 47
energy management 148
enrichment economy 27, 110–11
entrepreneurs 21
    Black 179–80, 181, 182
    Black women 177–8
    see also women
environmental change 69
environmental concerns 191
environmental destruction 200
environmental governance 24
environmental issues 15
environmental management 47
environmental sustainability 117–24, 163, 192
Equalitas 173–5, 183
Esquerre, Arnaud 27, 110
ethicality 166
exchange, moments of 27
exchange value 22
exclusion 77, 190
exclusivity 33, 113
experimentation 46
experts 34, 46, 179
    nature 118–21, 149
    place 101, 108, 110–11
exploitation 23, 191, 194, 199, 200, 201
    see also people
exports 91, 100, 169, 188
    see also value chains
exports, bulk 75
exports, South African wine 50–5

Fairhills 170
fairs, wine 150, 151–5, 195
Fairtrade wine 168–72, 183
Famiglie storiche 96
farmers 47, 48
farmers, smallholder 24, 45
farming 77
farmworkers 33, 170, 200
    see also people
feedback loops 24
females 165, 194
    see also women
festivals 104

finance 118–21, 198
financialization 17, 39, 197
fine wines 74, 99–102, 110–12
flexibility 46, 75
flexitanks 40
Fondazione Gamero Rosso 120–1
food safety 108
Fourcade, Marion 26
frameworks, analytical 28–32
France 35, 41, 77, 99, 125, 143
frauds 101
funds, mutual 40, 101

Gade, Daniel W. 95
Gambero Rosso 111
gatekeeping 34, 190
gender 23, 24, 69, 182–3
    capitalism 193–4
    exploitation 164–75
genuineness 143
geographical indications 74, 79, 188, 190
geographical indications and appellations 78–81
Gereffi, Gary 15, 29
Germany 150
globalization 40, 81, 85, 91
Global Networks 17
Global North 24, 27, 47
Global Reference Framework for Sustainability in Wine 124
Global South 187
Godard, Oliver 157
gold 20
governance 29, 158
    nature 158
governance and power 14–19
Gradin, Sofa 24
Graeber, David 25
Gramsci, Antonio 17
grape production 40
grape varieties 132
green commodities 15
greenhouse gases 148
growth 21, 49
guidelines 117
guides 120
guides, tourist 112
guides, wine 111

Hannan, Michael T. 87–8
Hastings, Thomas 48
Havice, Elizabeth 23
health issues 140–1
Heinich, Nathalie 26
herbicides 132
heritage 33, 143, 188, 190
    Amarone 95–6
    place 83, 91, 105, 113
    Prosecco Hills of Conegliano and Valdobbiadene 92–5
    South Africa 96–9
Herman, Agatha 170, 171, 179
heroic viticulture 106–7, 147
Hilton, Paris 82
historically disadvantaged people (HDPs) 176, 178–82
homogenization 73, 75, 81, 85, 113, 196
hospitality 103, 105
human rights 123, 166
Humphrey, John 29
hybridization 80, 88
hybrids 148–50

idealization 191
identities 190
Iliopoulos, Panagiotis 17
illegal manoeuvres 79
immigrant labour 163, 183, 190
immigration 166
incentives 150
inclusiveness 190
Indicazione Geografica Tipica (IGT) 65–6
industrial world 30
inequalities 19, 21, 77, 182, 190, 198–201
    capitalism 194–6
influencers 110, 120
infrastructure 45
initiatives 182
initiatives, community 179
innovation 21–2, 86, 147–51, 193
    value chains 41, 45, 49, 61
inspired world 30
institutionalization 79
institutional power 16, 187
institutions 74, 79
Institut National des Appellations d'Origine (INAO) 43

Integrated production of Wine (IPW) 121–2
integrity 93
intellectual property rights 22
International Federation of Wines and Spirits (FIVS) 117
International Organization of Vine and Wine (OIV) 117
International Standards Organization 26000 118
International Sustainability Standards Board 118
interventions 79
investment 47
investments 74, 179, 197
   international 111
investment wines 39
investors, foreign 57, 176
irrigation 130, 192
Italian wine
   brief history and recent trends 61–5
   Prosecco and Valpolicella 66–9
   regulation 65–6
   wine tourism 66
Italy 35, 75, 106
   capitalism 188, 195
   labour relations 164–8
   see also nature
Itçaina, Xabier 45–6

Jevons, William Stanley 19
jobs 147
judgements 29, 34
justification 28, 30, 32

Kaplinsky, Raphael 22
Karpik, Lucien 27, 111
knowledge 22, 77, 108, 181, 188, 195
Ko-öperatieve Wijnbouwers Vereniging van Zuid-Afrika (KWV) 46, 165, 176, 177
Krüger, Anne K. 25, 28
Kurniawan, Rudy 101

labels 117
   Sustainable Choice 119
labour (labourers) 23, 47–8, 144
   Black 46
   capitalism 191, 193, 195–6, 199

   certification 168–75
   chains of value 19–20, 24
   conditions 41, 194
   exploitation 74, 164–75
   surplus 22–3
   see also farmworkers; immigrant labour; people
land appropriation 136, 192
land ownership, BEE 178–9
landscapes 92, 104, 190, 192
Lang, Juliane 17
law enforcement 173
Lazonick, William 197
legislation 80, 106, 165
legitimacy 17–18, 34
lifestyles 146, 191
   see also place
livelihoods 24
logistics 57, 108, 120, 145
logos 152–3
luxury items 27, 41, 74, 100, 111, 191

machinery 192, 194
Mahutga, Matthhew C. 18
Malorgio, Giulio 62
marginalization 190
marketing 39, 85, 136
   destination 105
marketization 192
markets 26, 44, 91, 157, 182
   fine wines 100–1
   international 171
markets, domestic 51
markets, international 54, 61
markets, local 180
market world 30
Marshall, Alfred 19
Marx, Karl 22–3, 163
Matthews, Mark A. 78
Mauracher, Christine 129
Mazzucato, Mariana 21
mechanization 130, 165, 196
medals 34
media 139, 166
   see also social media
media, specialized 34
media, traditional 33
memories 78
metrology (measurement) 26–7

Milanovic, Branko 198
monocultures 132, 142
monopolies 21, 22, 118–21, 173
Monterescu, Daniel 84
morality 26, 29, 190

Napoleon III 41
narratives 7, 160, 201
   place 78, 80, 110
   value chains 24, 27
   see also stories
natural environments 201
   see also nature
natural resources 15, 21
natural wines 142–4, 159–60, 192
nature 15, 23, 69, 115–16, 200
   capitalism 191–3
   conclusion 161–2
   ecology, biodiversity conservation and beauty 124–42
   limited valorization of sustainability at wine trade fairs 151–5
   natural wines 142–4
   regulation and governance 117–24
   wine and climate change 144–51
   worlds of valuation and value struggles 155–61
nature depletion 195
nature, value of 23
Negro, Giacomo 87–8
Neilson, Jeff 24
Net Farm Income (NFI) 55
networks 181
New World countries 115
   place 77, 80, 99, 104
   value chains 35, 40
niche products 51
non-governmental organizations (NGOs) 9, 14, 137, 193
   people 165–6, 183
nostalgia 78, 86, 106, 191

oak 54
Old World countries 35, 40, 77, 79, 80, 104
online platforms 101
online purchasing 34
online source 33
opinions 110, 112, 157, 190
opinion, world of 30

organizations 49
organic wine 124–8
organization, intergovernmental 199
outsourcing 17, 196, 197
ownership 41
ownership, land 47–8, 136
Oxfam 166

packaging 33, 75, 108, 118–21, 123, 145–7
Pappalardo, Salvatore 139
patents 22
peer advice 110
people 69, 163–4, 200
   capitalism 193–4
   conclusion 183–5
   ownership and control 175–82
   racialized and gendered labour exploitation 164–75
   worlds of valuation and value struggles 182–3
pest control 47
pest control (management) 170
phylloxera 46
Pickles, John 23
Piketty, Thomas 198
place 4–5, 7, 73–4, 163–4
   capitalism 188–91, 194–7, 199–201
   conclusion 112–13
   and fine wines 99–102
   heritage 91–9
   nature 128, 130, 160–1
   placeless wines 74–7
   tasting of, tradition and authenticity 77–91
   wine tourism 103–7
   worlds of valuation and value struggles 107–12
   see also value chains
placeless wines 107–8, 188, 195
place, sense of 54, 66, 69
place wines 108–10, 188, 190
platform economy 21
platforms, online 101
Platter 76, 121
Plumecocq, Gael 157
political identity 77
Ponte, Stefano 15, 17, 18
populations, Black urban 52
Porto Agreement 59–60

post-colonialism 163
postcolonialism 24
power 26, 112
    capitalism 187, 196–7, 201
    and governance in value chains 14–19
    people 164–5, 171
practices 80, 130
praising 30
premiumization 54, 75, 188
price premiums 169
prices 19–20, 188
Pritchard, Bill 24
private cellars 48
privilege 190
prizing 30
producer cellars 48
producers 87
    New World 45
    wholesalers 49
production 40, 182, 192, 196
    place of 42
    South African wine 50–5
productive consumption 21
productivity 44
professionals, Black 100
profitability 55–6
    South African wine 55–7
profits 39
property development 39
property, intellectual 201
property theory 198
Prosecco 66–9
    (re)invention of 81–4
Prosecco and Valpolicella 127
    environmental value struggles 138–42
protests 107, 166
pruning techniques 54
publications 110, 138, 140

quality 29, 34, 58
    place 75–6, 82, 84, 108
Quentin, David 22
Quesnay, François 20

race 69, 171, 172, 182–3
    capitalism 193–4
rankings 99

rare wines 39
rarity 74
rationality 29
reality 28
Reckwitz, Andreas 27
recognition 39
recyclability 146
redistribution 196
Reduce, Retrench, Respect (RRR) 141
reforms 46
regulations 26, 158, 165, 191
    Italian wine 65–6
    place 83–5, 88–9, 93
    South African wine 57–60
regulators 87
Reinhart, Martin 25, 28
reinvestment 199
rents 20–2, 108, 110, 198
Report 83, 139–40
representations 41, 190
reputations 33
resistance 148
restaurants 181
retail 40
retailers 47, 87, 108
reviews 99, 112
Roger, Antoine 45–6

scandals 79, 82, 88, 101
scores 34
Shin, Jang-Sup 197
Shiu, Jing-Ming 17–18
Single Common Market Organization 44
Sistema Prosecco 84
Sistema Qualità Nazionale Produzione Integrata (SQNPI) 122, 140, 142
slavery 164
small and medium enterprises (SMEs), Black 177
Smith, Adam 20
Smith, Andy 24, 45–6
Smith Maguire, Jennifer 143
social conditions 193
    certification 168–75
    see also farmworkers; people
social interactions 19
social labour 21
social media 100, 110, 111, 112, 190–1

social movements 14
social stability 17
social values 103
soils 130–1, 138, 139, 148
solidarity 108, 190, 196
Solms-Delta 179
Sour Grapes 101
South Africa 150–1, 154, 169–70
　capitalism 188, 194
　confronting climate change 145–6
　labour relations 164–8
　place. *see* place
　see also Black Economic
　　Empowerment (BEE); nature
South African wine
　brief history and recent trends 46–8
　geographical indications 84–5
　heritage 96–9
　production and exports 50–5
　profitability 55–7
　regulation 57–60
　value chains characteristics 48–9
　wine tourism 60–1
South African Wine and Brandy Company
　(SAWB) 177
South African Wine Industry Information
　System (SAWIS) 96
South African Wine Industry Trust
　(SAWIT) 176, 181
South Africa (SA) Wine 49, 133
Spain 35, 125
standards 18, 47, 95, 170
　capitalism 195, 200
　nature 115–17, 123–4
Staricco, Juan Ignacio 18
Stark, David 25, 28
start-ups 21
status 39, 92, 97, 144
Steiner, Rudolf 128
stockpiling 44
stories 192
　heritage 67
　people 171, 181
　place 76–7, 83, 106
　value chains 42, 55
storytelling 33, 91, 136, 152–3, 166
Sturgeon, Timothy 15, 18, 29
subsidies 44, 45
supermarkets 34, 39, 127, 181

suppliers 24
supplies 44
supply chains 199
support 46
support initiatives, business 179–82
surplus value 23
sustainability
　capitalism 191, 193
　chains of value 15, 17
　environmental 41
　people 169, 174–5, 185
　place 98, 102, 108
　value chains 47, 50, 56, 69
　wine fairs 151–5
　see also environmental sustainability;
　　nature
Sustainable Supply Chain Initiative
　118
Sustainable Winegrowing New Zealand
　115
SWR 118, 123
Systembolaget 119–20, 145, 166, 173

tariff quotas 59–60
taste 34
taste, democratization of 99–100
taste of place 78
tastings 60
　wine tourism 103–7
　see also place
taxes 56, 142, 197
tax optimization 39
TDCA 59
technologies 147–51, 165, 194, 199
Teil, Geneviève 78
telecommunications 17–18
temperatures, high, resistance to 98
terroir 8, 10
　capitalism 188, 190, 195–6
　see also nature; place; value chains
Terroir Specific Wines 59
testing 29
Testo Unico Vino (TUV) 65
Theory of valuation 28
Thévenot, Laurent 28–30, 157
Thompson, Siobhan 152
time, surplus labour 22–3
tools 119, 123, 145
tourism (tourists) 40, 54, 136–7

tourism, wine 34, 112, 180, 190–1
   Italy 66
   South Africa 60–1
   tasting wine in place 103–7
trade 14, 35
trade agreements 46
traditions 33
   Amarone della Valpolicella (Amarone) 88–91, 95–6
   capitalism 188, 190–1
   or flexible bricolage 85–8
   place 74, 77–85, 105, 112
training 130–1, 192
Transformation Units 49
transmission mechanisms 15, 16
transparency 143
transport 119–20
Troiano, Stefania 129
Tups, Gideon 17
typicality 33, 43, 87, 91

undocumented workers 166
   see also immigrant labour
uniqueness 33, 195
   see also place
United Nations Educational, Scientific and Cultural Organization (UNESCO) 91, 92–5
United States of America (USA) 35, 39
unproductive entrepreneurship 22

Valdobbiadene 66, 77, 81, 92–5
   see also Prosecco and Valpolicella
Valpolicella 66–9, 87
valuation 33, 86, 101, 108, 112
   and sociology of value 25–8
   worlds of 28–32
value added 20, 22, 56, 187
value capture 21
value chains 5–8, 13, 40, 187
   global 196
   governance and power 14–19
   sociology of value and valuation 25–8
   South African wine 48–9
   value in 19–25
   worlds of valuation 28–32
value creation 21, 196
value extraction 21

value in 19–25
value of nature 23
value struggles 23–5, 46, 69, 87, 108, 112
   class, race and gender 182–3
   nature 155–61
variability 77
Veronelli, Luigi 111
vertical differentiation 88
vertical integration 61–2, 63
Vilakazi, Thando 17
vineyards 44, 45, 87, 132–3
Vinitaly 144
Vino da Tavola (VDT) 65
violence 165, 168
Vision 2020 176–7
viticulture 164, 172, 190, 192
   see also nature; place; value chains
viticulture, heroic 147
viticulture, regenerative 128–32
V.I.V.A. Sustainability and Culture 123

wages 23
Walras, Léon 19
water consumption 47, 98
water management 136, 148
water systems 145
wealth 21, 198
wealth distributions 197
weather 145
website 112
Western Cape 54
wholesalers 49, 56–7
Wine and Agricultural Ethical Trading Association (WIETA) 172–3
Wine Arc 180
wine cellars 154, 172, 178
   see also value chains
wine estates 49
wine funds 39
Wine Kingdom: Celebrating Conservation in the Cape Winelands, The 134
winemakers 63–4
winemaking 40
Wine of Origin (WO) scheme 58–9
wine shops 34
Wines of South Africa (WOSA) 60, 133, 134
Wine Spectator 111

wine, value chains for 33–4
    global 35–46
    Italian 61–9
    South African 46–61
    what's next 69
Wójcik, Dariusz 17
women 164, 170, 172, 180, 181
    Black 177–8, 185
    see also females
workers 47, 167
working conditions 48, 172
work, manual 33

World Biodiversity Association (BWA) 137
worlds of valuation 28–32, 107–12, 113
    capitalism 194–6
    class, race and gender 182–3
    nature 155–61
World Trade Organization (WTO) 44
World Wildlife Fund (WWF) 133, 134, 135

Zaia, Luca 83–4, 92
Zelizer, V. 26